Rough Magic
First Plays

ROUGH MAGIC

Rough Magic theatre company was formed in 1984 and has since produced more than fifty shows, over half of which were Irish or world premieres. The company has commissioned ten new plays and launched six new writers all of whom are represented in this anthology.

Rough Magic comprised initially of seven core members – four actors (Anne Byrne, Helene Montague, Arthur Riordan and Stanley Townsend) two directors (Declan Hughes and Lynne Parker) and an administrator (Siobhán Bourke). Many other actors, designers and musicians subsequently became part of the ensemble. From the beginning the emphasis was on diversity and pluralism, both in style and content. The company quickly forged an outstanding reputation for presenting Irish premieres of British and American plays and well as new interpretations of the classics.

In 1988, Rough Magic presented its first piece of new Irish writing, Donal O'Kelly's one man show *Bat the Father, Rabbit the Son* to critical acclaim. The following year, the company commissioned Declan Hughes to write his first play *I Can't Get Started* which was produced in 1990. In 1992, Declan was appointed Rough Magic's writer-in-residence and from this point, new writing became central to the company's policy and programme. Rough Magic has toured to the UK, Australia and New Zealand, the US and all parts of Ireland, winning many prestigious awards and developing a reputation for diversity, innovation and excellence.

POM BOYD

In the 1980s, Pom joined the Grapevine Theatre Company where she wrote comedy sketches and children's plays. She later moved to New York, gathered material and embarked on a solo comedy career. Back in Dublin in the early nineties she wrote and performed *La Rossa Gialla*, a serious piece, based on her experiences in New York, and *The Mad One With The Hair,* a one hour comedy show which played the Dublin Theatre Festival, the

Edinburgh Festival, London and New York. *Down Onto Blue* was written in 1993 and received a Stewart Parker award in 1994. Currently she is co-writing another play for Rough Magic and writing a feature film.

DECLAN HUGHES

Declan Hughes was born in Dublin in 1963. He is writer-in-residence with Rough Magic Theatre Company, which he co-founded. His plays include *I Can't Get Started* which won the Stewart Parker Award and the BBC Northern Ireland Television Drama Award for 1991, *Love and a Bottle*, his adaptation of George Farquhar's play of the same name (Project Arts Centre, Dublin; Tricycle Theatre, London), *New Morning* (Bush Theatre and Project Arts Centre, 1993) and *Halloween Night* (Andrews Lane Theatre, Dublin and Donmar Warehouse, London, 1997). Declan Hughes and Rough Magic were *Time Out* award-winners in 1992 for *Digging for Fire* and *Love And A Bottle*. His most recent play, *Twenty Grand*, played at the Peacock Theatre, Dublin in 1998.

A collection of four plays, *Declan Hughes: Plays: 1*, was published by Methuen in 1998.

PAULA MEEHAN

Paula Meehan was born and lives in Dublin. She has published four collections of poetry and been translated into many languages. She has written for theatre, film and for contemporary dance. In 1996, she received the Marten Toonder Award for Literature; in 1998 she received the Butler Award for Poetry.

GINA MOXLEY

Gina Moxley is a writer and actor. *Danti-Dan*, her first play, was commissioned by Rough Magic and produced in Dublin in 1995. Following a national tour it transferred to the Hampstead Theatre in London. Her play *Dog House* was commissioned by the Royal National Theatre as part of the BT/National Connections initiative and was showcased at the Cottesloe Theatre in 1997. For CoisCeim Dance Theatre/Abbey Theatre she wrote *Toupees and Snare Drums* (in collaboration with David Bolger) which premiered at the Peacock Theatre in 1998 and was followed by a national tour. In 1995 Gina received a literature bursary from the Arts Council and was winner of the Stewart Parker Trust Award in 1996.

DONAL O'KELLY

Donal O'Kelly is an actor and playwright. His first solo play *Rabbit* was followed by the highly successful *Bat the Father Rabbit the Son* (for Rough Magic) which he performed in New York, Australia and New Zealand as well as on tour in Ireland and Britain. His third solo play *Catalpa* won a fringe First at Edinburgh 1996 and played the Gate Theatre, Dublin and the Melbourne Festival 1997. Other plays he has written include, *The Dogs, Asylum Asylum!, Maimie Sighs, Hughie on the Wires* (also broadcast on RTE Radio); *Trickledown Town* and *The Business of Blood* (with Kenny Glennane); *Mulletman and Gullier* (with Charlie O'Neill) and most recently *Farawayan*. As an actor he is best known for his performance as Bimbo in the film production of Roddy Doyle's *The Van* while recent roles on stage include Joxer in the Abbey Theatre production of *Juno and the Paycock* and Beckett's solo play *Act Without Words I* in the Gate Theatre's Beckett Festival in the Lincoln Centre New York.

He is a founder director of Calypso Productions and is a director of the justice and peace organisation AfrI – Action from Ireland.

ARTHUR RIORDAN

Arthur Riordan is a founder member of Rough Magic and *Hidden Charges* is his first commission for the company. As a writer Arthur has scripted and performed in numerous sketches for RTE's *Nighthawks*. In the 1992 Dublin Theatre Festival he appeared as MC Dev in his self penned one man show *The Emergency Session* which was a hit with audiences and critics and subsequently toured Ireland and played in Glasgow. His one act play *The Last Temptation of Michael Flatley* was commissioned by Macra na Feirme and has been hugely successful on the amateur drama circuit.

As an actor, Arthur has performed in many Rough Magic shows over the past fourteen years. Arthur has also appeared with the Passion Machine, Druid and the Abbey Theatre as well as in various films including *My Dinner With Oswald, Before I Sleep, Ink,* and *Angela Mooney Dies Again*. He recently performed in his own play *Love Me?!* as part of the Corn Exchange's Award winning *CarShow*.

ROUGH MAGIC: FIRST PLAYS
First published May 1999 by
New Island Books, 2 Brookside, Dundrum Road, Dublin 14, Ireland
ISBN 1 874597 37 5

Published in August 1999 in Great Britain by Methuen Publishing Limited
215 Vauxhall Bridge Road, London SW1V 1EJ
ISBN 0 413 74030 7

Peribo Pty Ltd, 58 Beaumont Road, Mount Kuring-Gai
NSW 2080, Australia, ACN 002 273 761
(for Australia and New Zealand)

The publishers would like to thank Faber and Faber for their kind
permission to reproduce *Danti-Dan* by Gina Moxley and Gallery Press for
their kind permission to reproduce the poem 'Mrs Sweeney' from *Pillowtalk*
by Paula Meehan. Cover and inside photographs reproduced with kind
permission of Amelia Stein.

A CIP record of this book is available from the British library.

**New Island Books receives financial assistance from The Arts
Council (An Chomhairle Ealaíon), Dublin, Ireland.**

The Arts Council
An Chomhairle Ealaíon

Cover photograph: Amelia Stein
Cover design: Public Communications Centre
Typesetting: New Island Books
Printed in Ireland by Colour Books, Ltd.

Rough Magic

First Plays

I Can't Get Started
Declan Hughes

The Dogs
Donal O'Kelly

Down Onto Blue
Pom Boyd

Hidden Charges
Arthur Riordan

Danti-Dan
Gina Moxley

Mrs Sweeney
Paula Meehan

Edited by Siobhán Bourke

New Island Books
Dublin

Methuen

ACKNOWLEDGEMENTS

Special thanks to the following in the preparation of this anthology: Ciara McGlynn, Sinead McAodha, Jobst Graeve, John Fairleigh, Alexandra Cann, Peggy Butcher, John Sutton, Rough Magic Theatre Company and New Island Books.

*

PERFORMANCE RIGHTS

All professional and amateur rights in these plays are strictly reserved and applications for permission to perform them must be made before rehearsals begin. For *I Can't Get Started* please apply to Curtis Brown Group Ltd., 4th Floor, Haymarket House, 28/29 Haymarket, London SW1Y 4SP. For *The Dogs* and *Danti-Dan* please apply to Alexandra Cann, 12 Abingdon Road, London W8 6AF. For *Down Onto Blue, Hidden Charges* and *Mrs Sweeney* please apply to Rough Magic Ltd., 5/6 South Great Georges Street, Dublin 2.

CONTENTS

For past and future audiences

Editor's Note

New Irish writing is one of the hallmarks of Irish theatre in recent times and Rough Magic, along with many other independent theatre companies around Ireland, rose to the challenges it presented. What prompted the publication of this collection was my desire to record a body of work that emerged from Rough Magic's commissioning policy during the early to mid nineties of encouraging first time writers.

The thrill, danger and emotional charge of live performance is of course its addiction. It also makes for an ephemeral existence. In theatre, after the last performance, a play only exists in the collective memory of the audiences that saw it, and the actors and production team that made it happen. Its future life can only be secured through publication.

The company's guiding principal with writers was 'tell the story you want to tell' along with a practical requirement that the cast size should not be more than seven! As a producer my wish is for these plays now to engage new audiences in other places and other media. This anthology ensures a permanent presence for the work in the public domain.

I have included production photographs and production credits to reflect the collaborative effort involved in presenting drama and as a backdrop for the company experience in those years.

Siobhán Bourke,
Dublin,
February 1999.

(Siobhán Bourke was Executive Producer, Rough Magic Theatre Company from 1984 - 1998.)

INTRODUCTION

Rough Magic was formed in 1984, began by producing premieres of contemporary work from the UK and the US and went on to mount new interpretations of world classics. That implies a fairly broad spectrum, but one common factor seems to emerge, namely that the genesis of a Rough Magic show is a written play. Whatever elements are subsequently added, the playscript is the map of the show and the authoritative sensibility is that of the writer. In 1989 we decided that it was time to start putting the experience of our first five years into new work generated by writers commissioned by the company.

There is no unifying theme or style to these plays and that perfectly reflects Rough Magic's emphasis on diversity. But it is interesting that all of them are written either by performers or practitioners of theatre. The very word playwright, with its suggestion of hands-on craftsmanship reminds us that the theatre is a very practical art. It helps if you know how it feels to tackle and engage a live audience.

Producing new work is a difficult and dangerous business. By definition it has no existing reputation, particularly when, as was the case with all the plays in this volume, the writer has never undertaken a full-scale stage play before. The company makes a major commitment in terms of its energies and resources to produce and market the work. But the rewards are equally substantial. New writing opened some very significant doors for us. It took us abroad to Australia, the US and the UK and introduced us to inter-national scrutiny. It established valuable relationships with prestigious theatres in London, such as the Bush, the Tricycle, the Hampstead and the Donmar. Even more importantly it opened up the potential of the work itself. The glory of new plays is that they are not limited to contemporary matters. They can deal with any theme, enter any world, tackle any subject matter. So plays in this volume are set in 1930's Hollywood or 1970's Cork because that is where the writers wanted to take us. They speak in naturalistic vernacular, extreme stylisation and any degree of artifice in between. What they do have in common is an authentic and original vision and a story worth telling.

Declan Hughes' first play *I Can't Get Started* – the star-crossed love affair of Dashiell Hammett and Lillian Hellman, haunted by the spectres of a hard-boiled film noir – was an important breakthrough for Rough Magic, written, directed, performed and produced by members of the company. The following year Declan adapted *Love and a Bottle* from George Farquhar's play and wrote *Digging for Fire*, both of which gained the company prestigious awards. From this point he became the company writer-in-residence and new writing commissions became a focal part of our activities.

The Dogs can be described as the twin hells of Christmas and the Troubles as experienced by a Dublin family and a posse of cartoon animals. This was Donal O'Kelly's first full-scale play needing other actors to inhabit his extraordinary imagination. Not only had they to hop between Toontown and grim naturalism, they had to negotiate the mind-boggling post-Joycean language he uses in over half the play. It was a great adventure for the company and absolutely no-one else could have written it.

Pom Boyd's skill as a performer has an enormous influence over her approach to storytelling. The Fox family's never-apologise-never-explain attitude is portrayed with a sure-footed sense of theatre and a superb ear for the betrayals of casual speech. *Down Onto Blue* is a moving, beautifully crafted examination of a very typical and typically dysfunctional family where an accidental visitor becomes a catalyst for a black comedy of exposure.

It was obvious from Arthur Riordan's *The Emergency Session* – his one man de Valera rap musical – that here was a uniquely creative imagination. His work dances between the real and the surreal, both musical and furiously satirical, dissecting human nature with a laser intelligence. *Hidden Charges* plays on the tensions between town and country, the ability of someone's family to cause them profound embarrassment, and the dangerous power of the euphemism and the secret.

Cork 1970, summer holidays, kids going crazy with heat, boredom and frustration, and sex is the great mystery to be explored. When Gina Moxley joined the company as an actor we had discovered her talent for inventing characters and asked her to try her hand at straight drama. We were prepared for the sharpness and wit of her writing but not for its darkness and compassion. *Danti-Dan* is an astonishing debut, not least in that it treats adolescent sexuality objectively and reverses the gender stereotypes usually associated with stories of aggressive sexuality.

Paula Meehan's reputation as a poet could not be more impressive. *Mrs Sweeney* is a celebration of the voices of women in the front line of the drugs war, and a wonderful dramatisation of someone who has lost verbal power. As Lil attempts to come to terms with their daughter's death her husband starts to behave like a pigeon. It is a study of madness in an insane world, told with wit, humour and acute anger.

Most new plays are produced under pressure. It is very much the nature of the beast and, actually, it is part of the fun. What made the production of these plays so enjoyable was the collaboration of the people who were at the cutting edge of the great experiment. It is a tribute to the casts and crews of these shows that the collective experience was such a pleasure. From the Rough Magic regulars of *I Can't Get Started* to the new recruits of *Danti-Dan* they pulled together. Part of this esprit de corps comes from the privilege of being the first ever group of people to embark on a particular journey. They also benefited from the sanity, generosity and good humour of the writers themselves.

Two of these plays arose out of a particular initiative. The women's playwriting competition was thought up by Siobhán Bourke in an attempt to address the gender imbalance in play writing. Both as a statement and as a mechanism for creating new work it was extremely important. *Down Onto Blue* and *Mrs Sweeney* came from that initiative.

Quite simply, new writing is the future, and any company with its head screwed on will be keen to invest in it. It has to be handled carefully, if courageously. It's a scary thing, taking a plunge into the dark, especially if you have talked a dozen or so other people into taking it with you. But I cannot remember when our buoyancy deserted us for more than a moment. Ultimately we all believed in the destination, and in the captaincy of our rookie writers. It is no surprise to us that all of them have gone on to produce other work with growing confidence and authority. We are ridiculously proud of them and of the splendid plays in this volume.

Lynne Parker,
Artistic Director, Rough Magic Theatre Company.
February 1999.

Foreword

Irish theatre at the end of the 1990s is so strongly orientated towards new writing, with the well-subsidised venues and the smaller independent companies vying with one another to discover and nurture fresh talent, that it is hard to recognise the recent past when writers of obvious stature often had to struggle to be heard. Stewart Parker's first play, *Spokesong*, which ended up on Broadway and is still in regular performance around the world, saw the light of day only because friends raised the money to stage an independent production at the 1976 Dublin Theatre Festival. There were of course a few institutions, most notably The Abbey, which saw themselves as resident midwives to the new work needed to revitalise Irish theatre, but outside of these relationships the options for the aspiring playwright were few.

All this was to change in the early 1980s when confident young graduates from the university theatre studies departments and the drama schools no longer seemed content to wait respectfully around the usual places in search of jobs; instead, they hustled their way into opening their own venues and taking upon themselves the whole exhaustive business of presenting plays. In this new and burgeoning world of Irish theatre, the writer was no longer the suppliant at the artistic-director's door, but someone sought out and cherished.

Early on the scene was Rough Magic, a collective of ex-students so smitten by the theatre bug that they could think of doing nothing else. In the spirit of their youth and energy they wanted to take on new texts, but their name – carefully drawn from Shakespeare and *The Tempest* – signalled what for them was the context for contemporary work; their repertoire would be a free mix of theatre classics, modern masters and whatever new plays they thought worth doing. Any new script tackled need not be measured against a Sheridan or an Oscar Wilde, but they were granting no anarchic merit to a writer or a production team ignorant of the classical repertoire. Nor was there to be an elevation of any one of the alchemy of skills needed to bring a text to life; this was not an actors' nor a writers' nor a directors' company – when a new play was being done, everyone shared in the broad collaborative process.

It happens that many of the new texts successfully revealed in company productions have come from its own actors.

Perhaps the trust borne of many workings together made it easier for the actor-turned-writer to welcome scrutiny, and even mediation, in developing a text through to its faithful realisation on stage; while even first-time writers will defend what they have written from amendments suggested by other imaginations, there are technical and structural hazards lying in wait which can be averted through sensitive intervention by other specialists. It is this concentration of theatrical skills to support and release a new text which has been Rough Magic's greatest gift to the writer. When everything comes right on the night, the audience go home elated, knowing they have seen something which will live long beyond this first production. But never do they feel that they have shared in anything less than a skilled blending of the many component crafts that must come together in a thoroughly competent theatrical presentation.

For the writer, what greater opportunity can there be? And now that the works are gathered and published, they are ready for exploration by other voices and in other venues. The memory of a play fades all too fast after the closing night of that first production; print gives an extra breath of life which can sustain it on to its next destination. This collection marks the combined achievement of Rough Magic's writers, but no less the achievement of a company of artists who have sacrificed individual ego in the sustained production of work whose theatrical magic is never less than refined.

John Fairleigh
Secretary of the Stewart Parker Trust
March 1999

I CAN'T GET STARTED

Declan Hughes

To my mother and father

Rough Magic produced the world premiere of *I Can't Get Started* at the 1990 Edinburgh Fringe Festival and Dublin Theatre Festival at the Project Arts Centre. The US premiere was at the Stonybrook International Theatre Festival in 1991. The production had the following cast and production team:

Lillian Hellman Anne Byrne

Dashiell Hammett Arthur Riordan

Daniel Webster Stanley Townsend

Sylvia Bryant Helene Montague

Ethan Bryant Miche Doherty

Betty Friedrich Bairbre NiChaoimh*

Albert Friedrich Jonathan White

Curtis Bryant Jonathan White

Nell Kilcoyne Bairbre NiChaoimh*

Bill Jonathan White

Bob Miche Doherty

*The part of Betty Friedrich and Nell Kilcoyne was played by Carol Scanlan in Dublin and at Stony Brook USA.

Directed by Lynne Parker

Set Design by Barbara Bradshaw

Music Composed/Arranged by John Dunne

Lighting Design by Stephen McManus

Costume Design by Marie Tierney

Production Manager Padraig O'Neill

Stage Manager Marie Tierney

Produced by Siobhán Bourke

Photo: Stanley Townsend as Daniel Webster ©Amelia Stein

Dramatis Personae:

The Life
Dashiell Hammett, A crime novelist
Lillian Hellman, A playwright
Elisabeth Friedrich, A screenwriter
Albert Friedrich, A screenwriter

The Story
Daniel Webster, A private detective
Sylvia Bryant, A girl
Ethan Bryant, Her brother
Curtis Bryant, Her father, a governor
Nell Kilcoyne, A good old girl
Bill, An American soldier
Bob, An American soldier
Jim, A waiter

Time: 1930 – 1951
Place: Diverse locations, USA

Act One

Scene One

The Light Fantastic

*Music: 'I Can't Get Started' by Bunny Berrigan and His Orchestra
Light:* **Dashiell Hammett** *and* **Lillian Hellman** *are dancing to
the music. The light plays about the stage, and about their faces. It's
like a dream.*

Hellman: You never told me you could dance.

Hammett: You never asked me. Besides, a man should
never tell a woman everything.

> *Pause.*

Hellman: We're doing alright, Dash, aren't we?

Hammett: We're doing fine, honey, just fine.

Hellman: It's good to dance. Look at the light, how it
moves as we move. (*Pause*) How will things turn out, do you
think?

Hammett: Lilly, dancing isn't about talking. It isn't about
anything except dancing. That's why it's the perfect thing.
Do you see?

Hellman: I think so.

Hammett: Thoughts. Who needs 'em?

Hellman: We don't.

Hammett: No, we don't. We don't need anything else now.
We don't need anything at all.

> *The music swells, and they dance like angels.*

And ...

Scene Two

If I Had A Hammer

1952: **Hammett** *delivers a speech. Only his face is lit.*

Hammett: Good evening Ladies and Gentlemen, and welcome to this Benefit Dinner in support of those who have refused to collaborate with the House Committee on Un-American Activities. (That's quite a mouthful for a sober tongue to get around, believe me.)

I'm not much practised at speaking out, but – I went to jail because I refused to name names, names I didn't know in the first place. If I had said: 'I don't know the names', it's possible that I might have remained, ah, 'at liberty'. But I didn't believe then that anybody had the right to ask me for those names. Nor do I now. Some people say that the refusal to name names, to collaborate, is an act of principle. I don't know. To me, that suggests that you had a choice. Few of us had a choice, we never even considered collaboration as an option. What is a principle anyway? What does it cost? To be principled, to have a code, must you forfeit something of yourself, of your humanity? Can you be principled and yet trust others? Is a principle not the most selfish of things?

So I believe I went to jail as much out of stubbornness as out of principle. I believe that stubbornness to be an authentic American attribute. My belief may be old fashioned, but then, judging by the recent example of the United States Government, adherence to the Bill of Rights and the Constitution is equally old-fashioned, so maybe there's a moral there somewhere ... something to do with democracy, and no judge or cop or politician telling you what democracy is, ah ...

They send you to prison to change your mind, but prison doesn't change anybody's mind about anything, ah ...

I'm working on a new book, yes indeed, yes ... at last ... I'm through with all that hard-boiled crime stuff, it's a menace. This book ... will be a novel ... based on life, and the need to embrace, embrace the ...

It's about the beginning: the boy in the house ... and the end: the man on the island ... his life with the woman ... what they believe and what they feel, what keeps them together.

The man needs to remember how it started, so he can see how it's going to come out, so that he can embrace ... embrace the ... contradictions. (*Pause*) I'M THROUGH WITH ALL THAT HARD-BOILED CRIME STUFF, IT'S A MENACE!

The lights begin to come up on his room, where he has been all along.

And ...

Scene Three

Ghosts

Hammett *alone at his desk.*

Hammett: What a life is worth, ah ... the boy in the house, he hates his father ... and then the man – he wants to go and live alone on an island ... but he wants the woman also ... and so he's caught between the two. The man ... doesn't know what the fuck he wants.

The moon begins to rise. A match strikes, and light pools around **Daniel Webster**, *Private Detective, smoking a cigar.*

Webster: Hello Hammett.

Hammett: Go away, you spook.

Webster: Oh no. I believe it's time.

Hammett: Believe what you wish, my friend, just believe it elsewhere.

Webster: (*Reading note*) 'Novel idea – Daniel Webster, Private Detective – Governor Curtis Bryant – 'A politician is the devil's quilted anvil' – Centre of the story: Sylvia Bryant, the governor's beautiful daughter – Daddy's little girl – who is she, what is she? A New Departure – A Family Plot.'

Hammett: It's a menace!

Webster: Novel idea? I'll give you novel ideas: The hero of the book you should've been working on is left to cool his heels for 21 years 'cause you couldn't get your ass in gear to *write* the fuckin' thing, is that novel enough for you? You fucking *fake*. (*Aside*) This was gonna be my *opportunity*. I should be up there with the rest of 'em: Sam Spade, Ned Beaumount, Nick Charles – only he couldn't … Hammett, you need this now more than ever.

Hammett: Are you insane? I need you to leave me alone, Dan. You're a relic from a stupider age. A fossil. An outmoded myth.

Webster: Uh oh. I am going nowhere. Call me a spook? You're stuck in here making speeches you're never gonna deliver, promising new novels you're never gonna write, you're the only spook 'round here that I can see.

  Pause.

Hammett: Alright Dan, you want it, you do it. Let's get it over with, once and for all.

Webster: Just like that?

Hammett: Just like that. But don't blame me if it doesn't come out right in the end – it's your party. Off you go now.

Webster: Right. Ah, where should I start?

Hammett: Well now, unless you want to get all modern on us Dan, how about at the beginning?

Webster: Right. (**Webster** *consults note*) It all started with Sylvia Bryant.

Sylvia *appears.*

(*Hard-boiled*) She told me her story, but it doesn't add up. She's either poison, or she's sweetness and light. She's coming clean, or playing me for a sap. She's in it up to her neck, or she's pure as the driven snow. It's time to find out. It's Truth Time. (*Pumped up*) Now Miss Bryant, you just wasted an hour of my time with a mess of nonsense, and I don't get paid by the hour, I get paid by results, and I don't get paid if I don't get results, and I don't get results if my clients tell me lies, so why don't we just take it once more from the top, Miss Bryant, if indeed that is your name.

Sylvia: I suggest you learn some manners, Mr Webster, or you'll lose all your other clients the way you've just lost this one.

Sylvia *walks out.*

Webster: What? Hey, wait a minute. You can't do that!

Hammett: Nice work, Dan.

Webster: Yeah, yeah, yeah.

Hammett: It's Truth Time. Jesus.

Webster: Alright, so I'm a little rusty. Just … need to get my bearings. (*Consults note*) Governor Bryant, blah, Sylvia Bryant the centre of the story blah blah blah, this is the standard recipe, right? So what's all this about a new departure?

Pause.

Hammett: The idea was, that it would be *about* the girl. It would be a story *about* Sylvia Bryant.

Webster: But that's absurd. I mean, the story is about *me*, right, about Daniel Webster, Private Eye, and then about what I *think* of her.

Hammett: (*Beat*) You're right, Dan, the idea was absurd.

Webster: Good. Now tell me this: what type of broad is this, ah, Sylvia Bryant?

Hammett: You got types?

Webster: Sure. I mean, basically there's two types of broad, right? You got your little blondes to run around with and your big brunettes to have children with. (Big blondes are to be avoided – there's a strong body of evidence suggests big blondes are not broads at all, they're another matter, perhaps indeed another life-form.)

Pause.

Hammett: Go on, Dan.

Webster: Hey, who am I telling – you know all this, you're the one who –

Hammett: Just – refresh my memory, alright?

Webster: Alright, so in the books you got two other types – there's the type she's … she's like one of the guys, alright, she likes a *drink,* prolly got a dirty *mouth,* she's … she can take a *joke,* what can I tell you. She knows how to take a joke. A Good Old Girl, right? Then there's the femme fatale type. Dressed to kill, alright, she looks hot – but inside it's ice, oh, brother, your soul'll burn in a hell on earth trying to keep a torch aflame for *that* babe. And you'll fall – tough to resist, she's a spellbinder, a beautiful witch. That's broads, right?

Hammett: Right.

Webster: Now, the next thing is, the detective. He's got to have a *code* –

Hammett: A code –

Webster: That keeps him straight, so he won't fall for the broad – ever. Pinkerton's Golden Rule – *Never Get Involved With Women.*

Hammett: Damn straight.

Webster: He's hired to do some work, and if it's halfway honest, he's got to do it. He keeps his distance and he keeps his head, and he stirs things up 'till he can sort them out, and then he walks away from it all, alone. (*Pause*) That's everything, right?

Hammett: What else is there?

Webster: Oh yeah – trust.

Hammett: The big trust thing.

Webster: *Oh* yeah. To keep straight, don't trust yourself, don't trust her, don't trust anybody.

Hammett: Goodness Dan, you're the son I never had. Now, get the fuck out of here.

Webster: I'm history.

   Webster *goes.*

Hammett: The man wants to go and live on an island – but he wants the woman also … the man wants the woman … but what does the woman want? What the fuck does she *want?*

   And …

Scene Four

Flaming Youth in the Waste Land – An Introduction

Autumn 1930. The garden of a large house in Hollywood.
Hammett *is drinking scotch. We hear music from the party inside.*
Lillian Hellman *comes out. He is 35, she is 24.*

Hammett: Well hello there Mrs Kober!

Hellman: Hi.

Hammett: And how are you this evening?

Hellman: Fine.

Hammett: Fine, that's fine! That'a a mighty pretty dress you're wearing, what is it made of, is it chiffon?

Hellman: Silk.

Hammett: Silk, oh my, well of course there's nothing like silk now is there, when it comes down to it, down to fabric, you have the Number One Choice – Silk – and then – everything else! That is an exquisitely made garment, Mrs. Kober, right down to the stitching, would you like a little drink?

Hellman: I'd like a big drink. (*She drains her glass. He pours a drink, dancing and mincing the while*) Must you do that?

Hammett: Do what? Oh, my *steps?* I'm sorry, do my steps *offend* you? You see, I've got a skating audition tomorrow with Mr de Mille; now I *know* I've got what it takes, but: Confidence Can't Buoy Up Poor Technique; so I practice while I work. Cigarette?

Hellman: (*Taking one*) Do you intend to keep this up?

Hammett: (*Southern*) I'll keep it up as long as I can, Ma'am, but I *have* been drinking, so –

Hellman: Listen! I've just prised my way out of a debate on Swimming Pools in the Home; dodged an intense conference on Poodle Shearing; and evaded a bunch of drunken screenwriters singing football songs who wanted me to cheer-lead for them; is it too much to ask for a tranquil, ordered moment? (*Pause*) I'm sorry.

Hammett: No –

Hellman: My head – sometimes it just gets …

Hammett: Clotted?

Hellman: *Clogged.* (*Pause*) It's all the inane chatter of this town, words with party hats on – it confuses people. Last night, my husband, a good and sweet and smart man, said to me 'Lilly, why can't you just make small talk?' I said: 'Arthur, don't worry, you watch me at that party tomorrow night: "*Hello* my *dear, love* that *dress,* you paid *how* much, why that's for *nothing!*" I won't let you down.' And he said: 'No, I don't mean at the party, I mean here with me, just the two of us.' (*Pause*) Make small-talk with my husband? I said: 'Arthur, making small talk is what I got married to avoid!' You see what I'm saying?

Hammett: He wants you to be a social occasion.

Hellman: And I'd prefer to be the silent partner.

Hammett: Words with party hats on yourself.

Hellman: I suppose you think what I said about Arthur is disloyal.

Hammett: No, I –

Hellman: Well it is. But you see I'm as fucked up as he is. I come to a dumb party full of phonies looking for a decent conversation, then I get mad when I can't find one.

Pause.

Hammett: What did you make of the gold-plated Aztec-style bathroom?

Hellman: Is it a little gaudy?

Hammett: You could say that. You could in fact say it was the single most vulgar item you'd ever seen in your life.

Hellman: You could.

Hammett: But then you wouldn't've seen Clara Blow's genuine replica Cistine Chapel-style bathroom.

Hellman: Ah.

Hammett: Or Jean Harlow's Egyptian pyramid shaped Cleopatra-style bathroom.

Hellman: No, I –

Hammett: Maybe I should pen a cunning little monograph on the topic. 'The Bathroom: An American Obsession; and its Apotheosis among the glorious (and hygienic) Hollywood elite.'

Hellman: Do you think we could have a decent conversation?

Hammett: (*Beat*) Sure. What do you want to talk about?

Hellman: 'The Waste Land' by T.S. Eliot.

Hammett: (*Beat*) 'The Waste Land'?

Hellman: Yeah.

Hammett: (*Beat*) Okay. Shoot.

Hellman: What is your opinion of 'The Waste Land' by T.S. Eliot?

Hammett: I think it's very nice. (*Pause*) Okay, alright, I think this. Eliot sees sex as disgusting and irredeemably corrupt. As he sees sex pretty much everywhere in the world, he therefore sees the world as irredeemably corrupt. I think the spirit life is the life for him. Now he is also a great writer, which means that what he thinks isn't nearly as important as *how* he thinks, how he *writes*. And he writes like ... well, if I thought I had a soul, I would sell it to write like that.

Hellman: Do you think the world is irredeemably corrupt?

Hammett: Does it matter what I think?

Hellman: Yes, it does.

Pause.

Hammett: Uh, corrupt yes; irredeemably so maybe – but I don't think sex has got much to do with it one day or the other.

Hellman: I see that poem as a gauntlet thrown down to us all. If the world is corrupt, for whatever reason, then writing

... like an angel isn't going to get us very far. We've got to *do* something.

Hammett: A *gauntlet?*

Hellman: Yes. What's wrong with that?

Hammett: (*Pause*) I worked for Pinkerton's as detective, and one time I was sent to the mining town of Butte, Montana. Butte was a typically corrupt Company town – wages were low to begin with, and then you could only spend them in Company stores, on over-priced Company goods, 'cause there weren't any other stores around. And there weren't any other jobs around. And if you made a name for yourself as a union agitator – a Wobbly – well, they made sure you'd never get work again. It was a kind of blacklist.

But the Wobblies refused to give up without a fight. They were determined to *do* something. Anyway, I was working down there, and I was approached by a high ranking official of the Mine Company and offered $5000 to kill Frank Little, the Wobblies' leader. The Company figured I had the guts for the job, thought I was their man.

Well I didn't get the $5000, but somebody did, because two days later Little was found dead, hanged by the neck from the trestle right outside his boarding house. People say his balls had been cut off, but I don't think that's true. There was a warning pinned to his chest, and it said 'THIS IS WHAT HAPPENS TO ALL WOBBLIES AND UNION SCUM – SIGNED, THE MONTANA VIGILANTES.' Frank Little tried to do something, and a business man offered me a fortune to murder him. And when Coolidge was president, he said that the business of America is business. So I don't see much of a future in trying to do something.

Hellman: You wouldn't have been asked to kill Frank Little unless you were working for the mine company.

Hammett: That's right.

Hellman: So what were you, a strike-breaker?

Hammett: Something like that.

Hellman *walks away from him.*

Hammett: Now why do you think I told you that?

Hellman: I think you told me that so I would fuck you. Is that true? I would be moved, and so impressed, and so I would fuck you. That is true, isn't it?

Hammett: No it's not true. Not the whole truth anyway.

Hellman: Well, we'll see. Now this may sound too much like Flaming Youth on the March for you, but … well, three things. First, it's important to, I believe this – to have an idea from which to proceed. Otherwise, you have no centre, you fall apart. You need to measure what you do against a notion of how things should be.

Hammett: Well, I don't know.

Hellman: Well I do. Second, you *have* those ideas, you have *convictions.* You wrote Red Harvest about Frank Little, didn't you, about a system so sick only harvest of blood could cure it. You *know* what a writer thinks is every bit as important as how he writes. And Coolidge is gone, and Hoover can't last, and a lot of people *need* to do something.

Pause.

Hammett: You're right. It does sound too much like Flaming Youth on the March. What's the third thing?

Hellman: Of course I'll fuck you. I want to. Why do you think I came out here in the first place?

Suddenly the music stops, and the lights in the house begin to flash on and off. We hear commotion from the guests. The colour of the sky deepens.

Hellman: What is this, some kind of melodrama?

Hammett: I think our host is telling us the party's over.

Hellman: Oh. Class act, isn't he?

Hammett: He's a *Producer.*

Hellman: Right. How well do you remember 'The Waste Land'?

Hammett: Remember it? We're living in it.

Hellman: No, I meant –

Hammett: I know what you meant. But you'd go off me if I started quoting poetry at you.

Hellman: No, I wouldn't.

Hammett: Well, I'd go off you. And that isn't what you meant at all, is it?

Hellman: (*Approaching him*) No. No, that isn't it at all. This is.

She kisses him. He responds.

And…

Scene Five

The Woman

Lights on **Sylvia Bryant**.

Webster: (*Aside*) It all started with Sylvia Bryant. Now Miss Bryant – how do you think I can help you?

Sylvia: I *hope* you can help me, Mr Webster. You're my last hope. (*Pause*) My father is Governor Curtis Bryant. He's seeking re-election, as I'm sure you're aware, in a month's time. It is, needless to say, very important to him to win, and, as his daughter, it is equally important to me that he should. Anonymity is a disgraceful position for anyone to hold, don't you think? It is cowardice, isn't it? I have received four of these … *letters,* Mr Webster, the fourth this morning – no postmark, nothing to indicate the sender's identity – listen:

*'If you would know corruption, look not to the world,
but instead to your father's heart.*

   *The sins of your father will return. They will haunt
you and your brother as they have haunted and will
haunt him.*

   *You have lived in a false innocence for long enough.
It is time you learned the truth – the awful truth about
him.*

   *Why did Edward Kilcoyne disappear? Is he dead or
alive? Ask your father. He may know.'*

Sylvia *gives* **Webster** *the letters.*

Sylvia: Mr Webster, I want you to find whoever is sending
these letters and put a stop to it. Money is no object, but …

Webster: But?

Sylvia: But my father must not be involved in any way.
Any kind of scandal could destroy him.

Webster: I assume you have no idea what these sins the
writer alludes to might be.

Sylvia: I have no idea and I don't believe there is an idea to
have. It's absurd.

Webster: Who is Edward Kilcoyne?

Sylvia: What difference does that make? I'm not asking you
to investigate the letter-writer's allegations, I'm asking you
to find her out and put a stop to it. (*Pause*) 'Ned Kilcoyne'
was the head of the, oh, Printing Union I think. He
supported Daddy in his last election. He disappeared
suddenly, and people tried to link Daddy to the
disappearance, but nothing ever came of it.

Webster: The letters mention a brother.

Sylvia: Yes, Ethan. Ethan is … well, we're twins, Mr
Webster, but we're not close. Ethan has had a 'history of
mental illness', as they say. He rarely speaks to me, and
never to Daddy.

Webster: So you suspect he may have written the letters.

Sylvia: Yes – no – I don't know. Oh I feel so disloyal telling you this, it is a betrayal, but – when I showed Ethan the letters, first he laughed, which was unusual in itself, and then he said: 'Let's hope Father's man enough for the road ahead.'

The lights turn red. **Hammett** *brings two goblets of red wine on. He presents them to* **Webster** *and* **Sylvia,** *they each both take a sip, and then he takes them away again. It should look something from a dream.*

Webster: Do you know what he meant by that?

Sylvia: I have no idea, and he refused to explain himself. He just began to laugh, and the angrier I became with him, the more he laughed – wild, unrestrained laughter, it was horrible.

Webster: Miss Bryant, what makes you think these letters were written by a woman?

Sylvia: Do I think that?

Webster: You said you wanted me to find *her* out.

Sylvia: Did I? Well, I suppose it's a women's kind of thing, isn't it? Spiteful letters? A woman's revenge.

Pause.

Webster: Right then, Miss Bryant, give me a couple of days and I'll see what I can turn up.

Sylvia: Thank you, Mr Webster. I hope this will be enough to cover you for the time being.

She hands him a cheque.

Webster: Yes, that's enough. It's more than enough.

Sylvia: Good. Here's a number you can reach me at, day or night.

She makes to leave.

Webster: Oh, Miss Bryant?

Sylvia: Yes, Mr Webster?

Webster: Is your mother still alive?

Sylvia: (*Ice*) My, my, my mother died three years ago. And her death is of no significance to this …
in … vestigation, Mr Webster, so, I, I, I would prefer if we didn't speak of her again.

She's gone.

And…

Scene Six

Dash and Lilly Play House

Key Largo, Florida. Summer 1933. **Hammett** *is working.* **Lillian** *sings, off, then comes on and presents* **Hammett** *with a plate of food.*

Hellman:

> *Sing a song of sixpence, pocket full of rye,*
> *Four-and-twenty blackbirds baked in a pie,*
> *When the pie was open the birds began to sing,*
> *Wasn't that a dainty dish to set before a king.*

Hammett: Lilly, what did we say about baby talk?

Hellman: That's not baby talk, Dash, that's a nursery rhyme. (*Pause*) We said as long as you paid me not to, I shouldn't.

Hammett: That's right. And I've been counting out my money, so –

Hellman: So you better count out some more. What are you, cheap or something?

Hammett: No more baby talk, honey, or I go straight back to mother.

Hellman: 'Yes dear.' (*Pause*) So d'you wanna go fishing this afternoon?

Hammett: 'M working.

Hellman: Okay. I'll see if one of the local boys is interested. *Raoul* looks bored ...

Hammett: Lilly, did you taste this meal?

Hellman: What? Oh, no.

Hammett: It tastes like burnt rubber, it's horrible. How can you cook a meal without tasting it?

Hellman: It looked horrible when I was cooking it. That's why I didn't taste it.

Hammett: You know what my mother said about a woman who couldn't hack it in the kitchen?

Hellman: She said she probably wouldn't be much good in any other room in the house.

Hammett: That's right.

Hellman: So I'll send for her, shall I?

Hammett: Who?

Hellman: Your mother. She could live with us, and fill in for me in those rooms in which I can't 'hack it', would that suit you better?

Hammett: Hey piano, piano.

Hellman: Piano up your ass, cook for yourself in future if you're such a fucking gourmet.

Hammett: Lilly, I only –

Hellman: Or I know, you *teach* me how to cook. You can improve me Dash – teach me how to cook, how to write plays, how to drink – and then you can sell me at a profit. Then I could be grateful and you could be wise.

Hammett: The food's fine Lilly.

Hellman: No it's not. Give me.

She tries to take the plate.

Hammett: (*Holding on to it*) No.

Hellman: Yes. (*Tug of war*) Because if we don't like our food, then there's only one thing we can do. (*She gets the plate and upturns it over him*) Now, does that taste better?

Pause.

Hammett: Lilly, is this not a bit of a cliché?

Hellman: I am not your fucking wife, Hammett, and don't think you can treat me like one. If you want a wife, go out and get one. You'll recognise her by the demure way she lets you get away with murder.

Hammett: I've already got a wife, remember? Could I have a towel?

Hellman: Well get another, bluebeard. Buy three and get one free. Here.

Hammett: Thank you. Food still tastes like shit.

Hellman: Good.

Hammett: And anyway, the guy I bought you from told me you'd grow into a proper wife in time.

Hellman: Well you were had. You should've known by the clothes. *Women's Wear Daily*, Dash, you've got to broaden your reading.

Hammett: I know.

Hellman: Now, today, par example, I sport the 'Free Spirit' sun dress, indicating that I am Modern Girl.

Hammett: Is she anything to Flaming Youth?

Hellman: One and the same. Modern Girl is confident, independent and vivacious. She is bold, but not a virago –

Hammett: Ho ho ho.

Hellman: She likes to laugh, but she knows her own mind. Which reminds me, O Great One, when you read my first play *Four Days Ago*, did you think it was any good?

Pause.

Hammett: I thought it was very good, Lilly. I really think you're a writer.

Hellman: (*Rapture*) You really think it's good?

Hammett: I really think it's good. I do have some notes …

Hellman: Let's celebrate first. A big drink?

Hammett: Yes ma'am.

Lillian *fixes drinks, they toast each other.*

Hellman: Why don't we get married?

Hammett: Because I asked you and you turned me down.

Hellman: (*Outrage*) You know that's not true. We talked it all out and we decided –

Hammett: Well there you are, you see. Memory is the first thing to go, but it's sad to see it in one so young. You talked it all out, and you decided, and while you were thus occupied, I went out and got drunk.

Hellman: And that's how you can remember it so clearly, I suppose, because you were plastered at the time.

Hammett: What do we need marriage for, we have such peace and harmony without it, we don't want marriage to spoil this bliss now, do we?

Hellman: WELL I'D LIKE TO GET MARRIED.

Hammett: WELL SO WOULD I.

And …

Scene Seven

The Blood of the Bryants

Lights up on **Webster**.

Webster: Before I could make another move, Ethan Bryant called and asked to see me.

Ethan: I thought I'd better come and see you. Because of my sister. Because of, of, of what she might have said.

Webster: And what do you think she might have said?

Ethan: Uh, more what she, she, she didn't say. About our Mother. And other things.

  Pause.

Webster: Well I'm on the edge of my seat here, Ethan. Why don't you tell me about Mother. And other things.

Webster: Well, I want to, Mr Webster. And I will.

  Hammett *comes on. He has a smallish brown paper bag with him, the kind you get sandwiches in. He sits at a desk adjacent to* **Webster***'s, takes a white table cloth out of his pocket and spreads it out over the desk top. He puts the bag on the cloth, opens it, takes out a red apple and puts it on the desk.*

Webster: Ethan?

Ethan: Mr Webster, our Mother had an affair with a man. She and Father did not always see … eye to eye, and they had disagreements. Then she had an affair. With a man.

Webster: What was this man's name, Ethan?

Ethan: He was Mr Kilcoyne. They would meet at home when Father was not at home. They would sometimes meet in Mother and Father's room. And sometimes in a Guest Room. And sometimes they would go driving. In a car.

Hammett *takes a vase with a single red rose out of the bag and puts it on the desk.*

Webster: Keep on the track, Ethan.

Ethan: In a car. One night they went out driving in a car. But they didn't go a long distance. Because the car blew up. There was an explosion and the car blew up. Then, then, then my father came. He cleaned things up. Men came from my father's job and together they cleaned everything up.

Webster: What does that mean, 'clean things up'?

Ethan: It means, ohhhhh … it means, Mr Kilcoyne was reported as a person who had got lost, and our Mother was buried as a person who had died of, of, of natural causes. A doctor helped. Father and his men cleaned it all up.

Hammett *takes a red cloche hat out of the bag and puts it on the desk.*

Webster: You say your parents had 'disagreements': what kind of disagreements?

Ethan: Father got cross. He disagreed with Mother. He would say she let him down and that she didn't consider his position. 'You let me down,' he said. 'You don't consider my position.' I heard him say that.

Hammett *takes a half-drunk glass of red wine with lipstick stains around the rim out of the bag and puts it on the desk.*

Ethan: Then he would hit her. He hit her on the face, and he hit her on the tummy, and he hit her on the back, on the bottom of the back, and then he hit her … and then … between the legs. He hit her there. Sometimes with his hands, and sometimes with sticks. He would sometimes hit her with sticks.

Pause.

Webster: Who was Mr Kilcoyne, Ethan? What did he do?

Ethan: He worked for the Union, in the … Printing Press Union. He was a Union Man.

> **Hammett** *takes a string of rubies out of the bag and puts it on the desk.*

Webster: And how does Sylvia come into all this?

Ethan: Sylvia went away to school. Then she came home. They were in the Guest Room one night. Then Sylvia came home. She went into the Guest Room. The three of them were in there for a minute. Then Sylvia came out. She was angry. Then Sylvia hated mother. When Mother died, Sylvia was happy. She was happy.

> **Hammett** *takes two lighted church candles out of the bag and puts them on the desk.*

Webster: Ethan, when your sister showed you the anonymous letters she received, she told me that you said: 'Let's hope Father's man enough for the road ahead.' Why did you say that?

> **Hammett** *takes a red bible out of the bag and puts it on the desk.*

Ethan: I didn't say that. I never said that, Mr Webster.

Webster: Then why did she say you said it?

Ethan: I don't know. But I can tell you what I did say. Sylvia came into my part of the house and gave me the letters. And I read them. And I said: 'Good. I hope Father is found out, and drops dead.' (*Music*) That's what I said, Mr Webster. I said: 'Good. I hope he drops dead.'

> **Ethan** *stands up and smiles.*

Webster: Ethan. Did you write those letters to your sister?

Ethan: Mr Webster. I live in the same house as my sister. If I want to say something to her, well, I do. I don't need to

send her sentences through the mail. I'm going now.
Goodbye.

He goes. **Hammett** *takes a red crucifix out of the bag and puts it on the desk. Then he sits back and presents the desk to* **Webster**. *There are two lighted candles with a bible and a crucifix between them. There's an apple and a string of rubies and a cloche hat and a glass of red wine with lipstick stains and a red rose in a vase, all arranged on a white table cloth.* **Webster** *looks at the display. The music builds to a crescendo.*

And ...

Scene Eight

The Great Man At Work

1934. **Dashiell Hammett** *sits at a table, in front of a typewriter. On an occasional table to one side stand Scotch bottle, soda siphon and glasses; on a similar table to the other side stands a telephone.* **Hammett** *puts paper in the typewriter and stares at it. He brings his hands forward and types two words. He sits back and looks at what he has written. He looks at the Scotch. He looks at the typewriter, and cranks it up for his next line. He stares at it. With his fingers, he begins to tap out a typing rhythm on the table, humming 'Dixie' the while. He stops suddenly, closes his eyes and clenches his fists. The telephone rings. He looks at it, then walks over and picks it up.*

Hammett: Yeah ... this is he ... yeah ... how does $1000 sound? ... No ... yeah, I know all about the Screenwriter's Guild, I'd just prefer not to join ...'cause I'd prefer not to ... listen, I'll just send the cheque, alright?

He puts the receiver down. He stands a moment, then walks to the Scotch, pours off a shot and knocks it back. He winces, stretches himself a bit, steadies up and returns to the table. He sits down and stares at the page. He puts his head in his hands, his elbows on the table. He takes his hands away, looks at the page again, and suddenly tears paper out of the machine and crumples it up

*into a ball. He throws the ball away and fixes himself a big drink,
with soda this time. He sits back down and puts a new page in the
typewriter. He drinks, sits back and sings:*

Hammett:

> I wish I was in Dixie,
> Away, Away,
> In Dixieland I'll make my stand,
> I'll live and die for Dixie ...

*He drains his glass and grins. The whiskey has connected with his
hangover, and he has a sudden rush of bliss. He slides over to the
scotch, fixes another big drink and brings the bottle and siphon
with him to the telephone, humming a dance tune as he goes. He
puts his luggage down with difficulty, picks up the phone and gets
the operator.*

Hammett: Hello, yes ... no, not yet.

*He replaces the receiver, takes little black book from breast pocket,
finds a number and repeats the above procedure, entangling
himself in bottle, glass and siphon as he does so. There is an air of
self-conscious pantomime about all of this.*

Hammett: Hello, yes, could I have Hollywood Boulevard
1934-959. (*He gives a Groucho Marx Twang to the digit nine*)
Thanking you. (*Charm*) Hello *Angel* ... This is *Dash* ... Well,
I'm calling *now* ... I don't recall any incident ... No no no,
must've been another Dash .. or maybe my twin brother ...
You don't? Well we might just pop round together, then
you'd have your hands full ... well I'll pay for the glasses ...
so I'll pay for the *crystal* ... and a new rug ... no, I'm off the
sauce three straight weeks now ... Yeah, this is the big one,
angel, this is the best yet, and angel: You're in it! ... No, I'm
not kidding, one of the characters is modelled directly on
you ... Oh now Angel, you know I like a girl like you ...
Well, I thought the Brown Derby for drinks, maybe a little
dinner, and afterwards – who can tell, Angel, the night is
ours ... she's out of town ... sure I'm sure... yes I know she
gets mad, but she's back East, Angel, don't fret ... About
nine then ... I promise, not a drop ... Bye.

*He pours another drink. The bliss has worn off, and he's
beginning to feel sick and tired. He sits down again, and stares at
the blank page, and then pulls it out with care. He pushes the
typewriter back, puts his feet up on the table and sings the chorus
of 'Dixie' again, but slower this time, more wistfully. As he sings,
he forms the page into a paper aeroplane, and at the climax of the
song, he sends the aeroplane into space.*

And ...

Scene Nine

Governor Bryant Speaks His Mind

Webster: I went to see Governor Bryant deliver a campaign
speech.

Lights on **Curtis Bryant**. *The sound of the crowd.*

Curtis: Now let me pose you all a question. What is it that
makes this country great? Well, let us agree straight off on
what it's not.

It's not the obsession with Labor rights that enables
irresponsible, highly paid workers to bring our country to a
standstill with yet another strike, for yet another greedy
wage demand.

It is not the obsession with relief, that enables the work-
shy, the idle and the criminal to live like lords at the expense
of the honest citizen.

It is not the obsession with free speech that ten years ago
would have had us ruled by a Hitler, and that today would
have us controlled by the war-lords of Moscow; free speech
in support of a system that would deprive us of free speech is
a con-trick in my book, and I know what country my book
was printed in. None of these obsessions – and that is what
they are, folks, sick obsessions – made this country great.
Aren't you just a bit sick of them? Sick of the bleeding heart
liberals, who do very well for themselves I can tell you,
lecturing the rest of us about what we should do, what we

should think, and, worst of all, how much we should be prepared to give, presumably for the privilege of living in a land we call America, but which the bleeding heart liberals would soon christen 'The Union of UnAmerican Socialist Republics'.

I'll come clean. I'm sick of them. Sick of their UnAmericanism. Sick to the back teeth. Tell you what. Let's send them all some messages, ladies and gentlemen.

To the union man who spends more time on strike than at work (and that's all of them): If you don't want your job, Mister, there's plenty waiting to take your place.

To the work-shy Welfare sponger: Count yourself lucky to have gotten away with it for so long – your number is up.

To the communistic, fellow-travelling liberal whingers: If you don't like this country, well then get the hell out. Go on over to Russia, and see how far your free speech gets you there. We've learned our lesson: The New Deal ... was a Raw Deal. Always remember about the New Deal: while idealistic speeches were being made on the front porch, the Reds were being paid off round the back door.

Oh yeah – that New Deal was a raw deal alright.

What made America great, and what will make it great again? Success.

That's strange – I didn't hear anyone applaud. If you won't applaud success, ladies and gentlemen, what will you applaud – failure?

Rumblings from the groundlings.

Oh no. What made, and will once again make, America great – Success!

The crowd roars.

I believe in the success ethic, ladies and gentlemen. I believe in the vigorous American who creates the wealth we all desire; he employs others and so produces wealth for others.

The communists of the New Deal tell us the worker is the people's hero. I say NO.

I say in a successful America, the successful man, the businessman, the wealthy man is the people's hero. He holds the position to which we all should aspire, and he gives us the freedom to achieve that aspiration; his success is a beacon to light our way, light our way to freedom – the freedom to fulfil our dreams.

Wild applause.

Webster: That's Daddy.

And ...

Scene Ten

Those Foolish Things

1936. **Hellman**'s *thirtieth birthday. A party in* **Hammett**'s *hotel room.* **Albert** *and* **Betty Friedrich**, *two screenwriters, are there.* **Hellman** *enters. In half light.*

Albert/Betty: Surprise! Surprise!

Hellman: I don't believe this!

Lights: Party Hats, Presents, Hugs and Kisses etc.

Hammett: (*On a chair*) A toast, ladies and gent., a toast.

Hellman: Oh Dash – stop him, somebody.

Hammett: To Miss Hellman, on the occasion of her second 29th birthday. I hope this will be the second of many such, and I hope also that *Days To Come,* her new play, enjoys the acclaim and success it deserves. Let us hope Miss Hellman appears once more in her rightful place as the brightest star in the Broadway firmament.

Albert/Betty: Amen to that!

Hellman: Get me a bucket! Thirty years old already, and still I can't keep this shitheel away from me.

Hammett: We're adhesive folk, we Hammetts, we stick around to the bitter end.

Hellman: We'll see, you old shitheel, we'll see. I am not enjoying any of this!

Betty: Oh cheer up Lilly. Thirty isn't the end of the world.

Albert: No, it's just the end of your life.

Betty: Albert!

Hellman: Thanks Bert, you're a tonic.

She unwraps the gift **Hammett** *has given her. It's a fur coat. She doesn't say anything.*

Betty: Oh my God. Albert, do you know what that is?

Albert: Well dear, I think it's a coat.

Betty: It's a mink coat from Bergdorf's, it's exquisite. I think every woman should have one. What do you think, dear?

Albert: I think I think … what you think, dear.

Betty: Lilly darling, I hate you.

Albert: Thanks a lot, Hammett, there goes my spring fishing trip.

Betty: And now, my husband and I present – Lilly's Birthday Surprise!

Albert: Honey, are you sure?

Betty: Don't honey me, Albert. I will brook no honeying. Remember this and we may still be married tomorrow.

Albert: Ladies' choice.

Betty: As ever.

Hellman: A toast – to Elisabeth and Albert and their very happy marriage!

They drink their toast in silence.

Betty: You alright, Lilly?

Hellman: 'Course I'm alright. Now, where's my surprise?

Betty: An Infamous Tale of Drunk and Disorderly Conduct among the Lettered Classes.

Albert: Brought to you by Friedrich and Friedrich, Screenhackers for Hire.

Hellman: Drunk and disorderly, it's got to be Dash.

Hammett: I represshent that remark.

Betty: Interior: Day – The Famous 21 Club. It is noon. Mr Dashiell Hammett, the distinguished crime novelist, enjoys a bracing *aqua vite* with –

Albert: Mr William Faulkner, the *latest* Great American Writer –

Betty: Whose tales of Southern sweat have brought a tear to the eye of many –

Albert: And a dollar to the pocket of none.

Hellman: These guys should work in Show Business.

Betty: The rarefied talk is of Writers and Writing.

Albert: I'm Hammett.

Betty: And I amn't.

Betty: Marcel Proust?

Albert: Too French.

Betty: James Joyce?

Albert: Too Irish.

Betty: Joseph Conrad?

Albert: Too English.

Betty: He's Polish.

Albert: (*Beat*) Not Polish enough.

Betty: Johnny Walker?

Albert: Now you're talking.

Betty: And so on. Into this cerebral cut and thrust marches Bennett Cerf –

Albert: Publisher and fully paid up member of the Smart Set.

Betty: I'm Bennett Cerf.

Albert: I'm Hammett.

Betty: And I amn't. Hi Bill, good to see you; how are you Dashiell?

Albert: We're both fine, Ben, but what is this finery you're wearing, are you getting married again?

Betty: Oh you joker you. No, but later on, I'm having cocktails round at Alfred Knopff's – that's Alfred Knopff's – house.

Albert: Well I declare. Would that be in the nature of a little *soirée*, Ben? Just who all is agonna be there?

Betty: Well actually, Miss Willa Cather –

Albert: The significant lady writer –

Betty: Will be there.

Albert: Well Ben, if Miss Willa Cather –

Betty: The significant lady writer –

Albert: Is agonna be there, then we must be there too –

Albert/Betty: For we admire her work greatly.

Betty: Okey doke then, Bill, Dashiell, why don't you tag along with me? Where should I collect you?

Albert: Well how about here, Ben?

Betty: Well you'll hardly still be here, guys, now will you?

Hellman: Bom bom bom ...

Betty: The scene shifts ...

Albert: As scenes will –

Betty: To Bennett Cerf's car.

Albert: Exterior: Night –

Betty: Two bottles of scotch and counting. Now Mr Cerf is not best pleased –

Albert: He is disgruntled –

Betty: Well dammnit he has had it with these uncouth writer fellows –

Albert: These dirty, drunken writer fellows –

Betty: I cannot *believe* you've been drinking there for eight hours solid.

Albert: It's just a job like any other, Ben.

Betty: Well I don't know what Mr *Knopfffff* is going to say.

Hellman: I think I can guess.

Betty: Interior: Night. The gracious home of Alfred *Knopffffff*, publisher of the great Hammettski –

Albert: A select gathering of business folk, potential sponsors all –

Betty: The Publisher and his Begging Bowl.

Hellman: Oh my *God.*

Betty: I'm Alfred *Knopffffffffff* –

Albert: I'm Hammett –

Betty: And I amn't – Delighted to meet you, Mr Faulkner, won't you come in?

Albert: Missippi, fried chicken, cotton pickin' –

Betty: Hello Hammett.

Albert: Scotch 'n' soda, hold the soda –

Betty: Come this way, Mr Faulkner –

Hellman: Hammett, you can wait in the garden –

Betty: So Alfred does his best to ignore Hammett, who is stumbling around the place.

Albert: He takes down all his Faulkner first editions and asks 'Bill' to autograph 'em –

Betty: Which he does, and everyone's watching in rapt silence:

Albert: The Bankers, and the Captains of Industry, and the Society Ladies, all gazing at the Great Man At Work –

Betty: When all of a sudden, Hammett –

Albert: Scotch and soda, hold the soda –

Betty: Falls off his chair and passes out.

Albert: G'night honey.

Betty: Now our *soirée* is *horifiée*. Alfred is positively apoplectic; he stands over the snoring Hammett and goes:

Albert: Ta na ta *na* –

Betty: Outrageous conduct! This man Hammett is a disgrace. I give him advances but he will not write, he just drinks, he is drinking his talent away –

Albert: Well this is not how gentlemen behave in the South. Faulkner rears up, flings the books in the air and says: I will not sit here and suffer my friend to be abused, Sir. Hammett is a fine man, and a good drinker, and a great writer; and an

Eastern sissy like yourself is not fit to shine his shoes. I say: Good day, Sir.

Betty: So Bill turns on his heel and stalks off with great dignity, but a rogue carpet interrupts his flight – he hits the deck – and the Southern Sage remains Supine.

Albert: And it's closing time.

Hellman: Two Great Writers At Work And Play – A Still Life.

Albert/Betty:

> *Happy Birthday to you,*
> *Happy Birthday to you,*
> *Happy Birthday dear Lilly,*
> *Happy Birthday to you.*

Hellman: That is a *great* story.

She hugs both of them. The telephone rings. Eventually,
Hammett *answers it.*

Hammett: Hello … oh, hi … no … no, it's … yeah, that's right … alright … okay, Bye. Bye.

Pause.

Hellman: That your secretary, Dash?

Hammett: What? Oh, no. No, just a friend.

Hellman: It's funny really. Once I called Dash from New York, it was the night 'The Children's Hour' opened, and I needed to tell him how well it had gone, the way you do, so I called. This woman answered, and she said: 'Mr Hammett can't come to the phone right now' and I said: 'Who are you?' and she said: 'Oh, this is Mr Hammett's secretary' and hung the phone up. Then I realised that it was 4 a.m. California time, and I remembered that Hammett didn't have a secretary. It's funny really.

Pause.

Albert: Betty, should we –

Betty: Yes, we really should –

Hellman: And then, you see, we were going to get married. You didn't know that, you thought we didn't believe in it. You thought, because I *told* you, that we believed in, oh, 'love unfettered by bonds like marriage'. Percy and Mary Shelley sort of stuff. Marriage worked for some, but not for two as brilliant as Dash and me. Well, no, we were going to get married. We got rings, we set a day, I was even going to buy a dress. And then, with about two weeks to go, Dash threw a party. Sid and Laura Perelman were there. Dash put a hooker in his bathrooom and he told Sid Perelman and Sid went up, and then Dash told Laura Perelman and Laura went up, and there Sid was, screwing the hooker while his wife looked on –

Hammett: Lillian –

Hellman: Well Laura was so upset that Dash took her off to San Francisco, and in order to cheer her up, he fucked her ass ragged for the next four days.

Hammett: (*Comes at her*) LILLIAN!

Hellman: What're you going to do, Hammett? Hit me? Are you Man Of Action today, is that it? Come on, hit me. Or am I too good for that, is that what the girl on the phone is for? Or have you just forgotten what any of it is for?

Silence.

Hellman: I'm going now. (*She gives* **Hammett** *the fur coat he bought for her*) Dash, take this back to the store. I don't need it. I already have a fur coat. This coat. You gave me the same coat last Christmas. Don't you even remember? (*Pause*) Goodnight Betty, goodnight Albert.

She goes. The Friedrichs exchange a look, and then **Betty** *follows* **Hellman** *off. Pause.*

Albert: Dash, ah, would you like a drink?

Hammett: You guys belong to the Screenwriters Guild, don't you?

Albert: That's right. Why?

Hammett: Maybe it's about time I joined. Got involved.

Albert: Well the more members we have, the harder it is for the studios to push us around. And your name would be a big help.

Hammett: Well then, that's what I'll do. I guess it's a case of everyone getting together to do something, right?

Albert: Right.

Hammett: Good. Good then. (*Pause*) I'll have a large Scotch and soda.

And ...

Scene Eleven

Nell Kilcoyne – A Good Old Girl

Webster: I discovered Ned Kilcoyne, the Union Man, had a daughter – Nell – so I decided to pay her a visit.

He drinks and waits. **Nell Kilcoyne** *appears, déshabillé. A hot afternoon.*

Nell: Mr Webster, what can I say? When you're late, you're late. You'll forgive me though, I can see you're the forgiving type. Drink?

Webster: Scotch.

Nell: Scotch is the correct answer. I gave this hangover eight hours to vacate, but it's not budging. Guess I'll have to scorch it out. Here's mud. (*She downs a scotch, pours another and brings* **Webster** *his drink*) Now Mr Webster – how can you help me?

Webster: I'm a private detective, Miss Kilcoyne –

Nell: Nell.

Webster: Nell. I'm a private detective, Nell, and –

Nell: Short for Ellen, which I prefer, but I'm told it doesn't suit me so well. I don't mind what you call me, s'long as it's not –

Webster: Nellie? I, ah, knew a girl called Ellen once. Nell, I'd like to ask you a few questions about Ned Kilcoyne.

Nell: Ned Kilcoyne? Mr Web – oh look, what's your Christian name?

Webster: Daniel.

Nell: Daniel. Dan. Dan, yes, that's better, I can't call you Mr Webster all afternoon, it's an undertaker's name. So, Dan – in't this cosy? – what's your interest in Ned Kilcoyne?

Webster: I have reason to believe he may have been murdered.

Nell: Would that reason be Ethan Bryant?

Webster: How do you –

Nell: First day on the job, Dan? Gotta get that poker face in gear. So tell me, Ethan spun you a crazy tale about Curtis Bryant having his wife and my father blown up, right?

Webster: Right.

Nell: Well that's all it is, Dan. A crazy tale. Curtis has two kids, right? Sylvia is Daddy's little girl and always has been; Ethan is a great disappointment to his father and always will be. It's the usual father and son nonsense – with the added twist that Ethan is a certified June-bug loony tune. I hoped you noticed that.

Webster: How come you know so much about the Bryants, Nell?

Nell: Practically grew up with 'em. Alright, listen up: Tales of the Kilcoynes, Chapter One. (You wanna 'nother?) Ned Kilcoyne hit the top of the Print Workers' Union busting heads off of every rung. The men he couldn't screw, he'd screw their wives instead. He drank and he swore and he didn't give a shit. He was a Harp, what can I tell you? So Ned's meteoric rise brings him into close contact with Governor Byrant, and the two great men soon reach an ... *accommodation.* In short, they hit pay-dirt, and everyone else gets it in the ass. Chapter Two, Nell plays with the Bryant kids and their pretty toys. Only Sylvia doesn't want a pretender to her throne, so mostly I play with Ethan. *Weird* kid.

Webster: Chapter Three?

Nell: In Chapter Three, Ned falls for Mary.

Webster: Late wife of Curtis.

Nell: Private dick, right? Now, what we Irish've always lacked is a sense of proportion. We eat, we get fat. We drink, we get drunk. We fall in love, we fall, Dan. We are the fallen. Ned fell for Mary Byrant, and boy, was he lost. He thought she was a princess. My mother was just the wife, you know, just the baby machine, and she couldn't even do that right – she had me, a girl (wrong), then four miscarriages, (wrong, wrong, wrong, wrong) and then – a stillborn son that killed her. Wrong again. But Mary was the ticket to the land of hope and glory for Ned Kilcoyne. And then ...

Webster: And then?

Nell: Who knows, Dan? Maybe Mary ditched him. Maybe Curtis found out, warned him off, and Ned blew with a big stash. Maybe maybe maybe.

Webster: Maybe Curtis killed him.

Nell: Maybe he did? Who cares? Ned Kilcoyne may've charmed the pants off a truckload of broads, but he broke my mother's heart and he was an asshole to his daughter. All that Irish he-man crap, I figure he woulda stuck it in *me* if he'd got the chance. So – he disappeared, he died, big deal.

He fleeced the print workers for long enough to leave me plenty. And if I don't care, Dan, why should you?

Webster: Tough talk.

Nell: Tough life. Look, Curtis Bryant runs the cops around here. Runs 'em, he *owns* 'em. So even if he was a wrong 'un, there'd be nothing you could do. Except kill him. All on account of Ethan Bryant, registered crazy person?

Webster: And what about Sylvia Bryant. Is she crazy too?

Nell: Oh no. Sylvia's a shrewd operator, Dan. Daddy brought her up to take what she wants, and she does. Have you seen her yet?

Webster: I … saw her father speak last night. She was by his side.

Nell: That's how it's always been, Dan. Except for … alright, get this: Dennis Brand, rising assistant D.A., dies tragically in freak gas explosion at his home. Suspicious circumstances, open verdict. Peter Henry, intern at Willson General, dies tragically when brakes fail and his car skids over Leggett cliff. Suspicious circumstances, open verdict. Sylvia Bryant's name linked romantically to each shortly before death of each.

Webster: How do you know all this?

Nell: Drunken newspaper man makes a pass, I fend with silky skill, and surface with hot gossip. He was terrified I'd blab, had to swear me to secrecy.

Webster: I'm glad he did.

Nell: And now, in a vain attempt at beautification, it's bath-time for Nell-Nell. So you'd better run along – unless of course you'd like to stay and scrub my back.

Webster: Thank you very much, Miss Kilcoyne, you've been most helpful.

Nell: Story of my life. So long, Danny boy.

And ...

Scene Twelve

Glory

1942. **Lillian** *sits at a desk working. It's late.* **Hammett** *comes on, dressed in army uniform. He is gloriously drunk.*

Hammett: *(From off)*

> *Mine eyes have seen the glory*
> *Of the coming of the Lord,*
> *He is trampling out the vintage*
> *Where the grapes of wrath are stored;*
> *He hath loosed the fateful lightening*
> *Of His terrible swift sword;*
> *His truth is marching on.*
>
> *Glory! glory, hallelujah!*
> *Glory! glory, hallelujah!*
> *Glory! glory, hallelujah!*
> *Our God is marching on.*

Hammett *is on, glowing, doing a funny little dance.* **Hellman** *doesn't turn around.*

Hellman: Is that you, honey?

Hammett: *'I have seen Him in the watchfires'* –

Hellman: So what happened, you meet Bill Faulkner and re-enact the Civil War?

Hammett: *'Of a hundred circling camps'* –

Hellman: Or d'you go down the barracks and toast the troops again?

Hammett: *'They have builded Him an altar in the evening dews and damps'* –

Hellman: O my God – you've written something. You've finally –

She turns and sees the uniform. Silence.

Hammett: (*Still singing*) *'I can read'* –

She stops him with a wag of the finger.

Hellman: Now, my guess, my estimation, not least my hope, Mr Samuel Dashiell Hammett aged 47 years, is that you are clad in military attire for the purpose of attending a fancy dress ball, and all you require of me tonight is that I don suitable garb to accompany you to said ball. As your escort. Tonight.

Hammett *grins, shakes his head, opens his mouth to sing.*

Hellman: My second guess is that you met a soldier in a bar and you bet on the number of drinks you can drink and you won of course and he had no cash so he had to give you his uniform –

Hammett:

'His righteous sentence by the dim and flaring lamps' –

Hellman: And my third is that the army cracked at last and accepted you.

Hammett: *'His day is marching on!'*

During the next speech, **Hammett** *hums away while performing various military-style activities: marching, rifle drill etc.*

Hellman: I've never liked the kind of women who say this, and I really never thought I'd hear myself saying it, but it's the only cap that fits, so here goes: MEN! FUCKING MEN!

Hammett *turns, salutes her, and marches on.*

It is something I will never understand – why every American man – however cultivated – deep down, all he really wants to be is a redneck. A redneck *boy*. It's so …

godammnit, I knew this was coming; I just hoped because of your age, they wouldn't take you, and because of your politics, you wouldn't join, but … but but but. The army ups its age limit, Hitler invades the Soviet Union, and I'm a war widow. Just as well I look good in black.

Hammett: (*Approaches her*) Dance with a soldier boy, ma'am, dance with a soldier boy?

He is behind her. She smiles a stiff smile. He puts his hands on her hips and pulls her to him. He runs his hands over her breasts.

Hammett: Fuck with a soldier boy, ma'am, fuck with a soldier boy?

Hellman: (*Struggling*) Get off. Get the fuck off me! (*She pushes him away*) Hammett, six months ago you called this war a 'pro-fascist imperialist conspiracy'. Then the Nazis attack Russia, and all of a sudden it's an heroic confrontation between democrats and fascists? (*Pause*) It can't have escaped you that joining the army might just be a way of avoiding writing with a clear conscience. It hasn't escaped me that armies are trained to kill people and I don't want you to come back to me in a box. (*Pause*) Aren't you going to say anything? Do you not have a single word of any kind to say that might give me … a clue? A clue to unriddle all this?

Hammett: Lilly. This is the happiest day of my life.

And …

Scene Thirteen

Ethan Prays to his Holy Mother

Low strings play. **Ethan Bryant** *comes on.* **Hammett** *appears with a white sheet.*

Ethan: Hello? Is there somebody there? Sylvia? Father? Is there anybody there?

Silence. **Ethan** *kneels before the altar.*

Ethan: Hail Mary, full of grace, the Lord is with thee …

A man approaches. Music.

> Blessed art thou among women, and blessed is
> the fruit of thy womb …

The man draws nearer.

> Jesus. Holy Mary, Mother of all …
> Pray for us sinners now …

The man is right behind **Ethan**.

> And at the hour of our death –

Hammett *drops the sheet over* **Ethan**. *It covers him.* **Ethan**
*screams. The man shoots him six times in the face and neck. The
lights flood red. The music builds to a crescendo.*

Blackout.

End Of Act One

Act Two

Scene One

Family Plot

The Altar from Scene Seven. Ethan's Grave. **Curtis, Sylvia,** *and* **Hammett** *as a preacher. Night.* **Webster** *watches. Low strings play.*

Hammett: And it came to pass ... that God did tempt Abraham, and said unto him: Take now thy son, thine only son Isaac, whom thou lovest, and get thee into the land of Moriah; and offer him there for a burnt offering upon one of the mountains which I will tell thee of.

Webster: I bribed the morgue attendant.

Hammett: And Abraham took the wood of the burnt offering and laid it upon Isaac his son; and he took the fire in his hand, and a knife, and they went both of them together.

Webster: And two of Curtis' cops.

Hammett: And Isaac spake unto Abraham his father, and said, My Father; and he said, Here I am, my son. And he said, Behold the fire and the wood; but where is the lamb for a burnt offering?

Webster: Ethan was shot six times, his dick was cut off and stuffed into his mouth.

Hammett: And Abraham said: My son, God will provide; and they came to the place God had told him of; and Abraham built an altar there, and bound Isaac his son, and laid him on the altar upon the wood.

Webster: The verdict? Death by misadventure.

Hammett: And Abraham stretched forth his hand, and took the knife to slay his son.

Webster: He was cleaning his pistol, right?

Hammett: And the angel of the Lord called unto him: Lay not thine hand upon the lad, neither do thou anything unto him; for now I know that thou fearest God, seeing thou hast not withheld thy son, thine only son from me. In the name of the Father and of the Son and of the Holy Ghost Amen.

And ...

Scene Two

Mantalk

1942. **Hammett** *in Alaska with* **Bob** *from Brooklyn and* **Billy** *from Alabama. They are knocking back shot glasses of scotch.*

Bill: Take my wife.

Bob: Everyone else has.

Bill: Let Pop do the funnies, boy. At least when he do, they are funny.

They lower a shot.

Bob: (*Very loud*)

> *Ten men went to mow, went to mow a meadow,*

No.

> *One man went to mow, went to mow a meadow,*
> *One man and his dog, went to mow a meadow.*
> *Two men went to mow —*

Hammett: Bob. You may as well drink meths if that's all the music you can muster. Now son, you were suggesting that we take your wife.

Bill: As an *example.*

Hammett: Sure. Of what?

Bill: Of a woman who just ... lies there.

Hammett: Is this at all times, or ...

Bill: No, when you're ... when she's ... and you're ... you *know* ...

Hammett: Taking her.

Bill: Yeah. She ... just lies there. Still. As if she don't feel a darned thing. And silent. Like a ...

Bob: Sheep.

Bill: I'll tan your hide for you boy if you don't cut it out, you hear?

Hammett: Boys. Public warning No.1: This scotch is mine. It is intended to lubricate the vocal chords, but in an exclusively harmonious manner. Aggressive actions and unkind words will cause the bar, regrettably, to close.

They have another shot.

Bob:

> *Come peasants artisans and others,*
> *And soo de doo la de da oil,*
> *We have a something something something*
> *Drive the insolent from the soil.*

Hammett: Indolent.

Bob: What?

Hammett: The line is – Drive the indolent from the soil. Indolent. It means lazy.

Bob: So?

Hammett: You, ahh, sang 'Insolent'. Insolent means rude, unmannerly, obnoxious –

Bob: So?

Hammett: So there's probably a good argument for driving the insolent from the soil also, but this song has a sterner agenda.

Bill: It's not just her. Any woman. Except whores. Any woman I've been with. Just lie there. As if they were dead. Dead dead dead. (*Pause*) Do you believe in God, Pop?

Bob: Commies don't believe in God, Strawhead.

Hammett: I am a lapsed Catholic, William.

Bill: What's that mean?

Hammett: It means no, I don't.

Bill: Oh. Why not?

Bob: 'Cause he's a Commie, shut up.

Hammett: 'Cause I got along badly enough with the father I had, I figured it'd be pretty dumb to sign up with another. And just who told you I was a Commie, Bobby boy?

Bob: I just know it. I know it, see? So anyway Pop – if you're this great Commie and everything, why don't you sing the Internationale?

Hammett: Well, Bob, I've got this fixed idea that a body should be able to sing before he sings. And I can't sing.

Bob: And what's that supposed to mean?

Hammett: It's not *supposed* to mean anything ….

Bob: What you're saying is, you're saying to me, you can't sing, am I wrong?

Hammett: Are you wrong that you can't sing or are you wrong that that's what I'm saying to you?

Bob: I'm not wrong, I'm right.

Hammett: Right.

Bob: I'm right. D'you hear me? I'm right. Always right. You hear me?

Hammett: The folks back home in Brooklyn can hear you.

Bill: What would you do, Pop? To get her to ... to do something, anything, apart from just lie there.

Hammett: Well Billy, maybe what she needs is a little longer, you know what I mean?

Bill: A little *longer?* But Pop –

Hammett: Time. Longer time.

Bill: Oh, *time.*

Hammett: That's right. Like, how long do you take?

Bill: How long do I ... you mean, when I ... haw haw haw, what kind of a question ... how long does anyone take?

Hammett: How long?

Bill: Awww, about a minute, I guess. Ain't never timed myself, but I reckon a minute, 90 seconds or thereabouts.

Hammett: A minute?

Bill: Well, not always. Sometimes it's less. D'you think a minute's too long?

Hammett: A *minute?*

Bill: What's the matter with you? A minute's all the time a guy needs. Has it been so long you've forgotten, Pop?

  Bob *and* **Billy** *giggle.* **Hammett** *gets another drink in.*

Hammett: Billy boy. Women ... tend to need a little longer than a minute. Longer even than 90 seconds. Women need time ... *beforehand* –

Bill: Time beforehand for what?

Hammett: Time so that they can get aroused. Excited. *Hot.*

Bill: Hey, this is my wife we're talking about, not some two dollar whore, some cheap meat to jack off into.

Bob: And this is why she just lies there – *because* she's your wife. Whaddya looking for, some kinda … *nympho?* Because sure she'd holler and moan, and buck and roll, and then you'd go: 'Where the fuck'd she learn this?' and you'd go: 'When I'm not around, this bitch is gonna go sniffing after dick, no question', and you'd be living in some kind of fucking nightmare.

Bill: And then?

Bob: And then you'd kill her. You'd have to. So wake up, Bill – Women Don't Really Like It – except for sluts, (and you don't want to marry one of them), or whores that pretend to, (and you don't *need* to marry one of them). Am I right or am I wrong, Pop?

Hammett: No question, Bob.

Bill: I think I believe in God.

Bob: So come on then – give us the Internationale, Pop.

Hammett: Who told you I was a Commie, Bobby?

Bob: Some guy, I don't know, looked a bit like an M.P., only different. This is a couple of weeks ago, he comes up to me and goes: 'You know Corporal Hammett?' and I go: 'What if?' and he goes: 'You know he's a commie, don't you, he's a Red?' and I go: 'Well I figured there's something weird about a guy that joins the army one when he don't got to, and two when he's an old guy.'

Hammett: And what else did he ask you?

Bob: He asked me if you were going around trying to convert the boys into commies. So I said: 'Look – if all the commies in the world drink like Sam Hammett, they're never gonna make it out of bed in the morning, let alone convert us.' And if I'd've known, I'd've said – he *can't* be a Red – he don't know any of the *songs.*

Bill: So Pop. Betty Grable.

Hammett: Yes.

Bill: You was in Hollywood. You meet her?

Hammett: Yes.

Bill: Does she ... do you think she ... well ... what we was talking about?

Hammett: I don't know, Billy. I don't know if Betty Grable just lies there or if she screams the house down. I didn't do it to her, and I didn't listen to anyone else doing it to her. So I can't tell you what kind of a girl Betty Grable is.

Bill: 'Cause you know, *actresses* ... I heard a lotta talk about how actresses, you know ... they get *around* ... and with all different guys and stuff, but ... well they just look so ... so darned *pretty* on the screen, I can't believe those girls can be cheap or nothing.

Bob: They're different, actresses, they're ... it's a different thing. Actresses are completely different from just ... *women*.

Hammett: And that's why Hollywood is such a magical place, guys. Everything is different, even the air ... sparkles. Heck, I just love it. And you know – I miss it too.

Another drink.

Bill: Hey Bobby – in the office, General Barnes came around, asks Pop: 'Why does your paper only report the Russian troop advances? Why is there no coverage of our army's progress?' And Pop says: 'Well Sir, this paper has a policy not to publish any ads.'

Bob: And I'm supposed to believe a guy like that can't manage one lousy Commie song.

Hammett: That's it. On your feet: Bobby from Brooklyn, and Billy from Alabama, and Sam from St. Mary's County.

They all stand. They are all plastered.

There's only one song I feel like singing, and if you don't like it, Bobby from Brooklyn, well you can go and fuck yourself. And you too, country-boy. One drink now, and one for when the music's over.

They stand, a glass of whiskey apiece, swaying in anticipation. **Hammett** *clears his throat, and sings, without irony.*

> *O beautiful for spacious skies, for amber waves of grain,*
> *For purple mountain majesties above the fruited plain.*
> *America, America, God shed his grace on thee,*
> *And crown thy good with brotherhood from sea to*
>   *shining sea.*
> *O beautiful for patriot dream that sees beyond the years,*
> *Thine alabaster cities gleam undimmed by human tears.*
> *America, America, God shed his grace on thee,*
> *And crown thy good with brotherhood from sea to*
>   *shining sea.*

The two boys' eyes are damp. **Hammett** *raises his glass, and they all drink.* **Billy** *falls right back – out cold.* **Bobby** *makes an 'I'm going to puke' gesture, and runs outside so to do.* **Hammett** *pours another drink, sits down, and sighs.*

Hammett: Well, I don't care what anyone says, there's nothing like a night out with the boys.

And …

Scene Three

The Sins of the Fathers

Webster: (*Aside*) I called Sylvia Bryant. She said she couldn't see me. I told her if she didn't see me, I'd see her father. She saw me.

So let's talk about Ethan's death, shall we?

Sylvia: I don't know …what are you talking about?

Webster: You hired me to do some work, Miss Byrant. I'm doing it. I know about Ethan's death, and how it was kept quiet. How did it happen? Were you told?

Sylvia: He ... was cleaning his gun and it ... went off.

Webster: You see the body?

Sylvia: No, I ... Daddy thought it best if I ...

Webster: Yes, I'm sure he did.

Sylvia: What do you want from me, Mr Webster? I asked you to drop the case. We should be left alone in our grief now, my father and I.

Webster: Ethan came to see me. He told me things about your father and you.

Sylvia: (*Beat*) What things?

Webster: Many things. Why was his death hushed up, Miss Bryant?

Sylvia: The scandal, what with the election coming and everything ...

Webster: No. No, that won't do. That won't do at all.

Sylvia: What did Ethan say to you, Mr Webster? What were these 'things' he told you? You know Ethan wasn't well, that he –

Webster: Who are Dennis Brand and Peter Henry?

Sylvia: I don't know. Is that a riddle? Who are they?

Webster: Tell me about Nell Kilcoyne.

Sylvia: Nellie Kilcoyne. Is she involved ... did she write the letters? Yes, that would make sense, she never liked me, she always wanted to turn Daddy against me.

Webster: And why did she want to do that?

Sylvia: Because she was jealous. She was jealous of me, because, I, I, I was the best little girl in the world. (*Pause*) What did Ethan tell you, Mr Webster?

Webster: He told me that your father murdered Mary Bryant and Ned Kilcoyne, and that you were glad when you heard of your mother's death.

Sylvia: What?

Webster: He told me that when you showed him the letters, he said: 'Good. I hope he's found out, and drops dead.'

Sylvia: *What?*

Webster: You heard. Your brother was murdered, shot six times in the throat. Then his ... six times, shot six times. There was no 'accident', Miss Bryant.

Sylvia: No, I –

Webster: There's something rotten going on, it stinks to high heaven and you know more about it than you're telling.

Sylvia: Rotten, rotten, the only rotten slut in my family was that bitch, Mary, she shames the Bryant name, she was a cruel and wicked father to us both, to Ethan and me both.

Webster: A cruel and wicked father to you both?

Pause.

Sylvia: Did, did, did I just say that?

Webster: Yes. Yes you did.

Pause.

Sylvia: I'm scared, Mr Webster. I don't know what's happening with, with, with things in my own life anymore.

Webster: Why did you come to me? The police are all controlled by your father, they could've investigated the letters without any danger of scandal.

Sylvia: I came to you. I had bad dreams, they began to get worse. I was frightened. I ... the letters came ... and they seemed familiar. It was as if I knew all about them ... but I couldn't remember ...

Webster: And so ...

Sylvia: ... and so I had to do something, make a change. And Ethan just laughed at me, he said: 'You know all about it.' I couldn't go on on my own. I came to you. Here I am.

Pause.

Webster: Would you tell me one of your dreams, Miss Bryant?

Sylvia: Yes. Yes, this is one I have all the time now. I'm standing in the driveway of our house. It's a bright, sunny day, and my Daddy is starting up his car. There's a little girl sitting on the car seat beside him. I shout: 'Wait, please wait for me, please don't leave me alone.' And my Daddy and the little girl turn around and smile and wave. And the little girl is *me*. Then they drive away, laughing, and I'm left alone, standing. I begin to scream, but no sound comes, and anyway, there's nobody at home to hear me. Then there's a gap, I don't know what happens, and then, very suddenly, I'm on the grass, on the clay, and I can't lift my face up. Someone or something is forcing my head, my face, down, deeper and deeper into the clay. Then I wake up, choking, as if I'm going to suffocate. At the end, I'm so relieved to be alive again, just to breathe.

The lights change as the love duet from Madama Butterfly *swells up.* **Webster** *brings* **Sylvia** *to a table in an Italian restaurant. They drink red wine from goblets* **Hammett** *has brought.*

Sylvia: Ah, Puccini.

Webster: Beg pardon? You know one of the waiters?

Sylvia: No, Puccini wrote this music. *Madama Butterfly.* The opera?

Webster: Right. (*Pause*) Miss Bryant, what Ethan told me: does any of it sound familiar to you?

Sylvia: I don't remember, Daniel. I know it sounds absurd, but I have no memory of my own of what happened ...

Webster: Just what your father told you happened?

Sylvia: That's right. It's like the things people say you did when you were a baby – soon you believe you can actually remember them yourself.

Webster: And did your father baby you a lot, Sylvia – call you the best little girl in the world, call you his little princess? (*Beat*) You alright?

Sylvia: I'm sorry, I ... I get this powerful urge to attack you, to defend him. Anyone who ever said a word against him ... I'd fly at them in a fury. He used to say, 'I can count on you Sylvie. I can count on your loyalty. You'd never betray me, would you? You'd never let me down?' No Daddy. No Father. No Sir. I can't remember anything else, Mr Webster. I'm sorry.

Webster: You're different. Not as sharp, as careful ...

Sylvia: Yes, well, something is happening, isn't it? Something is changing.

Pause.

Webster: Miss Bryant, Ethan said your father used to beat your mother –

Sylvia: Oh Ethan built an altar to the bitch, he revered her like an angel instead of the whore she was, bringing that animal Kilcoyne into the house, doing it in their bed, rotten stinking slut. (*Pause*) You're going to have to be patient with me, Mr Webster. Sometimes a voice bursts through and I don't know who it belongs to, it just ... smothers me.

Webster: It's alright. We'll take it slow. It's alright.

The music plays.

Sylvia: Listen. It's a sad story. Do you know it?

Webster: No.

Sylvia: Madama Butterfly marries an American soldier – name of Pinkerton.

Webster: Oh yes?

Sylvia: She loves him deeply – but he's not in love. She's a geisha after all, and only fifteen. He just wants to sow some exotic wild oats, before he settles down with a nice American wife.

Webster: It doesn't come out right in the end, I guess.

Sylvia: You guess right. He leaves her, then returns with his new wife. He discovers Butterfly's had a child, 'his' child, and so he sends his new wife to ask his old wife for 'his' child.

Webster: Yes.

Sylvia: And Butterfly sends her away, and commits hara-kiri with her father's sword.

Webster: Yes.

Sylvia: Here though, he thinks he loves her. He's carried away by her beauty. But it's a lie. It's the story of a woman who loves too much a man who cannot love at all.

And **Sylvia** *leaves* **Webster** *alone at the table as the music plays.*

And ...

Scene Four

Crack-Up, Break-Up

1947. A bar. **Hammett** *drinking.* **Hellman** *arrives.* **Hammett** *stands, wobbling, and he tries to kiss her. She gives him her cheek, keeping him at a distance.*

Hammett: You want a drink, honey? (*He summons a waiter*)

Hellman: No thanks, nothing.

Hammett: Oh have a drink.

Hellman: Alright, a club soda –

Hammett: A club soda? That's not a –

Hellman: That's what I want, please.

Hammett: (*To waiter*) A club soda, and another one of these, Joe.

The waiter goes. **Hellman** *is eating olives from a cocktail dish.*

Hellman: Is that a double?

Hammett: It's a tribble. Are you counting?

Hellman: Are you? (*Pause*) So what would you like to do on this, ah, date?

Hammett: Well, we could go get something to eat.

Hellman: I've already eaten.

Hammett: Or we could have a couple drinks and, you know, see where they leave us.

The drinks arrive. **Hammett** *tips the waiter.*

Hammett: Way to go, Joe.

Waiter: Thank you, Mr Hammett, sir.

Hellman: So that's what you'd most like to do, is it? Have a 'couple drinks'?

Hammett: Oh, I guess so. Is that alright?

Hellman: Sure it's alright, it's fine. Just fine.

Pause.

Hammett: How are rehearsals going?

Hellman: Oh, you know. They're going.

Hammett: Good.

Hellman: The cast ask after you.

Hammett: Do they? That's good.

Hellman: Oh yes, you made quite an impression.

Hammett: Well, that's good to know. Good to know I didn't make quite such a fool of myself in front of 'em as you seemed to think. (*Pause*) How's my little girl Pat making out?

Hellman: Patricia Neal is not your little girl, she is my discovery, she's a very talented young actress, she's going to be superb as the young Regina and she *never* asks after you. (*Pause. A flicker*) How's the writing going?

Hammett: Oh, you know …

Hellman: No.

Hammett: What?

Hellman: No, I don't know. I don't know how the writing's going. In fact, I assume it isn't going at all.

  Pause.

Hammett: I, ah, have this idea, this new idea … I've been working on it, kicking it around for a while now … this guy, none too young, gets out of the army and finds he can't settle, all his friends, his *wife* … have changed … or maybe he has, he doesn't know … anyway, he decides what he really wants to do is just pack up and go to an island, go live on an island. (*Pause*) But I haven't done that much work on it yet … what with all these meetings, and speaking engagements, and my *teaching* …

Hellman: And that haircut …

Hammett: What?

Hellman: Well you got a new haircut, didn't you? I reckon that must've taken up, oh, three days at least, what with planning the haircut, having the haircut and then getting drunk to celebrate the haircut. Oh yeah, I can see how tough it must be to get writing done under that kind of pressure.

Pause.

Hammett: (*Yells*) Joe, I'll have the same again. And bring the lady some more olives.

Hellman: Hammett, I don't want to see this any more.

Hammett: Well shut your eyes. The pain just ... floats away.

Hellman: Don't want to see you ... you're a drunk. That's all you are right now. You used to be a writer who drank –

Hammett: So did you, darling, don't forget, so did you.

Hellman: I only drank to keep up with you. And I never could, and I suddenly realised I didn't want to, I didn't *need* to drink like you to be ... a writer, to be my own person –

Hammett: Oh pardon me while I puke. What is this, d'you read *The Schoolgirl's Guide to Freud?* I don't *need* this ladies' magazine horseshit ...

The waiter brings the drink and a dish of olives. **Hammett** *beams at the waiter and gives him another tip.*

Hammett: You pay to play, Joe, am I right?

Waiter: Absolutely, Mr Hammett, sir.

Hellman: Alright then, let's just put it like this: I don't drink any more, and you don't do anything else except drink. And I need to save myself here. I don't want to sit around and watch you commit slow suicide.

Hammett: I've told you why I drink –

Hellman: Oh yes, you told me because the world is bad enough drunk but even worse sober, or because you can't figure out why people's words and their deeds don't tally, or because a bunch of other reasons, but finally, you don't need a reason – you drink because you drink, and it's ugly, and deadly, and I don't want any part of it. I want to live.

Hammett: Well fuck off then. Go fuck yourself, lady, go off and live. I don't 'need' you. Don't need anyone.

Hellman: And it's not suave Dash and cute Lilly any more, Hammett, it's not some romantic prohibition fantasy. I've helped you bleeding from the gutter, I've sat quiet while you roared and hollered and made a fool of everyone around you –

Hammett: (*Loud*) Oh Joan of Arc with the flaming ass –

Hellman: Like that, yes and I got Mary taken away from you because you couldn't cope with her on your own.

Hammett: Of course I could cope, what do you –

Hellman: She had black eyes, and bruises, and the two of you always drunk and screaming at each other –

Hammett: So she's her father's daughter, that annoy you?

Hellman: It annoys me that she wasn't just wild, she was sick, and that you were too drunk or too crazy to see that; Jesus, your own daughter.

Hammett: Jesus, your own daughter what? What is this shit? Are you accusing me of something? You and that psychological fuckmate of yours, Paulie, you got it all worked out between you: 'D'you ever have a sister?' 'D'you ever have a daughter?' Is that right? 'What does any Daddy *really* want to do to his daughter?' Is that right? Is that from the Schoolgirl's Guide to Freud as well? Is it? What sort of man do you take me for?

Hellman: I'M *SORRY.* I'M CRACKING UP HERE HAMMETT, ALRIGHT? I'M SORRY. I'm sorry this is happening. But there's nothing ... nothing to look forward to. Why could you never speak your love for me? Only in letters ... all the times we'd be apart, during the war, always such loving letters, such love ... and then when we'd meet, and I'd be expecting, no, hoping, so much ... and you'd go –

Hi. Hello Lilly. And I'd go blah blah blah, walla walla walla, in such a panic, you know, such a fool, and you'd look at me like 'Oh for Christ's sake' … such love … where did it, does it go? It's like you wrote to an imaginary woman, and then I turn up, claiming to be her, and it's no good … I don't fit the picture you had in your head.

Hammett: Oh very pretty, Miss Hellman, very poetic, quick write it down, it's perfect for one of your wonderful plays.

Hellman: Why can you never say it?

Hammett: Because saying it –

Hellman: Lessens it, well, maybe. And maybe I'd've settled for less.

Hammett: No you wouldn't. No you wouldn't.

Pause.

Hellman: The cast ask after you because they can't believe you'll last much longer the rate you're going. The average waiter does not expect a hundred dollar tip, which is the amount you've given this one each time he's served you. And this one's name is Jim. Not Joe. Jim.

She gets up to go. He grabs her arm.

Hammett: Don't you fucking leave this table.

Hellman: Let go.

Hammett: Don't you fucking dare leave this table.

Hellman: Hammett, you're hurting me, let go of my arm.

He lets go.

Hammett: Don't leave …

Hellman: Thank you for a lovely evening.

Hammett: Lillian … I have something to say … but I can't find the right words … I *want* to …

Hellman: (*A flicker*) I know. I know you do. (*Pause*) I'm sorry for what I said about the haircut. It's a nice haircut.

Hammett: Don't leave …

Hellman: I've got to. I'm suffocating.

Hammett: Lilly – please don't leave me alone.

Hellman: Bye bye. (*She goes*)

Hammett: Joe! (*The waiter arrives*) Joe, is your name Jim?

Waiter: Yes sir, Mr Hammett sir.

Hammett: Well, I'm glad we've got that cleared up. Now, 'Jim', how about bringing me another drink?

Waiter: Don't you think, Mr Hammett, that maybe you've had enough?

Hammett: You're absolutely right, 'Jim', I have had enough. More than enough. Now bring me another fucking drink, alright?

Waiter: No sir.

Hammett: What?

Waiter: No sir, I won't do that.

Pause.

Hammett: Okay. I'm just going to sit here for a minute, 'Jim' – and then I'm going to go. Okay?

Waiter: That's fine Mr Hammett.

Hammett: Good. Jim?

Waiter: Yes, Mr Hammett?

Hammett: Jim, d'you ever have a daughter?

And …

Scene Five

Webster Roughs Nell Up

Webster *and* **Nell**. **Nell** *looks like a rough weekend.*

Webster: Nell.

Nell: Danny boy, come in, sit down, feet up. You wann –

Webster: Cut the cackle lady. Now you sit down and hear me out. I want the truth and I want it fast – or your portion's gonna be a truckload of grief.

Nell: 'You'll never take me alive, copper.'

Webster: (*Slaps her into a chair and grabs hold of her*) Listen, you two-bit tramp, if you wanna get back to swapping your tail for a couple of whiskey sours, you'll spill. Otherwise, I'll fix you up good, you can count on that. For starters, Ned Kilcoyne is still listed as missing – so his money is off limits. You're living high on the hog here Nell – whose is the bankroll? Then, there never was a Peter Henry or a Dennis Brand for Sylvia Bryant to murder. Just a Nell Kilcoyne, and a trail of loose ends. Like a set of anonymous letters that somebody sent to Sylvia Bryant – somebody so jealous of the little princess and her dashing father that she wants revenge, Nell? Or like Ethan Bryant, the crazy person with the big mouth – dead, Nell, murdered and mutilated since we last spoke. So if all this is your way of getting back at folks who live on the hill, the curtain's just dropped, Nellie – it's time to talk. And hey – the tears might fool some barroom dupe, but not me.

  Nell *is crying.*

Oh come on Nell, you're not gonna get away with that old crap. It's really not you.

  She gets worse. He cracks.

Oh for Christ's sake, what? What is it?

You want a handkerchief?

Nell: *No.* (*She sobs*)

Webster: Here, just take it.

Nell: Thank you. (*She blows her nose*) I didn't know Ethan was dead. That bitch must've killed him too, Jesus.

Webster: *What?*

Nell: Alright – I made up about those guys because I knew that Bryant bitch was guilty and I wanted you to know it too. Now. Now. When my Daddy 'disappeared', Curtis Bryant came to me. He said he was so upset about Ned, and that he wanted to do something for me.

Webster: And what did he do for you, Nell?

Nell: *Money,* Dan; he gave me money. *Gives* me money. So I go (to myself, needless to say): This doesn't figure. Curtis is a well-mannered guy and a gentleman and everything, but he doesn't need to shell out like this. So then I go: *What has he got to hide?* But the cash curbs my curiosity, so I drop it. Until Ethan comes and tells me that his father killed Ned and Mary Bryant, which makes no sense whatever.

Webster: Why not? You got Curtis pegged for sainthood Nell?

Nell: Look, Ned was worth more in votes alive than dead, and all his votes went to Curtis. And a politician doesn't mess with votes. So I figure it's got to be Princess Sylvia. And, ah, seeing as how we're coming clean here, I should also say that I rang Curtis and told him about Ethan shooting his mouth off.

Webster: And now Ethan's dead, Nell. So what do you think, Curtis hired Sylvia to do the job? The murderer cut Ethan's dick off, Nell, cut it off and stuffed it in his mouth.

Nell: If you'd seen that bitch as a child, Dan, so vicious to Ethan and to me, so … kittenish to her Daddy – you'd believe anything of her. *Anything.* She the one who hired you?

Webster: I don't have to –

Nell: I know you don't, but maybe you should. What to do?

Webster: (*Shows letters*) To find out who wrote these. They look familiar?

Nell: (*Looks at them, whistles*) Apocalyptic stuff. I'd say Moses wrote them. Well, rules me out anyhow – Catholics don't know shit about the bible, we've got the Pope instead.

Webster: If Sylvia Bryant is bad, why would she've hired me?

Nell: I don't know, but Curtis knows a hell of a lot about you, Danny boy. And I didn't have to tell him. You look a bit shook, Dan.

Webster: I'm alright.

Nell: Sure you are.

Webster: Nell … your father … you said before he'd probably've stuck it in you – but he never got the chance.

Nell: Did I? Well half of that is a lie, Dan. Take your pick which half. Do you want your handkerchief back?

Webster: No. No, it's okay. I'm … sorry, Nell.

Nell: Don't be a sap. Just watch out for snakehips, alright? She's gonna destroy you.

Webster: Yeah. Bye. Ellen.

Nell: Bye bye.

And …

Hammett *joins* **Webster**.

Hammett: Well Dan, how's your code?

Webster: It's fine.

Hammett: Good. I see you got your two types of broad, anyhow.

Webster: Yeah. Except …

Hammett: Except?

Webster: Yeah, I got 'em.

Hammett: Good. (*Gleefully, sensing* **Webster***'s confusion*) The man wants to go live alone on an island, but he wants the woman also, so he's caught between the two. The man … doesn't know what the fuck he wants.

And …

Scene Six

Private Life, Public Life

1951. **Hammett** *is sitting.* **Hellman** *appears with tea things. There is a phone between them.*

Hellman: They call yet?

Hammett: No.

Hellman: I made some more tea.

Hammett: Oh good. None for me thanks.

Pause.

Hellman: Well the conversation certainly deteriorated last night after you stormed out. I think they figured they were being too flippant, so they started in on McCarthy and the House Committee, the whole bit.

Hammett: Well goodness. What did your English writer pal have to say about that?

Hellman: Oh, what you'd expect. He doesn't care what a chap's politics are, so long as a chap's not a bore. Being a bore is the most grievous sin a chap can commit.

Hammett: He should know.

Hellman: I thought, God Lilly, and we used to think we could clever-talk with the best of 'em.

Hammett: Clever-talk. Who needs it?

Pause.

Hellman: Dash, do you remember, when we first met, can you remember what we talked about?

Hammett: Well, among other things, we talked about T.S. Eliot.

Hellman: I don't *believe* you remember.

Hammett: I have never forgotten it. The reason being, you called the poem, 'The Waste Land', a *gauntlet.*

Hellman: I what?

Hammett: Yeah. A challenge to … somebody or other, to do … something or other.

Hellman: I never said that.

Hammett: Yup.

Hellman: I *couldn't* have.

Hammett: Yup.

Hellman *moans with embarrassment.*

Hellman: Oh, and now I suppose you think you cured me of all that nonsense.

Hammett: I like to think I tried, Lilly. I like to think I tried.

Pause.

Hellman: Well, I just remember about our first meeting that you were drunk, and extremely pleased with yourself.

Hammett: I was King of the Castle in them days. And I suppose you think you cured me of all *that* nonsense.

Hellman: And I remember we quoted 'The Waste Land' at each other.

Hammett: No we didn't.

Hellman: We did.

Hammett: No, you wanted us to, but I put a stop to it. Forward thinking. So that, down the road, we'd be spared the embarrassing recollection that once, we were the kind of people who quoted verse at each other.

Hellman: I was *sure* ...

Hammett: Well, I guess one day you'll write about how we met. Then you can tell it any way you like. And knowing you, you will.

  Pause.

Hellman: Dash?

Hammett: No.

Hellman: How can you say no before you know what I'm about to say? (*Pause*) We're doing well, aren't we? For now.

Hammett: Lilly ...

Hellman: Just answer. Say *something.* It won't kill you. (*Silence*) How about a cup of tea?

Hammett: Oh yes please. A cup of tea would be very refreshing.

Hellman: You know, the doctor didn't believe you when you said you were going to give up booze.

Hammett: But I gave him my word.

Hellman: Do you always keep your word?

Hammett: Oh yeah. It's easy. You just never give it.

Pause.

Hellman: Can we go over it again?

Hammett: There's no point.

Hellman: Well, there might be. Let's go over it anyway.

Hammett: I don't see the point.

Hellman: The *point,* the fucking point *is,* is that that phone is going to ring, and you're going to answer and say: 'Yes, I'm taking the Fifth Amendment, I'm pleading the right to silence', and then tomorrow you're going to jail. And I need to know exactly why. I need to understand.

Hammett: (*By Rote*) Eleven Communist Party leaders were sentenced under the Smith Act and four of 'em jumped bail; that bail was supplied by the Civil Rights Congress, of whose bail fund I am a trustee; ordinary people contributed to the bail fund and tomorrow I'm expected to name their names and I'm refusing so to do.

Hellman: You don't know any of the names.

Hammett: No –

Hellman: So why don't you just say that? More to the point, why don't you speak out, Dash? Say: this is a witch-hunt, it's an abuse of democracy, it's wrong. Then people might understand what you're doing, the stand you're taking.

Hammett: People – who needs 'em? (*Beat*) Lilly, the last people I heard talking about 'taking a stand' were Albert and Betty Friedrich, and look what happened to them.

Hellman: Don't –

Hammett: We believe in freedom this and democracy that and then they name half the Los Angeles telephone directory.

Hellman: But if you *are* taking a stand, you could make it public – think of the effect it might have.

Hammett: The only possible effect it might have is on a handful of Hollywood liberals, so big deal. Anyway, I'm not taking a stand.

Hellman: Well what the fuck are you doing going to jail for six months?

Hammett: I'm doing … look, you know this kind of talk makes me sick, but … I just know they're wrong and I'm right, not in principle, just … I just know it. They have no right even to ask me for those names … so I won't answer 'em, and I'll be proud not to answer 'em … and if you really need a big idea for all of this, let's just pick democracy, and say it's because of that, and because I won't let any two-bit politician or judge or cop tell me what democracy is.

The telephone rings. They look at each other. **Hammett** *picks it up.*

Hammett: Hello … just a second … (*To* **Hellman**) It's your secretary.

Hellman: Yes … Oh hi Paulie … no … no, look, I'm, ah, expecting a call, let me, ah, call you back, alright? Yeah. O.K. bye.

Hammett: I thought you'd dumped him.

Hellman: I'm still trying. Anyway, if you can't even get jealous, just shut up about it. (**Hammett** *laughs*) When did they think up this dumb phone thing?

Hammett: Couple years ago. They need 12 hours notice of what way you're gonna go.

Hellman: So they can give you a harder time?

Hammett: No, so they can warn the papers and TV and get a lot of attention. John Wayne suggested it to 'em.

Hellman: Horray for Hollywood. (*Pause*) Hammett, this is not a Western. All you're saying to me is … fuck, is just Boy Learns To Be A Man prairie shit. I can't respect that.

Hammett: I'm not asking you to respect it.

Hellman: I can't even understand it.

Hammett: I thought it was just Boy Learns To Be A Man prairie shit.

Hellman: Your going to jail in silence is an action of worth to one person only, and that one person is you, and that is not good enough.

Hammett: Well, sorry.

Hellman: (*Mounting frustration*) What's so bad about having an effect on liberals anyway? Why not try and change them?

Hammett: Because liberals don't matter a damn, that's why. I've thought this for years, ever since I saw Frank Little lynched, only then I didn't think anything could be done, and now I do. But it's gonna have to be a little bit more radical than a bunch of liberals deciding to be kind to the poor. And we've had this out over and over –

Hellman: And I still don't think it's any excuse for not doing what you can, for not taking power into your own hands.

Hammett: No, that's just wrong. We don't have any power. They have the power. We want it. If we think we have a little, the way we live now, then we're just deluding ourselves. Which self-delusion suits those with power very nicely. And why do you need to hear all this again?

Hellman: Because … because, you're not going to be around to say anything at all for the next while, and because … oh Christ, forget taking a stand, and liberals, and democracy, and all other ten dollar words, because I need

something for *me*. I need something ... to hold, a reason, an
excuse, a promise ... a *something* to hold onto for the time
you're away. So I go over and over the same old stuff, in
case a new detail might slip out and make sense of it all.
Because I've known you for twenty-one years, Dash, and
you're still like a complete stranger to me.

Pause.

Hammett: Lilly, you *know* that I ... that I'll ... Lilly, I ...

They are both very upset. The telephone rings. **Hammett**
answers it.

Hammett: Hello ... this is Dashiell Hammett speaking ...
I'm insisting on my right to silence.

He puts the phone down.

Hammett: Lilly, I ...

Hellman: Tell me the story of how Frank Little was
lynched, Dash.

Pause.

Hammett: I worked for Pinkerton's as a detective, and one
time I was sent to the mining town of Butte, Montana.

And ...

Scene Seven

Webster Stirs Things Up

Curtis: Mr Webster, we meet at last. Sylvia, sit down dear.
Sylvia has told me such a great deal about you, Mr Webster
... such a flattering interest in our family, are you an orphan
by any chance? (*Pause*) Webster ... you will doubtless be
familiar with the writings of your dramatist namesake?

Webster: 'A politician is the devil's quilted anvil.'

Curtis: Yes indeed, yes indeed, 'He fashions all sins on him, and the blows are never heard ...' John Webster dear – the Jacobean poet of doom and despair.

Webster: You wear your learning a little more lightly when you speak in public, Bryant.

Curtis: A hit, Mr Webster, a palpable hit. You saw me don the weeds of populism, no doubt, the better to move the groundlings. Rhetoric is a wonderful device, is it not? If you have nothing to say, say it in threes nonetheless, and leave your audience weeping.

Webster: Oh you had something to say alright. Something about success being the dream, and welfare spongers and the New Deal commies and striking workers being the nightmare. Is that what you really believe?

Curtis: I cut my cloth, Mr Webster. I cut my cloth. People are happier believing that the enemy lies within. It fosters an agreeable illusion of disorder. So I keep them looking down – at the blacks, the Jews, the unemployed, always looking down –

Webster: For fear that if they started to look up, they might see what you are actually doing.

Curtis: Come now, Mr Webster – 'really believe', 'actually doing', what kind of phrases are these? You sound dangerously like someone with political convictions. I wish people would understand that politics is not about convictions, it's about getting things done, about managing the world the way it is. There's nothing hidden, no 'real' truth to be revealed – things are as they appear. You have your life, I have mine; politics is about not interfering. But you're not here for a debate, Mr Webster, so let's get on to the true purpose of your visit, shall we?

Webster: I think you have something hidden, Bryant. I think you have a real truth waiting to be revealed. Who murdered your son Ethan? And why'd you pretend it wasn't murder, and then hush it up anyway?

Curtis: Mr Webster, you understand you are here as a favor to my daughter. You must also understand that this privilege does not entitle you to indulge in personal abuse of your host –

Sylvia: Daddy, was, was, was Ethan murdered?

Pause.

Curtis: My son was a sexual degenerate of the more promiscuous and degraded variety. He was murdered by a casual pick-up – shot six times in the throat.

Sylvia: Oh God.

Webster: And then?

Curtis: I think that's more than enough, don't you?

Webster: Do you want me to tell her?

Curtis: The murderer then sliced off Ethan's ... genitals, and placed them in the corpse's mouth.

Sylvia: Oh my God. Oh Jesus. Oh God.

Curtis: I'm sorry, Sylvie princess, I kept it quiet for your sake. You can appreciate why any man might want to keep such an incident a secret, Mr Webster. It's a father's cross, and I had hoped to bear it alone.

Webster: And what kind of cross made you pay Nell Kilcoyne off all these years since her father 'disappeared'?

Curtis: Edward Kilcoyne fled, leaving his only daughter destitute – I took pity on her, Mr Webster. A 'good deed', you might say.

Webster: Your only son told me that you had Ned Kilcoyne and Mary Bryant murdered after Sylvia found them in bed together.

Curtis: Yes indeed, and Nell Kilcoyne probably told you Sylvia murdered them and I covered it up to protect her, and I might tell you Ethan murdered them, and then roasted the bodies on a spit and ate them, and which is true? Do you distrust me and trust Sylvia? And if so, what, exactly, is guiding your judgement? It seems to me that the 'actual truth' for you is just whatever truth you favor. You aren't sure that Sylvia didn't lie to you, Mr Webster. In fact, you don't seem very sure of anything at all.

Webster *looks at* **Hammett**, *who smiles and shrugs.*

Webster: You're absolutely right, Bryant – but it's the truth I favour or no truth at all. Sylvia, why did you write these letters about your Daddy?

He tosses them at **Curtis**.

Sylvia: What? I, I, I, didn't … how do you …

Curtis: Sylvia?

Webster: You wrote them, *Sylvie,* didn't you? And then forgot, or pretended someone had sent them to you. Why did Ned Kilcoyne disappear? Ask your father, *Sylvie.* If you would know corruption, look at your father's heart, *Sylvie.* You've lived in a false innocence for long enough, *Sylvie.* The sins of your father will return. They will haunt you and your brother just as they have haunted and will haunt him.

Curtis: Sylvie, did you write these?

Webster: And then you told me, *Sylvie,* remember what you told me, you said he was a cruel and wicked father to you both.

Curtis: Sylvie, did you say that? Did you betray me to a total stranger? Did you write these wicked lies?

Sylvia: No, I … don't know, I can't remember …

Webster: It's time to put an end to the bad dreams, Sylvie, time to stop being Daddy's little princess – What happened in your dream, Sylvie? You saw a little girl with your Daddy, but you were screaming. And then your face, forced down into the earth, choking. The sins of your father won't haunt poor Ethan any more, Sylvie, but then how could you have known that Curtis would murder his own son?

Curtis *has produced a gun, which he aims at* **Webster***, ready to shoot, but his daughter's scream makes him stop.*

Sylvia: *Daddy?*

Then at last, she remembers. We hear her voice, quiet but clear as a bell.

Sylvia: Don't do that to Ethan, Daddy, don't hurt him like that ... I heard him screaming, Daddy, I heard him scream and scream ... Ethan said his bottom was bleeding, Daddy, that it was sore after you ... don't hurt him, Daddy, please don't hurt him please ... You bastard. You evil bastard.

Curtis: Sylvie, no, don't let me down now –

Sylvia: It wasn't me. Oh my God, it wasn't me. It was Ethan. You never touched me, it was Ethan you destroyed. Your own son. And then, then, then ...

We were twins, Ethan and I. But he turned against me, and now I understand why – because he thought I *knew*.

But I was afraid to remember, afraid it was me – and then you see, we had the same dream, yes, I had *Ethan's* dream ... *his* face, deeper and deeper into the clay ... you *animal*.

Oh ... I'm free now.

I never understood it. Why I'd always get Ethan's stammer when I'd try to remember. It's all true. You turned me against my mother, made me hate her, and then you killed her. You killed Ned Kilcoyne. You killed Ethan. *Ethan.* You destroyed him years before you killed him. Your own son ...

Curtis: It's not true, Sylvie, I swear it –

Sylvia: It's broken. It's finished. There's nothing left now. You trusted me, Mr Webster.

Webster: Not really, I –

Sylvia: Yes really. You trusted me even if you didn't want to. Take me away now. You've done what I wanted. Take me away from him.

They leave.

Curtis: Sylvie ... Sylvie princess, don't betray me. Sylvie ... please don't leave me alone.

He is alone. The lights are flood red. The altar appears. Music. **Ethan** *appears, carrying a tray with two goblets of red liquid.*

Ethan: Our Father, who art in heaven, hallowed be thy name. Thy kingdom come, thy will be done on earth as it is in heaven. Give us this day our daily bread, and forgive us our trespasses, as we forgive those who trespass against us. Lead us not into temptation, but deliver us from evil, for thine is the kingdom, the power and the glory, forever and ever, amen.

He and **Hammett** *drink from the Goblets as the music swells.*

And ...

Darkness. We hear an announcer's excited voice over the P.A.

Announcer: Ladies and Gentlemen – your Governor for an unprecedented Fourth Term ... Curtis Bryant!

Curtis: My fellow Americans – what is it we think of when we use the word 'democracy'?

And ...

Scene Eight

I Can't Get Started

Hammett *and* **Webster** *stand, smoking.*

Hammett:

> 'I thought ... I always thought there'd be a
> moment ... a galvanising moment to lift me up,
> to bring me back. Then it would all flow from
> me, again, the brilliance, the wisdom, the rush of
> it all. Life. But you prepare for that moment if
> it's to come, and I haven't prepared for it. I've
> just spent twenty years waiting to die.'

What do you think of that?

Webster: Is it from the island book, the, ah, man and the woman thing?

Hammett: What? Oh, no. No, I think there's too much life and not enough book in that. No, this is a speech for Lilly's next play.

Webster: How come you can write stuff for her, but nothing for yourself? (*Pause*) I guess I should really explain everything.

Hammett: What 'everything' exactly, Dan?

Webster: Well, what happened. Who did what and why everyone behaved the way they did.

Hammett: You're kidding, of course.

Webster: No. This is what the detective always does at the end of the story. He explains what everything means.

Hammett: So go on then.

Webster: I don't think I can. I only got about a quarter of it.

Hammett: Well that's not bad going. And you got the girl. Do you know what you're going to do with her?

Webster: No idea. But don't worry – having seen your form in that department, I won't be troubling you for any advice. 'Pop.'

Hammett: So what type of broad is she, Dan? Figure it out yet?

Webster: I'm through with all that types of broad stuff, it's a menace. How about you?

Hammett: How about me?

Webster: You figure yours out?

Hammett: You crazy? (*Beat*) I think the thing is that you get in a certain distance, and then you hold back ... you, what, *feel* something, then pull away, then try and start it up again ... and it keeps on going like that ... you can't be any other way. (*Pause*)

Webster: That's a big help, thanks.

Hammett: Any time.

    Sylvia *comes on as 'I Can't Get Started' begins to play.*

Hey Dan, isn't that your girl over there?

Webster: Yes. Yes it is.

Hammett: I reckon she'll be wondering where you've got to.

Webster: I reckon so. I guess I'd better go join her.

Hammett: I guess so.

    Webster *joins* **Sylvia** *centre stage. The music plays. They dance.* **Hammett** *watches.*

Webster: You never told me you could dance.

Sylvia: You never asked me. Besides, a woman should never tell a man everything.

    Pause.

Webster: We're doing alright, Sylvia, aren't we?

Sylvia: We're doing fine, honey, just fine.

Webster: It's good to dance. Look at the light, how it moves as we move.

Pause.

Webster: How will things turn out, do you think?

Sylvia: Honey, dancing isn't about talking. It isn't about anything except dancing. That's why it's the perfect thing. Do you see?

Webster: I think so.

Sylvia: Thoughts. Who needs 'em?

Webster: We don't.

Sylvia: No, we don't. We don't need anything else now. We don't need anything at all.

The music swells as they dance into darkness.

The End

Author's Note

Revisiting your first play is a bit like bumping into an old girlfriend: you feel fond, nostalgic, not a little proud of your shared secret history, but you're also continually sidelined by the question: What on earth could I have been *thinking*? As it's eight years since I wrote *I Can't Get Started*, I'm not even physiologically the same person who wrote it. So I can only speculate on the state of mind of the fellow who, having spent the grand total of five days in the USA in his *life*, chose to make his first play an American play.

Indeed, when I was thinking about writing *I Can't Get Started*, I was mulling over the plot of what was to become *Digging For Fire*, and it occurred to me that it would be far more appropriate for my first play to be, like the song on the Walton's radio programme, an Irish one. However, since a good part of *Digging For Fire* was dedicated to exploding the notion that Irishness was in any way a meaningful signifier (We Are All Americans Now) and since 'Appropriate' has recently become virtually the watchword of every *faux moderne* puritan and moralising roundhead, I'm kind of glad that I got started with an inappropriate, unIrish play about one of the greatest and most influential writers of the century, about a messy, impassioned, unconventional love affair that for years had been to me a kind of inspiration.

Yes, well. One of the dangers of writing about real people is that, since you didn't invent their lives, there may well be stuff you don't know. So imagine how I felt when I read John Mellen's extraordinary 1996 volume, *Hellman and Hammett*, and discovered that the stuff I didn't know included Hellman aborting Hammett's child, Hammett's daughter Mary not really being his daughter at all, and Hellman being in reality such a thoroughly hypocritical, selfish, stingy, spiteful, grotesque that her role in the play is a kind of conscience is, to put it at its mildest, absolutely ridiculous.

But I was writing a play, not a biography, and I guess I always knew that if anybody's messy, impassioned and unconventional love affairs were being dramatised, it was my own, although I do think that spending quite so much time obsessing about writer's block in my first piece of proper writing amounted not so much to tempting fate as to sticking my head in its maw and bellowing Christmas Carols up its inner ear.

A year after the first production, on board an Aer Lingus 747, headed for New York: the producer, director and cast of *I Can't Get Started*, all members of Rough Magic, the theatre company I had founded in 1984 with my friend Lynne Parker. The play had been invited to a theatre festival in Stony Brook, Long Island, all seven original Rough Magic members were present and correct, it was the first time the company had been to the US, and it was a play one of us had written that was taking us there. 'This,' I thought, midway through one of what can only be described as 'many' drinks, 'this is certainly what I was thinking.'

Declan Hughes
Dublin
August 1998.

THE DOGS

Donal O'Kelly

Rough Magic produced the world premiere of *The Dogs* for the 1992 Dublin Theatre Festival at the Project Arts Centre and the Scottish premiere for the Festival of New Irish Writing Glasgow 1992 with the following cast and production team:

Turkey / Maurice Arthur Riordan

Robin / Mother Bernie Downes

Rebel / Terry Martin Murphy

Pax/Terry Anne Byrne

Rat / Father Joe Savino

Directed by Lynne Parker

Set & Costume Design by Blaithin Sheerin

Lighting Design by Rupert Murray

Original Music & Effects John Dunne

Production Manager Padraig O'Neill

Stage Manager Annette Murphy

Produced by Siobhán Bourke

Photo: Anne Byrne as Pax and Martin Murphy as Rebel © Amelia Stein.

Dramatis Personae:

The Dogs is performed by five actors, three male and two female. Each actor plays the part of a human character and also of an animal. Suggested doubling up:

Actor A (female), Terry and Pax

Actor B (female), Mother and Robin

Actor C (male), Father and Rat

Actor D (male), Maurice and Turkey

Actor E (male), Benny and Rebel

Place: Macken house

Time: Early nineties

The set consists of a relatively large area stage left and downstage, serving as the livingroom, and a relatively smaller area, slightly raised, upstage right, which serves as the kitchen.

In the livingroom, there is a table of five chairs, a fireside chair (possibly two or three of the other chairs combined) and a window with window-blind upstage centre.

In the kitchen, there is an oven, a windowsill, and a window and back door giving out onto a garden upstage.

Act One

Scene One

A large turkey sits with his head sticking out of a black bag on a tabletop. He is surrounded by similar bags, which rustle and utter approval at appropriate moments.

Turkey: Naked, limp and plump I lie, vacuum-plucked – indignity! Still frozen from my fridge-time, but warming to my coming feastery, surrounded on the good butcher's fleck formica by my turkey-brethren, – my disciples, my prophets, my leaders, my followers, my fellows, my rivals, my one-in-all, my all-in-one, my partners in the Trystfist.

I spread myself among the ovens of the Trystian world. My feet are bound. My hole is stuffed. Potatoes in tinfoil surround me.

Every year ye welcome me, ye heat yere fours.

Every year ye prepare and embellish me, ripe for the feast.

Ye have flamed me, ye have taken nourishment and pleasure from my hot flesh, year after year ye have enjoyed my meat.

I do not mind. I feel no pain. My sacrifice is done according to my will.

Eat of my breast! Wrench my legs asunder! Sink yere teeth and dentures into my thighs ye are wont to call my drumsticks! Devour my burnt remains! Leave only the bones, the bones, the bygones, until the next year, again the ovens, again the consume, again the throw out the bones, sowing the seeds for the do it again the next year again from the flames we arise, phoenix-lick, the eternal regeneration of the Trystkiss bird, each year triumphant again for ever and ever.

Turkey Voices: Amen.

Turkey: My turkey-brethren, heed my prayer.

Turkey Voices: Yes we will. Indeed we heed.

Turkey: Lying supine ye will roast. Let them taste! Drowning in oils ye simmer and splash. Wait till they lick that finger! The children squabble to break your breasts for a wish. Yea, ecstasy! For it is not we who splinter and crack, nay it is they who are won to our Trystfist fold.

Turkey Voices: Yea, oh yea, oh yea!

Turkey: They think we are the victims of their orgy of consumption, but they, unseeing creatures fumbling in the dark, are yearly et up and shat out by the Trystfist. 'Tis Trystfist Eve. Victory is nigh once more. They shall kill the turkey and they can't stop the Kissed-pissed! Chrismismschism!

Scene Two

A standing chorus of **Mother**, **Father**, **Maurice**, **Terry** *and* **Benny** *all engaged in preparing-for-Christmas activity.*

Terry: My biggest worry is to get Benny just to come along, you know, just to come along and meet my mother and my father for the day and have the Christmas dinner and he'll see that they're just confused ordinary people like ourselves rooted in their own peculiar ways and they will see – similar in him, and just through getting used to the sight and the sound of each other they'll – lose the fanatical fear they each have of the other, but of course it won't be any picnic.

Father: No stomach for it anymore, too much disruption and fuss, and the Benny chap this year on top of all the rest, Maurice swaggering from London picking squabbles with Terry the same as ever it was, the two of them too much alike my mother always said, I'm not able for it anymore, fading in and out where once I would have banged their heads together with the sheer – incision of my arguments, but not any more, ah well, last big ordeal before I go in for the tests, no stomach for that, no stomach left, but still and all it's Christmas.

Mother: Only once a year thanks be to G how did I put up with it all the years and this year of all years Jesus Mary and Jo how will I break it how will I say about Terry and the Benny chap together for good and all and Jesus Mary and Jo and the baby on the way he'll flip the lid he'll flip the lid completely but what can I do it's up to me it's always up to me on top of the usual Jesus Mary and Jo the turkey the presents the pudding the ham and bloody good cheer all round and geein' him up for the tests to come and then Maurice as well no help oh no help at all with his London ways and graces blast! What'll I do?

Maurice: I dread it, I dread it coming back every year to the same tale of woe, dad's back and bowel, mam's worried looks, new bigger locks on every door, dying to see their son turning out a credit to them in the way they'd wish, disappointed every year and this year the worst of all, where's the girl to go with the car and what about settling down, and now Terry gettin' plumped just in case we'd have a chance of avoiding unnecessary fuss and on no no fear of a Joe Soap oh no for Terry it has to be hard to be right it has to be pain, she has to pick a Bogside vigilante veteran to ignite the Christmas dinner for the good of all of us. Good-night!

Benny: Never thought I'd see the day – gotten used to spending it alone – not accountable to anyone, sheer bloody bliss, used to love it up at home of course, fry for breakfast big excitement queuing for the da to open up the sitting-room aw yeah, but this a different proposition, the trouble is it drags on and on with the drop of drink hope it doesn't – musn't let it spill into tangled arguments – don't mention the North the motto for the day and everything is ro - sy co - sy!

Terry: And of course I won't be able to drink it's hard to know for better or worse but then again maybe one or two wouldn't do a lot of harm have to keep a reins on the comments and maybe make a little list of conversation items to defuse – a few jokes to get a laugh?

Mother: Thank God for Pax at least the dog can hold his tongue and anyway he's thick enough to boss a bit thanks be to G there's one, a quare bloody family whatever was to blame, something in the genes my side was fine, stubbornness and loud mouth.

Maurice: Why do I have to sort out their sordid little quarrels when I've spent my adult life trying to leave all that behind? It's baggage, it's rot, it's irrational personal flak from the past that's holding Terry back well hard bloody cheese but it's not going to suck me down in the misery pit as well.

Benny: Maurice maybe not as bad as the picture Terry paints – nobody completely unsusceptible to ordinary warmth, maybe hit it off in an offbeat way you never know the way the – chemistry will work, stranger things have ha-ha.

Father: And I feel the thing Terry's carrying along with the Derry fella getting very strong as if not enough already on my overcrowded plate – blast! – too many brains my mother always said, Terry's great retention powers a blessing to be watched, how right she –

Terry: Wish I knew I could rely on Benny not to make a scene or not to help in the making someone else will start, because as sure as eggs –

Benny: Terry won't relax and be herself, always trying to prove some lost point to the clan I'd give it to them straight but there's the crux.

Mother: Benny isn't all bad, he has a gentle smile but Jesus Mary and how does Terry pick them is he safe or could he be – what's the? – taken in and given back?

Maurice: Silver lining is – Benny'll take the glare of inspection well away from me, he's certainly – absorbing as a specimen of – hood-man!

Father: Maurice will he worry now I wonder re the will though he always said he didn't want to know about legacies inheritance or any such but now with Benny on the scene well you never know, funny if –

Terry: Benny Maurice, Maurice Benny, – make chalk and cheese synonymous!

Mother: Mustn't let them rub one another up in such a way that – Jesus is there any hope?

Benny: I'm going to face a three-pronged attack – mustn't get defensive!

Maurice: Joyful and triumphant, come ye oh co-ome ye ...

Terry: Benny behave! The rug from under me Do Not Pull!!

Mother: We'll have to pull together – see the business through.

Benny: Terry back me up! Don't leave me iso – lated!!

Father: Have to face the Benny chap, rejoice! Re - joice!!

Maurice: If it comes to the crunch –

Benny: Keep the head at all costs –

Terry: Maurice'll help –

Maurice: Play dumb, don't get involved –

Mother: All together for the –

Father: Last time –

Maurice: Deep breath –

Terry: Take the plunge –

Benny: No qualms –

Maurice: Painted grin –

Mother: Mother of God –

Terry: Little to lose –

Benny: Face the squad –

Father: Please God –

Maurice: No escape –

Benny: Fuck it!

All: Happy Christmas!

Scene Three

A dog enters the kitchen area. He is a sensitive, puzzled-looking brown-and-white wirehaired terrier. He barks, twice, shakes his head, barks again. After a few barks and headshakes, he finds his voice.

Pax: Pax! Pax! Pax! That my name. That my doggy name. Nice name. Nice. Like the stuff my mammy put on fish. Fis. She call it fis. Paxo on a piece of fis for my pal Pax. Lovely. I lovely that. Rare. My mammy is a very nice. My fada o-k-too. He a bit big-boom-bom-bom big leda shoe. – Oh – I like to lick the polish off can't help the self – nice mell, get de toe in de mush poor bluggy nose hide it in de liddle gap aside de cooker where he no can get. It a dog's life.

I toth for da many years my name come from the fis-crumb, but one day I learn the no. Watch.

He throws his head back wolf-like and gives a call. Capitals indicate stress.

AilliliuaPEELertrinaCREENacrynaRAPareetheCROP pyboynaPITCHcapBLACKandtapaRACKrent CRUCifixionHELLorwalkingGALLowallow ALlowpuillePUCKaladdieailliliowowowowoWOW!

Pause while he waits.

Sorry. Sometime the nothing. We try again a minute. My mama nice. My fada okay for de walky or the out for the leak, I can put up with da fuck. And den der Terry. Terry only liddle baba when I first came a liddle pup. We grow

dagedder, me de doggy, she de liddle girl. But Terry gone
now. All gone wid de Benny fuck. Some melly bedzit, say
mama all cry an blow de nose. Lod of cry de late. And lod
of fada moan, aboud da bowel an de back. I pud de head in
de gap aside of the cooker half od da fucky day. So. That
mama, fada, and Terry, and too there was Maurice go away
de long time gone. Alway come back wid de shiny point on
the shoe, and da smell of da lavender shavy foam.

Da house I alway like. Many room in de fada's mansha.
Bright de fron, dark de baci, every de room have a million
differ smell. Nigh to just lie a let de waft-waft cross de tip de
nose. A ting-tingle, de longa stay, de bedda dey get. Gimme
de ereck-reck. I a boy. But de fada-fucka took me da de vet.
Only de time I ev ate de steak. Mama gev it doomey after.
Sub consummation. Nev ed de meat again. Jus meebe
mince no de lumps. Cos de deeth. I no mo de yung turk dog
nose. Ah fuck, no mench de turk. Nod dis time de year. Ev
Kissma de same. De fuss over de stuffy de bird. Same
allway back to Rebel time, he estoll me. Ah, Rebel wait we
see if he come now. (*Head back again*)

AilliawilliaSTANDwithinanIrishCOFFinshipspoTATofam
ineCAPtainBoycottESSexPEELinPITTitititCROMcruwilli
amIReTONtontontonto-
theBOWowowilAILLilowowowowoWOW!

Pause while he waits.

Oh-oh. Maybe I no can call 'im back no mo. Me
soopernodderel pows are leavin' me. Mebbe I try too hard.
Thadda comm mistake de day an age we live I do bell even
doe post Freud an Jung an Laing an all. Take for a himmel
da Kissma fuck. I haida haida haida fuckyoke, so say
alladay – womamanadog – I ev hair say. Bud da mama an
da fada, oh no, dey hafa do de do. Plum puddy,
Kissmakake, Kissmatee an kib, wid de stadoos an de
humelous hangels, de fucky binky-binkies an de corations,
an de tinsel-bickies and de wurstufall de wurstufallfall de
shiddy epigramma wellowoe de fucky bird. Dah bird, da
Kissma furkey id a furst fall of foe to leaf us failing in its
fake. Kissma suppo ta be da time a peacealove, bud de

mama and da fada every ear bing de e-fill fedderting an pud it in de baisded dray an garland id wid eeky ashers an oist id wid emon an dey do prey yey oh yey dey do prey on dey knees ad dee e-phill altaroven o de pince o de powl, an e rosens an lows ehind de lass, an dey run de rivulets o ravy down is raked rest, id a curse, a retcha curse untilla las bitsashit are it. Sonowyanoh.

   Tima peacealove me hearse. Anyway, de peacealove, like de booty, id in de buy o de bolder. Anow I like a cha wid Rebel. I call 'im back f'om de dead. (*Throws his head back*)

   AilliliuaBULLetbuilleBLOODysunderindeTERNemine QUALaqualaKILLyencoilleMOTormanaHUNGerstricke DIPelockaCHUCKyPUCKinBRITstabitsaRIPrallyRArally RATSRebelRATs!

   Rebel *appears. He is a taut alert black and white cocker spaniely kind of a dog. Pointed nose, sleek coat, pricked ears. A real live wire, except that he is old.* **Rebel** *bounds in, leaps onto the 'couch' and stands up on the back as if looking and barking out the window at the rats.*

Rebel: Kauf, Kauf, Kauf, Kauf. Ow, Sheshusshoice, foot the hearsh croshwaysh in me. Long the way back, lesh able than I wash. An alwayssh the falsh hellorum. I shick o the shoke. Shtale and shour hafter sho many shears brodir. Rats not shaggin shtewpit. I shaw them shunch upon a shimes, shinning around the shockery, oh dishgushtin. But my Kauf Kauf Kauf off the kindow shooed them ashtray. Now ey ony shnake out in the night, no shign when shun shine. An ey hide ehind trellishin, the nigh shites! But I shtill have to do the Kauf Kauf for the mama and the fada. Kauf Kauf. Kauf Kauf.

Pax: Hey Rebel, Rebel, relax Rebel relax. Wadaboudabidafun? You an me. Rebel and Pax. Dog, the trix I hada learn afta you. Nearly wen daft-daft. Uranellofanact to follow!

Rebel: Ah don debean yourshelf. Dey luv you too. I can bell well tell.

Pax: Nada hame way. Dey ove me uggly-duggly-og-dey-owe dey hafta uvey dey neykadoo udder. Budoo dey ubh adan eero, oo dey adore as a dog. Oh de way dey id tok o Rebel! A wonder I idn't iv up as a pup!

Rebel: (*Suspicious*) Oh de fludderin fladdery! I mell a rat! Y u caul mee back, Pac?

Pax: A chah! A chah!

Rebel: Chatofah? Chatofah?

Pax: Otie, newtie, swapa de tories, cross da paws ...

Rebel: (*Sniffs and looks around*) Hey, shiddy monger-elle, id fucky Kissmatime, idnit?

Pax: I sorr, Ebel, I no cacatake id alone. I haul u back to helm me. Hu is side u on?

Rebel: If de one ting I nodable to shtick, ida Kissma schmuck. De mama an de fada tae de luna sea, dey utter de rage, dey loose de rational elves. I lead a long time now, too far de udder higone. No hanoi me. Kissma beyond me. Have hum hence.

Pax: Da fudda furkey cud idda da kitch – I cana know de whaddafud I do.

Rebel: I lef it all ehind a hong time along. Don estroy e lidabid ehentment I enyoy, Dog yelp me.

Pax: (*Pause*) Den I woe wid you, Webbel, allaway! If you no hum to heel, den I foe to de hound, an no num nack no ney neve, no ney neve no moe, will I rove de wet nose, no ney neve no moe.

Rebel: (*Trying to encourage*) Ura hung dog, ura dong dog.

Pax: No hung no moe, I hold; no hong no moe – I heak, hick, handilap wid a no fron heeth the mange itch de back an de fron allover, de eye side faidin fast, ney de hength nor de hill du pud up wid no moe, especial de Kissma hill me.

Rebel: Poor Pax. Urin a bad way.

Pax: I wanna go, doggit, an I wanna woe it my way.
Warking ad de weal o de mo-mo, jus like dey say u did
Rebel. I wanna fizzle in a faze of fiery. Puddin id up da da
hubcap, de Wover or de Wolvo or de Wolkswagen Basset,
my tongue again de rim of de rubber tyre, de yung Turk
again fo de las few secs, den shtick de neck out. Nex ding,
de ryever at de reel torn in two – one, keepy de kids in de
baci no let see de doggy sigh 'n' die, de udder, wanna see da
damage da da fender geda owner of de mongrel fuck da pay
frew de fucky nose. Pax in pace. Pip.

Rebel: U shadden me, ut de shoice is sures. Mebbe on de
far shide, Pax an Rebel riv as run.

Scene Four

Mother, *back to audience, looks out back window. She turns
away.*

Mother: Poor Pax. Rebel went at Christmas too. Life
repeats. (*Looks out window again*) I hope he doesn't get a
dose like he got after Rebel's burial. If he'd only wear a hat.
That shovel's too short. He'll crucify me with his back.
(*Turns back again*) Poor Pax. The cheek of the bitch. If you
didn't drive so fast, I said, you have us crucified on that
main road. My solicitor will be in contact, she says. Poor
Pax. His tooth fell out God help him lying beside his eye.
It's not the damage it's the trauma she says. Trauma! Pax's
head hanging from my arms. His face in a grin. Grinning
aw my poor beloved dog.

   Father *comes in from the back. He grimaces with pain as he
bends himself into his fireside chair.*

Mother: The back!?

   Father *nods.*

Father: Blast!

Mother: (*Imploring intercession*) Jesus Mary and Joseph.

Father: No use crying over spilt milk. We'll have to get on with the living now Ruth.

Mother: Who do you think you're telling!? I've got a turkey to organise!

Father: Where is it?

Mother: It's arriving at the door by delivery. It's late! Benny's arrangement, if you don't mind. Isn't he good? Sausage-stuffing, potato stuffing, breadcrumb stuffing. And no turkey to stuff!

Father: We'll have to put the mouse trap down. This is the very weather. They want to come in to the warm. And now with Pax gone – have to take precautions. Have you any cheese?

Mother: (*Bitterly*) As much as you like. A platter-full.

Father: Good. I'll put it on the back doorstep to get them coming in.

Mother: I'm airing Maurice's bed, so leave his blanket on at one. Pickle. Maurice likes Ploughman's pickle.

Father: (*Righteously*) I thought you'd left it on by mistake.

Mother: Leave the running of the house to me. Please! Now what else?

Father: Is Benny coming for the dinner?

Mother: Of course he is. (*Sarcastically*) Terry couldn't spend a whole afternoon without him.

Father: Would he not go up home to his own?

Mother: (*Significantly*) Well now, that's enough of that. Ours is not to wonder why ...

Father: I see.

Mother: It's not for us to judge, and anyway, what could we do? Terry's picked him out for better or worse. (*Looking at Christmas cards*) St. Anne, you know, I'm sure, wasn't too pleased ...

Father: Hm?

Mother: Mary taking up with Saint Joseph ...

Father: He was a carpenter like me. What's wrong with carpenters?

Mother: Oh I don't mean his occupation. But his age. Very old. And Mary only a young girl. And yet how well it worked out.

Father: (*Pause*) Benny's not old.

Mother: No, but I think there's a caring streak there all the same.

Father: Do you think it's serious?

Mother: Oh it's serious all right.

Father: How do you know?

Mother: I know by the look in her eye.

Father: Ah serious my granny! He's a chancer Ruth, nothing but a chancer. I know. I know what we were like in my day and nothing ever changes. So don't come whinging to me.

Mother: I'm not whinging. We have to give him a chance. You'll have to find it in you to let live and forgive.

Father: (*Pause*) I see. Well. I better find it in me to make my forgiving quick.

Mother: Now don't be getting your back up. Isn't it a lovely time for it to happen. Christmas. And isn't it lovely that she can come to her own home for love and support. And won't next Christmas be lovely with a little baby on the floor for Pax to play with – auh –

Father: Dry up, woman. Pax is dead. I'll show this little Gerry Adams where he stands as regards my home, my daughter and my property.

Mother: Now. Don't upset yourself Denis. Save your energy for going in for the tests.

Father: Poor Terry. She's drifted very far Ruth. Maurice is over in London, yet he's hardly gone at all. He comes back at Christmas-time, everything's the same. But every time that Terry calls, she's drifted a little bit more. And that whelp Benny is the one tugging her away.

Mother: It's no use casting blame. You can't blame everything on Benny.

Father: That's where you're wrong.

Mother: Ah no. You were the one set her adrift from here. Fair's fair now. Own up.

Father: What are you blathering about, woman?

Mother: Well. You hit her. You punched her when she stayed out without her key.

Father: I gave her a cuff on the side of her head for waking the house at two in the morning. She was only nineteen. She was still subject to the rules of this house.

Mother: Jesus Mary and Joseph the rules! Not everybody wants to live by your set of rules, Denis. And you gave her hard enough a crack to break the bridge of her specs. That's hard.

Father: What was she doing until two in the morning? Damit, it doesn't matter now, but the same blooming failing still letting her down.

Mother: Now you don't mean that. (*Pause*) God help her she was only nineteen. If you saw the state of the flats we looked at. Oh stinking! Country people can be terrible mean. And her with the purple eye and elastoplast. She's been fattening landlords ever since. (*Pause*)

Father: I'm sorry now. Bloody mistakes always rising up to beat you from the past. (*Pause*) Maybe it's inevitable. Maybe it'll do her good. Maybe even have a moderating influence on him.

Mother: Oh it will. It will. Now you're talking. Nature's way. A whole change of life.

The doorbell rings – ding dong.

Mother: That'll be the turkey.

Mother *goes out to open the door. Her voice is heard offstage.*

Mother: (*Impressed*) Oh, my, you're a fine big brute of a bird!

The fine big brute of a turkey walks in, God-like, with a baking tray strapped to his back like a trojan shield. **Mother** *follows him in.*

Father: (*Mildly interested*) Looks good!

Mother: (*Matter-of-factly*) Park yourself on the table like a good big bird 'til I do a job on you.

Turkey *effortlessly flops himself onto his back in the middle of the table. He swivels a little in his baking tray on the tabletop.*

Mother: (*Checking*) Now. Three stuffings. Sliced lemons. Oils and spices. Scissors and thread. We're all set. (*To* **Father**) A nice bit of breast off this fella'll fatten you up for the tests.

Turkey: Oh yes! Oh yes!

Father: Aw shut up about the tests.

Mother *sets to the surgical business of preparing the turkey.*

Mother: Well now turkey how would you like to be done?

Turkey: Well. Do what you do, do well.

Mother: You're a fine plump bird. We better pop you in the oven straight away or you'll have me up halfway through the night.

Turkey: Strip me, stuff me, put me in the oven, cook me.

Mother: Wait 'til I pull out your gizz-gizz. Pooh the smell. I'll open the backdoor as far as the chain will let. Allow a bit of air to circulate.

Turkey: Ye oils and unctions wash me, bathe me in thy tides. Soon I will be cut and eaten of. Wash me, ye juices, streaming down my sides. Ye hackrevisers spice me, sugar me and pepper me for plate to palate bearing. Soon I enter the holly-of-hollies, the flaming tabernacle of the New World. After which, consume my flesh, scatter my bones, arise and follow turkey.

Mother: Poor Pax would have got all excited tearing into your giblets, Mister Turkey.

Turkey: Call me master, slut!

Mother: Now you're nearly done. Stuffed to the breach.

Turkey: Oven! The oven! I long! Turn on the oven to burn me!

Mother: Now Denis. Time to start the bird. Help me put him in.

Father: (*Standing up*) Christ, the back! Oh Christ, the wretched back.

Mother and **Father** *carry the turkey on his baking tray to the kitchen and place him in the oven.*

Turkey: Suck - cess! Suck - cess! I have made it to the chrismkitchTurkeybredabu!

Scene Five

Terry and **Benny** *in their flat.*

Terry: So what are you going to do about it?

Benny: About what?

Terry: Your dream – your nightmare.

Benny: You can't do anything about a dream. A dream happens to you.

Terry: You could talk about it.

Benny: I don't remember it.

Terry: I don't believe you.

Pause.

Benny: In Castlereagh you'd offer me a cigarette at this stage.

Terry: Who's Cora?

Benny: Coronation Street?

Terry: You screamed her name, Benny. Very loud.

Benny: A bit of fluff. On the side.

Pause.

Terry: Why can't we talk?

Benny: We are talking.

Terry: You're not talking. You're mouthing.

Benny: We talk plenty, Terry.

Terry: When do we talk?

Benny: I've never kept a list.

Terry: You talk about day-to-day things, but you keep your deepest thoughts to yourself.

Benny: You credit me with more depth than I deserve.

Terry: Flattery! You're hiding something.

Benny: Yeah. Present.

Pause.

Terry: Do you love me?

Benny: I'm going to your folks for Christmas dinner, amn't I!?

Terry: Do you feel love in your heart for me, or does it stop at some kind of comradeship?

Benny: More than both together, Terry.

Terry: You're a wriggly worm.

Benny: Too many nights in Castlereagh.

Terry: It's not a virtue, Benny. It's a sad legacy.

Benny: (*Sharply*) You don't need to tell me that!

Pause.

Terry: Tell me about that!?

Benny: What?

Terry: Whatever brought that on.

Benny: Nothing to tell.

Terry: There is something to tell.

Benny: I'm tense. Nervous about tomorrow.

Terry: You'll be fine.

Benny: Easy for you to say.

Terry: Just relax and be yourself.

Benny: And keep my mouth shut.

Terry: Just – maintain a guarded discretion. (*Slight pause*) But not with me!

Benny: You want a talk machine you can switch on and off!

Terry: I want a relationship.

Benny: I hate that word!

Terry: I'm not surprised. Hatred of the unknown.

Benny: It's the word I hate, not the concept.

Terry: You keep secrets from me.

Benny: Do you want to rip me open and inspect me!? Would that satisfy you!?

Terry: Why are you afraid?

Benny: I'm not afraid. I resent it! You don't trust me!

Terry: We're meant to share our lives.

Benny: Sharing is a nice voluntary act.

Terry: So you're clamping up again.

Benny: If that's what you want to call it – yes!

Terry: Then it's all a charade.

Benny: Right! Let's cancel tomorrow.

Terry: Cancel tomorrow and you cancel everything between us.

Benny: You said there's nothing between us.

Terry: Ah there's a whole lot of things between us but I don't think it adds up to a relationship especially if you won't even trouble yourself to meet the – grandparents of the – baby you're going to – become a father to!

Pause.

Benny: (*Full of dread*) Why is it so important for me to be there?

Terry: It's fucking vitally important!

Benny: But it's hypocritical to present a nice cosy family image when we don't even have a (*Mouths*) re-lat-ion-ship! Isn't it!?

Terry: You work on the relationship! You're one half of it!

Pause.

Benny: If I went tomorrow what good would it do?

Terry: It'd be the next best thing to a wedding as far as they're concerned.

Benny: The next worst thing to death as far as I'm concerned.

Terry: Jesus! Do what you like! (*Throws present*) Happy fucking Christmas!

Benny: (*Throwing present*) Happy fucking returns!

Scene Six

Scene opens with **Father** *and* **Maurice** *in a close embrace, melodrama on* **Father***'s side, embarrassment on* **Maurice***'s.* **Mother** *looks on, 'significantly' pleased. Eventually,* **Father** *disengages.*

Father: You've made a good choice, Maurice.

Maurice: (*Puzzled*) What choice?

Father: Opel.

Mother: Oh it's beautiful Maurice, is it quiet?

Maurice: I think so.

Father: A good buy. German. A good time to be buying German. High performance engine and attention to the bodywork too. You can't beat the Germans.

Maurice: I decided to buy new. I checked, you know. It cost me exactly half what it would here.

Father: Half. I'm not surprised. We're bet. We're nowhere. We're not in the park at all. You're right to buy new. You don't want to inherit someone else's problems.

Mother: The white will show the dirt though. But you wouldn't mind that.

Maurice: The least of my worries. How's Terry?

Pause.

Mother: Ah sure, you know Terry. But she's keeping well, thank God. All well, we can't complain, sure we can't Denis?

Father: Well there's feck all use moaning about anything, it won't make it go away.

Pause.

Mother: You know he's in for more tests. The week after next, please God.

Maurice: Just tests? Well then ...

Father: Once they get you in there ...

Maurice: Still. It's the right thing.

Mother: (*To* **Father**) Now. Don't start fighting it again. Maurice even says it.

Father: Was it calm coming over, son?

Maurice: Like glass. The only bump was coming up the gangplank.

Father: Good. Good.

Mother: That's the glasshouse effect, I bet it is.

Maurice: I brought a crate of wine. For the dinner.

Father: (*To* **Mother**) Wine?

Mother: Lovely. Benny will be delighted.

Maurice: I'm looking forward to meeting Benny.

Mother: (*Shrilly*) I want no politics in this house tomorrow.

Father: You'll get it whether you like it or not missus.

Mother: I won't have it. I won't.

Maurice: Don't worry Mam, there's plenty of things we can talk about for the few hours.

Father: Yeah. Billy Smart's effin circus again. Why is it Christmas seems to tie a knot in everybody's tongue? A morbid bloody occasion.

Mother: Denis!

Maurice: It's for the kids really, isn't it? Still, it's a great excuse for us all to see each other again.

Mother: Ah yes.

Maurice: And this year is doubly special. (*Pause*) I mean with Benny, and Terry, and their news.

Father: Yeah. You must have seen the star and followed it across ...

Mother: Stop that. It's good news, now, Maurice, no matter what. It's always good news, for God's sake, a baby, isn't it Maurice, no matter what the circumstances, even the Pope says that.

Maurice: Of course. It's fantastic news. I'm dying to meet Benny. Why wouldn't it be good news?

Father: Ah blast it Maurice, don't play the baby you! You know well there's a problem with Benny.

Maurice: Come on Dad. You know what love is. It can overcome politics. Remember how you used to hate Granny Sheehan, but you got on great with her in the end.

Father: The woman was a bloody tyrant. I weakened, that's all.

Mother: Dad's back is at him.

Maurice: Oh not again.

Father: What do you mean 'not again'? You'd think it was you who had it.

Maurice: Sorry, have I ...

Mother: Dad had to do a job out the back today Maurice. It was a sad job.

Maurice: A sad job?

Mother: Yes. Poor Pax, Maurice, oh, I'm afraid you'll get upset ...

Maurice: Did he die?

Mother: (*Nodding*) Poor Pax left us this afternoon. A bitch of a solicitor ran him over. Oh, if you saw the brooches on her!

Father: I buried him in the garden. The bloody shovel's too short. The cursed back has me crucified.

Maurice: Try and take it easy.

Father: Take it easy? At Christmas? Are you all there Maurice?

They laugh uneasily, stalling a little.

Maurice: Listen, why don't we open one of the bottles of wine? To celebrate.

Father: Celebrate what?

Maurice: (*Slapping* **Father** *on the back*) Ah buck up Dad.

Mother: Mind his back. Go on Maurice. A glass of wine will help us unwind.

Maurice: I have it out in the car. Just a sec.

Maurice *goes. Silence for a few seconds.*

Father: He's doing – well.

Mother: He's settled there now. A car and all. To go with the flat. Oh he's set up now. We needn't worry Denis.

Father: No sign of a girl ...

Mother: No. No. Well, I think Maurice is – contented with himself.

Father: I suppose I was late starting myself ...

Mother: And the way you had to be dragged.

Father: Ah dry up. Have we any wine glasses?

Mother: Oh good idea. I have a set put away for a wedding gift.

Father: Wedding? Fat chance.

Mother: Oh I didn't mean Terry. Just any wedding. A gift for any wedding. God, will Christmas ever end?

She goes out and gets the glasses. **Father** *on his own, immobile, thinking about his body.* **Maurice** *comes back in with the box of wine bottles.*

Father: Don't mind your mother. Christmas has her all upset.

Maurice: We'll all feel better after a glass of this. A fella called Ginger in the office got it for me. He's a connoisseur. Used to play cricket for Wales. Nice guy. Says he'll take it back if it doesn't measure up. Have you got an opener handy?

Father: Is it for a cork? Not in the drawer, no? Put it away. We don't need wine.

Maurice: (*Quietly, pointedly*) We're going to toast that baby if I have to smash the bottle open on –- on –

Father: Smash it on Benny's face, the face that launched a thousand, a thousand what?

Maurice: (*Sharply*) Dad! (*Pause*) I don't like him any more than you do, but you have to face the fact that he exists. Terry is an adult and Terry's made a choice. He's going to be around for the foreseeable future, so you better adapt to the situation.

Father: (*Hears* **Mother** *coming*) I'm not taking sermons from you, me bucko.

Mother *enters armed with glasses.*

Mother: Now, isn't this lovely?

Maurice: Where's the opener Mam?

Mother: An opener. An opener. Wait 'till I think. The kitchen, I think, the kitchen.

Maurice: I'll get it. Just tell me where.

Mother: Oh tell me where, tell me when, won't you tell me all about men ... (*Goes out again*)

Pause.

Father: Have you met the Benny fella?

Maurice: No. But I feel I know him pretty well from the look in everyone's eyes when they mention his name.

Father: He's the lowest of the low, a slime, a leprous scab spreading its blisters over Terry 'til we can hardly recognise her anymore.

Maurice: He's not THAT bad. He's a human being, for God's sake. Give him a chance. He deserves a fair trial. Terry says you haven't even met him yet.

Father: I know enough. I've been through the university of life and I know. I know. Let him carry on all he likes in his own life, his own place, his own shabby corners. But he's not going to upset the love and cohesion I've built up in this family over all these years. Not on your nanny.

Mother *returns with the corkscrew and tackles bottle.*

Mother: Maybe you'll think different, Denis, when you talk to him.

Father: Shut up woman. Shut up. By Christ I won't let him in. I'll stand up to the pup on the doormat. I'll give him boobytrap and I'll give him armalite, as God is my judge I will.

Mother: Now you see. Politics. Would you for God's sake stay off it.

Father: This is not politics. This is life.

Mother: Aw sure, that's worse.

Maurice: But he's down here and he hasn't been back for ages. He's not up to anything now. He's fixing televisions, nothing mysterious about that. (*Tentatively*) There were – there was – an extreme situation back in those days up

North you know, in some places, fairly rough ... a lot of young fellas, harem-scarem, knew no better ...

Father: A bloody TV repairman. For our Terry, I doubt he can even do colour.

Mother: Oh God I know it's terrible but what can we do? She's gone now. She's made up her mind. Our bed is made and we may lie in it.

Maurice: What about the orange boxes?

Father: What?

Maurice: All the stories that you used to tell us about starting off making furniture out of orange boxes that you picked out of the gutter on rainy days down at the fruit market. TV repairs is a step above that.

Mother: Ah that was different Maurice. Your father put his heart and soul into giving us a decent standard of life.

Maurice: Terry might be saying that in ten years time – about Benny and his televisions.

Father: Ten years. Ten years. Oh yeah, anything's possible in this monkey puzzle of a life. Some glamour girl might be saying it about you and your beds.

Mother: Oh. Beds.

Maurice: I don't make beds Dad. I programme the computer for a bedding company..

Father: And what programme would that be now? Have you a programme in mind for the property you bought?

Mother: Oh the flat. Is it really just half a house? Just the top half. Separate doors of course?

Maurice: Yeah. Don't worry. I'm not gone back to squats.

Mother: And is it very expensive Maurice?

Maurice: Well, there's two of us sharing it.

Mother: Oh?

Maurice: Remember Stephen? You met him at the ferry last year.

Mother: Oh yes – from the North, wasn't he?

Maurice: Portstewart.

Mother: Did he come across with you?

Maurice: No. He came early. Some – domestic stuff to see to. Difficulties. Has to look after his niece for the week.

Mother: Oh.

Father: But it's in your name?

Maurice: What?

Father: The house. The half-a-house. Whatever it is. When you want it all you can get him to leave?

Maurice: Don't worry, it won't come to that. We've a good, sound arrangement.

Father: The heart is a lonely hunter, but you can never tell when it's going to strike. One of these fine days, me bucko ...

Maurice: Well, let's drink to that. One of these fine days – here's to the heart and its hunt.

They drink.

Mother: Lovely. Now. What's next. (*She points at* **Father**) Don't forget the trap. Poor Pax. Well! At least the turkey's doing fine, thanks be to G.

Scene Seven

Lights up on red-floored kitchen. Music to suggest the surreal world of undead animals. **Pax** *and* **Rebel** *are both shaking, leaning against each other for support.*

Pax: How dun I no cunno believe. An orrible rick to lay. I can see, I can ear, I can mell, I can feel 'e floor aneath I paws – I low I not lead.

Rebel: I try to shtick myshelf on the toashtin-fork, no use. I try de harvi-carvi, bud de knave juzz parr me vleshanvlud an mage no lashin marg. I try to eat the geraniums, I hear they poison, bud I feel fine, fuggit. Now I shtuck, Pax, I no can see a way ta da other shide. I nidder lead ur alie, an I dun e'en merit dinky-abowd afar a de pebble o de mansha concern, becep as mebbe de mented hauntinoises of a boldy-ghost.

Pax: Da deed id done. Id no use kyin ober mink pelt. Now we godda puddur deads dadegger to egape de limbostate.

Rebel: Id eady for u to day! U led me baginduda leperlimboland. Ura fuddin iconbedend. Lud at me! Eben de body I half-have is decrabbit, wold an' wounded. There was a time I de prince o' dogs. Maurice an' Terry an' de udder kids dey laughed an' lowed to see Rebel ki' de ass o de bastard rats.

Pax: Oh ay, no deny ...

Rebel: De pebble gimme de bones a de back doors, dey wub me on de welly, say guddog, Ebel guddog. Or de pebble dey feel sorry fo' me wen dey see me menacin' aboud i de rainy-day, gimme de shelleh an de bowl o warm milk, lemme wax de weapon an leddle me lie by de fire.

Pax: Strew, Rebel, Dog nose estrew, bud now we godda make a flan ...

Rebel: Bud after a long time, de pebble ged sic o me, sometime I shiddy on de fudpad, or I digaholedahideabone ina garden den furgeddabuddit, dey geddabid peeved, gimme de slapa de nose, bud now id wursanever! I no can go back, I no can go o'er. An u no fuddy whelp, Pax!

Pax: Id no use lamin' me! Id ur own faulta haze urhelf ho high! Alla pebble hadda high de hopes o u, den u ged hory, huggly an hold, an no can ged de pebble clap an ding no mo. Bud we bode gonna haffa help addudder frew de kissa fuck, see de turkey fugou de back wid de rats de soona de bedda, bing de mama an de fada back da da senses, den mebbe have a chance da be at pease. Now I gonna whiddle fo' de toport o' de doggybredder o de neighbourhood.

Rebel: De doggybredder!?

Pax: Our own kine, f'om de born da de partied an de uncordinates de like of us who dangle in bedean f'om de Kissma bliss! Now! Shuddup an lemme whiddle!

Rebel: Okay! Whiddle away! Up u dump o de dindowill!

> **Pax** *leaps up on the windowsill and starts to whistle to the doggie brethren, alive and dead, and undead. The sound, of course, is silent to the human ear, but there is no question **Pax** has to put great effort into the whistling. Lights fade up on **Turkey** baking in his tray, ladling oil on his belly and chest, like a big man enjoying himself in a bathtub. He hums contentedly. Lights fade down on **Turkey**, fade up on **Pax** and **Rebel** on their windowsill.*

Pax: I am all izzy f'om e whiddling, Ebel. I mud ake a rest. Ooh da hyperventilation! I buffer de boss o balance.

Rebel: Ow many bredder banda da bawl!?

Pax: (*Counting*) Enuff ta ways a wuffle!

Rebel: Now we ha godda galvanise 'em into a horse fo' hange.

Pax: Lemme adem! I'll zing 'em to zeal!

Rebel: U de gre waffler wid de gif o de gab okay. U peak, I p'ompt u f'om ehind. Off u go, Cicero!

Pax: Lemme jus gadda me dots. We godda gedda doggies da use de canny-sychic powers on da mama, win 'er back f'om de turkeybird obression, an' allow us da lie an die of normalady.

Rebel: Dad'll do fo darters. Go. Go.

Pax presents himself to the doggies. Sound effects (fx) polite applause.

Rebel: Hey! U gedda good hound of paws!

Pax: (*In oratorical tones*) Ye dogs, ye dogs, livid an dread, I peak at you nod as a puperior, bud as a wellow-wog an wufferer.

Rebel: Good. Good.

Pax: In da hend, we all muz go da da same state, da state o' death. We mun all aid eedudder do dis end. Da denial o da rite o death is a turremulous crime agen da doggy rites!

Rebel: Hey! How how how you ackira da tilken tongue!?

Pax: (*Aside*) Id in me mongrel past, da libberador, da leader, I hujest wid humadamy.

Rebel: Wow on! Wow on!

Pax: We mun help Ebel da da resting place, he hanno ho on in da half-dyin hate! We mun help him da bury hisself in pieces as he say he wish.

Rebel: Thadda nodda point! Geddada point! Truss e trucky ou!

Pax: For us all to av a wappier wife an wealth, I eggport u da help us woo da muddadadamansha da E-JECK da kissma gobblezegob an all 'is pops an gravy!

Sound fx: doggies cheering.

Rebel: E-jeck! E-jeck! Chey is chantin an cheerin ta chucky!

Pax: Don' worry, doggyfolk, dad id mean no mo kissma-bones ta grinda teeth an molars on! Don' worry, buddybarkers, dad id mean no mo luscious guts an organs o de fowl dad we doggies crave!

Rebel: Fugg it Fax u effusem.

Pax: Don' worry, pawsers, dad id mean dad de coniberous pebble will furn fallow da da vege-cult an spurn da carne! Diz we muz egg-peck! We godda make a hackrevise!

Rebel: We ha hackrevised ouhelves to hymndom hum! Ged de fuggies da do de biz!

Pax: My canines, pud ur arts an mines dagedder to imbress wid allofourmite our e-jection o de mama's predilection wid de turkeybiz whit caud us doe much obression an bain of our lives.

Rebel: Da da duff! Okey-dokey! Da da ninety-duff!

Pax: Led us bay, dreary bred, for Rebel an Pax, wow, andat we bow before death. Ye dogs, bay da da mama-pusson, dat she may 'ear an cindercede on our wee-half.

Sound fx: a low hum or some sort of internal doggy-noise. **Rebel** *and* **Pax** *are both engaged in drumming up the psychic powers of the dogs.* **Mother** *enters the kitchen.*

Mother: Damn it I'm addled. My mind is gone. What's this I'm looking for? Go back and think again! I'm – oh, the excitement, I suppose – has me reeling! Now! Wow-wow. Wow-e-wow-e-wow! Rrrrr! The turkey, yes, the bird, the bird, the king of all birds! Queen-i-o, too high, too low, inchy big, or inchy no! Turny-wurny, one, two, three, gas – mark give-a-guess, yes, six! Why ... not!!? Wowsers, my head is fit to split! Ow, ow, ow! Ow, ow, ow, ow! (*Holding her head*) What a Christmas cracker – ouch!

Sound fx: Wave of doggy-noise from out the back.

Turkey: Ssss! Sssss! I sizzle to excess! What become the mad dame that she foment me so!? Bloody erse-'n'-two-legs don't know what's good for 'em. My succulent flesh is toughening dry! I must despatch my odour-code that my forces of Trysm may heed me!

Turkey *blows. Sound fx: another wave of doggy-noise. Suddenly a rat pops up out of a dustbin in the back yard (upstage).*

Rat: Ssh! Ssssh! Something rotten's cookin'! My lord turkissmaster strong-smelly beckons. Burns he? Chars he too far? My night-sights slit the starlight. Nothing my vision eludes. Scaaaaaaaaaaaaaaaaaan the dark! (*Pause as he scans*) Ah! A trap! In the trip of me special squat-run! Blockin' me shaggin access! To splatter me intended! M'turkissmaster immolation-threatened! Stranded I stand, rockery-bound, unable to save 'im! (*Pause as he growls*) Dogs may be dead, an' dogs may be buried, but I am a rat, and I smell a dog! Dogsadabuddumodisnodowd!

Pax *and* Rebel *on the windowsill.*

Pax: Hey, bruddeRebel, gedda mell!?

Rebel: I'm busy bayin!

Pax: Gedda mell o turkremating moke!? Pooh ... duddy-bud!

Rebel: Burnt offrin deidea!

Pax: Nod burnta cinders! Nod burnda duzzd! Our cindercession swinnin!

Rebel: Naw! De mama luzz de cracklin. 'Well done' she say, alladay.

Pax: Ah shuddup an say de bay! Nuddin can stop im bin burnt da da bones an bagged i' da bins ou da back! Ack-ack!

Fade up on Robin *on the back doorstep.* Rat *watches him from the bin.* Robin *turns around, feeling he is being watched from the bin.* Rat *closes the lid.*

Robin: Here li'l c'umb, hc'e li'l c'ust, he'e li'l heel of 'e Hovis, oh, nada. Nowhere in 'e yard, I canna find a li'l b'eadc'umb to feed my iddle tummy. I only eat like a bird. Breadrest fo' the robin redbreast. Wo-wo didn't sweep 'e kitchen floor today. Poor robin hungry. I love the lovely b'eadc'umbs spread i' front of the (*Sings*) k-k-k-k-k-k-k-kitchen door. But today, when I get there, the cupboard is bare, and so I poor thing, get none.

> **Rat** *raises his head slyly from the bin.* **Robin** *turns.* **Rat** *disappears.* **Robin** *continues looking for crumbs.*

Robin: He'e li'l c'umbs. He'e li'l c'usts. Maybe lef' over from yesterday – even stale, it okay, because at Rhesus-time, alltheways hard to come by breadbits only scraps of turkeyflesh, and oh c'umbs, I know it sound silly, but I feel it like eating one of my own – you know, birds of a feather, I cannot do it, my tummy won't allow, even though a turkey would walk all over a sweet li'l robin like me and peck me to death, poor thing. What a stroke of luck that a turkey can't fly! So you see my f'iends the c'umbs. Gull is good. Gull watch over us all the time, his eye is gull-seeing gullover.

> **Rat** *raises his head slyly from the bin again. This time* **Robin** *sees him and freezes.* **Rat** *tries to grin, and points to the piece of cheese on the mousetrap.*

Rat: Cheese! Cheese! Mmmmmm! Cheese!

> **Robin** *ignores him like a child who knows not to talk to strangers.*

Robin: Oh I must search the step again, because I wonder have I the strength to fly to my nest without a bit of sustenance –

> **Robin** *turns around nervously to check on the rat again.* **Rat** *grins, and points determinedly at the cheese in the mousetrap.*

Robin: Ah! I don't believe my bright liddle eyes, a morsel of cheese on that wooden block, oh I can't tell you how pleased cock robin will be when he sees you cheese, and me, you could from delight, now piece of cheese, my cheddary rock, let me peck you on ch-

Blackout. Slow fade up on back doorstep. Musical suggestion of a terrible accident. **Rat** *pops his head out of the bin.*

Rat: Eek! Judas! Tragic!

Robin: Nearer my gull to thee, nearer to thee, I feel my head is cracked, the good eye gone, I can only see the sky. It's a dirty grey sky, such a dirty day to go. Poor cock, it'll be a nasty shock. I'm coming to you gull, with my robin skull smashed. The bit of cheese my downfall, gulp me. Soon I'll go where all the robins go.

Rat slithers out of the bin and approaches **Robin** *who is caught in the trap on the doorstep.*

Rat: Tough luck robin! Didn't see the trap! Some heartless dogs knocking around!

Robin: Don't eat me mister rat! Let me die a-lying.

Rat: Eat you!? I'm a scavenger! Sca-ven-ger! What a scavenger eats has got to be dead. You've nothing to fear. Cheer up!

Robin: Thank you, mister rat.

Rat: Must run – too many dogs around. Can't stand still.

Rat crawls over **Robin** *and surveys the kitchen he is about to enter.*

Rat: I wouldn't touch it 'til it's dead! Feathers everywhere, peck me in the eye with the broken beak – mess-y! Now! To enter the cook-pit! Turkey-flesh a-plenty waiting to be scoffed. I come, I serve, I claim my just reward. (*Sniffs*) Oven calls! In the immortal words of a true rat! I'm going in! Snout up and scuttle! Who Dares Wins! Oops! Don't forget to roll the lips back and show the warlikes!

Lights down on back yard. **Robin** *off.*
   Rat enters the kitchen, traverses the floor by a backward circling motion, and takes up position in a gap beside the cooker. Fade up on **Pax** *and* **Rebel** *on the windowsill.* **Pax** *is frantically drumming up the doggy chorus. The humming rises and falls*

with his efforts. **Rebel** *is dumbfoundedly looking down from the windowsill at the spot where the rat just hid. He nudges* **Pax** *urgently, and points with his paw to the gap beside the cooker.* **Pax** *immediately turns and redoubles his efforts with the doggy-chorus, evincing a swell of humming from the back garden.* **Rebel** *scowls at him, disgusted. Suddenly,* **Mother** *enters.*

Mother: (*Decidedly doggy*) Ooh! Wow-e-wow-e-wow-chah! My head is in bits! Here kitch-kitch-kitch-kitch-kitchy the kitchen, yes the kitchen! Whuh! Whuh! (*Shakes her head dog-like*) Now! What was it I came for to the – whuh! Whuh! – to the kitch-kitch-kitch-kitch-kitchy – whuh! Whuh! My God it's hot in the ki-ki-ki-ki – it's hot in this room. Out the door! Out the door with the hot! Out the door! Throw it out! The cause of so much – HOT! Out out out! Open the door and get rid of the – (**Pax** *is boggle-eyed trying to raise the doggy psychic transmissions*) – get rid of the – Open the door wide and get rid of the hot!

> **Mother** *throws open the kitchen door and staggers as she sees* **Robin***, a little ball of feathers in the mousetrap.*

Mother: Oh!? Feather in the mousetrap! Jesus Mary have mercy my poor little robin destroyed. It wasn't meant for you, sweet cheerio. Don't move, my love, stay still – aw your poor beak is broke, my love, the bold bad cheese led you on. I'll put you in the mansize tissue-box, soft and warm in there, squatting, and I'll scrunch up a tissue to support your wounded head. Then I'll get the eye-dropper from the medicine chest and fill it up with Christmas sherry. Let you sip the drops. You're drooping. Now, rest, little feathery lovely thing. The world – so cruel at Christmastime. Please God let tomorrow be a day of peace! Jesus Mary and Joseph I'll have to go to bed.

> **Mother** *carries* **Robin** *out.* **Rat** *scampers out from the gap beside the cooker.*

Rat: Hey, Prince of Fowl, m'Lord, can you hear me through the oven wall? Speak to me! Speak to me! Tap with your drumstick on the – the – side. I'll ask you humble questions, if the answer is 'yes' tap once, if the answer is 'no' –

Turkey: I hear you rat. Remove your spats, rat, you are in the presence of the burning bird. As in your infamous plague, my extremities are blackening, I am struggling to hold my temper with you all. I should be out by now!

Rat: Dogs. O my sizzling beauty! Do I have to kiss?

Turkey: Open the door! Your claws will not burn. Come, open, and you may gorge your reward.

Rat: I'm a bit freaked of the dogs, m'lord.

Turkey: It is your special duty, you are the chosen one. Fear not to be harmed, they are at bay.

Rat: What if the woman comes?

Turkey: To Hell with the woman. She is addled with the dog-biz. Give me air!

Rat: I am coming, m'lord Gobble, soon I will fan your cool and save you.

Turkey: Push the handle in and turn it to the right.

Rat: There! I dared, and I have won.

Turkey: Oh holy Gobblegod that's lovely. Oh fan me, fan me. Rat, thou hast excelled thyself. Take thy reward.

Rat: The gorge?

Turkey: Gorge thy fill, but leave no marks lest they betray your presence to my future eaters.

Rat: Therefore I will suck. The stuffing I favour the most. Hey, the baking-tray scorches not my feet. Neat!

Turkey: Ah! Your fur doth tickle my drumsticks. Freeze, squat rat and suck!

Rat: Turkey I adore you. Oh the leisure. O delickus. O delickus. My tongue edduce thy paste.

Turkey: My humble rat, you I have chosen to save my trystkiss. When you have done, I charge you to eliminate the limbostate half-dogs which have caused me to be hotfired.

Rat: But how will I eliminate a foe I cannot see? Mmm. (*Sucks*)

Turkey: Ask me not, just go and rid me of these cursed dogs, trained as you are in the arts of conflict, after which the trystkiss will remain in my domain.

Rat: Oh crap! I have done a shite on the baking-tray.

Turkey: Incontinent fool! A rat-crap!

Rat: Too much pleasure all at once. The muscles go limp.

Turkey: Remove the turd lest it put them off the eating me.

Rat: Oh, no I couldn't touch it. Here, I'll hide it under a spud. I'm off to hunt the half-dead dog.

Turkey: The dogs must die!

Rat: Beggin' your pardon, m'lord, but the only way the dogs will die, knowing how the mad cur thinks, is when your good turkeyself remove for goodenall from the heat of the kitch.

Turkey: Insolence!

Rat: I incline to your aim, O lord, and make haste to make paste of the whelps.

   Rat *scuttles off into the gap beside the cooker.*

Turkey: Maybe it were better for me were I unhanded of these troubles. But, the comsummation of the Trystkiss demands I bear the trials inflicted on my hormone-buttressed breast. Such is the turkey's sad yet glorious lot!

   Rebel & **Pax** *on the windowsill.*

Rebel: Thish id nod wurging ow! Id id a fudile ack. Da doggychorush make no mada. There'd ony one way da'd

we dogs can die down an go go in peace. We godda
FUCKOU da kissma bird, an we godda do id now!

Pax: Hatience, Hebble, hatience. Fuckou da kissma bird
bing down da rod o da mama an da fada. We godda bing
aboud da cumdishes whiddle make e mamma an da fada
fug id owd emsells. Den we return da da noderel order, den
da kissma ardificial will be gone, an den we can leep de
everlastin leap.

Rebel: Shteppin shtones! Ah da dioretical crap! Blow da
shie ouda da cuckie.

    Rebel *makes to climb down from the windowsill.*

Pax: Wade, wade, wade. Id id wurgin on da mama's
psyche. She id nodda so obesed wid a bird, she id leddin id
burn.

Rebel: Naw, da rat widda sucky sicksation ha' rebibed da
bird. Dahony plan is da blow out da flame what keeps him
cookin, an fill da kitch widda natural gas. Id id da ony
physical act da which I can perform – da breath id lef in me,
an da shall be my weapon. Breath.

Pax: Don do it, Rebel.

Rebel: Don u coundermand me. Didid wahr! Wahr! I am
hadvancin to da hoven.

    Rebel *jumps down to the floor.*

Pax: Luka da damage u ha aready dun. Da robin id dyin.

Rebel: I din do dat! Da fada pud da trap down, budda fault
lay widda kissma shit an da advent o da bird.

Pax: Leddim burn to bones, he will be flung on da stones if
u bud wade.

Rebel: I will gas him. Poison his system.

Robin: My brain is still alive. My beak shattered. One eye
gone to shie. I hope cock come lookin' for me now, I li'e a
li'l comfortin in my hour o need. He still dozin in a nest,

unsuspeckin. Wakey-akey, cock, come an' have a drop of sherry, come an console your flighty-obin wub my wing, I am callin you. I am so appi 'ere in tintinsdel in de kitchen. Don't worry about li'l me because I am so happy. There is a rat in the room, but I am not afraid, gull look after me because I am a good robin.

Turkey: Heed me, Rat, my enemy draws near. He is cunning, we can see him not, smell him not, hear him not, but we can feel his evil breath. Hark, he approacheth the oven. Had he a shape, he darkeneth the door.

Pax: Rebel, u bing calamiddy upon us. Desist. Desist.

Rebel: Da deed ha godda be done, an id bedda id were done quick. I gonna blow ow da li'e.

Turkey: Heed me, Rat, he crawls upon my breast, I feel his hot breath.

Rat: Fear not, proturkeyrate, I have him in my ra-sights.

Robin: Oh! I feel disaster come! I feel the end is nigh!

Blackout, burst of music. Magnesium flare. Lights fade up. Smoke rises off the tattered **Robin**. *Fade up faint lament music.*

Rebel: I addended to mount da crest o' da breast, bud de grease made a fuddin' lippy, I lithered and lided, my four feet spread an I unwiddingly em-brace da fowlicreature. I wuz frying da kill da durkeyding, an I wind up riding on da yoke, two fron paws on is shoulders, two back paws clinging to its sides, a huffin an a puffin to blow oud da blue flamligh haloin is squintin ead. The bird beginda vibrate, an splashes o grease sputter out, which fan da blue cookerlie to da big whitenyella flambyshno. Den I feel de udder furry body fallin through my only-some-felt air. De squash o de impaq pousse da turbojet o breath ouda my blowpipe, whuh, an de flam extink.

Rat: To the protection of my behovened I scuttled, I pounced to puncture the crazed spirit-dog. yet I could only feel my enemy lightly, a warmth of stuffiness. Nowhere a jugular, no blood to draw, no bone to crunch. I slipped in the hot puddle of my earlier – falling – failing – my involuntary expulsion. The hostile airiness of dog was all around me; breathing it, I started to choke.

Robin: 'Twas a sweet release in the end. A rebirth rather than a sad and lonely death. The sherry was nearly complete and I was warm, dozing in my tissue box. Then a flurry happened over at the oven. I heard a crackle and sizzle, a silence, then a single tongue of flame anointed my head. Gull came for me then, smiling. He twittered, sweeter than I had imagined, and a flock of hummingbirds came and picked up the corners of the tissue that I lay upon and carried me away to lie upon the sky. Gull, how I love thee Gull, forever and ever, feather, a bob-bob-bobbin, robin.

Pax: Dandin on da dindowill I daw id all. Adagedy. Da durkey killed da robin, wid da grease-plash, an da rat's indervenshun fired da splash so far. Bud Rebel hafta bear a share o blamin' fo' lamin' in da flamin! Bedeen da dee o dem, poor Cock Robin ida widower. One ding I doe. Kissma never be da same again.

Cut faint lament music. Lights fade on kitchen, except for strange glow emanating from **Turkey** *in the oven.*

Turkey: In-gratitude! Ah-narcism! O-dieusness! My beaconlight extinguished, Kinsale gas in the darkness fills my ovenkitchentemple. My bodyflesh blackened before cools, toughens, is brushed by the alien gas. In-edible! Malignant! Poison-soiled! Still I will be feasted on. My lickey rat, once more into the breach! Trystkiss will arise! To battle!

Rat: I'm a clev rat, I have done your bidding in advance. The old trick of the viral canker, stock-in-trade of a vermin like me. I spread my empirical compound among the terrier immunity, pincer-like, 'til the two ulcered doggies suff the tummy-swell. Watch the two invisibles – they'll promise a pup and deliver eff-all and the sniffers on the lawn lie down for the nappedy never to wake to the dog-rally-call!!

Turkey: Onward Tristian rodent! Let sleeping dogs lie. The anti-trites will never drive us from our destined wrath. No sir, render us our due desserts, Rat, grant us feastery.

Lights down on **Turkey** *and* **Rat**, *up on* **Rebel** *and* **Pax**.

Pax: I know ur under stretch Ebel wid de chrisimation biz an de abnomalidy, but id id no accuse fo beldin ow de like o' dat.

Rebel: Id id regreddable but id id inebidable.

Pax: Whatabouda doggybred ouda back? Justa dey haida da durkey-in-d'oven so dey luvva de robin deadrest.

Rebel: Dey mememor me roary days. Dey know de why o de fight.

Pax: Id *me* dad after haulin em, id *me* dad hafta hanswer dem. Der howlin fo' de leaderin, dey look to me fo' de lash. U can hide, I godda haymake while the shi'e flies.

Rebel: I ha huffered me hill! Implizzoned on me mast! Dun accuse moi of shelderin shy! I ha been bulleted, blackened an dyed!

Flurry of many flapping wings in the sky upstage.

Pax: Cock Robin in de air now. A crabbin an a cryin. Kiggin up de worrowful wacket. An de birds o de air are a-wheelin an a peelin lamendin de sad fade of 'is love-bud. De basset neg door id wailin in wimpathy. A lodadda dead dogs spirid away ta da bye bye side. An de puggin odious allers from de vacant site are grimacin growlin at ME.

Rebel: U da orador! Channel deir ire a de source of de sobblin! De in-vadin occu-pyin fetter-creature bakin i' da hot shop!

Pax: Bud ow, ow, ow can I gedda birdiebuddies wailin in de air ta hear my prayer ta da mamapusson when u godda vacan' sigh' allers frettinin' da birdycull!?

Rebel: Calamadies are bad 'n' calamadies are sad, bud de birdies know dad der fellow-feathered fucky-fowl de claws o' de clobberin an' robininin! U godda vox-box! U can do de bark-lark! Led de tweeties 'ear de doggy-song!

Pax: (*Getting desperate*) Bud dey is a-sighin an' a-cryin on accounda de robin! Dey are in de flap 'n' fury o' de grievin'! An' de reason o' grievin 'n' scuse of ire u ha pandied to em on a plate!

Rebel: (*Darkening*) Grr. U soun like a Kissmaknave! Ur udderin da Kissmachah u shudderer.

Pax: Kauf! Fu Kauf! Fu kauf Rebel, kauf! I am haunch an' headfast agen de Kissmacult juzzazmuzazu! Ur dinderin me dance wid ur anticarmonical rowls! Lemme rouse de drowsies an' lemme ply de fliers o' de sky!

Rebel: Rouse an' ply! Rouse an' ply! Bon don geddindeway of me more bidrect exterimend!

Pax: Like de expendin' o' de doorstep-hoppin' Robin! Oh, birds'll flock to me call!

Rebel: (*Heated*) Fetters, wings, a beak, 'senuff. Ruddy redbreast, close enuff evolved in da Kissmashit, fuggin feathers 'n' fowl are symbols of obsession.

Pax: (*Intensely*) Now ur on ur own, Rebel. I ha rather stick in mid-misery than carry on wid you excusin da demise o' de robin.

Rebel: (*Emphatically*) Go on ur way, homedog, claws a plit atween ush.

Pax: We gotta tick together Rebel!

Rebel: No we don't. Rebel tock a different tick!

Pax: Wadaboud da slumberin' wuffs? Dey dwindle an' dwift f'om dewearywill.

Rebel: Enuff'll wade an whelp fo' me puposes.

Pax: Pithin i' da wind, Rebel. More wobins wasted.

Rebel: While I godda breath, I will puff it. Whuh!

Pax: Ur panickin.

Rebel: If panic wad id needed ...

Pax: Ur chasin ur tail, gun around in saorkills widout a lead or wurry aboud a mandead.

Rebel: Our mandaid id de pall o poultry 'moke 'mothering 'e kitchen. We godda mandaid da clear de air o' de ardificial malaise.

Pax: U canna win widou takin inda count de mama an de fada. Ur chasin ur tail.

Rebel: Bud idn't dat 'de quedon, Pax? Who de doggy an who de tail, an who of us do de waggle?

Pax: (*Screams*) Aargh!

Rebel: Whadda problem now!?

Pax: De pain! De pain!

Rebel: Were? Were?

Pax: Ah! me domach! Me baci! Id id da labour bains!

Rebel: Bud ur a boy, Pax, boy!

Pax: Ah! De everlastin labour o de puppy-bred invicted on me. Ah! Horror on harrow is biled! De agony med wurse by de know no puppy baba comin to atone. Ah! Me rocks! Ah! Me nethers! Ah me bullugs!

Pax *doubles up and rolls over in agony, watched by* **Rebel**.

Rebel: Hell on erd! Me bizizon is bizarre! All dad I wand is de RIP. An' all I godda dure da geddit! Wadin' trew de shid o' Kissma, pleadin' demise. I didn't axe fo' dis! Me doggybred blissed abouda rockery in da sickness o sleepinapathy! All de birds o' de air takin' da par o' de blackened featherbrether 'neath – woodenyaknow! – an' screamin' to be served de plattered Rebelhead, eyeballs spiced fo' peckin'! Me volover Pax ha' become a sticky customer an' I dunno wada do widim. Da gif o' da gab 'e god, no denyin', bud idun appear da be enuff agen da Kissma turkey an' da guarodent rat, now dey goddim ridin' deliri wi' deliverylay! Budenegen, de allers da bowel me

name f'om de vacant sigh mebbe double da trouble w'en lef'
off der lead! Oo, ow' I'd love ta doze an' av' a tink abouda
lemma, bud I daren't drop de lids in case I catch de
dormitory bug!

Pax: Ah! Me biddineys! Ah! Me bledders! Ah!! Me
trocities! Stop de airy vendilatin' ouda yer hole an' pud 'ur
tots to riddin' me o' de liver-wring o' de ulcermen! I beg a
pause. I crave a truce from dis bitch of a lockage. I demand
an epicendural. Now! Ow! Ow-ow-ow!

Turkey *glows ghoulishly in the oven.*

Turkey: Gasping, gaspipe airs stiffening my flesh, I ponder
my present necessitous predicament. Betimes, weakening, I
suffer doubts. Do the chrismeaters deserve my body-
benefits? *Why do I bother!?* Sometimes it beats me. I fail, I
fall, I feel alone in my cold furnace-cell, forsaken by my
bredderren, unbidden by my dinnions.

Pause.

But then I think of ing – ratitude! And the turkey of
tomorrow! And a table to set him on! and a mada to serve
him and a fada to carve him! And a tableful of gluttons to
devour him! And I think of all the turkeys of the gravy-
laden past, and the glories of their feasting, ripping and
peeling, gnashing and sucking to the pique de bonne
victoire, aah, the lore of the turkeybliss, I beg, I exhort, I
demand, I charge my delivery to epicury!

Blackout.

End of Act One

Act Two

Scene One

Livingroom. All assemble. **Maurice** *has just given* **Terry** *and* **Benny** *a lift to the house. The three visitors carry their presents – black plastic refuse sacks stuffed into shape. There is awkwardness, but it is overcome by the indomitable will to carry out all the little duties of the Christmas ritual.*

Mother: O-ho-ho, great to see you all, Happy Christmas Terry love, go inside Maurice, and Benny, welcome, come in, happy Christmas.

Benny: (*Long-prepared entrance line*) We're like the Three Wise Kings.

All accompanied, of course, by hugs and kisses, and appropriate responses. **Father**, *behind her, does the same, abashed, without fuss.* **Benny** *and he shake hands firmly man to man, eyeball to eyeball.*

Mother: Now Maurice, will you open one of those lovely wine bottles you brought, and we'll all have a toast together. Stoke up the fire there Denis, sit down now Terry, you take things easy, Benny pull up a chair, now we have the turkey on and he's doing nicely, and everything is ready so there's nothing left except to enjoy ourselves. Isn't that the way to have it?

Maurice: Listen everyone. I just want to get this bit of embarrassment out of the way, okay?

Mother: (*Alarmed*) Oh! What's wrong Maurice?

Maurice: I didn't bring an individual present for anyone, so please please please don't embarrass me by giving me something when I've nothing to give in return.

Mother: Would you listen to him! Maurice brought enough wine to float us all down the Nile and back to Alexandria.

Benny: Good man Maurice.

Terry: You're setting very high stakes Maurice. Look, Benny and me are giving joint presents this year because –

Mother: Oh for God's sake don't you be worrying about presents. You've enough on your plates.

Father: It's only an excitement for kids really – the whole presents business – silly really.

Mother: Still. Christmas is Christmas. Now. Don't anyone dare go into the kitchen. You know the way I am. There's only room for one.

This gives **Mother** *her cue to rush upstairs for her enormous pile of presents for everyone.*

Father: Excuse me just a minute.

He goes into the kitchen to get something.

Terry: (*In urgent whisper to* **Maurice**) They didn't mention Pax.

Maurice: Better say nothing until it's raised.

Terry: Did you hear that Benny!?

Benny: Happy Christmas Maurice.

He hands him a small black stuffed refuse sack.

Terry: It's nothing.

Maurice: (*Looking inside*) You shouldn't have ...

Benny: Something to stop you getting cold feet.

Maurice: Just what I needed. Honestly. The launderette sucks up one of every pair. I'm always wearing odd socks. That's wonderful. Three pairs. And they're lovely. Thank you very much. Both of you.

He kisses **Terry**, *nods to* **Benny**. **Father** *returns.*

Father: (*To* **Benny** *and* **Terry**) I'll talk to you two later.

He hands **Maurice** *a strange-looking kite-shaped object skilfully wrapped in a black refuse sack.*

Something for the car. (*Glances significantly at* **Terry**)

Maurice: It's really well wrapped. A shame to tear the paper.

Father: That's the carpenter's principles. Haven't I told you since you were knee-high? Preparedness, patience, precision and care. Applies to everything in life.

Maurice *opens it and sticks his hand in. He rummages, then peeks in. Puzzled.*

Maurice: (*Unimpressed*) Ve-ry use-ful!

Father: For cleaning the mist off the back window without getting out of your seat. I've got one myself and I find it a Godsend.

Benny: Happy Christmas Mr Macken.

Benny *gives him a middling-sized soft parcel.*

Terry: Something to make use of rather than something nice...

Father: I hope you didn't go to any trouble...

He opens it. It's a pyjamas set. He is disgusted.

Father: Pyjamas. Thanks.

Terry: Mam told us the ones you have are full of holes. And you're going in for the tests ...

Father: Everybody's very interested in my tests!

Mother *re-enters, laden down with huge presents.*

Mother: Oh look at the beautiful pyjamas. How did you know! Do you know that fellow is in-decent traipsing to the toilet at night. He's more holes than cloth hanging from his hips. How well you knew!

Father: It must have been divine inspiration.

Terry: (*To* **Father**) Anyway. Happy Christmas.

Father: Yeah.

Benny: Keep the fleas warm eh?

Terry: This is for you Mam. Happy Christmas.

Mother: That's bold now! I told you ! But thank you both very much.

She puts the present aside. She'll open it when they're gone and give it to somebody else before the season's out.

Now this is a little thing for you Maurice.

She hands him a huge parcel.

Maurice: For God's sake mam! This is really embarrassing.

Mother: Not at all. From your dad as well. And Terry, this is yours. Happy Christmas love. It's something you'll need in the very near future, because you'll find that time will not be on your side.

Terry: You've done it again Mam. We agreed only token presents. Now this!

Mother: It is only a token thing.

Maurice: (*Announcing in 'would-you-credit-it' tones*) It's a portable Hoover. How did you know that this is exactly what I need in the flat?

Mother: Because I'm your mother, that's how!

Father: Ideal for your little car as well. Keep it in good nick.

Maurice: Thanks Mam, you're brilliant.

Terry: (*Having opened and looked in at her present*) This is disgraceful Mam. It's fantastic. Benny it's a microwave.

Mother: You'll have both your hands more than full and there'll be no time for cooking. Everybody's getting them.

Terry: Mam you are too good! Thanks, but I could brain you for spending so much.

Mother: Ah sure for God's sake I can't bring it with me. And now Benny, happy Christmas to you.

She hands him a small soft present.

Maurice, have you organised the drinks for the toast?

Maurice: Oops! Forgot. Just a sec.

Benny: They're lovely, Mrs. Macken. Three pairs. Lovely colours and very soft. I have sensitive feet. Thanks very much and many happy returns.

Mother: Not at all Benny, you're welcome. Now. Are you right there Maurice, are you right, do you think you'll have them ready by the night ... (*She half sings*)

Terry: None for me thanks Maurice.

Mother: Now. I want to say something to you all. This is the birthday of Jesus Christ, a little baby, the Prince of Peace. We know we all love each other very much. We're a good strong family. And Benny, I'm sure you come from a good loving family too. Let us all put our love together today, and let it multiply to make today a celebration of the peace of Jesus Christ our Lord.

Father: Amen.

Maurice: Cheers.

They all decide to use this as the cue to toast.

Mother: Benny. In the kitchen please. Time to get the soup and make a start. Everyone else sit down.

Mother *and* **Benny** *head for the kitchen.*

Scene Two

The kitchen.

Mother: Funny smell. My head is gone daft. Daft!
However. Benny, a bit of advice!

Benny: Fire ahead Ruth!

Mother: Benny, Dada's not an easy man. But he has a little
bit put away. Not much. A little bit. He's willing to buy a
banger for Terry – and you.

Benny: A banger!?

Mother: Don't raise your hopes! Just four wheels and an
engine. He'll throw in insurance and tax.

Benny: That's very eh –

Mother: Generous – I know. He has his funny ways. I'm
telling you, it makes an awful difference with a baby – save
you all the getting on and off buses, and folding up the wet
buggies. Dreadful! Now. Don't let him rise you! Hold your
fire! For Terry's sake.

Benny: So I'm to keep my mouth shut.

Mother: Not completely. I'm sure you know what I mean.
Controversy won't help.

Benny: Okay. I get the picture. I'm not to mention the
north. I'm not to mention my family. I'm not to mention
my past. And I'm not to mention politics.

Mother: It sounds a bit excessive. Will you manage?

Benny: I'll suffer the simtins, Ruth.

Mother: – ... ?

Benny: The simtins. S.M.T.N. Spare Me The North! I call
'em the simtins. You know what they say – if you can't beat
'em –

Mother: (*Completely at sea*) Well, if you can spare them for
a short while –

Benny: Don't worry Ruth. It used to be called 'taking the king's shilling'. But this is only 'taking the dada's car'. I'll show you how low I can stoop. Give me the soup!

   Turkey *pops his head up.*

Turkey: (*To* **Benny**) Bollox! (*To* **Mother**) Bitch!

Mother: How's Mr Turkey? Pooh!

Benny: Take a look in the glass and we'll see ...

Turkey: And they looked! And they saw! And they said –

Mother: Jesus Mary and Joseph the stench!

Benny: That's no turkey!

Mother: Gassed! Rotten! Roddled! Burnt to look at! Raw to touch!

Turkey: You'll eat me anyway ...!

Mother: Too late to change! (*Shrilly*) The Christmas dinner destroyed!

Benny: Whad'd you do with it!?

Turkey: Left me to my fate! (*Looks at his feet*)

Mother: Once a year we try to do things right! What right have you to interfere and wreck it all? What right!!?

Benny: It's not my fault. I was sold a –

Mother: Not my fault!?

Benny: – turkey.

Mother: Angel Benny can do no wrong.! Blast you! Damn you! I could – !

BENNY: Easy on, Ruth. I was looking forward to a bit of bird just as much as you. That yoke is some sort of – mutant! The Consumer Protection ACT – must be a clause – false advertising ...! Throw it out!

Turkey: (*To* **Benny**) Claws will rip you! Throat to groin!

Mother: I've to face that man with no Christmas dinner!

Benny: He'll have to do without!

Turkey: (*Roars*) No!!

Mother: (*Roars*) NO! Denis will be livid! Forget about the car! Poor Terry! (*Decisively*) Heat the creature!! Light, gas, light!!

Turkey: (*As gas lights*) Clsk! Aauuh ...!

Benny: Take a drop of sherry, Ruth!

Mother: I don't need your say-so to take a little swig. Robin in the bin! My robin redbreast – dead! The sherry no good! The little beak smashed. Jesus! You darkened our door and look!

Benny: The robin – ?

Mother: Trap!

Benny: (*Reacts with pain*) Oh!

Turkey: Cook while you whinge, witch!

Mother: You're giving me a dreadful migraine. That turkey will be served and we will eat it. Bring the soup in, and everything is normal!

Benny: Ruth, you're over-

Mother: Baby! Car!

Turkey: Trystkiss!!

   Mother *and* **Benny** *return to the livingroom with the soup.*

Scene Three

The living room.

Mother: Now eat up everybody. Terry you're eating for two.

Father: Eat? It's not lumpy, is it?

Maurice: (*Mock*) Oh no! Disgraced again. Don't you know, papa, that you don't drink soup, you eat soup.

Father: I hate the lumps. That's all I know. Snotty.

Mother: Denis!

Terry: We know. You've been telling us for thirty years.

Mother: (*Ironic*) But did you listen Terry, did you pay attention?

Father: Clear soup. My mother, God rest her, made a delicious clear soup.

Maurice: Was that the one with the nettles?

Mother: Now now –

Terry: Consommé in French Dad. (*Pointed and speedy aside to* **Maurice**) The famine *did* happen. It was real.

Maurice: (*Aside to* **Terry**) Who's saying it didn't!?

Mother: The mother again –

Father: My mother knew nothing about French, of course –

Terry: Potage is the thick stuff.

Maurice: Anyone for more vin rouge ou blanc?

Benny: I'll have a drop of red, Maurice.

Maurice: Good man. Sell out a bit of sovereignty. Truly international at last.

Father: Wine. It's not bad I suppose. There was a time only the horsey set could get it.

Benny: (*Pointedly as ghaeilge*) Go raibh míle maith agat.

Mother: We'll all have a sup –

Maurice: You see? Old boundaries collapsing. We're all Europeans now.

Father: Findlaters was the only place to buy it. To go with their famous big cheese. My mother used to bring me in to get the smell and look in the mirrors. They didn't mind.

Terry: Progress is great, of course, Everyone should have the chance to drink any wine they like. But national self-determination is not exchangeable for –

Benny: Thirty cases of wine.

Maurice: Oh excuse me! Touché! We were talking about wine –

Benny: Flooding the market. Lakes of it. And Guinnesses are laying them off in droves.

Father: Nobody can blame you Benny.

Mother: Now. Will we begin?

Maurice: Wine comes from grapes. They grow on a bush. It doesn't have any politics.

Benny: Red grapes and green grapes! *Sláinte.*

Mother: Sláinte Benny. Was the traffic heavy?

Terry: It's an example of something Irish people can't control. It's a symptom of our lack of economic clout.

Maurice: We can't grow grapes because it's too friggin cold. What can you do about that?

Benny: But native industry is losing out. We're bombarded with their stuff, but they ignore ours.

Mother: No buses, so people rely on their cars.

Father: Aren't we doing well enough to keep a tight hold on to the coat-tails of the big fellas?

Terry: We can't compete with the big economic powers built upon centuries of colonial exploitation.

Benny: Our economy was never developed. Eight hundred years of occupation saw to that.

Mother: What's on telly Denis?

Maurice: The eight hundred years rears its ugly head again.

Benny: It's a long time, getting longer.

Father: And getting uglier by the hour. (*Staring at* **Benny**)

Maurice: Can we just drink the stuff and stop the agonising?

Terry: Who's agonising? You're the one started the analogies.

Mother: Now stop the two of you. Remember what I said. You too Benny.

Benny: It's just a bit of banter Ruth.

Father: If only it was ...

Mother: Grace. Who'll say it? Benny?

Terry: You say it yourself Mam.

Benny: No. It's quite alright. If Dev could sign the Oath of Allegiance I can say grace, isn't that right Denis?

Father: You may be sure Dev always said his grace.

Benny: When he was asking the archbishop of Dublin to bless his constitution!

Maurice: (*Laughing*) Nice one Benny nice one son!

Mother: And bless dada's constitution too. Now In the name of the Father and of the Son and of –

Benny *joins in. Simultaneously:*

Mother: – the Holy Spirit.

Benny: – the Holy Ghost

Pause.

Benny: Bless us O Lord, and these thy gifts, through Christ our lord, amen.

Mother: Which of thy bounty we are about to receive. Yes. Amen. Thank you Benny. Now.

Pause.

Father: You haven't much time for the prayers Benny? Too busy?

Benny: I'm a little rusty.

Terry: People have their own spirituality now Dad. It doesn't have to be institutionalised. Things have changed.

Father: That doesn't mean that they're right. Give me a good committed Protestant any day before the wishy-washy-can't-be-bothereds.

Maurice: What about good committed Atheists?

Father: No such thing.

Maurice: You're looking at one.

Father: Who?

Maurice: Me!

Father: Not at all. You're fooling yourself Maurice.

Mother: Please God. But there are some things that don't change Maurice. The sacraments. Marriage. Baptism. Everybody normal believes in them, no matter what religion. For the sake of the babies if for nothing else.

Terry: The future of the babies is for the parents to decide Mam.

Mother: Oh of course Terry. But the parents will be delighted to get the opinions of those who love them. Talking is always good.

Terry: So long as the parameters are clearly set from the start.

Maurice: A few preconditions Terry, eh?

Terry: Shut up Maurice.

Mother: No need to get aggressive Terry.

Terry: Who's getting aggressive? I'm just giving my point of view.

Mother: Oh who's this, who's that. You should try and get a rest after dinner. You're tired.

Maurice: Don't worry, we'll all nod off watching Superman III.

Father: There's a choice. Superman III, Chitty Chitty Bang Bang, or Carmen on Iceskates.

Mother: Chitty Chitty Bang Bang. Is that still on the go? The two of you loved that film.

Maurice: Don't start the harking back again Mam.

Mother: Excuse me, Mr Winecrate, I'll hark where I like in my own house on Christmas day. We didn't have much, but at least we were happy.

Father: Blast! We've missed the Pope's message.

Mother: We'll get it later on the RTE news. Urbi et Orbi. Latin. What's that Terry?

Terry: To the city and to the world.

Mother: God you were great at your Latin. The tails of the words all underlined in markers. Ooh-ooh-aah-ooh-ooh-aah – oh, a brainbox Benny. But wait 'til you see yourselves how much they can change, and not a thing you can do to stop it.

Maurice: For God's sake Mam, why act so sad? It's not all that hard to accept that grown-up adults want to organise their own destinies in life.

Mother: Wait and see. That's all I'll say.

Maurice: (*Quietly*) You're the one who'll be waiting.

Terry: Maurice is just saying that it happens every generation – the tug between traditional and – and – the way people feel they ought to run their lives.

Father: Tradition isn't a bad thing. It's served many a generation very well indeed, thank you. And you'll find in time it's a thing you might be damn glad to hand down to your own little brood.

Terry: We're all part of tradition whether we like it or not.

Maurice: Yes, but not always the majority tradition. There are minority traditions as well. (*Speedy aside to* **Terry**) And not always historically-based!

Father: And why should the tradition of most have to bow to the tradition of the few!? I suppose that's democratic!

At this point the turkey in the oven in the dark kitchen starts to redden and glow in throbbing, pulsating fashion. The turkey wants to be served, and is impressing this on **Mother**.

Benny: It's not a question of bowing. It's a question of accommodating.

Maurice: Remarkably tolerant of you Benny.

Terry: Why do self-appointed majorities have to feel so threatened by involuntary minorities!?

The turkey in the dark kitchen steps up the intensity of its glowing.

Mother: (*Standing up*) Ssh!

All pause momentarily. The strains of turkey music become faintly audible.

Benny: (*To* **Terry**'s *rhetorical question*) Can I answer that? (*A look from* **Mother**) Ah, why bother!

Maurice: No! I'll answer that!

Mother: (*Struggling to cope*) The – eh – time to serve the – the Christmas dinner ...

Short pause, **Maurice** *prepares to speak.* **Benny** *is in like a shot. Simultaneously, faint inky-blue light outside the kitchen window silhouettes* **Pax** *and* **Rebel** *howling in silence on the windowsill,* *drumming up the psychic powers of the dogs-out-the back to influence* **Mother**. *The doggy-noise becomes audible, and perhaps some dog-ears and howling muzzles bob above the windowsill level* (*shadow-puppets*).

Benny: The crucial difference is between dominant tradition and repressed tradition. Without dominance tradition wouldn't matter. Much.

Father: It's nice! Tradition can be nice!

Maurice: Nothing wrong with a bit of diddley-die...

Terry: To some it's more than diddley-die.

Maurice: Absolument! Die diddley-die! To some it's life, not death. Alive alive-oh!

Mother: (*Almost softly*) Maybe we should call the whole thing off.

Benny: Who mentioned death!?

Terry: (*Dryly*) ... the usual trap!

The turkey redoubles its reddening and glowing. The turkey music intensifies.

Maurice: Seems to follow you around Benny ...

Benny: So long as it doesn't catch up!

Father: Would you all shut up about death and let us have the bit of grub!

Mother: (*A little shrilly*) I take it from the empty dishes you all enjoyed the soup. Next course!

She prepares to clear up, and this sends the dogs into a frenzy of effort to avoid the carrying-in of the turkey.

Benny: Lovely Ruth.

Father: I always like the clear stuff.

Terry: Just like when we were small, isn't it Maurice?

Maurice: (*Resignedly*) The very same.

Mother: Oh no! When you were small it was so much different –

Father: A happier, innocent time.

Maurice: Drivel! Half the time it was Hell –

Benny: What's so different!?

Mother: Thank you Benny very nice –

Terry: It really doesn't matter –

Mother: Then why are you so unhappy, Miss?

Benny: Because she's constantly hounded and pressed to be something other than herself.

Father: Benny has the answer!

Mother: (*To* **Terry**) What about the times when you and Maurice – sitting in behind me in the armchair –

Maurice: (*In 'not-again' tones*) The concerts! –

Mother: Smothering your faces in the corners of the cushion –

Terry: Lovely, Mother, but it's –

Maurice: – Different now!

Mother: That's what I said!

Father: Correct!

Terry: But Mam you've such a sanitised, idealised –

Maurice: – picture of the past.

Benny: And the present!

Mother: Thank you Benny lovely –

Benny: Sorry, just –

Father: Getting in your clever spoke!

Mother: But you MUST remember the concerts on the armchair – in behind my bottom –

Terry / Maurice: Yes we do –

Terry: But you'll just get yourself upset because you can't understand why it's not like that now – and forever!

Maurice: Amen!

Mother: My God, prayers from Maurice! What next!?

Father: They never got to singing anything for all the skitting and laughing.

Terry: (*Sarcastically*) /
Mother: (*Delightedly*) That's right!

Mother: (*Cont.*) Giggling with their faces in the cushion and their bottoms shaking in the air –

Maurice: What I remember most is reading with my torch under the covers in bed.

Terry: Me too! (*To* **Mother**) You couldn't figure out why we never kicked up like other kids about going up to bed.

Mother: My brainboxes! I might have known!

Father: I got you those torches for Christmas one year –

Mother: The cheek! You never got – Jesus Mary and Jo the neck!

Benny: Santa Claus brought the torches.

Father: Good man Benny.

Terry: I had one as well.

Maurice: Reading Connolly by torchlight –

Terry: – with red and green filters on them –

Maurice: – when we should have been enjoying ourselves –

Terry: We *were* enjoying ourselves!

Maurice: – not much –

Terry: We were! That's why you remember it so well.

Maurice: We were full of youthful –

Simultaneously.

Maurice: – naivety

Terry: – enthusiasm.

Mother: Laughing in the armchair, couldn't sing a note!

Maurice: – the rotten applecart –

Terry: We were going to grow up to upset the rotten applecart.

Maurice: – together –

Terry: – the two of us together.

Pause.

Maurice: Mam's right. Different now.

Mother: Thank God (*Slight pause*) In some ways.

Father: (*Laughing*) Remember Nelson's eye!?

Mother: Nelson's eye! Oh, very funny, Benny!

Terry: It was cruel!

Maurice: They used to bring us in to the kitchen, one by one in the dark, blindfolded –

Terry: Then they'd put a pot on your head –

Maurice: That was Nelson's hat.

Terry: And a stick in your hand –

Mother: (*Laughing*) The poker, the poker –

Maurice: That was Nelson's wooden hand –

Father: (*Laughing*) And a big bowl of suet –

Mother: – gooey dripping –

Terry: They'd stick your hand into the dripping –

Maurice: – and that was Nelson's eye!

They all laugh, except **Benny.**

Benny: (*Simply*) Yous had it nice down here.

Maurice: Oh dear! Benny has a persecution outburst coming on.

Terry: He has his reasons.

Mother: Oh we all have our reasons.

Father: It wasn't all that nice and easy I can tell you Benny.

Terry: Dad! Not the –

Terry / Maurice: Orange-boxes.

Mother: The whole house, it's true Benny, he furnished the entire house out of orange-boxes.

Father: Long gone, of course.

Mother: Oh God, yes, proper furniture now.

Benny: The orange boxes turned to firewood – ?

Mother: Well, the marks, you see! Children, Benny! Wait 'til your own – !

Father: Soft wood ...

Mother: ... and hard treatment from these two.

Benny: Did you have a cane, Mrs Macken?

Mother: A cane!? No not at all!

Terry/ Maurice: Yes you did!!

Mother: I left all that to Denis.

Terry / Maurice: No you didn't!!

Father: We never had to use it much –

Terry: (*To* **Father**) You didn't need it!

Mother: I don't remember ever –

Maurice: That's what I mean – selective amnesia! Remembering what suits!

Benny: A common problem! Don't feel isolated Ruth, you're very trendy.

Maurice: As trendy as Benny's friends.

Benny: I don't have trendy friends Maurice. Wish I had ... I envy your success.

Mother: If it's trendy you want –

Father: – you're in the wrong house. We're traditional here. Will we have the dinner now Ruth!? Bring the turkey in!

Mother: Now! What about the wine, Maurice. You're in charge of the wine.

Maurice: Sure! Glasses everybody!

Father: What about the bird?

Maurice: Red, Benny?

Benny: Thanks, Maurice.

Mother: The turkey's not quite right, but –

Father: Not right?

Terry: Give it another few minutes, Mam, and we'll carry on with what we've got.

Father: Christmas isn't Christmas –

Mother: Without a turkey! I know!

Father: My mother, God rest her, had a great knack with the turkey. She used to –

Maurice & Terry: Dad!

Father: What!?

Benny: (*To* **Mother**) Don't worry Ruth, I'll be saying the same thing about you in twenty year's time.

Mother: (*Deadly earnest*) I hope not Benny.

Maurice: Let's hope we just have to take a Christmas pill at that stage.

Terry: *Sláinte*, everybody.

Benny: *Go mbeirimíd beo ag an am seo aris.*
[Trans: May we all be alive at this time again.]

Father: Indeed, Benny. More Irish than the Irish ourselves!

Benny: (*Shocked*) I *am* Irish!

Maurice: Don't be so defensive Benny.

Father: You're Ulster. Always contrary, the Ulstermen.

Terry: Dad!

Benny: Contrary! Maybe that's the problem –

Father: Historical, you see.

Mother: That's enough, Denis.

Benny: Historical!? Agreed! The inevitable product of colonialism –

Maurice: Blame the past! Blame the past!

Father: Look at the Craobh Rua cycle ...

Benny: What?

Father: You mean to say you don't know your own past!? Cu-chulainn, Cruth-hooer, Táin bo-Cool-inne – the heroes of Ulster.

Terry: When Dad looks back, he looks to the end of the line!

Father: The Ulstermen were the fiercest of warriors, but they didn't seem to have a lot upstairs. Contrary. Always walking into traps. One time they all got struck with women's labour pains.

Terry: Excellent idea! Dad you've made my day.

Maurice: Benny's chance to be a real hero.

Father: Another time they all fell asleep. Just dozed off by the dozen. The big reputation, you know – but shag all behind it when they're put to the test!

Benny: (*Completely at sea*) So I better put the matchsticks in for Superman III to show I'm not contrary.

Father: What!?

Maurice: And don't go into labour! Tough afternoon ahead!

Father: (*Disgusted*) Ah, you're missing my point entirely!

Terry: Nice story anyway, Dad. Reminded me of your bedtime efforts. You used to put yourself asleep, and then we'd sit up and read.

Mother: We had lovely turkeys here every single year, and lovely Christmasses too. This year has just been –

Maurice: – a coincidence –

Terry: – of sadness. (*Slight pause*) Sorry about Pax, Mam.

Mother: (*Struggling to hold back tears*) Now Terry, don't get too upset. In your condition –

Father: The future, Ruth, keep looking forward –

Mother: Oh, yes, my man Lot!!

Maurice: To dad's tests.

Father: (*With deep contempt*) You little imbecile!

Maurice: To their success!

Father: Bring in the bloody bird, Ruth. We'll cut it up and eat it.

Lights down on livingroom.

Scene Four

Urgent preparing-for-battle music as lights fade up on kitchen. **Pax** *is on the windowsill,* **Rebel** *is on the floor,* **Turkey** *in the oven, and* **Rat** *in the gap beside the cooker.* **Mother** *approaches the kitchen gravely in slow motion. Unbridled panic is rife in the kitchen, made more manic by the labour pains suffered now by all. As music fades, the wailing of* **Pax**, **Rebel**, **Turkey** *and* **Rat** *increases. All are on their backs.*

Rebel: (*To* **Pax**) De mama 'proach! De mama 'proach!

Pax: I know I know I know! OW!

Rebel: OW! The bloody birth – (*Loses breath*)

Pax: Pangs! (*In pain*)

Turkey: Hear that Rat!? The mother comes! Aw pain! The pressure unBEARable on my half-baked flesh!

Rat: Shaggit! Shaggit! Me rat-canker wild! AH! Its virulent sepsis reflective! Even I suffer the contractions – AH!

Turkey: Find an antidote!

Rat: No time! Must dress you for the mother's eyes!

Rat *climbs up and arranges* **Turkey** *in the baking-tray, placing rashers on his blackened breast and spuds around him.*

Pax: (*To the birds in the sky, desperately*) O ragin' birdies o' de skies, I beg ye'r ears! Bottle ye'r beaks an' close ye'r claws for a sec.

Flapping wings wheel above **Pax**'s *head. He ducks, but stands firm.*

Rebel: (*Scornfully*) Ah futilidy!! Time to ledde allers rip! (*Loud barks*) Kauf! Kauf-kauf! (*Short pause*) Kaufincountincallinallerallerallyrootinbello

beatedrumdadrumdadrumdumdumdumdump
adakadakadakadoom!

*A ferocious faraway growling and ripping sound is heard from
the vacant site. The flapping wings wheel again, angrily.*

Pax: I appeal to ur sense of animus. Lug ad us! Stug in
gizzmo, like de poor Thai budgies in de squash-box. Led us
paz is all I az, fezzerloves, elp to free uz all f'om de cells o'
Kissma an' de days o' de crumb-scatter re-turn agen!

*The flapping wings swoop again, forcing **Pax** down on his belly.*

Turkey: (*In the oven, to* **Rat**) The dogs gain the strength of
desperation. They are danger. Neutralise the Rebel one,
silence the talkee-one. Now!

Rat: (*Desperately*) Turkissmaster, you're a holy show! The
mother-one will not be fooled. You're a foul and rotten
bird.

Turkey: Go! Stalk! Kill! I'll psyche the mata when she
comes.

Rat *and* **Turkey** *both suffer a birth-pang simultaneously.*

Turkey & Rat: AAH!

*Rat is floored by the pain, but duty gets him back on his feet.
Rat moves around the kitchen floor with urgent stealth,
sometimes backwards, circling, sometimes almost bumping into
Rebel who is invisible to him, **Rebel** watches him, furious that
he lacks the physicality to attack.*

Rebel: Fo' teeth! Fo' jaws! For a fidin' body! Ah*!* (*He is hit
by a birth-pang*) I found id in me ta pousse a breath! Whuh! I
muz push to gain anudder ejection – da piss! Da which I
can make be a weapon!

Rebel crouches with his eyes clamped shut, trying to do a pee.

Rat: Eureka! If I mix one of my rat-farts with the warm
invisible air of the dog, 'twill give it a purple hue, presenting
a target at last for me dripping fangs.

Rat *slouches with his backside in the air, writhing to produce a fart.* **Rat** *and* **Rebel** *inadvertently wheel around each other.* **Pax** *is close to tears on the windowsill. He shouts at the birds.*

Pax: Juz mememor wad I said. Kissma incacarain us all! (*He adjusts his address to the dogs still slumbering on the lawn and rockery*) Wake, buddybarkers, wake! Roll off de rockery! Band up on de bawn! No dime fo' de 'lumberin'! Ur canisychic iffluenze on de mam I neeeed! Save me f'om de boddomless Kissmapit, an' save ursells as well! Wake, u bastas, wake!

Sound fx: A low noise of dogs humming is heard from the back garden.

Pax: (*Almost overcome, over his shoulder to* **Rebel**) Rebel! Day is wakin' da ma call! Dey is heedin' me!

Rebel: (*On his haunches still*) U keep gummin', dey keep hummin', bud in fear of fudilidy, I'll make me weapon work!

Sound fx: Fierce alsatian snarling is heard from the bottom of the garden, then the yelping of scarpering dogs.

Pax: Rebel! De allers are 'ere! Der scadderin de gladderin! De doggybred are riff torn ablunder! Me canny-corps is mashed! U bloody bollogdog! AH! AH! AH! AH!

Pax gets an attack of pangs close together. He falls over on his back, helpless. **Rebel** *also gets an attack.*

Rebel: AH! AH! AH! De pangs ha dunnit! A squirda piss effuse! Now de pitcher range! Now ta use me secretin' weapon!

Rebel *crouches trying to produce. But still evading* **Rat**.

Rat: (*Suffering a pang-attack*) AH! Ah! Ah! A fart! Just eploded hot from my chamber! Prepare the bites (*Gnashes teeth in practice*) for the purple dog-fog a-forming! (*Bares his teeth*) Rebel-sucker, (*Mock-kiddy*) – where –are –you!?

The tops of the alsatians' heads appear over the windowsill, snarling ferociously. **Pax** *backs away from the window as far as he can without falling to the floor.*

Turkey: O Rat! I am afeared of the fierce guard dogs. To be rent asunder by beasts such as them destroy the Trystkiss spell. My smell attracts 'em. They'll all rabid invade. Save me Rat!

Rat: Too late! The mother is here.

Mother *walks into the kitchen. She is a little faint-headed, from the sherry, the wine,* **Pax**'s *death,* **Robin**'s *demise, the strain of the Christmas dinner, and the effect of all the psychic attempts to influence her mind.* **Rat** *circles* **Mother**'s *legs trying to locate* **Rebel** *who circles out of range ahead of* **Rat.**

Mother: Blasted security firms! So-called! They think because it's Christmas the alsatians don't need to be fed.

Mother *pauses.* **Pax**, *lying on the windowsill, revives enough to say:*

Pax: (*Weakly*) Feed ... Turkey da da allers Mama!

Turkey: (*Panic-stricken*) Noooo!!

Mother: Maybe I'll throw them the bird.

Turkey: Shock 'n' gobble!

Rebel: Ah! I av a liddle dribba pizz. Muzz depoz id on de brez o de buzzard. (*He raises a leg and squirts a pee onto* **Turkey**) Dad'll show 'er wad de brood is like!

Mother *bends down to inspect the turkey.* **Rat** *and* **Rebel** *circle.*

Mother: Such a queer year! You brought sadness with you, big bird. And a lousy smell you're putting out! Oh, the colour of you! And the feel of you! Are you fit to serve at all?

Turkey: (*Desperately, fervently to* **Mother**) Think of your spouse – it may be his last. Will you deny him the breast he craves!? Think of your son, prodigal returned. Will you not serve the fatted fowl!? Think of your daughter, carrying progeny. Will you not offer her poultry sustenance!?

The alsatians outside the window bark ferociously again.

Pax: (*Weakly down to* **Rebel**) Rebel! De allers! Mo' dangar da *me* dan da *dem!*

Rebel: Shudduppup, Rebel too busy a-tickin' to tock!

Mother: (*Considering*) Hmmm.

Turkey: (*To* **Rat**) Rat, she vacillates. She should be eating me out of her hand by now. What's the matter with me!?

Rat: (*Exasperated*) Take a look at yourself and you'll see! Blackened, toughened, twisted, polluted, shitonpiston, full of hot mengasity! Less than appetising so surprising!?

Turkey: AH! (*Labour pains again*) Rat-pangs!

Mother: I don't think it's edible at all.

Turkey: (*To* **Rat**) Less of your verbiliosophy! Attend to your ratical ops. an' ouevres! See to my plattering! The mother – presentme!

Rat: Zilch I can do to better your presentment! Already stretched countering uncanny flaged dogs. Can't clean your breast *and* wipe away the pest.

Turkey: (*Pleading*) Think of the rewards ridin' on your strivin'!

Rat: (*Disgruntled*) Is it worth my risks of duty tour, que!? (**Rebel**'s *dyed outline now becomes visible to* **Rat**) Ah! (*Labour pains strikes*) My fart-effect works! The airy dog is dyed! Ah! (*Another pang*) Inspiration strikes! Into the gap! An explosive light dawns to cure all our ills!

Rat scuttles into the gap beside the cooker, **Rebel** *follows him.*

Turkey: What do you menial!?

Mother: Slices off the edge maybe ...

Pax *revives himself for a last assault on* **Mother***'s sensibilities.*

Pax: Mama, swee', mememor ow Pax an' Rebel afore 'im beaudify ur days 'n' nighs? Memor 'ow I med u 'mile, an' Rebel trill u wid 'is trix? Memor 'ow de famil eak de fugall-livin' in de bye-gones, appi wid der pets rollin' ada kiddies' feed? Memor all de joys de doggies jiv'd. Now we doggies beg ur indercision da negate de Kissma guggly below, an' 'umbly pray u spray de tray 'pon de lawn fo' de puravinous allers to eat.

Pause. **Pax** *fawns.* **Mother** *hesitates. The* **Turkey** *trembles.*

Mother: Oh Damn it, it's disgusting. I'm going to throw it out.

Mother *bends down to pick up the turkey in the tray. Suddenly* **Pax**, *seeing* **Rat** *and* **Rebel** *down below, freezes.*

Pax: (*Shrilly to* **Rebel**) Rebel! Beware! Rat chews de power supply! Disengage!

Turkey: (*Panicked*) Nibble rat nibble like fuck!

Rebel: I'll sizzle de rat!

Pax: No! De madaccept me message an' agree –

Suddenly, **Pax** *having moved too near the window, a ferocious yellow-eyed rabid alsatian with saws for jaws rises with a blood-chilling roar to the windowsill and drags* **Pax** *out clasped between his jaws.*

Mother: (*Half-aware of a happening at the window*) Jesus Mary and Jo –

Pax*'s severed head is flung up through the air outside the window, followed by his torso.*

Turkey: I beg! I beg!

Rebel: I spy! I stalk!

Rat: I nibble! I gnaw!

Rebel: I leap!

Rat: I sever! (*Lights waver*) – nearly!

Rebel: I – hnh – piss!

Rat: I dodge! – Too late! The purple fog is on me. He wets me!

Rebel: I see – too late! – the green, the red, the orange-and-black.

Rat: The naked fuses uncovered –

Rebel: The piss-sodden fur –

Rat: The wet –

Rebel: The electrical –

All: (*Terrible shocked short scream*) Ah!

> *A blinding explosive magnesium flash, followed by black-out except for turkey shape glowing in the oven, looking ravenous in the darkness.*

Turkey's voice from the dark: Thanks be to gobble that's over! Now to be carved and devoured!

Mothers voice from the dark: The fuses gone again! Funny always Christmas! Overloaded I suppose. Oh, to Hell! Never let it be said we didn't make the effort. Turkey come here to me.

> *In the darkness, the glowing-turkey-shape in the baking tray traverses the stage, and is placed on the dinner-table in the livingroom.* **Turkey** *voices from the dark give forth a full-breasted rendition of the chorus of the turkey song as they parade turkey to his table-place.*

Turkey: (*From the tabletop*) Searching in the dark, they seek the carving knife. My breast, heaving in anticipation, awaits the metal tip. (*Pause*) Let me sermonise a spell. (*Pause*) Why the dogs had to die! (*Pause*) Hallowus antisepticate with rapture the truthmask beast. For the preservation of the ter-er-ist masqued fast, a fist enjoyed by all, exceptional pleasures are squawled for. In the execution of these pleasures, one dutiful rat suck-bummed herodically at the hands of faceless dogs. These dogs cannot be allowed to roaminise alive the trivilised fuckunity of 'aters at the trystkissmad innercircle! Mad bow-woo-ers must be cast from the feast lest they fist the feasters into fasting. That the eaters feast, the dogs must die. Weep no tears for two curseless. Those who live the dog's life must die the dogs' death. Such as they now are may all who hate us be. RIP.

Pax's sorely battered head appears on the kitchen windowsill, followed painfully and slowly by the rest of his body.

Pax: Oh, woe, woe, woe, woe is me! Why was I born a dog? Left a lone dog now, Pax the last of the pack.

*As **Pax** laments, **Rebel** drags his electrified presence out from the gap beside the cooker.*

Rebel: Pax!?

Pax: Rebel!!

Rebel: Dey may think they kill de Rebel –

Pax: Bud nada Rebel rever-rie!

Rebel: See!? W'en u dink me gone, u miss me an' howl fo' me lack, ha-ha!

Pax: Does id av' to be a joist bedean I lamendin yer emdy space an' shuddinupanpuddinupwidanydinugodda – gimme!

Rebel: Ah u soun' like an oul bashed bitch!

Pax: Dis oul bashed bitch had de mama vinced undil your barmalantics me doin' undid in a flash.

Rebel: Your doin'!? I did in de rat-at-at!

Pax: Pip-pip! Pip-pip! A plague o' vective rats to take his space!

Rebel climbs up onto the windowsill level.

Rebel: U an' ur lazin' dogs o' de lawn impeded me bedient allers from a-polishin' de sittin' turgey da da bone-bags.

Pax: Ur bloody-end allers loss me me-doggy-pack so dividicult to wake. Tink widda head an' nod widda bones dad are buried! (*Alluding to* **Rebel***'s secretive weapon*)

   Rebel *pins* **Pax** *to the windowsill, his paws on* **Pax***'s chest.*

Rebel: No mo de talk! No mo de vaselination! Dese bones, bones I have buried in the backers of me past, one bone, word a billion boken words of fou-fou-fools and bow-wow-booers!

Pax: No mo bones! Bones again bones'll splinter an' crack an' degener to ash-coloured crumble.

Rebel: De bones o' de past point da da pad ahead!

Pax: De turkey abouda reveal his own big bones as da fada carve.

   Faint sound of barking dogs in the distance.

Rebel: Me alloy-allers come ta cyst. I candallow de Pax-vox to hinder 'em. Apology, Pax. Regreddable bud inebidible!

   Rebel *is choking* **Pax**. *The barking gets louder.*

Pax: (*Struggling for breath*) Rebel lackin' Pax a malicious ghost-pest. U won't survive widout me.

Rebel: I will! I will! I will revive as long as claw-fowled fetterer drum-stick de pebble o de kitch in da knavery o Kissmabonds. De fools! De fools! Dey ha left us, maddened in da kitch, wid noddin to lose bud our half-led loves in the larderficial lovence.

   Pax *almost done. The barking noise is now outside in the back garden.*

Pax: Dad nodda allers – id da buddy-barkers barrackin'!!

   Rebel *releases his grip on* **Pax***'s throat.*

Pax: Day ha led de allers offaraway an' offer me der yelp in stoppin de carve. Wada turn-up for de barks!

Rebel: (*Helplessly*) De nigh side, Pax, gemme da da nigh side. Me ferrantic antagonistivities shown ta be tardin' our roguerest. I bow an' vow ta bellow in your wake wid de waked wuffers.

Pax: (*Thrilled*) Now a chance for me to sing unbadcomp'nied da da flappin' airbornes.

Lights fade down on kitchen.

Scene Five

In the darkness we see and hear the dogs-out-the-back move from outside the kitchen window to the livingroom window. The turkey sits glowing in the middle of the dinner table. Sound fx – fade up turkey music. The five diners glare daggers at one another. Their anger rises as the turkey music swells and the turkey's glow intensifies.

Mother: (*To* **Terry**) A fine turkey! A fine turkey indeed!

Father: (*Glaring at* **Mother**) The knife is blunt! It wouldn't cut butter!

Maurice: Use your carpenter's hands! Wrench the edibles off!

   Mother, Father *and* **Maurice** *all glare at* **Benny**.

Terry: (*To* **Mother**) Blame Benny for every mess! It wasn't him who cooked it!

Maurice: (*To* **Terry**) Blame Benny!? Oh no!! Blame the turkey, Terry, blame the bloody turkey!

Mother: (*To* **Terry**) I cooked that bird the way I've cooked every bird in this house since before you were born.

Benny: (*To* **Mother**) You didn't pay attention. You let the bird burn.

Terry: (*Turning on* **Benny**) She's my mother! Leave her alone!

Father: (*To* **Benny**) Bloody expert!

Maurice: (*To* **Benny**) Benny the arsonist speaks.

Benny: (*To* **Terry**) Look at the state of the bird! It's somebody's fault!

Mother & Father: But not Benny's!

Terry: It's not his fault!

Maurice: It's everyone's fault but Benny's!

Father: (*Re* **Turkey**) It's black, it's raw, and it stinks.

Mother, Father & Maurice: But it's not Benny's fault!

Benny: You all sicken me.

Terry: Benny! Don't!

Mother: Charming!

Father: Delightful!

Maurice: (*To* **Benny**) You smug little shit!

Terry: (*To* **Benny**) Don't give in to them!

Benny: (*To* **Terry**) You landed me in this! Now you expect me to sit mute like a dummy in the stocks!?

Maurice: You set yourself up to be pelted! You put yourself in the stocks!

Benny: You know nothing of me! Nothing!

Maurice: Shed a little light! We invite! Your secret life can now reveal itself in its magnificence!

Terry: You invite!!? You extract!! A confession by force!

Maurice: Confession my arse! This is compulsory instruction! How to carry out sectarian elimination.

Benny: You don't need such instruction! You turn a blind eye to the sectarian elimination machine of generations.

Maurice: Confess your secret crimes!

Terry: Confess your own secrets you hypocrite! At least Benny's not afraid to state his beliefs.

Maurice: I hear no statements of belief.

Father: We're sick of being subjected to his animal beliefs!

Mother: Sick!

Maurice: Is the kitchen too hot, Benny?

Benny: Don't patronise me, you closet faggot shit!

Terry: (*To* **Benny**) No Benny! Don't!

Father: (*To* **Benny**) Don't address my son in your vulgar gutter terms.

Benny: (*To* **Father**) Your son loves men! Your son's secrets will disgust you! Your son –

Terry: (*To* **Benny**) I hate you!

Maurice: (*Roars*) I love men! Therefore you must all hate me!

Father: (*To* **Maurice**) Shut up, you filthy animal! You're no son of mine! (*Pause. To* **Benny**) But you – are not – worthy – of the gift of life!

Mother: Despicable! Each and every one of you! After all my sacrifices! This is how you thank me! Ungrateful pigs!

Maurice: (*To* **Terry**) You're going to live your life with this Fascist bastard!?

Father: This fucking bird is uncutable and this knife is blunt!

Terry: (*To* **Maurice**) Yeesss!! He shouldn't have said, – but you're forcing him! You're all forcing him! (*To* **Benny**)

Keep that fucking tongue of yours controlled!! Jesus! Hatred!

Mother: Christ! You're foisting him on all of us! You're foisting him on our grandchild! You bitch!

Benny: (*To* **Mother**) Don't fucking talk to her like that!

Maurice: (*To* **Benny**) Don't fucking talk to her like that!

Mother: (*To* **Terry**) You're going to let that Derry dunce run the rearing of the child you bear him!? Jesus are you mad!!?

Maurice: We've always known she's mad!

Mother: (*To* **Maurice**) Choke on your tuppenceworth!

Father: We'll have to pass it round and rip it with our teeth!!

> *Sound fx: the doggies out-the-back increase their humming efforts. Lighting fx: fade up blue outside livingroom window. The five diners all slump slightly as though released from invisible bonds.*

Mother: Whuh! Wuh-woosey! (*Coughs dog-like*) Kauh! Kauh! Everybody all right...? (*Fixing on* **Turkey**) Oh yuck!

Father: (*Confusedly embarrassed about* **Turkey**) Maybe it's too far gone ...?

Benny: (*To* **Terry**, *as if punch-drunk*) Maybe it's time we were off ...?

Maurice: (*Uncertainly*) Does anybody find the wine a bit – I dunno – a bit –

Terry: Maybe we should have a nap... – Superman III ...?

> *Sound fx: fade up turkey music, drowning out dogs-humming-noise. Lighting fx: turkey's glow intensifies. The five diners straighten up again and glare at each other.*

Maurice: I want to ask the macho patriot how many people's brains he's blown away!

Terry: This is Christmas, for fuck's sake –

Father: No better time to get an explanation –

Mother: The Prince of Peace is listening –

Terry: (*To* **Maurice**) I hope you're proud of your kangaroo court!

Maurice: (*To* **Terry**) I'm giving him the chance to speak! More than his victims got! Why are you afraid to let him speak!?

Terry: You call this a fair hearing!? You're condemning him to death before he gets the chance to speak!

Maurice: Let him speak! No censorship! A Christmas truce! We all want to hear the brave Benny speak! Speak! Benny! Speak!

Mother: I never want to hear the evil devil speak!

Father: Shut up woman! Maurice has the fucker where he needs being put!

Terry: (*To* **Maurice**) Do you want to crucify him!?

Maurice: (*Shaking his head*) Too good! This is better! (*To* **Benny**) Volunteer Benny-bollox, tell us what your pretty hands have gripped!? Tell us what your smiling eyes have watched!? Tell us what delightful things you've done for united fucking Ireland!

Benny: (*Raging*) Ye-e-e-sss!!! I've blown brains away!! Ye-e-ee-sss!!! This hand has squeezed a trigger! This hand held a throat! Ye-e-e-e-sss!!! I blew his brains away!

Maurice: (*Victoriously, hatefully*) You sadistic scum!

Terry: (*To* **Benny**) Shut your fucking face!

Father: (*To* **Terry**) You'll cover for him all your life, you stupid fool!

Mother: Brains! Jesus! And he's sitting at our table!

Terry: I won't cover for him! No I won't! I hate it too! I hate it, but you won't even listen why somebody like Benny can have done those things! You won't even hear! Listen now, you bloodhounds! Listen!

Maurice: I'm all fucking ears!

Father: I'd strap the rabid dog in flitters!

Mother: Let God above judge the animal!

Father / Maurice: Speak! Benny! Speak!

Terry: Bury yourself in fucking glory, Benny, – you – mad – fool!!

Benny: (*To* **Terry**) At least you've chosen which pack you're running with, you turncoat tout!

Mother: (*To* **Benny**) Don't speak to her like that!

Terry: Shut up, you bitch! I'm closer to him than to you! I hate you more!

Maurice: Benny!! Tell us about the brains!!

Benny: (*Suddenly roars*) Cora!! Cora!!!

Sound fx: the doggies-out-the-back increase their humming efforts. Lighting fx: fade up blue outside window. The five diners slump again as though their strings have been cut.

Mother: Oh God! I have an awful feeling we'll regret – an awful lot of this ...

Father: I don't think there's any point in pulling at the bird ...

Benny: Nightmare! A nightmare! Monsters in the dark ...

Maurice: Enough is enough ...

Terry: Enough is too much by far ...

Mother: Maybe we should stop –

*Sound fx: fade up turkey music again, drowning out doggy-hum. Lighting fx: **Turkey** glow intensifies and pulsates. The five diners sit up straight again and the war goes on.*

Maurice: Who the fuck is Cora? Some Provo stooge who spread her legs at the sight of your massive Armalite!?

Benny: (*Roars*) Co - ra! Co - ra!

Father: (*To* **Maurice**) No more dirt from you – we've had enough of it, you shit! (*To* **Benny**) Don't attempt to take the mickey out of me and my family!

Benny: (*Roars*) O - ra! O - ra!

Terry: (*To* **Maurice**) You've got him to talk! Do you want him to sign!?

Maurice: I've heard nothing yet! Come on, Benny, fill us in with the *War News* page three glamour!

Benny: Shivering like *fuck* because the cold – fucking <u>cold</u> – snow blowing in the open garage door, my fingers numb but the barrel pressed behind his ear but he was *wriggling* like *fuck* because the oil – puddle of oil in the middle of the floor – I pulled his fucking hair to make him stay – bastard screaming at me, spitting in my face, his hair too fucking short to get a grip. He kicked. Steel caps lashed my shins. Steel caps I knew. My head got hot.

Mother: (*Hands to her ears*) Stop him! Stop him ranting!

Maurice: So you did the decent thing, you psychopathic cunt!

Terry: (*Screaming*) Benny shut up!!!

Benny: My knee was on his chest. A smell of shit. Still kicking. Slipping on the oil. I pinned his head to the concrete with the barrel. He was a fucking eel. Slithering, kicking, wriggling like fuck. Crying. Spittle on his neck an chin. Had to do it quick. Then he started. (*roars*) Co-ra! Co-ra! Co-ra! Not calling! No! He was saying something to me. Something incomplete! Cora this! Cora that! Cora what!?

Maurice *goes dead quiet and white.*

Benny: He couldn't get the sentence out. Bent on survival. Like an animal. Squirming. A hand got free, trying to poke,

trying to blind me. He got it off. Cold air on my pouring
face. He screamed into my eyes, Cora, as if I didn't
understand, Cora, as if I was stupid, I squeezed the trigger,
he slipped, I fired, then – 'O-ra, O-ra, O-ra'. We ran. It was
a clean operation. *War News* said we made good our
getaway.

Terry: (*Recklessly, hopelessly*) Don't let me hear any of your
glib liberal inanities! There's a fucking war on and *that's* the
reality. People shoot each other. It's been done since time
began. Don't get on your moral fucking hobby-horses –

Benny: Cora was six. 'Distraught widow Gladys held the
hand of daughter Cora, six years old.'

Maurice: (*Roaring into* **Benny**'s *face*) You – mad – dog!

Benny: (*As if in a raging trance*) I'd met him once before. I
saw him from a hedge. I couldn't move. It was wet. I could
see the steel caps stand beside the car. It was on its roof. A
door was ripped off. Smoke. They pulled Willy out. His jaw
was shot away. Steel caps bent over Willy and shot off both
his knees. Willy wailed a terrible noise. Then steel caps shot
his prick away. Then he pushed him to the ground and steel
caps stood on Willy's jaw until I heard his skull splinter and
a sound like brown sugar being crushed. (*Roars*) Willy
wasn't in the Ra!! Steel caps thought my brother was me!!

Maurice: Steel caps stories make the Christmas crack! Let's
have another one! My lover Stephen has a brother too. Not
like loveable Willy-not-in-the-ra! Stephen hates his brother.
He says he's a bigoted pig. But even bigoted pigs need to be
fed when they're let home at Christmas. Because Stephen's
bigoted pig of a brother only possesses a third of his brain.
A Rebel shot out the rest! Didn't like his footwear! So
Stephen puts a bib on the bigoted pig with the steel caps and
feeds him baby-food. And because it's Christmas he'll have
to bring the pig's daughter to the local youth disco. (*Into*
Benny's *face*) His daughter Cora doesn't mix very well!!!
Cora's what you call a troubled kid!!!

Benny: The grief of children is a part of war! I was at war! He was in uniform. I saw him torture the life out of Willy. I saw him crush his head! (*Roars*) It's not my fault!

Father: (*Bitterly ironic*) Nothing's Benny's fault!

Sound fx: the doggies-out-the-back redouble their efforts and start to overcome the turkey music. **Mother** *starts to hesitate.*

Mother: Sssh! Listen! Ssh! Something's changing. Something's moved.

Pause.

Terry : (*Takes* **Benny**'*s hand and* **Maurice**'*s hand*) Secrets. Fester if left in the dark. Evil growth. Let light in!

Father: (*To* **Benny**, *lashing out*) Eat the turkey!

Mother: To hell with the turkey! No-one has to eat it.

Pause. Exchanged looks.

Father: Leave the thing alone. It's a rotten carcass. We'll throw the damn thing out.

Sound fx: the doggy-noise drowns out the turkey music. Lighting fx: fade up blue outside window – dog shadows silhouetted.

Mother: Let's play instead. A game. Any blasted game. A game from the armchair days. Some stupid bloody happy thing. Nothing to do with the – turkey. We'll play a fecking party game! Let us not eat the turkey!

Sound fx: the doggy-hum reaches a howling crescendo, and flapping wings cross the window. Lighting fx: – the turkey-glow fades gradually until it's non-existent. Silence as the five diners slump, then gradually recover their emotional equilibria as though released from thought-custody. Pause as all glance remorsefully at each other. Then all speak together.

All: I think I owe you all an apology.

Pause.

Mother: (*Pleased*) Well! That's the best thing that's been said all evening!

Pause.

Father: Weren't we wise to get out of that cul-de-sac!?

Pause.

Terry: I'm exhausted.

Benny: Maurice ...

Maurice: Benny ...

Pause.

Terry: (*Intensely*) It's got to stop.

Maurice: (*Staring into* **Benny**'s *eyes*) No!

Benny: It's got to start.

Maurice: (*Nodding*) All sides.

Benny: (*Nodding*) Every side ...

Terry: (*Nodding*) A way to – change ...

Benny *and* **Maurice** *look at each other. Pause.*

Benny & Maurice: Sorry.

Pause.

Mother: A cup of tea?

Terry: There's no need for anything at all Mam.

Mother: (*To* **Terry**) Are you all right love?

Terry: I'm fine now, thanks. (*Referring to her tummy*) I think she's gone for a little doze.

Benny: (*Self-deprecatory*) That's my daughter!

Mother: Who'd blame the little angel after what she's had to listen to!?

Terry: Thank God she's no more Christmas to endure.

Maurice: Hear hear! Though it's great to see you all.

Father: It's great to see you too Maurice. You're a good son. You're good to come home to see us. It's a long long trip for you I know.

Maurice: I'm glad I came and I'm going to stay to see you in for the – the extra week.

Father: The tests will be easy now I have a nice pair of jajas to wear chatting with the smokers in the corridor. Thank you Terry. Thank you Benny.

Mother: We'll help each other through the hard part of winter now. Lonely. We'll miss poor Pax.

Father: Well, when the baby comes –

Mother: It's your baby and we'll be delighted to see you both bring her over any time that suits.

Maurice: How do you know she's going to be a girl?

Benny: We don't. She's whatever she wants to be.

Father: It's a pity she's asleep for this bit.

Maurice: She'll only remember the nightmare part.

Mother: Oh she'll take it all in.

Terry: By – osmosis.

Mother: Brainbox! Osmosis –?

Terry: Yeah. Tolerance osmosis. Living things enrich themselves by sucking up the moisture from well-tended soil.

Sound fx: The faint noise of a helicopter becomes audible, getting gradually louder. The turkey starts to glow again, but this time in a low pulsating way.

Maurice: (*To* **Benny**) Maybe we can have a –

Benny: Frank discussion!? Overdue! I'd be delighted.

Maurice: Up front.

Benny: No holds barred.

Terry: Admitting all doubts.

Mother: Confessing all omissions.

Father: Owning up to past mistakes.

Maurice: Revealing secrets.

Benny: Finding a way to express remorse.

Terry: Moving away from old rotten hatreds.

Father: Understanding change.

Mother: Desperation for change.

Maurice: And resistance to change.

Benny: Desperate resistance to change.

Terry: Because we've all been guilty of posturing with the vivid flags of absolutes –

Benny: On a twisted mound of tortured doubts –

Maurice: – as if they're solid matter.

All: Me as much as anyone.

The helicopter noise has reached its zenith. Suddenly, the turkey starts to hover and rise off the table. The helicopter noise changes from stationary sound to moving sound. The turkey rises and rises as its erstwhile consumers watch from below until it disappears from sight.

Mother: It's a Christmas miracle.

Father: Who said turkey's couldn't fly?

Terry: You did!

Maurice: I did!

All: We all did!

Benny: It's flying, look, it's flying!

Father: I never thought I'd see the day –

Mother: It's changing!

Terry: To what!? To what!?

The chakka-chakka of the helicopter noise starts to incorporate a tune in among its rhythm as engine noises often do. It becomes clear after a few bars – 'There Once Was an Ugly Duckling' as immortalised by Danny Kaye. The five are still watching the turkey flying in the sky off in an upstage direction.

Maurice: A swan! A swan! He's become a swan!

Mother: A swan!

Father: Our turkey a swan!?

All: Ah, go on!

Terry: It is! It IS a swan!

Benny: Look! There's two more have risen to the sky!

The window blind on the livingroom window shows three swans (like the children of Lir) flying across the sky together into the distance.

Mother: It's Pax and Rebel! Wave! Bye-bye Pax! Bye-bye Rebel!

All: Bye-bye Pax! Bye-bye Rebel!

Mother: May they all be happy swans away on the swan side, may ugliness never touch them, and if it should, may they find a way to turn their ugliness to beauty as they have today.

Sound fx: Fade up 'There Once Was an Ugly Duckling' over helicopter noise fading down. Lights fade to blackout. Lights up for bow with music. Still playing. Lights down. Lights up for encore. Music. Still playing as audience leaves theatre.

The End

Author's Note

WHY THE DOGS HAD TO DIE

That was the headline in *The Sun* newspaper on September 8, 1988. The first line read: 'DOGS of war deserve to die like dogs'. It referred to the three IRA members shot dead by the SAS in Gibraltar. It referred to them as 'dogs'.

I decided to write a play about two dogs called Rebel and Pax. They were called after my Auntie Ellie's dogs. When Rebel died in the winter of '72, she got a new dog on the weekend of Bloody Sunday and called him Pax for peace.

The play takes place at Christmas, when family faultlines quake. The Macken family is split like any other, and everything is compounded by the tension of Christmas a-coming. You have to sit around the table and consume the damn turkey yet again.

The action of the play takes place around the conflict between the Macken family trying to carry out the turkey-eating imperative, and the two ghostly dogs Rebel and Pax trying to prevent its consumption.

The difficulty is compounded by the inability of the family members to hear the dogs talk. They talk in their own cartoony doggy-language, a theatrical device to parallel the distortion of communication brought on by censorship laws at the time.

The mad unstated questions that underpin the play are: Why do we eat the bloody turkey? What if we could hear the dogs talk? What if the turkey could turn into a swan and fly out the window and up into the sky?

Well, I think in the past two or three years the messed-up turkey that was stuck in the oven of Northern Ireland for generations has given some welcome indications that it can indeed turn into a glorious smooth-necked swan. And Rebel and Pax can rest in peace, having no need to come back to life and live in struggle with the dreaded Kissma-biz.

The bad old days of media censorship which smothered debate about the Northern Ireland conflict so fatally are gone. It played a big part in creating the atmosphere that allowed papers like *The Sun* to justify summary execution by depicting people as dogs. The ceasefires and the peace process have allowed the breathing space where listening can and must take place. And what seemed like a demand for a miracle has become an achievable end, due to many ordinary people thinking the most imaginative thought of all – there's got to be a better way!

The actors who performed *The Dogs* displayed heroism beyond the call of duty. The risk factor was enormous. The play had no chance of successful communication without total commitment to its style and vision from everyone involved under Lynne Parker's wonderfully astute direction. For that, and the incredibly skilful application of it, sincere thanks to all. And let's hope that this bizarre journey of the Macken family and their half-dead dogs to miraculous happy ending is mirrored in reality on this doggy-shaped bit of moss in the Atlantic to which we find ourselves clinging.

Donal O'Kelly

16 February 1999

DOWN ONTO BLUE

Pom Boyd

Rough Magic produced the world premiere of *Down Onto Blue* at the Project Arts Centre in May 1994 with the following cast and production team:

Julie Fox Deirdre Donnelly

Frank Fox Peter Caffrey

Joey Fox Michelle Houlden

Shane Fox Peter Hanly

Chris Farrell Des Nealon

Airport Staff Corina Gough & Bryan Harten

Directed by Lynne Parker

Set & Costume Design by Barbara Bradshaw

Lighting Design by Paul Keogan

Production Manager Padraig O'Neill

Production Co-ordinator Kate Hyland

Stage Manager Susanne O'Halloran

Produced by Siobhán Bourke

Photo: Michelle Houlden as Joey © Amelia Stein

Dramatis Personae:

Julie Fox, A woman in her mid fifties

Frank Fox, Julie's husband in his mid fifties

Joey Fox, Frank and Julie's daughter, in her mid-twenties

Shane Fox, Frank and Julie's son, in his early twenties

Chris, An ex-pilot in his early sixties

Place: Dublin Airport and Livingroom, Fox household.

Time: Mid nineties

Act One

Scene One

An Airport bar. **Frank** *and* **Julie** *are sitting with their drinks, a whiskey and a gin & tonic in front of them.* **Frank** *is observing everything around him. There is something childlike in his interest.* **Julie** *is looking about too but with an alertness that comes from apprehension. There is a childlike air about her also. Jazz music is coming softly over the airport speakers. Every now and then it's broken by airport announcements which* **Julie** *tries to hear. As the lights fade up* **Julie** *has taken a cigarette from her pack and is looking for her lighter.*

Frank: (*Looking at the seats around him and rubbing the sides of his own*) Chairs are comfy aren't they Jewel?

Julie: (*Ignoring him*) Can I have my lighter please Frank?

Frank: (*Reaching into his pocket*) Odd sort of colour though. What colour would that be Jewel?

Julie: (*As he tries to light her cigarette*) I'll light my own cigarette thank you. (*Looking at the chair*) Shit brown.

Frank: (*Pondering*) Shit brown mmm, a civilised person would have said ... Chocolate mahogany ... toffee ... rich brown even.

Julie: Revolting.

Frank: (*Looking at a huge plant just behind them*) That's an extraordinarily big plant. Where did that come from I wonder? Course it could have landed off a plane from anywhere ...

Julie: It's not real.

Frank: You think I'm imagining it? God I hope not. Look I'm touching it. It is real.

Julie: It's plastic.

Frank: I don't know what you'd call it, the soil looks wet.

Julie: (*Feeling the plant*) It's plastic. Why are they watering it? What time is it Frank?

Frank: (*Looking at his watch*) Just gone four. I'll finish this, then I'll go and check arrivals. (*Casually spotting*) Looks like Chris Farrell over there.

Julie: Where?

Frank: God he's gone very grey.

Julie: Where is he Frank?

Frank: My God he's aged.

Julie: I can't see without my glasses.

Frank: Poor old Chris never married.

Julie: Oh he was an awful little creep. Never would acknowledge me. All over you of course. I'm sure he's homosexual.

Frank: Ah Chris wasn't the worst.

Julie: He never gave us back our rake.

Frank: Christ you never forget.

Julie: Well it's true. I'd love to ask him for it back.

Frank: You'll have to find him first.

Julie: Where is he? I'm going to go over.

Frank: He won't remember. Poor fella looks like he wouldn't remember his name.

Julie: Course he remembers. He was as guilty as sin about it. Speeding past me in his car. I'd like to let him know –

Frank: I'll buy you a new rake –

Julie: – that we're not pushovers. It was a good one too.

Frank: Jesus you're your father's daughter. It's not him anyway.

Julie: Is it not?

Frank: I think it's a woman actually. (*He sees* **Joey** *struggling in with her bag and roars*) Here she is! Here she is!

Julie: (*Trying to see*) Is that her?

Frank: (*Shouting*) Joelle! Joelle love! Here we are! (*He goes to help her with her bag and they embrace*)

Joey: Dad! Hello (*She kisses him*)

Frank: (*Gesturing towards* **Julie**) There's your mother.

Joey: Hi Mum.

Julie: Hello darling. Oh it's so lovely to see you.

Joey: It's lovely to see you. (*They embrace*)

Julie: Poor pet you look exhausted.

Frank: (*Hovering*) Can I get you a drink love?

Joey: I'm not too bad, have you been waiting long?

Frank: No we haven't.

Julie: Two hours, we got the time wrong.

Frank: Bit of a mix-up.

Joey: Oh no!

Julie: I wrote it down and everything. Stupid.

Joey: You've been here two hours?

Julie: Frank got confused between fourteen hundred hours and four o'clock.

Frank: Your mother's writing. Can I get you a drink love?

Joey: Oh God I'm sorry.

Frank: Not at all, we've been having a great time. What'll you have to drink pet?

Julie: Sure it wasn't your fault.

Joey: Drink here?

Julie: G&T for me please Frank.

Joey: Are we staying?

Julie: We have to wait for Shane.

Frank: What'll you have love?

Joey: Shane's got the car? Em, Gin & Tonic please Dad. Have we to wait for him?

Julie: Yeah. He should be here soon. Shoes are lovely, were they expensive?

Joey: Not really. I didn't think you'd like them. That's a nice cardigan. Did you get a new ring?

Julie: Terry gave me that. Swapped it for the big jade one. I wouldn't have worn it.

Joey: I would have.

Julie: Would you? Oh I'm sorry. She loves it.

Joey: So did I.

Julie: Well, if you're not here.

Joey: I could have put a bid in over the phone.

Julie: I'll remember next time.

Joey: So what else have you flogged?

Julie: Not much (*Trying to remember*) A few books. Oh, the dining room table.

Joey: Really? How much did you get?

Julie: Around two hundred I think.

Joey: It was worth more.

Julie: No, the leg was broken.

Joey: Oh. I can't believe I'm here. I started to cry as we came in to land ... I was mortified

Julie: It's been too long love. We've missed you terribly.

Joey: It's amazing how quickly the time has gone though. I can't believe it's three years.

Julie: It feels like an age to me. You're young of course, such a full life. Lucky.

Joey: Mmm. Well between work and –

Julie: How do you think your Dad looks?

Joey: Fine. Why?

Julie: He hasn't been great, he was in for tests.

Joey: For what?

Julie: They didn't really say.

Joey: Did you not ask?

Julie: I think his liver has ...

Joey: Drowned.

Julie: Been a bit over-used, but he's fine.

Frank *arrives back with the drinks.*

Frank: (*Southern drawl*) Now Ma'am one gin with the tonic beeside! That'll be twenny dollars. Thank you an' have a nice day.

Joey: (*Smiling*) On the side.

Frank: Excuse me Ma'am but where I come from we like to speak proper English and we say *beeside*. (**Joey** *laughs*)

Julie: (*Also putting on accent*) Thank you honey and you have a nice day too. Do they always say have a nice day?

Joey: Only when you're giving them money. The terrible thing is it's catching, I've caught myself a couple of times even though I'm doing me best to keep me accent.

Frank: Good girl, let them see you won't become Yankeeised. (*Raising his glass*) Welcome home darling. *Sláinte.*

Julie: (*Lifting her glass also*) Welcome home pet.

Frank: How do you think the Jewel looks Joey?

Joey: I think she looks great.

Frank: Isn't her hair lovely?

Julie: Oh she made a mess of it.

Joey: It's lovely Mum.

Julie: Oh no, it's too blonde

Frank: I thought a woman could never be blonde enough.

Joey: Jesus what a thought.

Frank: I'm only saying what I heard.

Joey: Don't know where you heard that.

Frank: I think we learnt it at school.

Julie: Wouldn't surprise me.

Joey: So why does Shane have the car?

Frank: Oh I think he needed to pick up something or other.

Joey: Did he not know that I had to be picked up?

Frank: 'Course he did, he should be here shortly. He just didn't want to hang around.

Julie: Are you nervous about tomorrow?

Joey: No. I'd have mixed feelings if I got it. I'd have to come back.

Julie: (*Hurt*) Would you not like to come home?

Joey: Well I'm not sure the –

Frank: What exactly is the job? What would you be doing?

Joey: Everything I'd say. Deciding the menu, getting the image and decor of the place right, organising importation of the stuff you can't get here. Basically they'd be paying me to rip off ideas I've seen there and bring them here. I think it's the first of its type in Dublin.

Frank: I thought we had a few Mexican places.

Joey: It's not Mexican. Cajun. From New Orleans.

Frank: Good God.

Joey: (*Looking at* **Julie**) I mightn't even get it Mum.

Julie: They paid your flight.

Joey: That doesn't mean ...

Julie: (*Suddenly*) There's Shane! That's him isn't it? Shane! Yoohoo Shane!

Shane: (*Coming over*) Could you not shout a little louder Mum? I don't think the people getting on that plane out there heard you. Hey Joey! How's my big little sister? (*They embrace*)

Joey: (*Giving him a big kiss*) How's my big little brother? Jesus you've got thin boy!

Julie: Sure he won't eat.

Shane: I'm ten stone.

Julie: It's not enough.

Joey: Jesus Shane, fatten up wouldja?

Shane: I got the car. It nearly wasn't ready.

Frank: Great. Can I get you a drink?

Julie: Is it OK?

Shane: Fine. It's gonna cost though.

Julie: Oh God, how much?

Frank: (*Irritably*) Jesus Julie! Will you quit worrying about the car. What'll you have son?

Shane: I don't want a drink.

Joey: What's wrong with the car?

Frank: Nothing. Same again Joey?

Joey: No, I don't want anything.

Frank: Julie?

Julie: Gin & Tonic please Frank.

Joey: What's the deal? Are we spending the evening in the Airport?

Julie: He wants another one.

Frank: (*Getting up to go to the bar*) We're celebrating.

Joey: Gosh isn't it marvellous to see the change in him now? Febbulous. Totally different but completely the same. If you know what I mean.

Shane: I do Mary I do and I'll tell you another thing, Mammy doesn't drink now either. She just gets the one gin and Daddy buys fresh tonic all night. Isn't that right Mammy?

Julie: (*Coldly*) That's right.

Shane: It's amazing how one gin can last. A week sometimes even. Can't it Mum?

Julie: Belt up Shane.

Shane: Ah sorry .You can't help being thirsty all the time and far be it from me to say, there's plenty of water in the tap.

Joey: OK, Shane. (**Shane** *shuts up*) What's with the car?

Julie: Nothing. There's nothing wrong with the car, why?

Shane: (*Laughing at her*) Jesus mum you're so subtle. There's nothing wrong with the car. Why do you say that? There's nothing wrong with it I tell you! Nothing. Nothing! It's a good car, an old car, a car with family values. (*Himself again*) No Mum's right, there's nothing wrong with the car ... because it's been fixed.

Joey: Why? What happened it?

Shane: Oh not much. Dad just had a little accident. Did a little damage to it ... wrote off two other cars and was done for drunken driving.

Joey: For fuck's sake!

Julie: Lucky he wasn't killed.

Shane: Lucky?

Joey: Jesus he could have killed somebody else. When did it happen?

Julie: About three weeks ago. He's still a bit shook.

Shane: He is in his arse. He doesn't even remember it happening. He fell asleep coming on to the roundabout. It's amazing nobody was killed.

Joey: Oh ... my ... God.

Julie: Nine lives.

They fall silent as **Frank** *returns.*

Frank: (*Putting G&T down on the table*) There you are Jewel.

Shane: Mum's tonic.

Frank: (*Sitting down*) It's a pity you two aren't having anything. Well we'll drink this up quickly and then we'll all go home.

Julie: No we can't delay, I've a chicken in the oven.

Shane: Oh! Can't keep the chicken waiting. (*He lifts an empty glass*) Well I'd like to make some toast ... to my sister ... welcome home Sis.

   Blackout.

Scene Two

The Airport bar as before. Everyone is in good form. The jazz music is still playing but it shouldn't be intrusive.

Frank: I must say the idea of Cajun food doesn't greatly appeal to me. What is it? Mainly fish. Well there'd be no problem getting hold of some fish, but isn't it a special kind of fish? I suppose they'll be able to adapt the recipes to Irish fish ... and of course if they want snails we've got a garden full of them. Jewel could collect them and bring them in on the bus, couldn't you Jewel? That would be a nice little job for you. They have a recipe that sounds like it might taste like your Granny's Wellington don't they? What's it called? Gumbo I think, isn't that right Joelle?

Joey: That's right, fillet Gumbo.

Julie: Sounds divine. What is it?

Joey: Kind of a fish stew.

Julie: (*Making a face*) Ugh!

Shane: And does it really taste like your Granny's Wellington?

Joey: Not as much flavour.

Shane: Ah it's true what they say. You have to come to Ireland to really sample the delight of an old boot washed down by a lovely –

Joey: Packet of Tayto Cheese & Onion. (*They laugh*)

Julie: Did you miss crisps Joey?

Joey: No Mum, I didn't.

Frank: Oh dear, the crisp farmers will be very upset.

Shane: Ah go on, you did. You can tell us, we're your family remember.

Frank: Your brother has been busy losing his respect for us while you've been away Joey.

Shane: Have I? Didn't think I'd any to lose.

Julie: Did he tell you he repainted your room?

Joey: You didn't?

Shane: I did and it was supposed to be a surprise.

Julie: Me and my big mouth. Sorry darling. He really worked hard. (*Looking at her watch*) Oh God the chicken will be dried up ... ah to hell with it, it's not every day my daughter comes home from America. (*Leans over to touch* **Joey** *affectionately*)

Joey: (*To* **Shane**) Why did you paint it?

Shane: What you mean why?

Joey: I mean why? I'm only home for –

Frank: (*Interrupting*) Yes the Jewel does have a big mouth. I couldn't even begin to count the times she's nearly had me thrown in jail or beaten up or beheaded because of it. Never mind the amount of times it has caused acute embarrassment.

Julie: Well you're still here dear so it's obviously not big enough.

Joey: You've certainly made a big impression on everyone in the restaurant Mum. Everybody's catch phrase now is 'call your old Ma'.

Shane: You didn't say 'her old Ma'?

Joey: She did.

Julie: Why not? I knew they'd love it. Donna seems nice. Is she the one whose mother jumped out the window?

Joey: No, that was Nina.

Shane: What was wrong with the door?

Julie: Tragic. Poor girl.

Joey: Yeah it was awful.

Frank: What was that? Whose mother jumped out of the window?

Joey: This friend of mine from the restaurant, Nina. One day she got a phone call to say her mother was dead. Her body had been found on the street below her apartment window ...

Shane: Whose apartment?

Joey: The mother's. She'd jumped six stories. When we got back to Nina's place after the morgue, there were literally dozens of messages from her on the machine. She was trying to find Nina but she couldn't remember where she worked. She was sobbing her heart out ... completely bombed.

Frank: Good God. And did you go to the morgue? That must have been very harrowing.

Joey: I didn't see the body. I waited outside. They gave her a plastic bag with all her jewellery and she kept a piece of her hair.

Frank: A lock.

Joey: A lock. A lock of her hair.

Shane: As opposed to her hairpiece.

Frank: (*Getting up*) Excuse me ladies and gentlemen while I go for a pee. (*He exits*)

Julie: The poor woman. She must have been really desperate. To do that to your kids. Is Nina bitter?

Joey: No. I don't think so. She's got her apartment now, it's huge and cheap and her mother was ...

Shane: Small and expensive.

Joey: She was. It was kind of on the cards, she was a very screwed-up unhappy woman, she caused a lot of unhappiness. I saw what Nina had to put up with. She did them a favour really.

Julie: That sounds very hard Joey. Is that what you think? That problem-parents should just bump themselves off?

Joey: If they're ruining everyone else's life then probably yeah.

Julie: That's a wonderful attitude to have.

Joey: Well so many parents wreck their children's lives.

Julie: Do they now?

Joey: Yeah.

Julie: And what about children who wreck their parents lives? Do you think they should kill themselves for the sake of their parents?

Joey: Dunno, hadn't thought of that.

Julie: Because I can tell you there isn't a parent in this world who would want that to happen no matter what they are going through with their child.

Shane: I dunno, Robert McAle's parents would be fairly pleased to be rid of him I'd say. (*To* **Joey**) He spent every penny they had in the bank forging their signatures, and then he'd thought he'd help them out by trying to burn down the house so they could collect the insurance.

Julie: Are you joking me? His mother will stand by him to the bitter end. Lie for him and everything. It's a mother's instinct, you wouldn't understand.

Shane: That's true, she won't have a word said against him. It's probably her fault he is the way he is.

Julie: Oh blame the Mother of course.

Joey: Did he really burn down the house?

Shane: Yup. They had to move out, rebuild the whole lot.

Joey: God almighty, but he was always a pyromaniac, remember he set the hen shed in the convent on fire.

Shane: That was you as well.

Joey: I just hid in the bushes. I thought it was a great idea.

Shane: I remember the two of you running back to our house, and telling me I had to call the fire brigade and confess to the crime. I was only four. I didn't even know what a hen shed was. I remember thinking it was this enormous big thing in the shape of a hen. And you kept saying to me just tell them it was an accident, but don't tell them your name.

Joey: (*Laughing*) And then myself and Robert started to worry that they'd know it was us by our fingerprints, but then we thought no, that as there was no shed anymore there'd be no fingerprints, but then we decided we must have left footprints, so we swapped shoes to throw them off our scent.

Shane: Not that the cops would have come anywhere near us looking for culprits. It was probably some kids on the estate that got the rap for it.

Joey: I don't think anyone cared about it that much Shane, it was only an old shed.

Julie: This is all news to me. How come I never knew about this?

Joey: (*Vaguely*) Dunno.

Julie: Mother's always the last to know.

Joey: Only if she wants to be.

Julie: What's that supposed to mean? (*Pause*) I've always been there for you Joey.

Joey: (*Sharply*) Oh please. I hate when people say that.

Julie: Oh dear, you've come home in a charming mood or maybe the gin doesn't agree with you. Better not have anymore.

Joey: I'm sorry but I'm just off an eight-hour flight and I'm still sitting in the bleedin' airport.

Julie: (*Becoming sympathetic*) I know love. We're going now.

Shane: Yeah, c'mon let's go.

Julie: We'll just wait for Frank to come back.

Shane: (*Sees **Frank** coming back with a tray of drinks accompanied by a small man*) Oh for fuck's sake.

Frank: (*As he's walking to the table*) ... and the beauty of it was I didn't have to change a thing ...

Chris: Are you sure I won't be intruding?

Frank: Not at all, they'll be delighted to see you, we're celebrating my daughter's return. (*Reaching the table*) Jewel! You remember Chris don't you? Chris Farrell.

Julie: Frank, we were just about to leave, what the hell are you doing?

Frank: Trying to put the tray on the table my love. Could you move that bottle please? Chris you remember my wife Julie? (*He knocks over a bottle of tonic water*) Oh damn! Don't help whatever you do Shane. And my daughter Joey who's just arrived from cowboy country, and my son.

Shane: Shane.

Frank: Shane.

Chris: (*Offering handkerchief to* **Joey** *who's been doused by the tonic*) Hello, pleased to meet you Shane. I remember you Joelle – only a little thing of course – and Julie, very nice to see you again. (*Sensing an atmosphere*) I hope I'm not imposing. I haven't seen Frank in a long time. We used to play tennis together when we were young men, twenty years ago would it be Frank?

Frank: Oh it's at least that. Frightening isn't it? You haven't changed a bit though Chris.

Chris: Oh indeed I have. Lot more grey hair.

Frank: It suits you very well if I may say so.

Chris: Still full of charm Frank.

Shane: Is that what it is? Oh.

Julie: (*Friendly*) What brings you to the airport Chris?

Chris: I have a sister living in Canada who was flying back today. She was here for a visit. Won't see her now for another five years.

Julie: Oh that's sad.

Chris: Well it is but she has her own life out there now.

Julie: Is she married?

Chris: No. No. She's not married, she's eh ... a single lady.

Frank: (*Moving a chair round for* **Chris**) Sit down on this Chris.

Julie: Frank, Joey wants to go home.

Frank: 'Course she does but sure we have to drink these first. Chris insisted on buying a round.

Chris: He's an awful man, I didn't you know.

Frank: What do you think of these chairs Chris? We were remarking earlier how comfortable they were.

Chris: Yes. Yes indeed they are very comfortable.

Joey: Jesus. I can't drink this.

Frank: Can you not love? Is there something wrong with it?

Joey: I just don't want it.

Frank: Shane, are you not drinking yours?

Shane: I didn't ask for it and I don't want it.

Frank: I see.

Shane: Why don't Joey and me leave now and you can follow us later?

Julie: What you mean follow you? How would we get home?

Shane: Taxi.

Joey: Yeah, I'll pay.

Julie: But sure we'll be going in a minute.

Frank: That's a ludicrous suggestion. We'll all go home in the car together.

Joey: Maybe Mum and Dad, you could ride home with Chris?

Shane: Yeah, why don't you ride Chris home?

  Joey and **Julie** are amused but try to hide their smirks.

Chris: Eh no, in actual fact I was hoping to take a lift home with Frank, (*Little laugh*) heh heh, if that's alright with you Julie?

Julie: Oh, did you not bring your car?

Chris: I didn't, no. I was afraid it might get stolen.

Frank: Sensible man. If you're going anywhere by car nowadays the best thing is to go in somebody else's and leave your own at home.

Shane: And just keep it for washing on Saturdays.

Frank: That's right.

Chris: Well the car I'm driving at the moment is quite special, it's an eye-catching little car.

Shane: What kind of car is it?

Chris: It's a Jag. An E-type. I've spent the last two years doing it up.

Shane: Oh lovely. They're beautiful little cars.

Chris: They are.

Joey: Oh I remember you now. You used to drive a little red sports car and you lived in the house beside the traffic lights.

Chris: Yes, well that was my mother's house. Sold now. A few years after you moved away.

Joey: We used to call it the pilot's house. Was that true, are you a pilot?

Chris: I was, yes.

Frank: And a bloody good one too.

Julie: How do you know dear?

Frank: Everyone knew.

Shane: Retired?

Chris: Yes. Yes I retired early. It's quite a taxing job.

Shane: I'm sure it is ... especially when you're about to take off.

Chris: Yes that's right.

Joey: Where do you live now?

Chris: I have a house in Ballsbridge. A small house.

Frank: Testicular Viaduct.

Joey: Very nice.

Julie: Does it have a garden?

Chris: It does yes.

Julie: Your old house had a beautiful garden.

Chris: My mother's house. Yes she liked gardening.

Joey: Is it big?

Shane: Ah now Joey, that's a bit personal.

Joey: Your garden.

Chris: No it's only pocket size.

Joey: Easier to keep.

Chris: Yes.

Julie: Do you like gardening?

Chris: I do actually, I like to do a bit.

Julie: (*Pause*) By the way ... ahm Chris, you wouldn't still have our rake would you?

> *Everybody freezes.* **Joey** *and* **Shane** *cringe while* **Frank** *stares fixedly in front of him.*

Joey: (*Under her breath*) Oh good Jesus.

Chris: Your rake?

Julie: Yes our garden rake. It was a lovely light one with ... em ... it wasn't like the other ones, it had long springy sort of prongs.

Chris: (*Embarrassed*) I'm afraid I have no memory of it ...

Frank: Sure it was a useless bloody old thing.

Julie: Oh come on now Chris. You borrowed it and never returned it.

Joey: (*Under her breath*) She's – completely – fucking – barking.

Chris: (*Flushed and embarrassed*) A rake? I borrowed it did I? And I didn't give it back? Gosh that's terrible ... most embarrassing ... I'm afraid I've no memory of it at all ...

Frank: 'Course you don't, we've all forgotten it.

Julie: I haven't.

Frank: She's always had an extraordinary memory Chris.

Chris: Julie, I must apologise, I must have forgotten about it. It shocks me to think that you've had this ... grievance against me for so long ... and rightly so ... rightly so ... I'm profoundly sorry, profoundly sorry.

Frank: Not at all Chris, don't even think about it.

Chris: (*Taking out his cheque book*) You must allow me to make it up to you.

Frank: Chris put that away! Don't be ridiculous!

Chris: (*Writing cheque*) No Frank, Julie will be doing me a favour.

Frank: No, no this has gone far enough.

Chris: (*Handing cheque to* **Julie**) Please take this Julie with my sincere apologies.

Julie: (*Taking the cheque*) Thank you.

  Joey, Shane and **Frank** *look at her in disbelief.*

Frank: Jesus Julie!

Julie: I'm not a petty-minded person Chris but I believe in putting old wrongs to right.

Chris: Well you are absolutely right. Now in the absence of a peace pipe I insist that we all have a drink together. (*He gets up*)

Frank: Not at all Chris, sit down.

Chris: No, must have a peace pipe. (*He exits*)

Joey: Jesus Mother, you are unbelievable.

Julie: (*Delighted with herself*) What?

Shane: How much did he write it for?

Julie: I'm not going to look now, it would be awful if he came back.

Joey: I don't believe this. Over a rake.

Julie: It's the principle.

Frank: Ah poor old Chris.

Julie: Well he's gone up in my estimation, I always thought he was mean. He must have genuinely forgotten. Well we can all forget.

Joey: The worrying thing is that you remembered.

Julie: (*Laughing*) I know, isn't it amazing? My attention to detail. You know Frank I feel a great sense of satisfaction. I hate feeling somebody has taken me for a fool.

Joey: Why did you never call over to ask for it back?

Julie: Oh I don't know. Frank lent it to him. I didn't know him all that well.

Joey: Yeah but if you thought you were going to stew over it for the next twenty years.

Julie: Oh really Joey, I don't know. I haven't been stewing over it. I just thought of it when I saw him.

Shane: Well now the family honour has been restored can we go?

Joey: We're having a peace drink aren't we?

Julie: Oh we're not. You're tired, let's go home.

Joey: What about Chris?

Julie: What about him? He can't expect us to stay in the airport all night.

Joey: Well somebody better tell him.

Frank: Ah Chris will understand. (*They all stand up to go.* **Frank** *puts his arm around* **Joey**) Come on, let's bring my Joey home. Have you got her bag Shane?

Julie: The duty free. Where's that?

Frank: I have it love.

Shane: Right, come on. (*He exits*)

Julie: I wonder will the chicken be OK.

Frank: If it's not I'll go out and get chips. Chips would be nice wouldn't they Joey?

Joey: Oh they'd be only gorgeous.

Julie: (*To herself distractedly*) I'll cook a proper meal tomorrow – have I got my lighter? Frank have you got my lighter?

Frank: I gave it back to you.

Julie searches in her bag but doesn't find it. She walks over to **Frank** *and puts her hand in his pocket and takes out the lighter.*

Julie: Liar. (*Exit everybody*)

The stage is bare for a couple of seconds and then **Chris** *returns. He is carrying a tray with a bottle of champagne on it and five glasses. He looks around to see if he can see the others, thinks*

*maybe he's gone to the wrong part of the bar, and then realises
they have gone. He puts the tray on a table and stands there
scratching his head.*

Blackout.

End of Act One

Act Two

Scene One

The interior of the house. The living / dining area. The kitchen is off stage left. There is a large wooden table centre stage. On it is the burnt chicken, a large wooden salad bowl with the remains of some salad in it, a teapot, empty cups and plates. Also the greasy brown paper from the chips, two cartons of duty-free cigarettes and a bottle of Jack Daniels whiskey. Pushed to one end of the table are old newspapers, bits of paper, bills etc. **Shane** *is wearing the NY baseball cap that* **Joey** *has brought him back.*

Shane: (*Enjoying himself*) And there's a bit where they're in the car and they're trying to look really cool. They're all wearing sunglasses and they've got the music really loud. And your man – not the other one – the little weirdy guy – and the other guy –

Joey: God this table –

Shane: – who's sitting in the front, decide they're going to swap places because your man the little weirdy guy says he gets car sick in the back...

Joey: Are you finished with your cup?

Shane: Eh yeah thanks. (**Joey** *takes the cup and walks out to the kitchen with it*) So they start trying to swap and your man driving, the fat guy, doesn't even notice he's singing away to the music looking at himself in the mirror...

Joey: (*Off*) Jesus are these here since this morning?

Shane: Eh probably – so anyway the two of them get completely stuck and your man the little guy starts (*Giggling*) sliding forward head first into your man's lap and he slides the whole way down till the other guy's chin is resting on his crotch ... well at this stage Macker had fallen on to the floor he was laughing so much...

Joey: (*Suddenly*) Jesus Christ does nobody ever clean this place? It's a mess!

Shane: Is it?

Joey: Look at it for Christ's sake! Old newspapers dishes in the sink, floor looks like it hasn't been done in months.

Shane: (*Looking around him*) Ah Joey relax. You're being neurotic. We did a big clean-up for you.

Joey: My God what was it like before? What do you mean neurotic? I'm not neurotic, I just like a bit of tidiness.

Shane: Oooooh I luv a bit of tidiness meself.

Joey: Ah fuck off. Pour me a whiskey. (**Shane** *looks at her*) Please. S'pose it was too much to expect things to have changed. (*Looking at a small antique table standing on some old newspaper*) Is he selling that?

Shane: Yeah I think so. (*Pause*) Do you not like being back?

Joey: Well the reality is different from the fantasy. I was dying to come back, I've been a bit homesick. Now I'm home and ...

Shane: You're slightly nauseous.

Joey *starts trying on different skirts for the interview tomorrow*

Shane: It'd be great if you got the job wouldn't it?

Joey: (*Distracted*) Mmm yeah. It'd be great to come back for a reason.

Shane: Mum was thrilled when she heard you were coming home.

Joey: Yeah she really seems thrilled... Oh God this is way too tight.

Shane: Ah she is Joey. It was her idea to paint your room...well to get me to paint it. She's been a bit down. She thinks Frank is having an affair.

Joey: Oh she doesn't. That's just a game Shane.

Shane: I don't think so, she gets really upset and stays in bed a lot.

Joey: Gives her a good excuse doesn't it?

Shane: I feel sorry for her.

Joey: I don't. Can't afford to. God, do these pants give me a huge arse?

Shane: (*In New York camp*) I hate to tell you this honey but they give you the butt of an elephant. What have you been eating?

Joey: Oh God do they? Fuckit I don't care. Sure I love a girl with a big arse ... Do you think Dad is having an affair?

Shane: No of course not. Who the fuck would have him? Are you going to put your hair up?

Joey: Why?

Shane: Dunno, more efficient maybe. I'd say he uses prostitutes though.

Joey: Sorry?

Shane: Prostitutes.

Joey: No!

Shane: Why not? They haven't done it in years, he has to get ... release somehow.

Joey: Shane my father does not use – God how can you even say it?

Shane: Oh c'mon Joey! Don't pretend to be so naïve. That's where he was coming from when he had the crash.

Why else would he have been round there at that time of night.

Joey: I'm not pretending anything, I just don't have a sick mind like yours. Jesus!

Shane: OK. Don't get upset. We'll put Daddy's hobby aside and talk about something else. The place has been like a morgue without you. I'm glad that you're back. I hope you get the job.

Joey: Well I haven't fucking got it yet.

Shane: I know I'm just saying ... we've missed you.

Joey: We're family, we're supposed to miss each other but I feel like I died by going away. That's not healthy.

Shane: (*Italian/American accent*) Healthy? Hey we're talking family here, where does healthy fit in?

Joey: Right. (*Pause*) So anything on the job front?

Shane: No.

Joey: Have you been looking?

Shane: Course I have. There's nothing.

Joey: What was the story with the newsagents?

Shane: No story, he just didn't want me to come back. He was a cunt.

Joey: Excuse me?

Shane: Sorry bollox.

Joey: Well did he say why?

Shane: No not really. I think he thought I was over qualified for the job mind you he was always telling me I was too slow ... actually come to think of it he probably thought I was thick. Who knows?

Joey: And what happened with the woman whose garden you were doing?

Shane: Dunno, she hasn't called me.

Joey: You can call her you know.

Shane: Ah fuck it, I don't wanna be some old bat's gardener.

Joey: Well what do you want?

Shane: Em I'd like to design furniture ... for budgie cages ... there are some very good courses.

Joey: (*Sighing*) Does it not drive you mad being at home all day?

Shane: I'm not at home all day. I do go out you know. Do you think I'm the strange son like some kind of Boo Radley?

Joey: I just wonder what you're going to do. I worry about you.

Shane: Well please don't. (*Pause*) I worry about you. All alone in a city with the biggest proportion of loonies in the world, highest murder rate, rape, crack, tall buildings falling on top of people.

Joey: I'm not alone. I have good friends. Sometimes I do get a bit overwhelmed by it all. It's good though. It's made me look at things differently. Shane do you think I exaggerate about getting slapped around the place by Mum?

Shane: Oh Joey I hate when you start talking about this.

Joey: Why?

Shane: What difference does it make?

Joey: You do. Everyone in this family thinks it's all in my head.

Shane: It's just you make such a big deal of it. I personally don't remember getting slapped. I think Mum was probably a bit harder on you being the eldest but I don't think we got ...

Joey: We?

Shane: You then. You got slapped any more than was the fashion then.

Joey: It was more. I remember being locked in a cupboard and not being let out for hours. I still dream about it.

Shane: You probably locked yourself in. You were always doing mad things.

Joey: Drop it. I'm sorry I brought it up.

Shane: I'm sorry.

Joey: Now you've made me want to hit you.

Shane: OK, go on, hit me then.

She mock hits him which turns into a play fight and ends with **Shane** *holding her wrists.* **Frank** *enters. He's wearing a NY baseball cap and a T-shirt* **Joey** *has given him over his own shirt. He's carrying an empty cup.*

Frank: The Jewel would like another cup of tea. (*Goes to pot and pours one*) Shane would you run up with this to her?

Shane: I'd love to Dad but the thing is I don't really run about the house anymore. I usually walk. I think it's more mature.

Frank: Mature? Mmmm maturing ... my old friend Victor Mature ... and is that something that concerns you hmm? Being mature?

Shane: Not unduly, no. But there are certain childhood practices I feel it wiser to try and shed. Temper tantrums, nappies, potties...

Joey: Being breast-fed...

Shane: Yeah, I stopped that a couple of months ago.

Frank: And what about running to your mother for sweets? Ever thought of dropping that one son?

Shane: Eh, no I haven't.

Frank: Well as long as you're still living out of your Mammy's purse I'm sure you'll agree it's not too much trouble to bring your Mother up a (*Suddenly roaring*) FUCKING CUP OF TEA!

There is a second's silence. **Shane** *goes rigid and stares at the floor.*

Joey: Dad!

Frank: Dad! Dad what? I'm sick of his supercilious sarcastic attitude. Who the fuck does he think he is? Sitting round on his arse all day. I asked you to have a look at the boiler three weeks ago. Three bloody weeks and you still haven't done it. Mr Cool, Mr Know All. Mr never has a penny in his pocket that his Mammy hasn't given him.

Shane: Well at least I don't get pissed drunk and get into my car and try and kill people.

Frank: That, Mr Smart-Ass, was an accident in much the same way you were – the thing is I can still drive the car but I'm not sure what use you are.

Shane: No use. No use at all.

Frank: Well we're agreed on something.

Joey: That's enough Dad.

Frank: Well you have the women on your side Shane. Congratulations. They hate of me course. I'm Mr Baddy. Mr don't let me drive I'll only crash, Mr Lover Boy who's screwing half of Dublin.

Joey: Jesus Dad!

Frank: Oh no it's true Joey, I'm sleeping with all the women in Dublin. Did your Mother not tell you?

Joey: Shut up! Stop giving me all this crap like some creep in a pub. What is going on in this house? Does everybody hate each other?

Frank: Just a family row dear. Happens in every family.

Shane: (*Standing up to leave*) I'll see you later Joey.

Joey: You going out? See you later. (*He exits*)

   Joey *gives* **Frank** *a look.*

Frank: Will you have another cup of tea love?

Joey: Why do you behave so badly towards him?

Frank: He behaves badly to me.

Joey: Oh God almighty. I keep making the mistake of thinking you're an adult.

   Julie *enters in her 'house clothes' which are a big old shirt of Frank's or Shane's and a pair of slippers.*

Frank: Ah there you are. Coming down to join us?

Julie: Mmm I was feeling a bit lonely there on my own, thought I'd come down to where the action is ... Is that my tea? Looks a bit on the cold side. What's that you're drinking Joey? Whiskey? Mmm I'd like something ... What about Irish Coffees?

Frank: Irish Coffees! A startlingly good idea Jewel. (*Gets up*) I'll stick on the kettle.

Julie: Oh let's make them with real coffee, I'll make a pot.

Frank: You see Joey, it takes Jewel to know how to do things properly. You know pet you're really looking wonderful. Have you changed your hair-do?

   Joey *and* **Julie** *laugh.*

Joey: No my hair-do's the same Dad.

Julie: Hair-do! Really Frank where have you been?

Frank: Well, whatever. I don't know these bloody things. Anyway, I wouldn't care if you were bald and had no teeth, you'd still be the loveliest daughter a man could have.

Joey: (*Fetching glasses, sugar, spoons etc.*) Ah that's nice. That little table is lovely. Is it finished?

Frank: Nearly. Nearly. It's terrific isn't it? I'll get £200 for that.

Joey: There'd be a big demand for those in New York.

Frank: Oh there's demand here.

Julie: Where's Shane?

Frank: Out. I think he had to see someone.

Joey: I think he said something about taking a contract out on a Frank somebody.

Frank: Better get me bullet-proof vest out of the attic.

Julie: Bullet-proof vest. What are you talking about Frank? (*To* **Joey**) Tired love?

Joey: Yeah a bit.

Frank: It'll take you a week or two to get over the old jet lag.

Joey: Yeah, I don't know if it's worse if you come and go back in such a short space of time.

Frank: Well how long are you staying anyway?

Joey: (*Hating saying it*) I'm going back the day after tomorrow.

Frank: You're not serious? You're going back the day after tomorrow? But sure that's madness.

Julie: You're not really going back then Joelle?

Joey: I am, I have to. I told you it was going to be very short.

Frank: Yeah but three days.

Joey: I know, but work and everything.

Frank: We thought you'd be staying ... well ... longer.

Julie: My God Joelle, I thought ... I understood that you were coming back ... I thought the interview was just a formality.

Joey: Ah no, there's other people. Anyway even if I do get it I have to go back and sort everything out. I can't just leave my apartment, clothes, everything.

Julie: Of course, it's just that we didn't really realise.

Frank: But they must think you're bloody good if they fly you over love. I'd say you've got it. I'd say it's in the bag.

Joey: Oh Dad don't. We don't know.

Frank: So you're only here till the day after tomorrow. My God.

Julie: It's hardly worth it, is it? It's very unsettling.

Joey: Oh stop. I'm only going to the other side of the Atlantic.

Frank: It's a big ocean love and a bloody long swim. Julie'd never be able for it.

Joey: Ah c'mon now. Let's have these lovely Irish coffees. Missus Julie will you take sugar in yours?

Julie: A half please darling.

Joey: Mister Father? Eighteen spoons?

Frank: Ah my daughter knows what her Daddy likes, but actually I'm cutting down – two will do.

Joey: My God, wonders will never cease. OK get me the coffee quick quick quick. (**Julie** *goes to get the coffee*) Cream where's the cream? Get me the cream please! Spoons! Where are the spoons?

Frank: (*Running to get the cream*) Oh barely back and she's giving orders. You haven't changed.

Joey: Nope and neither have you. (*Takes the coffee off* **Julie** *and pours it into the glasses*) Cream! Where's the cream? (*Taking it from* **Frank**) Thank you. (*As she pours*) Oh jaysus!

Frank: She's making a balls of it. Knew she would.

Julie: Leave her alone.

Joey: (*Stopping*) Eh, some music please. I need to do this to music. Mum?

Julie: Oh I don't know what to put on.

Joey: Go on, stick on something – there's a tape in there, play that.

Julie: (*Hits button. Music comes on*) Harry Belafonte. Who's been playing him?

Frank: I have.

Joey: Ah lovely. (*They all take their coffees*) Now! Isn't this lovely? (*She does a mock collapse, rights herself and takes a sip of her coffee smiling*)

   Blackout.

Scene Two

The interior as before. **Julie** *is sitting at the table drinking her Irish Coffee and smoking a cigarette.* **Joey** *is ironing her clothes for the next day.*

Julie: No but it was different with Shane from day one, sure I remember when I took him home from the hospital and I gave him to Frank – it was his first real opportunity to hold him you know – and he seemed so uneasy with him – which was strange, as with you he'd been so natural – and he couldn't wait to hand him back to me. Made some excuse about having work to do or something ... some lie. But you know after that every time he would come into the room, Shane would give him this look as if to say: 'who the

hell are you?' It used to make me laugh and even though he
was only a little tiny baby Frank would be quite
intimidated.

Joey: I don't understand why he was like that, you'd think
he'd have been thrilled to have a son.

Julie: I think, to be perfectly honest, that it was just
jealousy pure and simple. He was always very possessive of
me, hated me even talking to other men ... (*More thinking
out loud now*) ... very insecure ... I ... Course the other thing
is a second baby was an enormous pressure. We'd no
money at the time and he had this terror of not being able
to support his family and all his spare attention went on
you – well first child always gets more of everything.

Joey: That's true. So you think he was jealous? Of a baby?
His son.

Julie: Mmm I do, but he wasn't that interested in babies
anyway. That generation of men aren't. Mad about his
darling Joey though, he'd light up when you were around.

Joey: Would he really?

Julie: Oh you know he did, used to make me sick. I'd be a
frazzled mess at the end of the day and he'd come home
and take you on to his lap, in your nightie all pink and
ready for bed. And he'd say tell me about your day Mrs
McGregor and you'd chat away like a tiny adult. You were
a scream. He got the best of you really. I was always too
tired. I don't think he ever said a cross word to you.

Joey: He did so. Lots of times.

Julie: No I was left to do all the ...

Joey: Slapping.

Julie: Slapping? Oh don't be ridiculous, you got away with
murder for God's sake. The very very odd slap if you were
really bold.

Joey: Yeah the very very odd slap. And sure I only make up these things to keep myself amused, so anyway ...

Julie: Well you've always had a great imagination.

Joey: That's right I do. In fact I even imagine things have happened to me when they haven't. But that's because I'm completely insane.

Julie: Well we're all a little crazy.

Joey: Yes that's me. I'm a bit of a crazy and I love nothing more than to make up wild stories about being beaten and locked in cupboards as a child.

Julie: What? Oh we're so dramatic! You poor child, what an awful Mother you had. I don't know what to say to you love. You've really got a bee in your bonnet about all this. I never hurt you – the occasional tap.

Joey: (*Starts off calmly but the memory of it brings up strong emotion*) You did so hurt me. I remember being afraid to come home because I had forgotten to buy bread. We had all been out playing till late and I had missed the shop. I decided a good bit of strategy would be to bring Katie Lacey home with me thinking you wouldn't do anything in front of her. We came in through the back door (*Pause*) and you were there banging things down and I saw immediately you were in a bad mood so I just said it straight out – 'I forgot the bread' – and you threw your head back and screamed as if I had stabbed you or something and came flying across the kitchen. Your face was all red and you gave me an almighty crack over the head and then grabbed me by the hair – I remember it getting caught in your rings – and you yanked me round the kitchen hitting me and saying, 'I told you not to forget, I told you not to forget' and Freddie was barking at you trying to get you to stop and Katie Lacey was calling him in a stupid playful way as if nothing was going on – God she was thick – and then you stopped. You had strands of my hair still in your rings and you said, 'I'm very sorry girls', and you smiled at Katie like it was nothing.

Julie: That is a wonderful piece of fiction darling ...

Joey: It's not fiction.

Julie: And I'm sure if you wrote it down it would make a very good little story. But nothing like that ever happened in our house. My God! I don't know why you feel the need to make these things up. Maybe your job isn't creative enough and you're frustrated. Your imagination isn't being used enough. Would you do a creative writing course maybe?

Joey: I'm not making it up, I remember it.

Julie: You're always been a great little embellisher.

Joey: Why the hell would I make up a story like that?

Julie: I don't know. You tell me.

Joey: And how do we know it's just that you don't remember?

Julie: Because I don't forget things.

Joey: What? Bullshit! You mean to say with all the pills you've taken throughout the years – pills to make you sleep, pills to wake you up, pills to calm you down, pills to stop the side effects of taking pills – that your memory of certain events is not, to say the least, a little hazy?

Julie: All right dear, it's all coming back to me. I beat you black-and-blue every single day. You were only fed bread and water and you were never given any Christmas presents except one year when a kind old man gave you sixpence and in the end you ran away to America and became a big success. How's that for the truth – except maybe for the last bit?

Pause. **Joey** *is really stung.*

Joey: Thanks Mum.

Enter **Frank**. *He's been out walking the dog. He has the lead in his hand and an old metal kitchen draining rack that he's found in a skip.*

Frank: (*In his 'old farmer's' voice*) Hello ladies, hope you don't mind me barging in like this, but the door was open and I saw the two of you sitting there and I thought that mebbe one of you might like to rub me knee. (*Pause*) Everything all right?

Julie: Fine dear. Just fine.

Frank: Hmmm. Time for bed I think. You two ladies look like you need your beauty sleep – I don't mean that in any derogatory way of course – bloody dog wouldn't come in for me, cocked his arse at me and disappeared into the bushes at the lane ... little sneak. Look at this great yoke I found.

Joey: (*Dully*) What's it for?

Frank: Well I thought we could use it for making pancakes, mmm, don't know though, it might not work because it would be a bit difficult to toss them. So I'll probably just keep it for the apples in the shed.

Joey: Right. Good idea.

Frank: Shane not in yet, no? (**Joey** *puts away the ironing board*) Does he have a key I wonder? Mmmm, Julie does he have a key? (*Noises of someone coming in through the back door*) Ah there he is now. (*Looking at his watch*) Ah yes, well before midnight, Cinderella won't turn into a pumpkin.

Enter **Chris** *Farrell with the tray from the Airport, the bottle of champagne and the glasses. He is quite drunk. He stands there enjoying his 'dramatic' moment.*

Frank: Good God Chris, What are you doing?

Joey: (*Tentatively, sussing out his mood*) Hi Chris, nice of you to ... wander in.

Julie: We have a doorbell Chris.

Joey: And a door to go with it.

Chris: Sorry ... just a little surprise ... joke, I thought you would appreciate my spontaneity.

Julie: It's very late.

Joey: We only like spontaneity when we're warned of it in advance.

Frank: Yes it's very nice of you, Chris to come by with champagne and everything, very generous, but I'm afraid we're all a bit pooped. I've to be up in the morning, my daughter ... Joelle has an interview.

Joey: Oh, are you going to do it for me Dad?

Frank: (*Irritably*) No but we'll ... be getting up.

Joey: That's right Chris we've a busy day tomorrow we're all going to be getting up.

Chris: Yes. Yes of course ... You all just disappeared ... just left ... (*Mumbling*) I'd already bought it ahm yes ... never mind. Have it tomorrow. (*He looks around for somewhere to put the tray then changes his mind*) No. No! This is Captain Chris Farrell here, I insist – insist that we all have glass of this ... stuff ... before I take off. It is most important that we cruise at the absolutely right altitude – please.

Joey: (*Getting up*) Well I think I'll take my chances with the Captain. I like his style. Come on, let's open this bottle. Mum, Dad, go to bed if you want. Chris I'd like to apologise for our atrociously rude behaviour earlier.

Julie: Speak for yourself.

Joey: Abandoning you without even bothering to say goodbye. This is the peace pipe isn't it? Well let's drink it. Let's celebrate the rediscovery of an old family friend and my return to the bosom of that family.

Frank: You're right Joey. Captain Farrell you are welcome. Come on in and take us to exotic places. Julie, you going to come along for the trip?

Julie: As long as it's quite clear that I have no intention of being a hostess.

Frank: *An* hostess.

Chris: (*Delighted with himself now. He goes over and takes Julie's hand*) Julie we require nothing more from you than that you grace us with your presence, The Jewel among us, the pearl among oysters.

Joey: Dad, Chris just called you and me oysters.

Chris: Oh Joelle no! No. I didn't mean that. You're not an oyster and neither is your father – you're wonderful people.

Frank: (*As he put four wine glasses on the table*) You know Chris I think you're right about us. I think we do like spontaneity in this house. Sure that's what life is all about isn't it? This is marvellous. Course it's too generous of you. You shouldn't have bought it. Looks like a very good one too. Is it a very good one? I'd say it is although I must confess I don't know much about champagne. Are you going to open it now? Stand back everybody. Stand well back. (*In American accent*) OK Captain let's crack it open.

Blackout.

Interval

Act Three

Scene One

The interior of the house as before. Everyone has had a fair bit to drink. They have finished the champagne and are now on to the whiskey and gin. They all have a glass of Baileys beside them that **Frank** *is trying to make them drink. It's been left over from Christmas.*

Julie: Fuck, fuck, fuck ... I like the word.

Frank: Julie, please.

Julie: We're all adults aren't we Frank?

Frank: Chris doesn't like it.

Julie: Oh I'm sorry Chris, does it offend you?

Chris: No not at all Julie ... I tend not to use very strong language myself but I have no problem with, eh ...

Joey: She can't even blame it on Alzheimer's, Chris.

Chris: Heh Heh Heh, yes very good.

Frank: There wasn't so much cursing in our day was there Chris? I remember being horrified when I heard the expression fuckface for the first time.

Julie: Oh I don't like that.

Frank: I think it was you Joey, said it about someone.

Joey: I wonder who I was talking about ... But the one you really hated was dickhead.

Frank: Mmm yes that's a bit shocking also. God Chris aren't you lucky you don't have a family. And don't believe a bloody word you hear about the fairer sex – my wife and daughter have the foulest mouths, worse than any sailor.

Chris: There's a terrible one they use in the States, I've heard it quite a bit. (*He pauses*) Penis breath.

There is an awkward silence.

Joey: Chris, trust me when I tell you, you shouldn't say things like that. It doesn't really suit you.

Julie: Uhh! How revolting.

Frank: Well done Chris, (*Getting up*) you've managed to shock the ladies. How's everybody's drink? No sign of Shane yet?

Julie: Where is he I wonder? He never tells us anything.

Joey: Well the communication lines don't exactly hop in this house.

Frank: Oh I suppose you'd have us all going to therapy.

Joey: Well I think what you said to him tonight will help him to end up there.

Frank: God be with the days when a father could give his son a good boot up the pants to make him smarten up. It might surprise you to know Joey, that I consider it my duty to keep Shane in line.

Joey: The word was invented by a sadist to give respectability to abuse and cruelty.

Julie: Yes I agree with Joey. It's a horrible word. I've always hated it.

Frank: That's absolute poppycock Joey.

Joey: Dad, language please.

Frank: The most noble acts known to man are usually done in the name of duty. A captain going down with his ship for instance or ... Chris. Chris you'd be expected to go down with your plane wouldn't you?

Joey: You mean instead of jumping out of it and flying away to save himself?

Frank: Very funny dear, I mean as pilot he would have a duty to his passengers to bring them in safely.

Chris: Yes of course I would.

Julie: You've given up being a pilot though, haven't you Chris?

Chris: Yes. I don't fly anymore, I eh, lost my nerve.

Frank: Did you Chris? That's an awful shame. Dreadful thing to happen.

Julie: Why did you lose your nerve Chris?

Chris: I don't really know, eh ...

Frank: Ah it happens, very common I believe.

Chris: Is it common? I didn't know that ...

Frank: Well I'd imagine it is

Chris: Yes. Yes that's interesting. I didn't really like the responsibility, too many people counting on me. I thought when I trained that flying would be ... freedom (*Laughs*). I was young ... I found it a strain really. I'd be terribly nervous before a flight, I used to see all the passengers getting on and I used to feel it was ... wrong I suppose – that they were depending on me ... (*He trails off*)

Joey: But you could still fly planes without people, couldn't you? Cargo planes full of things – woolly jumpers ... apples ... rashers – I dunno whatever we shift around the world.

Frank: My daughter's knowledge of Ireland's export industry is impressive, isn't it Chris?

Joey: I mean you still have a licence don't you? For flying.

Chris: Well, eh, actually no. I don't.

Joey: Oh don't you. Oh. I see. Oh.

Frank: I'd imagine it expires much like any other licence would it not Chris?

Chris: Yes well it has to be ...

Julie: I love flying. Do you remember the time we went to Chicago Frank?

Frank: I do.

Julie: He was as sick as a parrot (*She frowns*) or is it a dog, anyway...

Frank: A parrot who's eaten a dog.

Julie: We were thinking we might move there, Frank's idea, I wasn't that keen. I was pregnant with Shane at the time and I'd been plagued with nausea, but do you know as soon as that plane took off it went and I felt great, and when I turned around to tell Frank, he was as green, (*Laughing*) as a ... whatever. I think he had absorbed it from me by a kind of osmosis. That's why you made sure to avoid me for the rest of the pregnancy, isn't it dear? So you wouldn't get sick again. Funny isn't it though? He got sick and I felt better.

Frank: Extraordinary Chris, my wife actually believes that I got morning sickness from her. The fact that as a member of the male species it is highly improbable ...

Julie: Oh shut up pompous eejit.

Frank: See what I have to put up with.

Chris: I would trade places with you today Frank, if it meant having that lovely lady as my wife.

Julie: How sweet Chris, but aren't you a homosexual?

   Joey and **Frank** *are horrified.*

Joey: That's none of your business Mum!

Frank: Jesus Christ Julie!

Chris *ignores the question.*

Julie: Well I'm sorry. I didn't think it was anything to be ashamed of. Sorry Chris, I've always had a bit of a mouth I ah ... think homosexuals are marvellous. Women usually get on much better with them than other ... you never married?

Chris: No. No I never married. I suppose I'm kind of a solitary person really. I never met – cigarette? (*Offers the packet to* **Julie** *who takes one*) – the right ...

   Frank, **Julie** and **Joey** *all at the same time:*

Frank: Woman.

Joey: Person.

Julie: Man.

Chris: (*Ignoring them*) ... type of human being really. I travelled a lot of course ...

Frank: (*Getting up, edgy and embarrassed*) Yes of course you did. No sign of Shane yet. Better get that bloody dog in. (*He exits, but can be heard offstage whistling for the dog*)

Julie: Well marriage is no guarantee against loneliness. Christ, you can be married with children and still be very lonely.

Joey: Nothing is a guarantee against loneliness except sleep.

Chris: I'd imagine New York can be a lonely place Joey?

Joey: For who? For me? Or for everybody?

Chris: It always seemed that way to me, but that was hotel rooms, one-night stops.

Joey: Oh hotel rooms on your own are awful.

Julie: (*Starting to sing*) All the lonely people where do they all come from ...

Chris: Yes they are.

Joey: Is that why you gave it all up Chris, all the travelling, everything got too much did it?

Chris: You ask a lot of questions in this family.

Joey: (*Taken aback*) Oh I'm sorry ... just making conversation really ... I'm not even that interested.

Chris: No I know ...

Joey: That sounds very rude but ...

Chris: Yes it does.

Joey: (*Coldly*) But it's very late and you did come barging in here uninvited after all.

Chris: So I deserve to be treated badly of course. (*Pause*) But you welcomed me with open arms Joey. (*Laughing softly*) But I think that was because you like champagne.

While **Joey** *and* **Chris** *are talking* **Julie** *has been putting on some music.*

Ah don't get uptight Joelle. Don't mind me. I'm a drinker ... that's why I'm not a pilot. (*He tries to turn her face toward him*) That's why I'm not a pilot, I'm a drinker. They took my licence, but anyway you're here with your family. You should be happy ... smiling you're all together again. Your father, mother, brother ... I remember you as a little girl, you liked reading didn't you? (**Joey** *looks at him a bit surprised*) Oh I remember little Joelle Fox ... Ah you're a wonderful family ... love your Father ... he's a gentleman ... he thinks I'm an eejit but I think he's a great man. Women found him very attractive you know ... 'course he is a very attractive man. They're a very attractive couple your parents, always were ... Julie is like a film star. I'm a bit afraid of her though, she can be a formidable woman. I thought she would have made the business work. Frank is too soft, but your mother ...

Julie *moves into the centre of the room dancing to the music. The other two pause to look at her and then she moves towards* **Chris**.

Julie: Dance Chris?

Chris *gets to his feet almost as if jumping to attention.*

Chris: With pleasure Julie.

They start to dance. He's quite a nimble dancer and **Julie** *and he start to enjoy themselves.* **Joey** *feels uncomfortable watching and gets up to leave the room. Before she does* **Frank** *enters and he and* **Joey** *watch the show.* **Shane** *enters and stands in the doorway.*

Frank: (*To* **Shane** *curtly*) Ah your home. Good. (*He exits to kitchen*)

Shane: (*Ignoring* **Frank**) Hi. I see we have a victim.

Joey: Where were you?

Shane: (*Looking at* **Julie** *and* **Chris**) Friend's house. Christ what's she on?

Julie: (*Over* **Chris***'s shoulder*) Ah there's my beautiful son. Chris have you seen my son?

Chris: Yes. Yes he's very nice. Hello there Shane.

Frank returns from the kitchen with a tea cosy on his head a cushion up his jumper and the kitchen squidgy mop. He takes up a position near to **Chris** *and* **Julie** *and pretending not to notice anybody starts to dance using the mop as his partner. He carries on a dialogue speaking a high pitched squeaky voice for 'her' replies.*

Frank: Ah missus you're looking lovely tonight

Mrs S: Oh, Oh thank you.

Frank: You're the best wife a man could have.

Mrs S: And you're the best husband a woman could ever want.

Frank: And your chicken casserole tonight was out of this world.

Mrs S: Oh do you really think so? There's more in the oven my sweet.

Frank: No. No, Missus all I want is you you you (*The dance is getting faster and building up almost to a frenzy*) I would marry you but my wife won't let me.

Mrs. S: Oh don't talk about that terrible woman. I hate her. I hate her. I HATE her!

Frank: Oh calm yourself Missus Squidgy! She might hear you and God knows what she might do to me. (*He stops, completely out of breath. Everyone is amused by him except* **Shane**)

Chris: Marvellous Frank! You should be on the stage. You must allow me to swop partners with you now though. (*He takes Missus Squidgy from him*)

Frank: (*He still has the tea cosy on his head*) Dance Jewel?

Julie: Oh no I'm tired now. Turn down the music somebody. (*She sits down*)

  Shane *turns down the music.*

Chris: (*Trying to keep up the party atmosphere*) Does Julie still sing Joelle?

Joey: Dunno. Why don't you ask her? Do you still sing Mum?

Julie: Oh I don't have much to sing about.

Joey: Well sing the blues then. Isn't that what you're good at anyway? The blues. I hate the blues.

Shane: Nobody hates the blues.

Joey: 'Course they do. Moaning put to music.

Shane: Yes right. Well we can see what kind of mood you're in. Sing Mum!

Chris: Yes give us a song Julie.

Frank: Yeah give us a song Jewel. Sock it to us. Sing for your supper. Sing for my supper. I'm feeling rather peckish, anybody want something to eat?

Julie: Well what do you want me to sing?

Frank: (*As he exits*) 'Baa Baa Black Sheep'.

Chris: Do you know 'These Boots Are Made for Walking'?

Julie: Yes. But that's not what I'll sing.

> **Julie** sings 'So in Love' by Cole Porter. It is a powerful performance. When she is finished she holds a 'dramatic pause' and they all clap.

Chris: My God terrific! Really terrific. You could be a professional Julie.

Shane: She was.

Chris: Really? I didn't know that?

Julie: Oh my voice has gone off a lot. Gave it up when I got married. In those days you didn't –

Shane: – have singing after marriage.

Julie: Frank didn't want me to anyway. He preferred me to stay home, cook meals, have babies. Not that I minded. I loved my children.

Joey: Note the past tense.

Julie: God you're getting as pedantic as your Father. Anyway I don't like talking about it. It's all water under the bridge ... I never felt I fitted in, they were all so boorish – ignorant people.

Joey: Who was? Everyone you met before you got married?

Julie: Everybody. Everybody involved. The crowds we played to, the musicians, they tried to bully me ...

> **Frank** *enters with a tray with cheese and crackers and biscuits.*

Frank: Anybody hungry? (*Clearing a space on the table*) Help yourselves. Julie tell you how I ruined her singing career Chris? Yes! I barred all the doors and kept her in an enormous chastity belt. That's why she never went out. Isn't that right Jewel? Now and again however she would break free the little monkey and she would beg and plead with me to be allowed to sing, and while I am a strict master (*Pause*) I am not a cruel one. So I would release her and she would get dressed up in her beautiful golden finery and flutter about the place like an anxious little lark, waiting to sing her tiny heart out ...

Julie: Yeah yeah Frank, I wasn't blaming you.

Frank: You were darling. But that's alright. I understand why you do that. Now where was I ...

Julie: Don't push it Frank. I'm warning you.

Frank: Oh yes. She would be all dressed up and I would have to get dressed up too and drive her to whatever Godforsaken dump it was this time, but when we arrived the same thing always happened. Julie would suddenly want to go home. She would get a (*Pause*) panic attack I suppose you'd call it. So I would bring her to the bar and give her something to calm her. And we would stay at the bar ... and while we were there we would look at the other acts, which were always appalling, my wife outshone everyone of them before she even got on to the stage. And we would wait for her nerve or whatever it was to come back and I could tell the man that she was ready. But of course they didn't like this as it made it very difficult to run the show, and then there was that famous time of course ...

Julie: Drop it.

Frank: Not now love, I'm just getting to the good bit.

Julie: Frank! I won't ask you again. Drop it.

Shane: What happened?

Joey: We know what happened.

Shane: I don't. What happened?

Joey: (*Impatiently*) Oh Shane you do! You've heard it before.

Shane: I don't. I haven't. What happened?

Frank: Your mother fell – she fell off the stage and on to the table of a couple who had just got engaged and I must say it was spectacular. I have never seen anyone fall off a stage so gracefully.

Julie: Thank you dear.

Shane: How did you manage that Mum?

Julie: Oh it was the bloody shoes and the ...

Joey: Drink.

Julie: Dress.

Joey: The dress! I meant the dress.

Shane: Is that why you never went back Mum? Singing?

Julie: Oh I don't know Shane ... my life just never seem to get straightened out.

Chris: Well it's their loss, no doubt about that.

Julie: And now let's change the ugly subject can we? (*Looking at* **Frank**)

Joey: I'm going to bed.

Frank: (*As she leaves*) Joelle. (**Joey** *turns*) Are you really only here for three days?

Joey: (*Pause*) Yes.

Frank: Mmm well that's bloody marvellous.

Joey: (*Pause*) Good night. (*Blackout*)

Scene Three

Interior as before. Everyone but **Chris** *and* **Julie** *has gone to bed. It is about three a.m. They are drinking the Baileys.* **Julie** *has the blanket from the couch wrapped around her as the lights come up. She is taking a sip of Baileys and grimacing.*

Julie: (*In a low voice*) Bastard. (*Looking around*) Where the hell did he hide the whiskey?

Chris: (*Holding his glass of Baileys*) ... but if they take me for a fool ... big mistake ... genius? No. No way! ... Not a fool .. (*Getting a bit more worked up*) No! No fool ... (*In whiney imitation*) 'Oh Mr. Farrell I'm very sorry the car isn't ready, I had to send to ... (*Thinks where*) Japan! For the parts!' Bullshit, s'cuse me Julie, con artist ... I know that I could get the parts tomorrow ... 'Oh we couldn't do that Mr. Farrell, different manufacturers ...'

Julie: Are you going to go on about this all night?

Chris: Sorry ... repeating myself ... just saying not a fool. No. Genius? No way, but I'm always polite (*In imitation of himself*) 'Thank you Mr Moore, Maguire, Mars Bar, I'm sure you're doing all you can', I'm always polite never let on that I know I can get the parts down the Navan Road ... tomorrow ... For free! No not free ... thinks I'm a pushover. Pushmeover push me under a bus if you want. Not a fool though. No. No fool ...

Julie: Yeah yeah Chris, I think I've got the message by now, you're not a fool but you are becoming a bore...

Chris: (*Turns and smiles at her*) Ah Julie, a hot knife through snow. (*Makes slicing noise*) Straight in there, bullet to the heart ... Everyone else (*Puts finger to his lips*) shhhh shuuush tip tip around Julie. (*Makes loud explosion noise and does a*

'Julie' *imitation*) Why's everyone whispering? (*He laughs and turns to smile at her again*)

Julie: (*Smiling*) You're right. Big mouth. Hate pretence, no time for it. Always want the truth. I have to be careful though sometimes too bloody honest. You can hurt people.

Chris: Yes yes. You can be too honest. You can hurt people.

Julie: I made the mistake of telling Frank I wasn't in love with him when we married. Big mistake ... I was so young and immature I didn't know what the hell I was talking about ... I think I only wanted a reaction. (*Suddenly getting up*) Music! Musica per la Signora! (*She goes over to the tape deck and puts on the overture from 'Lakeme' by Delibes*) Isn't this beautiful Chris? Shhhush just listen.

*She stands there completely enraptured by the music for a short while, then turns to **Chris**, stretches out her hand to him and brings him to his feet. She is lost in the role she is acting out. They dance in a slow, gentle, almost balletic way then **Chris** turns his face to hers and they start to kiss. They stop and look at each other in surprise and then smile. Unknown to them **Frank** has appeared in the door way and has seen the 'performance'. He claps softly and then walks over to them.*

Frank: Very nice. Very nice, but isn't it supposed to be a bit more like this? Mind if I cut in Chris?

Chris: (*Looking surprised*) No. No of course not, of course not.

*It looks as if **Frank** is going to start dancing with **Julie** but instead he takes **Chris** in an embrace and starts waltzing him round the room. He holds him tightly keeping his eyes on **Julie** the whole time. Then he presses his lips to **Chris'** and kisses him 'passionately'. **Julie** looks on impassively and then turns off the music. **Frank** stops and looks at **Chris** as if he was a stick of furniture for which he no longer has any use.*

Frank: You can leave now Chris, same way you crept in, back door.

Julie: He'll go to any length to steal the show. (*To* **Frank**) Well done dear. May I say you fitted the part. It just confirms everything as far as I'm concerned. (*She looks at* **Chris**) Is he the best you've ever had? Or do you find him like I do, mediocre? (*She walks over to* **Chris** *and kisses him long and full on the lips*) My husband is right, I think you'd better leave. I don't care which door you use.

   Chris *doesn't move to go.*

Frank: Go on, Chris bugger off.

Julie: Get out of our house Chris.

Chris: (*He is shaken and his voice trembles but gradually grows stronger and louder, shouting on certain words but not shouting the whole speech*) I just wanted ... I just thought ... I was lonely ... I just wanted some warmth, a bit of life. I thought to be with a family at a happy time, to share ... but ... My God! You're sick! You are sick people. You don't love anybody! You don't even love each other (*Shouting*) Joelle! Joelle! Get out of this house, it's full of sick people! Get out now while you can!

Frank: (*Roaring*) Leave my daughter out of this! (**Joey** *has appeared in the doorway*) Get out you pervert! Out of my house now before I call the police!

Chris: And as for your rake. You think I don't remember? You think I don't recall? Well I do. Of course I do. But I didn't wish to say. Would never have said. But now I will. Now I'll tell you what I remember about your precious rake Julie. I remember it very clearly, it had as you said light springy prongs on it and if I'm not mistaken a green handle. Anyway I did as a matter of fact try to leave it back, to put it in the garden shed as I had promised. It was late October, November, I'd needed it for the leaves, my own had disappeared. Anyway I found I was prevented from leaving it back. Do you know why Julie? Joelle do you? (**Joey**

shakes her head tersely) Well when I got there I heard noises, small little movements coming from inside. (*Puts his hand to his ear*) Wha's tha? I didn't know. Maybe a rat, maybe a dog but I didn't expect to see what I saw ... What did I see? I saw (*Making a grand gesture*) I saw this little girl, your daughter, in her white vest and pants sitting there with her book on the stone floor beside the lawn mower. She was cold and in the dim light I could make out red marks on her legs but she was not crying. She told me that you, Julie had put her there and that she was to stay there till bedtime. I asked her if she thought I should bolt the door again and she said she thought I should. So I did ... and I did not leave the rake. I must say, I was in a dilemma. I couldn't leave it outside in case it was nicked but if I left it in the shed you would have known that I had ... seen. I knew Frank you would have been ... put out, embarrassed perhaps, if you had known I had walked in on such a personal matter. Now I think I'll go. I never thought I would intrude on a family in this way ... I believe the family is sacred. Yes I do. Joelle, you're a wonderful girl. You'll bring quality and class wherever you go. Good night to you. (*He exits*)

There is a couple of moments silence after he leaves.

Julie: (*Breathing exaggerated sigh of relief*) God I thought he'd never go, did you Frank? Talk about overstaying your welcome. I could see it coming though, I knew he was very unstable. I think we just proved too much for him.

Frank: Ah poor old Chris. Nothing to go home to I suppose. Overstayed his welcome. C'mon let's get to bed. Milk bottles weren't put out were they Jewel?

Julie: No you better put them out Frank. (*Turns to* **Joey**) He woke you out of a sleep, I could kill him. You poor frozen baby. (*Gives her the blanket*) Put this around you love. Would you like if I brought you up a cup of hot milk or cocoa?

Joey: (*Softly*) Em, cocoa please.

Julie: Okay, darling you go on up. Blackie never came back did he Frank?

Joey *doesn't move.*

Frank: No, ah he'll be back in the morning. Sitting on the steps with a cold arse when we get up. Will you make a cocoa for me Jewel?

Julie: Course I will Frank, big or little mug?

Frank: Ah the small one will do me love.

Julie: Right, I'll make that then and I'm bringing one up to Joey.

Frank: Ah good.

Julie: Right.

Frank: Right.

Julie: Right.

Frank: Right.

Julie *exits to the kitchen.* **Frank** *and* **Joey** *stay standing for a moment.*

Frank: Right. Milk bottles. (*He exits*)

Joey *is left alone on stage.*

Blackout.

End of Act Three

Act Four

Scene One

*The house interior as before. It's Sunday, the day before **Joey**'s departure. As the lights come up the phone is ringing. **Frank** who has been sitting reading the Sunday papers gets up to answer it.*

Frank: (*Into phone*) Hello, 2803778 (*Pause*) Ahm I'm afraid Joelle is out at the moment, may I take a message? (*Pause*) Well she's travelling back to New York early in the morning ... (*Sounding interested*) Oh yes ... Ahh that's marvellous news! Oh she'll be delighted ... yes of course. Well I will tell her when she comes in and I'll get her to call you (*Pause*) at home? And she has the number ... lovely right so. When would she have to start? Oh that soon? Oh she'll have to get her skates on. (*Chuckling*) Well I'm sure that won't be any problem. OK, thank you very much for ringing. Bye bye now. Bye bye. (*He hangs up the receiver and opens the door into the hall*) Jewel! Wonderful news! Joelle got the job! (*Walking back into the living room*) Ah that's marvellous. Fantastic bit of news. I knew she'd get it. Good girl yourself.

> **Joey** *enters. She's been out visiting some friends and has her jacket on.*

Frank: Ah there she is! There she is! Jambalaya mi o mio. Mi o mio! Let me shake the hand of the young woman who is single-handedly responsible for introducing gum fish pie to this poor little nation of unsophisticated peasants. Pleased to meet you ma'am. You remember your ol' fella now don't you?

Joey: (*Laughing a bit puzzled*) What's up?

Frank: You had a phone call from a Geoffrey something.

Joey: Cunningham. What did he say?

Frank: You got the job.

Joey: Did I?

Frank: What do you mean did I? Course you did. I said you'd call them when you came in. Congratulations darling. I knew you would.

Joey: God, I didn't.

Frank: They want you to start as soon as possible. It's going to be a bit of a rush for you. Do you definitely have to go back and get your stuff?

Joey: Oh I do yeah.

Offstage sounds of **Shane** *approaching.*

Frank: Here's Shane. He'll be delighted with the news. Cheer him up a bit. (**Shane** *enters*) Joelle has great news.

Shane: Yeah?

Joey: I got the job.

Frank: She got the job.

Shane: Did you? Oh excellent! (*Gives her a kiss*) Well done. I knew you would. I know you hate me saying that but I knew you would.

Frank: The Cajun food queen of Ireland. (*As he exits*) Where's Julie, she's missing all the fun.

Shane: It's great news. Are you thrilled?

Joey: Mmm, more surprised really. I didn't do a good interview. Thought I came across a bit sharp, rude even. I didn't say it but I thought I had fucked up.

Shane: Well they must have been looking for someone rude and nasty 'cos you got the job. You're going to be the whipcracker round there telling everyone what to do, it'll be great.

Joey: Well they can give the job a fancy name but it's still going to be hard slog. Revolting customers, hopeless waitresses, alcoholic kitchen staff and to be mammy to them all.

Shane: Well just mind you don't bowl me over with your enthusiasm. (**Joey** *laughs*) It'll be great. Me and mum and dad can come in for free meals. Ah no we'll pay. You probably wouldn't like us coming in though would you?

Joey: Shane, you sound like a child.

Shane: Oh I'm so sorry.

Joey: Sometimes you seem very out of touch.

Shane: Oh this from the woman I can't mention the word prostitute in front of. (*He roots through* **Julie***'s bag and takes out her pill box*)

Joey: What are you doing?

Shane: Taking a smartie. Want one?

Joey: You don't take them?

Shane: Why not? Does Uncle Sam's niece disapprove?

Joey: When the hell are you going to wake up?

Shane: To what and why? You used to do these all the time.

Joey: When I was a teenager.

Shane: Oh and that's supposed to be better than me taking them as an adult.

Joey: Why are you so unhappy?

Shane: Oh please.

Joey: Why?

Shane: Back off Joey.

Joey: No I won't. Why are you so unhappy?

Shane: I'm not unhappy.

Joey: Well what are you?

Shane: Nothing. Empty.

Joey: Why?

Shane: God, and you tell me I'm childish. Why why why? Why is anybody anything?.

Joey: Well what do you want out of life? (**Shane** *gives her a pitiful stare*) What?

Shane: You should hear yourself.

Joey: You must want something or have wanted something at some stage.

Shane: I did

Joey: What?

Shane: I wanted to be a Turpin. Remember them?

Joey: The Turnips – yeah of course I do.

Shane: And you remember how we used to think they were the most disgusting people on earth. So boring and dull. Mum used to do an imitation of Mrs Turpin hurrying home from the shops, to have the tea made at exactly five o'clock every day. (*Pause*) Well I always felt that I should have been a Turpin. Still do.

Joey: Well there's nothing wrong with that ... I don't think.

Shane: I never said there was anything wrong with it, that's not the point. The point is ... the point is, that Alan Turpin is now making loads of money in insurance and I feel, that that should have been me and I'm very bitter about it. I feel I've been cheated.

Joey: You mean to tell me that all this time under that cool Fox exterior lies a little Turnip?

Shane: Yup. A disgusting little bore. I even said to Dad once, that in case he and Mum died, could he put it in his will that I was to move in with the Turpins.

Joey: What did he say?

Shane: He thought it was very wise of me to be making contingency plans and that he was thinking of moving in there himself. (**Joey** *laughs*)

Joey: I wonder why you and he can't get along.

Shane: Because he's a big bollox that's why.

Joey: I suppose it's natural. Fathers are always jealous of their sons.

Shane: That's as ridiculous as saying all mothers are jealous of their daughters.

Joey: Maybe they are.

Shane: Ah people are weird. The sooner Sellafield explodes and we all just dissolve the better.

Joey: That'd be a great solution Shane. (*Yawning*) God I'm knackered.

Shane: Well jet lag and then you had Chris Farrell keeping you up on your first night. God what a nut case!

Joey: I don't think he is. I'm glad that he came.

Shane: Oh God, I thought he'd never go.

Joey: He said that I was in the shed when he left the rake back.

Shane: He said he left the rake back? When did he say that?

Joey: Before he went. There was a row. You didn't hear?

Shane: No. There was a row? I didn't know that.

Joey: Well now you know. He said I was in there. I was locked in.

Shane: How did I not wake up? Was there shouting?

Joey: Yes there was lots of shouting Shane. He said I was only wearing a vest and pants ...

Shane: It must have started after I'd already been asleep for a while. That's the deepest part. Although I always wake up for Blackie ...

Joey: He said that there were red marks on my legs and that he didn't leave the rake ...

Shane: I didn't think I was such a heavy sleeper anymore. I wonder why I didn't hear anything?

Joey: You didn't hear anything you fucking fool because you'd sleep through a nuclear fucking explosion!

Shane: What the fuck is wrong with you?

Joey: I'm trying to tell you what he said. He said that I was –

Shane: In the shed. I know I heard you. (*Pause*) I heard you. (*Enter* **Frank**)

Frank: Julie's coming down in a minute and I'm just nipping out to the off-licence. We'll have a little celebration this evening. Celebrate you coming home. What would you like me to get you love? Shane would you like something?

Joey: Dad. (*Pause*) I'm not coming home Dad. I'm not going to take the job

> **Frank** *looks at her. He finishes putting on his coat and exits.*

> *Blackout.*

Scene Two

The Airport. **Julie** *and* **Joey** *sitting there. It's very early morning and they both look pale and tired. There is piped 'musack' playing very low.*

Julie: (*After a few moments*) Well we're in good time anyway.

Joey: Yeah.

Julie: Music is dreadful.

Joey: Mmm.

Julie: You didn't forget anything did you?

Joey: Eh no. I don't think so.

Julie: Sure we can always send it to you.

Joey: Yeah. Nothing vital anyway.

Julie: You look a bit pale.

Joey: I've a splitting headache.

Julie: Did you sleep well?

Joey: Yeah, I was exhausted.

Julie: Crying is exhausting.

Joey: Mmm completely. (*Pause*) 'S'posed to be good for you though. Gets rid of toxins.

Julie: Really? That's interesting. (*Pause*) I must be full of them. I never cry.

Joey: Which toxins ... or tears?

Julie: Toxins ... well both. (*They both fall silent*) What's keeping Shane?

Joey: Yeah I'm dying for a coffee.

Julie: And you go straight back to work tomorrow?

Joey: Yeah.

Julie: Wasn't much of a break for you was it?

Joey: Eh, not really no.

Julie: It was too short a time ... everyone was a bit over excited. We never got a chance to settle down. (*Tentatively*) When do you think you'll be back again?

Joey: I don't really know Mum. I don't know what my plans are going to be for the next while. When I've enough money I'm going to travel round a bit, I'd like to go to Mexico.

Julie: Sounds very exotic.

Joey: It's not. Everybody does it.

Julie: Don't kill it before you even do it.

Joey: (*Looking at her*) You're right.

Julie: I'd love to be going on a plane journey. I'd love to travel. Never even thought of it when I was your age. (*Pause*) So you don't know do you? That's where your life is now ... over there.

Joey: For the moment.

Julie: But you don't know. You could end up staying ... permanently.

Joey: I have a life over here too.

Julie: Well a family.

Joey: Yeah a family. My family.

Julie: (*With a little laugh*) Maybe not the one you'd have chosen but at least it's yours.

Joey: At least it's mine and it's paid for.

  Shane *returns with four coffees.*

Shane: There's an extra one if somebody wants it. I bought four by mistake.

Julie: We could bring it home to Frank.

Joey: And throw it at him, only it'd be cold by then.

Julie: Joey!

Joey: What? He deserves it. His behaviour yesterday was outrageous. Ruining the whole evening for everybody just because I made a decision he didn't happen to like.

Shane: C'mon Joey, it's not just 'a' decision.

Joey: What do you mean?

Shane: Well ... you're going away, you're leaving us.

Joey: Oh for fuck's sake Shane! Don't tell me I'm going to get it from you now. It's part of life. You grow up, you leave home. Have a little think about it some time.

Julie: Not another row please.

Joey: You'd think I was doing something awful to everybody. Christ he wouldn't even get out of bed to say goodbye to me.

Julie: That was bad. I'm cross with him over that. He just couldn't understand it. He thought that you wanted to come back. That you'd be back like a shot if you had a job. He blames it all on Chris Farrell of course.

Joey: I'm not going back because of that.

Julie: Are you sure you're not?

Joey: No of course not.

Julie: I'm relieved to hear that. I'd hate to think you thought we were awful parents. Irresponsible ...

Joey: I don't. You've given me so much.

Julie: Well I tried. I gave you the best ... all of what I had. You were well loved.

Joey: I know I was. (*Pause*) It's kind of amazing though.

Julie: What is?

Joey: Well, Chris knowing all that about us all these years. I'm really glad he said it. I just needed to hear someone say that I ... well it's as if he's broken a spell.

Julie: Say what?

Joey: Well the story about the shed and everything.

Julie: What story?

Joey: The story about leaving back the rake and me being in the shed.

Julie: Oh that! Such a load of nonsense. Did you ever hear such rubbish? Such an elaborate story over forgetting to leave back a bloody old rake. I though it was a scream. He's not stupid you know.

Joey: (*Slowly*) You think he made all that up?

Julie: Course he did pet. Don't tell me you believed him?

Joey: But I thought you said that Frank blamed him for me going back. That you were worried that I thought you were awful parents ... I thought it was because of that ... because of what he said.

Julie: No! Because of the awful row he created. Waking you up out of a dead sleep on your first night home. We shouldn't have let him stay. It wasn't fair on you.

Joey: I see. Right. It was a bit over the top alright now that I think about it.

Julie: Oh totally!

Joey: Actually it didn't ring true with me at all.

Julie: Did it not?

Joey: Not really no.

Julie: You could see he was making it all up. Couldn't you?

Joey: Ah yeah. It was so obvious.

Julie: Yeah it was so obvious. We didn't even have a door on our shed.

Shane: We did.

Julie: Not with a bolt on it.

Shane: It had a bolt.

Julie: No Shane. Definitely not.

Joey: What does it matter? It doesn't matter. Everyone has a different picture in their memory.

Julie: That's very true Joey. Will you pass me my bag please Shane? (*He passes her bag*)

Shane: Here you are you ol' bag.

Julie: Watch it.

Shane: I just said here's your old bag.

Julie: (*As she roots in her bag*) I can't believe it, I almost forgot ... I hope you like it ... weren't sure ... the size ... (*She hands **Joey** something small wrapped in tissue paper*) I hope you love it. (*As **Joey** unwraps the gift*) If you don't ... I'll wear it so don't worry.

Joey: (*Taking a jade ring out of the tissue paper*) No. No. I love it. It's lovely (*Putting it on*) It fits. Perfect. Eat your heart out Terry. (**Julie** *laughs*) Thanks Mum. Thanks a million.

Julie: And Frank. He went in on the bus to collect it.

Joey: Did he? Oh maybe he's not such an old pig ... tell him I said thank you ... and ... and nothing.

Shane: Do you have any cash on you Mother?

Joey: What do you want cash for?

Shane: We have to get petrol for the car Dear?

Joey: Oh.

Julie: I don't. I'll have to cash a cheque. I can do that here. I can cash Chris' cheque.

Shane: Oh yeah. How much was that for?

Julie: I don't know. I forgot about it.

Joey: You're not going to cash it?

Julie: I certainly am. (*Taking it out and looking at it*) He left it blank.

Shane: He left it blank? How much would a rake cost?

Julie: I haven't a clue. Twenty pounds?

Shane: Nah I'd say more like forty ... thirty make it for thirty.

Julie: It seems a bit mean.

Shane: OK. Fifty then.

Julie: No I mean to be doing this.

Shane: Then just do a small amount ... a tenner.

Julie: No. No it's not right (*Tearing up the cheque*) I can't do it. It doesn't feel right.

Joey: Smart move Chris.

Shane: Smart? Mum could have fleeced him.

Joey: Yeah, but she didn't. (*Pause*) So when are you coming over to me Shane?

Julie: Are you going to New York Shane? But you've no money.

Shane: That's sort of the whole point.

Julie: Oh and when will you?

Shane: Oh I don't know. Haven't a clue. It's just an idea maybe.

Julie: It's a good idea.

Shane: (*In surprise*) Do you think so?

Julie: Yes I do.

Joey's *flight is announced over the system.*

Shane: Jesus Joey that's you! Last call. Typical, we would have all sat here talking while you missed your flight. Have you got your boarding card? Passport?

Julie: (*To herself*) This is it then.

Joey: Fuck! Where's my other bag? The small one?

Shane: Here here here! I have it. Hurry up, you'd better go.

Joey: It's all right, they're not going to leave without me.

They all brace themselves for the goodbyes. She hugs **Julie** *first, then* **Shane**, *whispering something in his ear which he nods impatiently to. Then she starts walking towards her gate. Just as she is about to exit* **Frank** *appears. He looks wild and dishevelled and is very out of breath. He stands looking around for a few seconds till* **Shane** *sees him.*

Shane: Quick Dad! She's just gone.

Frank: (*Roaring*) Joelle! Joelle!

Joey: Dad!

Frank: (*Trying to keep control of his emotions but he is close to tears*) You forgot this. (*He holds up a toothbrush*)

Joey: That's not mine, it's Shane's.

Frank: Oh dear is it? ... And this ... (*Holds up a book*)

Joey: I'd finished it.

Frank: Oh Lord are you serious? I thought you'd want it for the journey ... I thought I'd miss you ... was worried that ... wouldn't have mattered in the end ... nearly broke me bloody neck over there, fell over some idiot's suitcase.

Joey: Oh God did you?

Frank: Did yeah ... lovely day for flying, you'll have a fantastic view ... Blackie told me to say goodbye, he was sorry he missed you.

Joey: Did he come back?

Frank: He did yeah. Strolled in this morning looking for breakfast, the little so-and-so.

Joey: Tell him I was very upset. (*Suddenly*) Oh Jesus I'd better go! I'm going to miss the bloody flight. (*She grabs* **Frank** *and hugs him*) Bye Dad ... Bye ... I'll be home again ...

Frank: Course you will, course you will. (*Softly*) You'd better go now love.

Joey: Yeah. (*She gives him another quick hug*) Thanks for coming out Dad. OK, gotta go! Bye.

Joey *exits as fast as she can with her bag.* **Frank** *goes over to stand with* **Julie** *and* **Shane***. They all move to the window to watch her plane take off. The three of them stand there backs to the audience. The music fades up, ' In the Morning' sung by Nina Simone.*

Blackout.

The End

Author's Note

Down Onto Blue is my first play. I had performed with Rough Magic as an actress so I knew about the ruthless analysis of character and plot that would go on in rehearsals. It was anticipating those awkward questions actors love to ask that helped me keep the plot tight.

I decided to write a play about a family. Middle-class Dubliners whose fortunes have taken a downward spiral and who live their lives without regard for the petty rules of respectability. I was writing about a world I had at that time never seen on the Irish stage and I had to keep reminding myself of the validity of what I was doing. But like the old maps used to say 'here be monsters'. I think there is an idea out there that the monsters lie only in urban hell holes or bleak rural townlands but not in tame suburbia. But having grown up in suburban Dublin in the Sixties and Seventies I knew it could be a dark and dangerous place.

Down Onto Blue has elements of lots of families in it. Every family has their own history. Every member of the family has their own version of that history. It seems to me that the more screwed up the family the more grimly they hang on to their sense of humour. It becomes a private language.

For the Foxes, humour has its own secret code that no outsider can crack. I felt the Airport was the right setting for Frank and Julie to do their double act. I hoped the buzz there, would emphasise by contrast the dullness of the house. I needed a device to expose Julie's selective memory – the borrowed rake was perfect. For some reason it was funny. It's so suburban and so ordinary. Small enough to be forgotten the next day but big enough to be remembered years later.

The music from Miles Davis 'Kind of Blue' informed the whole play. I listened to it over and over as I was writing. His jazz weighed with a sense of the past and helped infuse the play with a feeling of melancholy. Many pieces from it were used in the production.

This play wouldn't have been written without Siobhán Bourke in Rough Magic who encouraged me to submit an idea. My thanks to Siobhán and Rough Magic for giving me the best vote of confidence any writer can get – a commission.

Pom Boyd
Dublin
1998

HIDDEN CHARGES

Arthur Riordan

To Carol

Hidden Charges was first produced by Rough Magic for the 1994 Dublin Theatre Festival at the Project Arts Centre and subsequently toured to Kilkenny, Cork, Galway and Limerick. The production had the following cast and production team:

Mark Darragh Kelly

Carol Anne Byrne

Kitty Bernie Downes

Bill Donal O'Kelly

Voice of Fran Stanley Townsend

Voice of Derek Michael McElhatton

Directed by Lynne Parker

Set & Costume Design by Kathy Strachan

Lighting Design by Stephen McManus

Production Co-ordinator Kate Hyland

Production Manager Padraig O'Neill

Stage Manager Annette Murphy

Produced by Siobhán Bourke

Photo: Darragh Kelly as Mark © Amelia Stein.

Dramatis Personae:

Mark, A Journalist
Carol, A restaurant manager, in a relationship with Mark
Kitty, Carol's Aunt, and ex-showband singer
Bill, Kitty's friend, a property manager/handyman

Place: Carol's flat
Time: Mid nineties

Act One

Scene One

Enter **Mark** *and* **Carol**. *Pause.*

Mark: Well, one of us had better speak.

Carol: Oh I didn't know, the silence is kind of ... (*Makes a gesture: 'good silence'*)

Mark: Oh, silence, yeah? Right. Go on a bit tonight did I? Hm ... (*Pause*) Yeah this is ... this is a good silence. Nice and quiet. Mm-hm. Makes a change from all that bloody talk, doesn't it?

Carol: Mark –

Mark: Bloody Mark rabbiting on as per usual, blah, blah, blah, nobody the least bit interested of course –

Carol: I didn't say that –

Mark: Well, sorry, but I just couldn't let that guy away with what he was saying ... Seemed to think he was entitled to an opinion or something. (*Pause*) Come on, Carol, I wasn't that bad was I?

Carol: No, I love to see my friends getting treated like morons just because they happen to like a certain book.

Mark: No, but that book –

Carol: So Derek liked it, OK, that makes him an asshole. He also handles most of the big gigs in Ireland.

Mark: Yeah, I think he mentioned that a couple of zillion times.

Carol: And if I could persuade him to let me do the catering just once I know it would lead to other stuff. I

know you have some stupid prejudice against music
people –

Mark: No I don't –

Carol: But getting this extra work is really important to me.
You know how things are in the restaurant.

Mark: I don't have a prejudice, it was just ... when he went
on about how brilliant Jim Wells's book is –

Carol: Not again, please.

Pause.

Mark: *Hidden Charges.*

Carol: I know, lousy title, lousy book, not a patch on
yours.

Mark: My book has nothing to do with it.

Carol: Of course not. And neither does the fact that both
books are up for the Mulligan Award?

Mark: Do you really think I'm that petty?

Carol: Do you really want me to answer that?

Mark: Of course not. But I don't have any prejudice about
music people.

Carol: Really? Why exclude them?

Carol *goes to switch on the answering machine*

Mark: *Hidden Charges. What Price the Liberal Agenda?* Jesus,
Wells used to be depressingly right-on, but now it's like
he's, I dunno, post right-on? Feels someone ought to speak
out and stand up for the poor defenceless right-wing bigots,
that kind of thing.

Mark's Phone Voice: Hi Carol, Mark here, and ... you're
not there, so ... I'll probably see you with those lecherous
music-biz smeg-heads you're meeting. Love you, bye.

Fran's Phone Voice: Carol, Fran here. Howya doin'? Hope you're enjoying your night off, Listen, up to ninety here, animal.

Mark: Fran the man with the turbo tan. Fran the tightly trousered man.

Carol: Sshh.

Fran's Phone Voice: I'm even doing a few tables myself, ah, yeah, I'm not just the financial brain of this partnership, heh, heh, no, I'm having a ball here I swear, doin' great, well, OK, a couple of minor glitcheroos, but the customers are cool, just laugh it off, and yeah, I tell them they'd need a sense of humour to eat here, that cracks 'em up, well, most of them anyway. (*Off*) What? Ah, listen man, cool it, it was only a bit of chilli, here, I'll wipe it off ... oh ... well it doesn't look that bad ... Shit. Carol, I'll catch you later, OK? Ciao.

Carol: Shit.

Mark: Why do you put up with that wizened little reptile?

Carol: Because he's got the money.

Kitty's Phone Voice: Hello? Hello? Oh Carol, Hi, this is your Auntie Kitty. You've got a machine, aren't you great? Em ... let's see, what's the best way ... Em, yes would you ... tell you what, give me a ring OK? I want to ask you a favour and ... well, ring me, I'll be here, and I was wondering if ... Hah! Where's 'here' says you, easy knowing I don't often use these yokes. I'm down at home in Ballinscale. God bless us and save us, you'll be laughing at me when you hear this. More like you'll be saying get on with it you silly old cow, and say what you have to say. So anyway, listen, if you haven't given up and gone to bed by now, or gone off to work, or out disco dancing or whatever – oh say it Kitty says you – before the tape gadget runs out, if it hasn't already, I just want to ask a bit of a favour .... Oh it's spooky talking into a silence like this, but Carol ... do you think I can stay in your spare room for a few days? I want to go up and check on the house, see if Bill is taking care of the flats and so on, and I know you're probably saying I wouldn't impose on my other tenants like this and that's true, so if you want to refuse I'll understand. So that's it now ... there you have it. You'll give me a ring, won't you pet? Alright. Well that's it so. Bye Carol. Bye.

Mark: Oh Carol?

Fran's Phone Voice: Carol, Fran the man again, little bit of a to-do there but nothing too serious, listen – (**Carol** *switches it off*)

Carol: Shut up. God if it was always that easy.

Mark: Carol, that woman ...

Carol: Yeah, my auntie Kitty, why ... No, Mark, you are not taking that tape. You already have two of Fran.

Mark: Please? At least let me time it cos she wins the set of steak knives for duration alone, but what *was* she saying?

Carol: So she's not used to the answering machine.

Mark: Fascinating captain, a life-form that seems to be made up of pure bullshit.

Carol: You're not doing too badly yourself.

Mark: OK, fair point, but when she mentioned Ballinscale, was that because she actually lives there or was it all just part of the fun of talking?

Carol: Yeah she lives there. I've told you about her before. The one who used to be a showband singer?

Mark: Aunty Kitty ...

Carol: Kitty Coyne and the Glorydays: 'Been a bad girl now the bogeyman's coming for me'.

Mark: Ballinscale. Thought I'd finished with that hole for good. Mucksavages.

Carol: Oh, right, you were down there.

Mark: Yeah. Lily Maher.

Carol: The journalistic junket of the century.

Mark: No, I was the lowest of the low, it was one of my first jobs. Background stuff, how did her classmates feel about it, what guesthouse did the coroner stay in, what was the gossip in the pub?

Carol: So our intrepid boy reporter spent the weekend in the pub?

Mark: No, no, it was more like a week.

Carol: The mucksavages must have been impressed at your efforts to blend in.

Mark: What, was I supposed to commute back to Dublin every time I wanted a pint? So as not to intrude on a community's grief? Not this community. One big mountain range of slopey foreheads. We're talking slackjaw heartland here.

Carol: We're talking bullshit here. Just a bit of gratuitous culchie-bashing.

Mark: Yeah. You got a problem with that? Oh right, you're a culchie. But you don't act like one.

Carol: Doing well, am I? Thanks very much. So how are culchies supposed to act?

Mark: Oh, don't get all unreasonable now, you know that's my job. But you are quite presentable, I suppose, with your fancy restaurant and all.

Carol: A girlfriend you wouldn't be ashamed of. That's sweet.

Mark: That's nothing. I'll even go to bed with you if you like.

Carol: Are you staying?

Mark: That OK?

Carol: Sure.

Mark: Sure?

Carol: M-hm.

Mark: Thanks ... You must call round to my place again soon.

Carol: I know. Yeah, I must.

Mark: You never call round any more.

Carol: Yeah.

Mark: I'm not trying to push this or anything.

Carol: I know you're not ...

Mark: I'm not gonna say, 'nice place, huh? Want to come and live here?'

Carol: I know.

Mark: Do call round though.

Carol: I will. Thanks Mark.

Mark: So what's this auntie like? Barking mad prehistoric culchie like your folks?

Carol: Can we forget about culchies for a minute Mark?

Mark: If only we could. Sorry, what's she like?

Carol: I don't really know. She's not actually my auntie, she's a cousin of my dad's, so that makes her – I don't know, one of those once removed things. She'll probably tell you herself. I only met her a couple of times when I was a kid, but I remember being idiotically proud of her. My auntie the pop star, you know? Even now, I think, fair play to her for making a go of it. It can't have been easy for a young girl, back then, when ...

Mark: When showbands walked the earth.

Carol: Come to think of it, Mark, maybe while she's here it might get better if ...

Mark: If I didn't stay here?

Carol: Do you mind? I don't know how she feels about that kind of thing, and –

Mark: Well surely how she feels about 'that kind of thing' is her problem.

Carol: Agreed, sure, but she's only going to be up here for a few days –

Mark: It's up to you.

Carol: – there's no point in upsetting her –

Mark: It's your flat, you shouldn't let her intimidate you –

Carol: I'm not! Just a bit of consideration.

Mark: See, that's how people like that always get their way. We let them walk all over us. Sorry, forget it, it's your decision.

Carol: Yeah, it is. But I'd be happier if you didn't sulk about it.

Mark: I'm not sulking.

Carol: You sure?

Mark: Yeah, it's just ... nothing.

Carol: No, Mark, what?

Mark: No, it's just, have you ever noticed ...

Carol: What?

Mark: Have you ever noticed how much the human tongue looks like a dog's penis? (*Sticks out his tongue*)

Carol: Aw, you turnip! (*They kiss*)

Mark: And it's just for a night or two, yeah?

Carol: Yeah. Yeah, I guess.

Blackout.

Scene Two

Carol, Kitty *enter.*

Kitty: Lovely. Here we are in the ... the sanctum sanctorum is that the word, I think so. Your fella would know anyway Carol, oh brains! And he's not bad looking either – ah shut up Kitty, you'll have the poor girl blushing. He was telling me about the book. Politics is it or some such – I had to pretend I was listening. I remember the name though, the blackguard! *The Sacred Heart Bypass*, oh, that's very good, very clever, very sophisticated, shock a few holy Marys I'd say. Oh the sideways look. Might even shock your poor old auntie says you, well, maybe. You never know, it just might, and what harm if it did, as the fella says? (**Mark** *enters with bags*) Mark you're a great man, I was just saying it might do me the world of good to read that book. I'd be very interested.

Mark: Oh. Great. Kitty, would you like some coffee?

Kitty: You have him well trained Carol, fair do's to you. No, I have to go and meet Bill, but I'll put the kettle on for you two lovebirds first, no, I insist, and that's all about it. Earn my keep while I'm here. Never know I might even sing for my supper some time. Carol, you didn't tell me Mark was a fan. (**Kitty** *goes into the kitchen*)

Carol: Oh? ... must have slipped my mind.

Kitty: Very flattered I was when he told me about the tape.

Carol: What?

Kitty: Didn't he borrow a tape of mine off you? What was on it? Sure it must have been 'The Bogeyman', I suppose. That was the only big hit.

Carol: (*Sotto voce*) Bastard

Mark: They must have been great days, were they Kitty?

While **Kitty** *talks in kitchen,* **Mark** *and eventually* **Carol** *are stifling giggles.*

Kitty: Ah sure they were. It was a marvellous time for everyone though, the sixties. Showbands, mini-skirts, the property boom, your grandad did well out of that Carol; lounge bars and dancehalls sprouting up everywhere. And a bit of freedom of course, not the way out stuff you get now, but a nice bit of leeway, you know? And of course, I thought I was the bees knees. Oh a superstar altogether, up and down the country with the band, and me only out of school. Good money mind you, for the time. Ah but the time comes, even for the wildest of us, when you say to yourself, it's time to call a halt. How about ... this instant Carol?

Carol: Pardon?

Kitty: (*Emerging from kitchen with coffee jar*) Will this instant do?

Carol: Oh, yeah, that's grand. (**Kitty** *goes back into the kitchen*)

Kitty: You should get Bill to fix that drip in the sink.

Carol: Oh, Bill, yeah, sure. It's hardly worth bothering about.

Kitty: Ah, he'd be delighted to do it Carol, he's very obliging. Isn't it marvellous that he lives so near? He takes great care of the place, any work that needs to be done at all, or any trouble that needs sorting out, he's great. Ah, you can always depend on family. Of course he'd only be very distantly related to you now, is it second cousin once removed or first cousin twice I can never remember. Whatever. Third cousin maybe, no, I don't know. First three times removed, is that possible, or would that make him very old? Ah, what are you really saying Kitty, sure what difference does it make, he's family. Extended family anyway. And he'll be wondering what's keeping me, so I'd better get my skates on. Mark, I suppose I'll be seeing you later if you're staying the night? Oh, shut up Kitty, before you put your foot in it. God bless now.

   Kitty *exits.*

Mark: Wow.

Carol: Yeah.

Mark: Yeah.

Carol: Absolutely.

Mark: You OK?

Carol: I'm good. I'm good.

Mark: That was nothing. You should have heard her in the car! Jesus. Rewind and erase.

Carol: M-hm. Speaking of which –

Mark: What? Oh. Sure. (*Gives her the tape*) It doesn't do her justice anyway! The stuff she was coming out with, she's perfect! You know, I wouldn't mind so much that people like her lap up the sanctimonious barf that our more hilarious public figures dole out; no, the real killer is that when they're caught at their bed-leppin, she not only excuses it, she actually seems to admire them for it. She came out with a great phrase: 'It's a queer horse won't take his oats.'

Carol: Brilliant.

Mark: Isn't it though? The inference being that these pot-bellied drunkards are beating off floozies with a stick until they finally get exhausted and succumb. 'It a queer horse ...' Not a bad title for a piece on rural Irish values.

Carol: Oh, and they're uniquely rural values, are they? No double standards in the great metropolis?

Mark: Sorry, am I being a tad shrill?

Carol: And I thought I had you well trained. Are you staying tonight?

Mark: Would that be OK?

Carol: Looks like.

Mark: You're sure?

Carol: She said she'd probably see you later.

Mark: Yeah, but I thought maybe –

Carol: Look, do you want to stay here or not?

Mark: It's a queer horse won't take his oats.

Carol: And what would you expect from a pig but a grunt?

Blackout.

Scene Three

Kitty *sitting.* **Carol** *enters.*

Carol: Hi Kitty. Great you decided to stay another night –

Kitty: Ah, Carol, I'm just in myself. Listen, there are some messages on your thing and I didn't want to go near it. I think one of them is mine anyway.

Carol *goes to the machine.*

Carol: OK. Have a good time tonight?

Kitty: Lovely. Didn't Bill take me out to a cabaret, oh top style, God knows, I could get used to the big smoke, especially with a handsome young escort –

Answering machine starts.

Mark's Phone Voice: Hi Carol, Mark here. I'm in Doyle's with some of the lads, celebrating my nomination – yeah, again – and I'll be here for one more pint anyway, so, might see you here? Give me a ring anyway. Bye.

Derek's Phone Voice: Carol, ah, Derek, yeah? Interested. Very interested. Ah, now you know we have our own people that would usually handle the VIP catering but there's a lot of gigs coming up in the next few weeks so ... you never know, we might be doing business. Em ... nice one. Bye.

Mark's Phone Voice: Hi, Carol, Mark here again and I'm getting kind of settled here, so ... hope you can make it in and ... Bye.

Kitty's Phone Voice: Carol? Oh, you're not there either, that's grand so. I'm just ringing to say I'll be late back, so ... so don't wait up for me as the fella says. All right so. Bye.

Fran's Phone Voice: Carol, howya doin'? Fran the man here, listen, minor problemo, yeah? I locked up like you said, but guess what? Now, I'm sure I didn't leave the keys in the restaurant door but just in case – just in case, mind, I'm going to go back and check, OK? But if I don't ring back, would you bring in the spare set in the morning, and yeah, I know, it's your morning off, bummer an' all, but what can we do? Ciao.

Mark's Phone Voice: Hello? Hell-o? ... fuck. Carol? This is Mark, and I'm yes indeed you've guessed it, I'm celebrating my nomination and this wine is really foul, and (*Sound of phone dropping*) ... pardon me, hello? Oh, Carol, by the way, I'm sorry for slagging you off about culchies all the time, I know, it's not fair, but the thing is, the way I see it, you're only a culchie by an accident of birth, you know? Not by temperament. You don't ever ... you don't block up the footpath talking to your culchie friends and then take your leave of them by walking backwards into passers-by. I've never once heard you adjudging the crack to be either mighty or ninety lads, and you call yourself a culchie? No, if you were a real culchie you'd only have time for people who are 'ginuine', i.e. other culchies; your standard conversational gambit would be 'where are you from yourself?' and you'd know at least one guard. Real culchies say 'sarry' when they mean 'get out of my way or I'll give you a big culchie elbow in the ribs', real culchies are thick set, shifty-eyed, rosy-cheeked, knuckle-dragging, stale-smelling, pot-bellied, buck-leppin' grassroots who always give you that look, kind of suspicious or indignant, like you've just come all over their sangwiches? But anyway you're not like that, that's all I wanted to say, OK? Ah maybe I'm going overboard on this culchie thing a little, it's just, the last few days, having your flat invaded, having to put up with the ... the rhinestone cow ... anyway, now she's gone so why don't I just mosey over, hm? Hello? Hello? Oh. See you later.

During this, **Kitty** *has gone into her bedroom.*

Fran's Phone Voice: Carol, Fran here again, and you won't believe this! The keys were still there, sticking out of the door for every passing head-the-ball to see! Lucky I called back to check. Oh, by the way, your buddy Mark rang earlier, sounds like he's flyin'! Nice one. Jeez, those keys, can you imagine me doing a thing like that? I mean –

Carol *switches off the machine.*

Carol: Kitty? Would you like a cup of tea or anything?

Silence. Blackout.

Scene Four

Carol *is having coffee.* **Kitty** *enters with large bag of groceries.*

Kitty: Carol, love, you finally surfaced?

Carol: Oh, Kitty, all that stuff, you're brilliant. Look, I'm really sorry about last night.

Kitty: What, love?

Carol: Mark on the phone ...

Kitty: Sure that was only a bit of laugh. Bit of high spirits as the man says. Ah, I like Mark. Bit of life in him anyway. I've read his column in the paper a few times. Some very refreshing arguments.

Carol: That's our Mark. Arguments and refreshments. Kitty, about Mark staying here ...

Kitty: Ah, sure, you get used to seeing that kind of thing. Too busy going about my own business, as the man says. But Carol, would you mind if I stayed another night myself?

Carol: Of course not. Having yourself a bit of a wild time are you, Kitty?

Kitty: Oh, the twinkle in her eye, laughing at the poor ould auntie, but now I must say, Bill is going out of his way to keep me entertained. Lunch today, would you believe?

Carol: Think you've got yourself a toy boy there.

Kitty: What? Oh, go on outa that! A toy – oh that's very good. A toy boy! Bill! (*Door buzzer*) Oh, that'll be him now. My fancy man! That's desperate.

   Carol *lets* **Bill** *in.*

Carol: Hi Bill, come on in.

Bill: How're you doing, Carol? (*With great casualness*) Kitty, I was in the neighbourhood, and it occurred to me you might like to come for a lunch?

Kitty: Yes Bill.

Bill: Just thought it might be a nice idea. Lunch.

Kitty: (*Deciding to go along with his pretence that this wasn't pre-arranged*) Oh, lunch! What a lovely idea, aren't you great to think of that. Lunch.

Bill: She's in good form anyway, hah?

Kitty: Do you know a nice place, Bill?

Bill: I thought we'd try Fiancetto's. Do you know it, Carol?

Carol: Yeah, it's good. For lunch. Pricey though.

Bill: Money's no object to us property tycoons, isn't that right Kitty?

Kitty: Will you stop it you blackguard! That reminds me though. Carol, as I'm staying for another night at any rate, we'll forget about this month's rent.

Carol: Kitty, for goodness sake!

Kitty: No arguments now –

Carol: But that's ridiculous!

Kitty: My mind's made up.

Carol: I couldn't possibly – ah Kitty.

Bill: You hear that, Kitty? Wish I had a few tenants like that.

Kitty: No, fair is fair. Sure what would I be paying in an oul' hotel? Come on Bill, we'll be late for our lunch.

Bill: Should see some of the messers we have in my place. You'd sometimes wonder is it worth doing any repairs at all.

Kitty: Repairs! Oh, Bill, would you ever see to the tap in Carol's kitchen? There's a drip.

Carol: There's no hurry, Bill.

Bill: It'd be my pleasure, Carol. Would the weekend suit?

Carol: Well, great if –

Kitty: Right, we'll hit the road so. God, I'm famished now, I'm really looking forward to this. You couldn't have called at a better time, Bill.

Bill: Well ... it's lunchtime! See you at the weekend, Carol. (**Bill** *exits*)

Kitty: I mean it about the rent, now. I'll feel easier staying here, honestly.

Bill: Kitty, are you right?

Kitty: I'm coming! I'm coming! Bye, love.

Carol: I'm coming! I'm coming! My heart is full! My D-Cup runneth over! Lunch! Lunch! Lunch! Mark!

Mark: (*Off*) Uh.

Carol: They're having lunch! Auntie Kitty and Bill, they're out to lunch! The lunch of a ... of a lunchtime!

Mark: (*Emerging from bedroom, massively hungover*) You don't mean ... knowledge of each other in the ... prandial sense?

Carol: From soup to nuts. Well, look at you. Is da poo iddle sojer home from the wars?

Mark: Is he what.

Carol: Grievous bodily functions, huh?

Mark: The works, spazz attacks, sweaty conscience, bowel remorse, verbal diarrhoea not to mention no I won't, kidney jitters, banjaxed liver, cardiac suspended sentence, and my sinuses, well they are appalled, truly shocked and disappointed and rightly so. Am I still talking? Hello nice lady. Gastric boom, neural flutter.

Carol: Hello talking turd.

Mark: A brain of lead and a knob of butter. No wait, scratch that last one.

Carol: No thank you.

Mark: Oh. Yeah. Sorry about last night.

Carol: Yeah? That makes it OK then, I guess.

Mark: Carol, I thought Kitty was leaving yesterday. Otherwise I wouldn't have left that message, I swear. Did she hear it?

Carol: Do the washing up, Mark, will you?

Mark: OK. But only if you praise me for it at embarrassingly regular intervals.

Carol: Yeah, I'll tell them in work. He did the washing up! And he isn't even a professional.

Mark: All this and pert buttocks too!

Carol: Women all over the world send me hate mail.

Mark: And to think you're passing up the chance to live with me.

Carol: I wouldn't push that one this morning mister.

Mark: Aw, Carol, I was only joking. Yeah, right, like my great joke last night. Sorry.

Carol: Yeah, she was OK about it anyway. Too excited about lunch. They're going to Fiancetto's.

Mark: No less.

Carol: He can afford it. Have you seen that house of his up the road? The bedsit gulag?

Mark: Yeah, beautyboard city. Are he and Kitty having a thing?

Carol: No. No ... He's her cousin. Or second cousin. Or something. Is it half cousin once removed to the power of n, – Oh! Shut up Kitty! Lunch! Showbands! The Sixties! Valium! You should have seen her just now. Bill's obviously doing something right. I wonder ... nah. Anyway, she's staying another day.

Mark: Really?

Carol: At least. And she's letting me off a month's rent.

Mark: A month?

Carol: So no more crazy wacky phone calls, OK? It was really embarrassing.

Mark: Wash-up.

Carol: Right. I'll go check on Fran. See if he's turned the place into a shelter for starving bimbos.

Mark: You will keep Friday free, won't you?

Carol: Why?

Mark: Why?

Carol: Oh, your award thing! Yeah, thanks for reminding me. I must remember to do that. See you later! (**Carol** *exits*)

Mark: Yeah. See you.

Blackout.

Scene Five

Mark *is rehearsing his acceptance speech.*

Mark: ... And so – ladies and gentlemen – great pleasure – important award – blah blah – thank sponsors – lick lick – thank judges – bend over, yeah, yeah, yeah ... Exciting time ... There can be no doubt that it's an exciting time in this country, particularly in our line of work. A time of belated, tentative changes in our legislation ... eh ... belated, though nonetheless welcome, changes in our ... homosexuality, divorce, all that ... belated stuff, changes which many of us here tonight have argued for and campaigned for over a number of years. And because most of us here share a broadly similar, I would say, humanitarian outlook, it's all too easy, in gatherings like this, to be lulled into the pleasant belief that everyone in the country shares our outlook. Of course they don't. Conservatism hasn't gone away. Nor have stroke politics or the nudge and wink of the cute hoor

backwoodsman. They're all still there and still in the
ascendant. And so I find it ... distressing, when certain
elements in the media – yes, you Jim Wells, and your
Hidden poxy Charges – when certain elements in the media
... We haven't even tried the liberal agenda yet but already
it's being denounced as an intolerant orthodoxy. I would
suggest that these individuals, naming no names, should ask
themselves where the intolerance really lies.

Kitty *enters.* **Mark** *sits down quickly, riffles through notebook.*

Kitty: Just clear a few things away. Earn my keep as the
man says. Sorry, Mark, am I in your way?

Mark: Hm? Oh, ah ... no.

Kitty: Good. Won't be long ... Can't abide a mess. Not in
the morning anyway. (*Pause*) I suppose Carol would do it
after work usually, would she?

Mark: What? Yeah I suppose.

Kitty: I'd be the other way. I could come in at night now
and walk straight past the mess: dirty dishes, LPs out of the
sleeves, or CDs or whatever ... tapes, anything. (*Pause*) Old
newspapers, full ashtrays, I'd leave the whole shebang 'till
the morning. (*Pause*) That floor could be covered in – I don't
know what, any rubbish at all, you know the kind of thing?

Mark: Mm-hm.

Kitty: Oh, yeah. (*Pause*) Sweet wrappers, cake crumbs,
mouldy coffee cups ... would you like some coffee Mark?

Mark: No, thank you.

Kitty: You're sure now, or tea, or anything?

Mark: No, yeah. I'm sure.

Kitty: Right you be. (*Pause*) I could walk past a pile of
smelly old beer cans, and straight into the leaba. Even if I
had to push my way, or climb over them, into the leaba,
and lights out. (*Pause*) Not in the morning though. Different

strokes I suppose (*Pause*) for different folks. You're sure you won't have a coffee, Mark?

Mark: Yes. Thank you. I don't want a coffee OK?

Kitty: Oh. Right so. I'm sorry. I'll get out ... out of your ... excuse me. (*Starts to exit*)

Mark: Kitty? Em ... were you getting some for yourself?

Kitty: Well I suppose I could if ... yes, I actually was going to get some for myself anyway, yes.

Mark: Right then. Might as well take a break.

Kitty: You'll, you'll have some?

Mark: Yeah. Great.

Kitty: Lovely! Coffee is it?

Mark: Absolutely (**Kitty** *goes quickly to the kitchen*) Jesus. Day five.

Kitty: I suppose you're all set for the awards?

Mark: Ah, yeah.

Kitty: I though you might need a break at some stage. (**Kitty** *emerges with tray of coffee, cakes etc.*) *The Sacred Heart Bypass*. Ha! Great little title anyway.

Mark: Thanks.

Kitty: Deserves to win on that alone, says you.

Mark: Right.

Kitty: God it's great to be here where it's all happening. Though Ballinscale is beautiful of course. Shame it came to be associated with that poor young one of the Mahers. Poor child, to drown herself like that. God the hounding we got that time from the media.

Mark: Ah, The meeja.

Kitty: Oh, I'm sorry, no offence to you Mark, but this shower! Arrogant louts and trendy-boots down from Dublin to spy and jeer at us. We were only bog trotters of course, wonder the roads weren't littered with corpses as far as they were concerned, except when they were drunk of course. Then we were the best in the world, and the salt of the earth, and the producer would like to buy you all a drink lads. The poor child. God if we'd known she was expecting ...

Mark: They never found out anything, did they? Who the father was, or –

Kitty: No, nothing. I sometimes look out at the sea there and picture the poor creature, floating, in the pitch dark .... And I used to have such happy memories of that very spot. I remember one night, the Glorydays had done a gig in the local hall, and of course, it was very special for me, a homecoming, you might say, right after we'd done the single, but we had to drive back to Dublin that night. The rest of the band went in the van, but this fella, Drew, he was our saxophone player at the time, he gave me a lift up in his car. It must have been the spring. Or the autumn maybe, anyway the two of us got on great, you know? Ah we had good oul' crack, Drew and me, we could – we could say anything to each other, you know? We were ... quite close. So anyway the two of us drove off, out into the black night, well not black because actually there was ... was there? Yes there was a full moon. So off into the moonlit night, better still says you, and before we knew it there we were by the sea. That night Mark, and now that I think of it, it was actually summer, there was a ... warm summer breeze coming in from the sea, and us sitting on the cliff, hardly a cliff at all, the sea only a couple of yards below us, bright as day and our feet dangling down in the spray. And side by side we rocked gently, a little forward, a little back, a little forward ... just sitting there, rocking. Wonder we didn't catch pneumonia, or fall in. And the moon above us. Summer definitely, I think, and the sea below. So I don't know, that was a happy time, and a beautiful place, whether it was July or August or bloody Christmas, what does it matter, Paddy's day for all I know. And that was my memory of those cliffs, until ....

Mark: And what about the guy .... Drew? Do you ever see him?

Kitty: Oh, Lord no, not for a long time ... he was ... as it happens I didn't know it at the time, not that there was anything ... well, he was married. So there couldn't have been anything. Anyway, he left the band soon after that, I believe he's got a very successful business. So ... so that's it anyway. I'd better get a move on. Mark, you don't mind if I do a small bit more foostering around, do you?

Mark: No, no of course not.

   Kitty *goes to take the tray.* **Mark** *stops her and takes another cake.*

Scene Six

Carol *on phone.* **Mark** *enters.*

Carol: Yes, sure ... oh, I can, yeah. Oh, that's brilliant, thanks. Thanks a million. Mark, Mark, Mark! At last! Yes! (*She hugs him*).

Mark: What, is she leaving?

Carol: Ah, Mark, not Kitty!

Mark: Sorry.

Carol: That was Derek, remember? Max Promotions?

Mark: Oh, him.

Carol: Yeah, anyway, he's asked me to do the catering at the Megafleadh! This is it, Mark! I'm in! His usual caterers, great bunch, he'd always give them the first option, they know the scene, blah, blah, but they let him down at the last minute. Yes! Yes!!

Mark: That's brilliant Carol! When is it?

Carol: This Friday. It's going to mean a shitload of preparation, starting straight away, but – Mark? Is something wrong?

Mark: The Mulligan Award ...

Carol: What? Oh, shit, Friday night. Mark I'm sorry.

Mark: No, no, it's fine. You go and do your gig.

Carol: It's a pity though.

Mark: Yeah, sure, well, congratulations. It's great news.

Carol: But I was looking forward to your award thing.

Mark: The Mulligan Award.

Carol: Yeah, it's a real shame they both happen on the same –

Mark: Not 'my award thing'. I wish you wouldn't keep calling it that.

Carol: What?

Mark: Nothing.

Carol: Right. The Mulligan Award. I was looking forward to the Mulligan Award. Is that OK?

Mark: Oh, look, forget it.

Carol: No, no, it's obviously very important to you. Stupid Carol, can't even get the name right.

Mark: Carol, I'm really happy you got the gig. (*Pause*)

Carol: Right, well, I'd better go prepare.

Mark: OK.

Carol: And thanks for being so supportive.

Mark: What?

Carol: Well, I just got this brilliant news, but you couldn't give a toss.

Mark: No, it's great news. I'm sorry.

Carol: Never heard anything so selfish.

Mark: Look I'm disappointed you can't make it, OK?

Carol: I'd've thought you'd be relieved not to have to bring a thick culchie like me along. All I've been hearing the last few days.

Mark: What? Ah, Carol, you know I don't mean you.

Carol: But you don't mind giving my aunt a hard time. Jesus, Mark, couldn't you even make a bit of an effort? It is her place, and you're making it really awkward for me.

Mark: Yeah, well ... nothing.

Carol: What?

Mark: You wouldn't have that problem if you moved in with me.

Carol: Ah, not this. Not again. Look, I've got to go and prepare.

Mark: Fine. Don't even discuss it.

Carol: There's nothing to discuss.

Mark: No, there isn't, is there?

Carol: Don't do this. Don't fucking do this. I told you I need time!

Mark: For what? To see if I'm up to scratch?

Carol: Oh, for Christ's sake.

Mark: See if I'm as good as Richard? You moved in with him straight away.

Carol: Mark, please –

Mark: But not with me, no, you'd rather stay here with fucking hucklebuck psychogorgon than move in with me.

Carol: You're being stupid.

Mark: Yeah, you're right, I am. Stupid of me to think I was worthy, of course.

Carol: Can we stop this please?

Mark: It doesn't make sense, Carol, putting up with this place, your aunt calling round whenever she wants. And Bill.

Carol: And you.

Mark: What?

Carol: You think I enjoy this? You here all the time belly-aching and whining like a fucking child? Slagging off my friends, looking for attention, me, me, me –

Mark: Ah, Carol, that's not –

Carol: What's the point? Look, it was great for a while, I really thought, this is it, this is the one, the best ever, but now ...

Mark: What? What are you saying?

Carol: Why bother, Mark? It isn't working.

Mark: Oh, look, I'm sorry, I know, I shouldn't have brought it up again.

Carol: But you did, you always do, it's like, any time you can't think of anything else to say –

Mark: I know –

Carol: – fall back on the old reliable, we both know it by heart, Jesus, if I did move in with you we'd have nothing left to say to each other.

Mark: I'm sorry.

Carol: I can't believe we're back to this same old shit again.

Mark: Neither can I. Sorry.

Pause.

Carol: I just need a little bit of time. Can you understand that?

Mark: Yeah. So ... you aren't throwing me out?

Carol: Yeah, I'll pick you up and pitch you out with my raw red culchie fists.

Mark: Fine girl y'are.

Carol: Ya boy ya.

Mark: Fair play to you.

Carol: Howya horse.

Mark: Mighty.

Carol: Give us me coort, you big turnip ... (*They kiss*)

Carol: And I wish you could just forget about Richard. Living with him was a mistake, and that's why I'm wary of doing it again.

Mark: Yeah, I know. God, I hear myself going on about it and ...

Carol: This house is a touch overcrowded at the moment though, isn't it?

Mark: Ah, Kitty isn't the worst.

Carol: I'm sorry I won't be able to make it to the award with you.

Mark: Hey, the 'Mulligan Award'.

Carol: Yeah. So proud of you.

Mark: Yeah?

Carol: Course I am.

Mark: Shucks.

Carol: We'll celebrate when I get back, yeah?

Mark: Yeah, we'll celebrate Wells' victory.

Carol: You reckon.

Mark: Who knows?

Carol: One day that gobshite'll be found out.

Mark: Heh, yeah, the begrudger's prayer.

Carol: I'll be thinking of you Friday night.

Mark: Thanks. And I'll just have to find some babe to bring along instead of you.

Carol: Yeah, right.

Mark: I hope it goes great for you horse.

Carol: It better.

Mark: And sorry if I've been out of line with Kitty. I'll try and behave, OK?

Carol: Yeah. Come here. (*They kiss. Sound of door opening and* **Kitty** *enters. She's edgy.* **Mark** *can't hide his annoyance at her arrival*)

Kitty: Hello? Ah, full house again?

Carol: Hi Kitty.

Kitty: Bless us Carol will we ever get rid of this fella? Ah, sorry Mark I was only having you on, I'm sorry, that must have sounded awful, it came out all wrong.

Carol: So were you out with Bill again Kitty?

Kitty: What? Oh, yes, yes I was. Yes.

Mark: Good night?

Kitty: Em ... yes, oh, it was grand, grand. I think I'll just have a drink, and then hit the leaba early tonight if you don't mind.

Carol: Kitty, are you OK?

Kitty: I'm fine. Why wouldn't I be? (**Kitty** *goes into kitchen*)

Carol: I've got a big catering job on Friday night Kitty!

Kitty: Really? That's good. Isn't that the night Mark's award thing ...?

Mark: Oh, yeah, it is, but I'm hardly going to get in a sulk about that.

Kitty: No, no, of course ... Night so.

Carol/Mark: Night

Carol: (*To* **Mark**) Hucklebuck psychogorgon.

Mark: That was pretty good, wasn't it?

Carol: So, any particular babes spring to mind?

Mark: Hm, right, got to find a replacement for my usual culchie –

Carol: Your current turnip –

Mark: I don't know ... Actually ...

Carol: Oh?

Mark: Well ...

Carol: Thought of somebody have we? Go on ...

  Kitty *re-enters, unseen.*

Mark: (*Sarcastic*) Well, it's just a thought ... she probably wouldn't want to come anyway ...

Carol: Who?

Mark: I thought I might ask your aunty Kitty.

Carol: To the Mulligan Award.

Mark: Yeah. Think she'd like to come? If she's not busy?

Carol: I'm sure she'd oblige.

Kitty: Sorry, I couldn't help overhearing, Mark, do you need someone to go with you?

Mark: Em, well, I ...

Kitty: Oh, Mark, I'd be delighted! Oh, that'd be wonderful! If you really need somebody?

Mark: I ... I ...

Carol: Of course he does, Kitty. Don't you, Mark?

Kitty: That would really round off my stay nicely. Tell you the truth I was thinking of leaving tomorrow, going back to Ballinscale, but sure no, to hell with it, I'll stay on. Clothes, though, I need a rig-out. Show the Dubs we can put on the style down in Ballinscale too. Is it formal or semi? Let's see, I've a few things with me but I'm not sure if any of them ... maybe I'll splash out and get something really special. Carol, I'll need advice from you, now, because you know the scene.

Carol: Em, yeah, come on, let's look at what you've got. You're welcome to anything of mine of course.

Kitty: Mark, thanks a lot, it's really nice of you. (**Kitty** *goes to bedroom*)

Mark: Oh ... ah, right.

Carol *goes into bedroom leaving an appalled* **Mark**.

Blackout.

Act Two

Scene One

*Enter **Mark** followed by **Kitty**. They've been to the Mulligan Awards, and are dressed up but a little dishevelled after a night's drinking.*

Kitty: Sure it turned out a grand night anyway.

Mark: Yeah, yeah, it did. I had a great time.

Kitty: Good. You weren't upset about the award so?

Mark: No. I knew he'd get it.

Kitty: *Hidden Charges*, sure what does that mean?

Mark: Fucked if I know. Sorry.

Kitty: You're alright. So I didn't show you up in front of your friends, did I?

Mark: Heh, no, you were the star attraction.

Kitty: You thought I might though, didn't you? Might make a spectacle of you?

Mark: No, I –

Kitty: Ah, sure I wouldn't blame you. Saddled with an oul' bogtrotter like me. What was it? The rhinestone cow?

Mark: I'm really sorry about that. And you were brilliant tonight. You really were.

Kitty: Ah, sure, you can always get a bit of mileage out of the showbands. A lot of people are still fascinated by them. God knows why.

Mark: What?

Kitty: Desperate oul' nonsense they were. Oh, you could coin money out of them, of course, because there was damn all else around, but I can't understand why everyone gets so misty-eyed about them.

Mark: You're a peculiar creature, Kitty. Will we have the one more drink?

Kitty: Sure why not? Round off the night.

Mark *gets bottle, pours. They drink.*

Mark: The one more drink, ha.

He pours again.

Mark: Listen Kitty, what's the story between you and Bill?

Kitty: Ah, now you don't think he's really my fancy man, do you?

Mark: When you came in the other night, before I invited you to the awards, you'd been out with him again and you seemed upset.

Kitty: I suppose I was, yes. But it was nothing to do with Bill, really. I'd been ... sure there's no harm in telling you, do you remember the other day, I was telling you about the night down in Ballinscale, down by the cliffs ...

Mark: The cliffs where Lily Maher –

Kitty: Yes, but the night there with Drew, and the happy memories I had.

Mark: Yeah.

Kitty: Well, as it happened at that time, I was making a lot of money as the lead singer. Much more than the lads in the band. So, that night I got talking to Drew, about future plans and what have you, me thinking of course that he might include me in his plans, but no, he kept talking about a business he was going to set up, as soon as he could raise the money. So nothing would do the bould Kitty but to offer to lend him the cash he needed. Yes, he managed to be persuaded eventually, and I was delighted. And later, even when I'd found out that he was already married, I didn't begrudge him the money, because he'd used it to make something of himself. He's got a huge business now, and ... well, recently I heard Bill had had some dealings with him. So didn't I persuade Bill to take me to places where we might meet him accidentally mar dhea. So silly.

Mark: So did you meet him?

Kitty: That night I came back upset, I'd just met him. Oh, Mark, it was awful.

Mark: What, Kitty, tell me, it's OK.

Kitty: All I wanted to do was meet him, see how he was, and talk about the old days. I didn't mind about the money, and I wasn't even going to bring up about the wife he hadn't bothered to mention, I just wanted to see him again, I swear.

Mark: Right, and he didn't ...?

Kitty: He thought I was trying to blackmail him!

Mark: What?

Kitty: Well, when I saw him in the restaurant, I went straight over to his table and then I didn't know what to say. So I might have blurted out something about the night on the cliffs, and how I was glad to see he'd put the money to good use, and how were his wife and children?

Mark: Ah. Right.

Kitty: Then he was calling me the most awful names, and threatening to call the manager ... I just wanted to meet him Mark. I just wanted to meet him.

Mark: He sounds like a real shit, Kitty. Not telling you about his family –

Kitty: Sure, you know what they say, Mark. It's a queer horse won't take his oats. But, bless us and save us, I'm after putting an awful damper on your night, Mark.

Mark: No, Kitty, it's OK.

Kitty: Tell you what, put on a bit of music there, might cheer us up.

Mark: OK – any requests?

Kitty: I'll leave it to you.

Mark: These are all – oops – all Carol's. Must be drunker that I thought. Let's see, oh, we'll try this one. (*Puts on tape*) Here we go. I'd say you were a mighty jiver in your day, were you Kitty?

Kitty: Me? Oh, go away, you're fierce.

Mark: No, no, you must, I mean, the whole dance-hall thing, the whole down the country thing. I've seen them.

Kitty: What?

Mark: Oh, you know, the woman doing all the strenuous stuff, gyrating like an amphetamine juggernaut, contorting herself like something out of the *Book of Kells*.

Kitty: Oh, thanks very much. (*Music starts*)

Mark: – and the man just standing there, the odd judicious shuffle, flicking the wrist every so often just to keep the woman on course, but generally looking as if his mind is elsewhere – headage payments maybe, or is it time to fork out for another vat of Brylcream.

Kitty: Ah, that's awful, I must say though, there was a time though I say to myself, I could make a ... a passable attempt.

Mark: See? I knew it. What do you reckon, give it a go?

Kitty: What? Oh, bless us and save us, not now Mark.

Mark: Oh, come on, I've never danced with someone who can jive properly.

Kitty: Can you jive?

Mark: I presume so.

The music has the right tempo for jiving but is otherwise unsuitable. **Mark** *and* **Kitty** *attempting jiveish routines. A lot of stumbling, giggling. Music ends.*

Mark: So would I get away with this down in Ballinscale?

Kitty: Oh yeah, wouldn't do to have the culchies laughing at you, would it?

Mark: OK, OK.

Kitty: You're very hard on us culchies.

Mark: You really love it down there, don't you?

Kitty: I do ... you should come down. Yourself and Carol. I think you'd like it.

Mark: You reckon?

Kitty: Don't knock it till you've tried it, as the man says. There's more to the place than that oul' scandal, you know.

Mark: Yeah, I'm sure there is. Did you know Lily Maher at all?

Kitty: Only to see. Why?

Mark: Just curious ... Kitty ...

Kitty: What?

Mark: Nothing ... tell me what you know about her.

Kitty: Bless us and save us!

Mark: Just ... whatever you know about the whole thing. Anything at all.

Kitty: No more than anyone else ... she was in the pub till closing. (*A slow song starts up*)

Mark: Would you like to dance? (*They start to dance again. Slight bump*) Sorry.

Kitty: That's OK. Bit drunk I'd say.

Mark: So I'm drunk. Big deal.

Kitty: Not you silly. Her. Lily.

Mark: Oh. (*Giggles*) Lily. Go on.

Kitty: All right, well ...

Mark: Your hair ...

Kitty: What?

Mark: You hair smells nice. What is it?

Kitty: So that's all anyone knows, she –

Mark: No, what is it? In your hair?

Kitty: It's hmmmm ... it's called 'Dark Caresses', Mr Nosey.

Mark: Ha! 'Dark Caresses, Mr Nosey'. That's good.

Kitty: Do ... do you want me to go on?

Mark: Who was she in the pub with?

Kitty: Lots of people. No one in particular. She walked out by the coast road –

Mark: Did she leave the pub with anybody?

Kitty: Ah, no, not that I know of. Next thing anyone knows is, she is found floating, off the head.

Mark: What?

Kitty: Off the head ... the headland.

Mark: Oh. I thought you meant ... (*Strokes her hair*) That's right. Swept around the head.

Kitty: Because she would have gone in on the South side ...

Mark: Dark Caresses ... (**Kitty** *pulls away. Still dancing*)

Kitty: ... and the current must have caught her – (**Mark** *catches her*)

Mark: And dragged her ...

Kitty: Right around ... (*The do a slow twirl, coming closer*)

Mark: Along the bed. Abrasions down one side (*Runs hand down her side*)

Kitty: One arm

Mark: Both legs. (*He kneels, runs hands down her legs*)

Kitty: Mind my tights! Like a good man. Abrasions ...

Mark: Consistent with being swept ... (*Another slow twirl*) along the bed.

Kitty: And when they pulled her out of the water ... (**Mark** *lifts her*)

Mark: Half of her face ...

Kitty: Half of her face was ... (*They kiss, and go into* **Kitty***'s bedroom as the lights fade*)

Scene Two

Morning. **Mark** *sitting.* **Kitty** *emerges from bedroom.*

Mark: How do you feel? (*Pause, looks at her, looks away*). Yeah. Want some coffee or anything? (*Shakes her head*) Well, we really did it, didn't we? We really went and ... Yeah. Sure you don't want some coffee? (*She nods, grimaces with hangover*) You do? (*Shakes her head*) Oh. Ha! ... Talk about ... Shit, she could be back soon. Think I'm still drunk. This is very bad, isn't it? Well, no, you don't really need to answer that, no. Christ. Kitty? I'm sorry; it was all my fault, all my stupid fault. I realise that. But ... So ... Well, what are we going to do? Shit, do you have any headache tablets? No? Might be some in the kitchen. Jesus, I know, heh, worried about a headache, when, OK, I mean well, let's have a think. Like, what are the options right now.

Kitty: Mark, don't you think I feel bad enough without having to listen to this drivel?

Mark: What? Oh, right –

Kitty: Now we need to tidy up here.

Mark: Kitty, all this, it was all my fault.

Kitty: How could I have been so stupid?

Mark: Yeah, me too. Well, I mean ...

Kitty: And what do you mean it was all your fault?

Mark: Well, I ... just that I came on pretty strong, I suppose.

Kitty: And I couldn't have resisted, I suppose?

Mark: No, that's not what I meant, but –

Kitty: But an oul' one like me should be grateful for your attentions, is it?

Mark: No, of course not –

Kitty: Well, don't flatter yourself. It was my fault as much as yours.

Mark: OK –

Kitty: Takes two to tango.

Mark: Fair enough.

Kitty: Or jive, or whatever it is we were trying to do.

Mark: Jesus, yeah, and using Lily Maher as a chat-up line. Very classy. Jesus. What are we going to say to Carol?

Kitty: I wish you weren't enjoying this so much.

Mark: What?

Kitty: You are, you can't believe what an awful man you are, and you're delighted with yourself.

Mark: Wait a minute –

Kitty: I don't think you're sorry at all. You might be if it was some pretty young girl you picked up at a dance, but with me it's different. You're saying to yourself, I wouldn't have slept with her unless things were really bad. Oh, yeah, makes you a bit more interesting.

Mark: Oh, come on.

Kitty: So do you intend to tell Carol just to make yourself feel better?

Mark: I ... I wasn't going to tell her anyway.

Kitty: Right, let's tidy up then. And I'd better pack. Shouldn't have come here in the first place. Weren't you going to get headache tablets?

Mark: Yeah. Kitty, I'm sorry –

Kitty: Let's just try and put it behind us now, alright?

Mark: Alright. I – (**Bill** *emerges from kitchen*) Jesus!

Bill: Sorry, folks, for startling you, but I knocked and got no answer so I let myself in like Carol said. Sorry for invading your privacy like that. I'll be finished in a few minutes.

Mark: Have you been in the kitchen all this time?

Bill: We're on the ball this morning, hah? Yeah, I'm trying to fix this bloody leak.

Kitty: Oh, the leak, aren't you very good, Bill.

Mark: Yeah, that drip is really annoying at night. That's great Bill.

Kitty: Yes, Bill, that's marvellous!

Mark: Carol will be delighted.

Kitty: Yes. Great.

Bill: Well, nice to know my work is appreciated. Yeah, it's very irritating to have a little drip in the background all the time (*Looks at* **Mark**) You look shagged. Late night?

Kitty: Oh, we had a nice night, Bill, lovely, and then we came back here ... and –

Bill: You look a bit tired too, Kitty.

Kitty: Yes, well, I suppose we did stay up quite late, didn't we, Mark?

Mark: Well, yeah, we had a chat –

Kitty: That's right, oh, remember, we spent ages talking about that girl, Lily Maher, you know, Bill, that poor unfortunate down in Ballinscale?

Bill: Oh, yes, yes, an awful case.

Kitty: Yes, well, Mark was asking me, yes, all about that.

Bill: It's good to talk, though, isn't it? Great thing about the Irish, we're never short of a word or two. Even if it's bullshit half the time, what harm? Pardon me, Kitty. So you thrashed it all out between you, did you? That's great.

Kitty: Right, well, I'll just go and ... excuse me. (**Kitty** *exits*)

Bill: No problem, Kitty. One in a million, isn't she?

Mark: Absolutely.

Bill: Give her a good pumping, did you?

Mark: Sorry?

Bill: About Lily Maher.

Mark: Oh. Yeah. (*Going toward kitchen*) Excuse me, I just want to get something ...

Bill: (*Produces headache tablets*) These what you're looking for? You mentioned it a couple of times. (*Pause*) Talking about Lily Maher, hah? Never heard it called that before! (*Laughs*) Don't worry, pal, I'll say nothing. None of my business. Heh. I'd say you're a bit embarrassed, are you? Ah, I can see you are. See how you would be too, hah? I'd say you must have had a fair few scoops in you, did you?

Mark: Heh, I did, yeah. Listen, Bill –

Bill: The things we do, hah? Jesus, with Kitty though! No wonder you look fucked!

Mark: Look, I'd rather not –

Bill: Say no more, Mark, we'll drop the whole subject. Lily Maher though, that's priceless. I'll have to use that one myself. Hey, honey, want to come upstairs and discuss Lily Maher with me? Ah, you have to see the funny side, don't you?

Mark: I suppose, yeah. (*Sound at door*)

Bill: Here's Carol now. Don't worry pal, it's cool. (**Carol** *enters*) Carol, how are you?

Carol: Oh, hi Bill ... Mark, love, sorry about the award. I heard on the radio. Were you very disappointed?

Mark: No, it was a good night anyway. How was the gig?

Carol: Great, really great. Still buzzing. Two gigs next month, Mark, and loads more coming up.

Mark: Ah, Carol, that's great, that's really ... great. (*They embrace*)

Carol: So how about you and Kitty? Was it OK? Did you behave yourself?

Mark: Yeah, of course.

Bill: Carol, I'm tackling that drip right now.

Carol: That's great, Bill, thanks. (**Kitty** *enters*) Kitty, what are you doing with your bags?

Kitty: Ah, sure I can only handle the big smoke for so long, Carol.

Bill: Would you listen to her? I'd say there's very little you couldn't handle, Kitty?

Carol: I'm dying to hear about last night, Kitty. Did you charm the pants off them all? Come on, you'll stay on for lunch at least.

Kitty: I don't want to be getting under your feet here.

Carol: Don't be silly, you're always welcome here and you know it. You'll stay for a coffee anyway. Mark, make us all a cup there.

Kitty: Well, maybe a coffee, but I'll go then.

Bill: I wouldn't do that, Mark, if I were you.

Mark: What?

Bill: Not till I've finished fixing the sink. Oh and Carol, do you know what I have to tell you as well? There's something very dodgy going on in here. With the wiring. The ah, the sockets have seen better days of course. Do you mind if I take a poke around while I'm here?

Carol: Well, it hasn't caused me any problems –

Kitty: Maybe you could leave that till another day, Bill.

Bill: It won't take a minute. And as soon as I'm finished, I can run you down to the station, all right?

Kitty: Oh. Right.

Carol: Fine. Why don't you nip across the road and get us some coffee, Mark?

Mark: OK. Three coffees and ... Bill, what'll you have?

Bill: Whatever you're having yourself, Mark, and I can't go too far wrong, can I?

Mark: Right, four coffees. Won't be long. (**Mark** *exits.* **Kitty** *exits to bedroom*)

Bill: He's a great guy, Mark, isn't he? I'm a big fan of his column.

Carol: Really? I didn't think that'd be your style, Bill.

Bill: Ah, no, I pick up the odd newspaper once in a while, Carol.

Carol: No, I meant –

Bill: I know, I'm only slaggin'. No, you're right, Mark's stuff would be a bit left field for me I suppose, bit strong on the old liberal agenda. But fair enough, I suppose, if he really believes in it.

Carol: Of course he does.

Bill: Your man Jim Wells, now, he talks a lot of sense, too. He's not afraid to take on the trendies, the liberals, the Dublin four crowd.

Carol: Bill, they aren't exclusive to a single postal district.

Bill: Hm ... It's good to talk, though, isn't it? I think, it's when people stop talking, that's when you should start worrying. Take Kitty there.

Kitty: Sorry, what, Bill?

Bill: You said you had a long talk with Mark last night, what was it about again?

Kitty: Well, lots of things, you know how –

Bill: Lily Maher, wasn't that it?

Kitty: Yes for a while, but –

Bill: Can you imagine? Different generations, different backgrounds, spending the night calmly and seriously discussing a sensitive issue like that? Where else would you get it?

Carol: Kitty, I hope Mark didn't give you a hard time last night.

Bill: Whoops!

Kitty: Ah, no, he just asked me a few questions, and we ... both said what we thought – there wasn't anything to disagree on, really.

Carol: Really?

Kitty: Not at all, just a bit of a natter.

Bill: Ha! What a chancer!

Kitty: Sorry, Bill?

Bill: Whoever did this wiring. It's a joke.

Kitty: Very funny, I'm sure, Bill. I'll just get my bits and bobs together. (**Kitty** *goes into bedroom*)

Bill: So I'd say you'll be glad to have the place to yourself again Carol?

Carol: Sorry, Bill?

Bill: Oh, I don't mean any ... Kitty is the best in the world, nobody knows that better than me –

Carol: Yeah, she's great.

Bill: But at the same time, I'd say you'd need your own space, wouldn't you? A girl like you.

Carol: Mm-hm.

Bill: You and ... Mark, of course.

Carol: Of course, yeah.

Bill: He always speaks his mind, doesn't he? Must be embarrassing sometimes.

Carol: Sometimes, sure, but that's what I like about him.

Bill: I see. Of course. Seems to get on well with Kitty.

Carol: She's great if she's given a chance.

Bill: Yeah. And you're happy with how she's treating you here, are you?

Carol: Hm? Oh, sure, why?

Bill: I always like to deal straight with people.

Carol: What are you saying, Bill?

Bill: Well, Carol, sometimes, you meet someone and, I don't know, a chemistry thing I suppose, whatever, but it happens, and you're thinking ... do I have a chance, you know? On the other hand, they might feel just the same. Sorry, I suppose you're surprised to see this side of me.

Carol: I don't know. What side is it, exactly?

Bill: You mean you can't tell?

Carol: This is about you and Kitty, right?

Bill: What? Me and Kitty? Is that what you thought? Ah, you're only slaggin' me now.

Carol: Well, I must confess, you two were seeing each other so much, you squiring her all over town, Mark and myself thought maybe ...

Bill: Oh, did you? Ah that's very funny. Yeah, that's great, because... heh, brilliant. You're gas, the pair of you. But no, no, Kitty wouldn't be my style at all. Seriously. Cop on Carol. Me and Kitty? Ah, for fuck's sake!

Carol: Right. Thought there was a secret romance there.

Bill: I've no secrets Carol.

Carol: OK.

Bill: Anyway, ah, if you ever need anything, you know where I am, all right?

Carol: Sure, Bill.

Bill: Anything at all.

Carol: All right. Thanks Bill.

Bill: Seriously though, you're very easy to talk to.

Carol: Thanks.

Bill: Whereas Kitty, now, you don't always know where you stand. Mark staying here for example, I would have thought she'd disapprove.

Carol: No, that's no problem.

Bill: Hah, yeah, well, that's because she knows you, and any boyfriend of yours is ... ah, she's more broad-minded that you'd think ... (**Mark** *enters with coffees*) Ah, here's the man who can pin her down for us. Hiya Mark, wouldn't you say Kitty can be surprisingly accommodating?

Mark: What?

Bill: Oh, Carol and I have been having a great old chat here, haven't we Carol?

Carol: Oh, yeah, very interesting.

Bill: Oh, no big secrets or anything, don't worry. (*Winks at* **Carol**)

Mark: Right. OK, here's the coffees.

Carol: You look pretty shaky Mark, must have been a wild night, was it? All the usual symptoms? Spazz attacks? Appalled sinuses? What else?

Mark: Oh, heh, all that, yeah.

Bill: While the cat's away, hah? I'd keep an eye on him Carol. Ah, don't mind me, I'm only slaggin'. If you can't have the laugh you might as well pack it in. Amn't I right? No harm in it, just an oul' bit of fun. I love to knock a bit of crack out of people, you know? 'Cos we understand each other, and slaggin' is all part of that.

Bill: (*Shouts*) Kitty! Mark's back. With the coffee. I'd say you like an oul' slag yourself, do you Mark?

Mark: How's the work, nearly finished?

Bill: Ah, here she is now!

Kitty: Oh, the coffee! Come on Bill, we'll drink this up and go.

Bill: Right you be, Kitty, won't be long. We were just saying Kitty, how accommodating you are.

Kitty: What's he on about?

Bill: Just that you're great the way you keep up. The way you adapt to new attitudes, changing values.

Kitty: Sure I manage Bill.

Bill: Sure I know, Kitty. Must be tiring sometimes though.

Carol: Well able, aren't you, Kitty?

Bill: Do you ever wonder though, the way things are going, everybody jumping onto the bandwagon and into the bed, are we throwing the baby out of the bath water?

Carol: (*Laughing*) Yeah. Best policy is, leave it in the bath water.

Bill: That's not –

Carol: – Forever. Wasn't that bath water good enough for our parents and their parents before them? Why throw it out as if it was ... bath water?

Bill: You know what I mean, Carol.

Carol: Only slaggin', Bill.

Bill: Yes, well, there's a difference between patronising and slagging.

Carol: Is that the difference between dishing it out and taking it?

Bill: I wasn't talking literally about bath water, I thought that would be obvious. Personally I don't mind what people get up to. Let it all hang out, right, Mark? But ... but with Kitty here, it's different. Amn't I right Kitty? You remember a gentler time, a more innocent time, when people didn't go shouting about abuse and abortion, and what have you.

Carol: They just swept it all under the carpet.

Bill: Maybe that's your view, Carol, but there's no need to shove it down people's throats. Lily Maher!

Carol: Shove it down ... I'm not ... hang on –

Bill: Lily Maher, there's an example! Yes, yes, of course.

Kitty: Lovely coffee.

Bill: Lily Maher!

Kitty: Oh, let's not talk about that now Bill, God knows haven't we had enough about it?

Bill: That's what I'm saying Kitty. How things like that get blown out of all proportion. Lily Maher, Lily Maher, people going on and on about Lily Maher. I mean that kind of thing must upset you, does it?

Kitty: Of course, everyone was upset. That poor girl.

Bill: But aren't we sick to death of hearing about the poor girl?

Carol: Right now, I'm starting to be –

Mark: Yeah –

Carol: But there's no point pretending it didn't happen. Mark, you were down there –

Kitty: Mark, were you? I didn't know that ...

Carol: – And you felt it was important, didn't you? Because of the abortion debate. Now Kitty, I don't know how you feel about that –

Kitty: Well, we always understood if some poor girl had to make the trip to England, but nobody shouted about it of course.

Bill: More sense.

Carol: Oh boy. Put like that it sounds nice and folksy. Part of what we are.

Kitty: Mark, I didn't know you'd been down in Ballinscale.

Mark: It was ... part of my job.

Kitty: You did your job alright. Held up before the world as uncaring savages. God, if we'd known the poor girl was expecting, we're not such holy Marys that we'd have turned our backs on her.

Carol: Although that's what she must have thought.

Kitty: You never told me that, Mark.

Bill: Wouldn't you agree now Mark, that the media had their own reasons for going down to Ballinscale?

Carol: Well of course they did, same as they would if they were covering an oil spillage or an industrial dispute –

Mark: Carol –

Carol: To find out the truth if they can.

Kitty: They'd decided what the truth was before they came near the place. That we were a crowd of intolerant thicks who drove her to suicide.

Bill: Is that how you feel now, Mark?

Mark: Yes, I think now, maybe people in Ballinscale did get a pretty rough time.

Carol: So did Lily Maher.

Bill: But Carol, isn't Kitty after saying, they have their own subtle ways of dealin' with these things in towns like Ballinscale? It's nothing new for a young one to get into trouble, they know that. And the trip to England, that's as old as the hills. They know that in Ballinscale, just as well as the Dublin trendies know it. They just don't go round shouting about it, because their approach is more subtle. I mean, why should Kitty go and upset the parish priest and the local oul' ones by voting for abortion? Anybody who wants it can get it in England anyway, so why not keep the old biddies happy? You see, it's actually a very tolerant attitude.

Carol: So it's OK to have an abortion but not to vote for it?

Bill: It's just a subtler approach. Am I talking sense Mark? I'd say you see the merit in a subtle, softly softly approach, don't you?

Mark: Well, I see what you mean, but –

Carol: What?? Mark, this is bollox!

Bill: Fair enough, Carol, that's your opinion. Mark what do you think? About Lily Maher?

Mark: Maybe the less said the better.

Carol: Mark –?

Mark: I mean, there are a lot of people who em ... who feel uncomfortable with, em, with rapid change. People who are hurt and confused by it. Anyway it's boring, let's just drop it.

Bill: Exactly.

Carol: Hurt? Confused? Hello?

Mark: Well, yes, they feel –

Carol: Delicate flowers are they?

Mark: No, but they –

Carol: Jesus, Mark, it was bad enough when you thought us culchies were some kind of cute hoor evil empire –

Mark: I never said –

Carol: – but now you're insulting us even more. You think anyone born outside the pale can't handle the facts of life?

Mark: Well ... just ... they might find some of our attitudes a bit much to take on.

Carol: Come on, they're not thick.

Mark: No, no of course not, in fact, what Bill is saying is, in a place like Ballinscale, they actually have a more complex set of attitudes than they're given credit for.

Carol: Great, they're not morons, so why not pay them respect –

Mark: I am –

Carol: – and argue with them as equals – don't let them get away with 'hurt' and 'confused'. Kitty, are you hurt or confused by the very notion of divorce?

Kitty: Well, no, I –

Carol: Abortion? No, the trip to England's a grand old tradition obviously. Mark, what happened last night? What made you turn into Jim Wells?

Mark: No, I'm just trying to see it from a different perspective.

Carol: What, the one where your head is up your arse?

Bill: You see, Mark, that's how bad it's got. That's what scares me, that's the new tyranny.

Carol: Right, I'm being a tyrant because I disagree with you. Hurt and confused now are you? Mark, what are you at?

Mark: Nothing. How do you mean? I'm just ...

Bill: Mark knows how to make allowances for all the people of Ballinscale, not just Lily Maher.

Kitty: Now can we stop talking about Lily Maher?

Carol: What is all this about Lily Maher?

Mark: Sure who cares about her anyway?

Bill: I don't know Mark. She means something to me.

Kitty: Yes, I know what she means to you. That's a great laugh, isn't it? Talking about her when you mean something else. (*Pause*) I'm sorry Carol. (*Silence*) Come on, Bill.

Bill: I haven't finished, Kitty.

Carol: Leave it Bill, I'll see to it myself.

Kitty: Come on, Bill. Or do you have anything else to say?

Pause.

Bill: No. Not for now.

Kitty: ... Mark.

Mark: (*Suddenly animated*) Right, em, Kitty, it was great meeting you, might see you next time you're up, who knows? Yeah. Well. Have you got all your – great. If you like I'll carry ... no, grand. I'll see you Bill, good luck, and –

Bill: Lily Maher, hah?

Carol: Get out Bill.

Bill: What? I've said nothing. See you Mark. Carol.

Bill *and* **Kitty** *exit. Silence.*

Carol: Well, one of us had better speak. (*Pause*) No?

Mark: Heh, that Bill is a piece of work. I thought it was best just to go along with him ... Though, I dunno, maybe there was a bit of truth in what he ... I mean, I suppose in the past I have been a bit unfair on the em, heh, rustic element. You ... you'd be the first to point that out, right? No, I know, he was talking rubbish, absolutely. Getting all sentimental over people's double standards. And all that stuff about you ramming your opinions down people's throats, I mean, that's so typical, isn't it? Em ... but I felt getting into the whole, the whole Ballinscale thing would have been unfair on your auntie Kitty, you know? A bit ... inconsiderate. So the gig went well, did it?

Carol: What did she mean? About Lily Maher meaning something else?

Mark: Well ... I suppose it's true, isn't it? We all use people like Lily Maher for our own purposes. We ... we all appropriate her to ... to prove points, to score points, you know? That's all. And who wants to argue about it with somebody like Bill, anyway? Life's too short.

Carol: Right. Anything for a quiet life. That'd be you.

Mark: What? Carol, you're acting like ... I don't know... as if ... It was only a conversation, you know?

Carol: Yeah. Why didn't you say what you thought?

Mark: Look, can't we just forget it?

Carol: I don't know, can we?

Mark: Well, when you come right down to it, what's more important? Lily Maher or ... or us? Carol? Look, we're both tired. I'll ... I'll go, let you get some kip. (*Pause*) I'll see you later, all right?

Carol: Maybe if you stayed in your own house tonight ...

Mark: Sorry? Well, sure, no problem. Maybe meet you for lunch tomorrow?

Carol: Maybe yeah. I'll give you a ring, OK?

Mark: OK great. I'll see you Carol. (*He kisses her awkwardly*) ... Carol?

Carol: What?

Mark: Nothing. Bye. (**Mark** *exits*)

Carol: Yeah.

Phone rings, **Carol** *picks up.*

Carol: Hello? Oh, hi, Fran. What? Yeah, the gig was fine ... what? The mop? In the press behind the door, why, is there ... ? Oh. Well, have you got everything up off the floor? Ye-es , including the – why were the tablecloths on the ...? Fran, just how much water is there? ... I see. Right. Take it easy Fran ... Yes, I'm listening ...

> **Carol** *slowly puts the phone down, without returning it to the receiver, sits on sofa, and turns on stereo with remote control. Slow fade to black.*

The End

Author's Note

Rough Magic commissioned me to write a play some time in 1992. Before that I'd regularly written sketches for *Nighthawks* on Network 2, and, evolving out of those, a one-man show featuring myself as Eamonn de Valera singing rap songs. So I approached my first full-length play with some aptitude for satire and an unhealthy love of smart-arse one-liners.

Hidden Charges started out as an attempt to satirise two conflicting, though equally stupid attitudes to rural Ireland: one, the downright hostile; the other a sentimental, folksy, special pleading guaranteed to set my own rural teeth on edge. I also wanted to address in some way the inevitable backlash that was occurring in the face of recent liberalising.

In this scheme of things, the Kitty character was going to be a figure of derision, an anachronistic buffoon on whom I could drape a few of my own prejudices. Perversely though, she grew into someone much more complex, and, I think, appealing. She also became the germ for a proper play.

It still wouldn't have ended up a proper play without the encouragement, input, and endless patience of the cast and, especially, Lynne. With this invaluable support, I was able to bring more vivid life to characters and story, and still hold onto the one-liners!

Arthur Riordan
Dublin
August 1998

DANTI-DAN

Gina Moxley

Danti-Dan was premiered by Rough Magic at the Project Arts Centre, in March 1995. The play subsequently toured to Everyman Palace, Cork, Belltable Arts Centre, Limerick, Hampstead Theatre, London, Backstage Theatre, Longford and Hawks Well Theatre, Sligo. The production had the following cast and production team:

Dan (Danti-Dan) Alan King

Ber Dawn Bradfield

Cactus Sophie Flannery

Dolores Eileen Walsh

Noel Donal Beecher

Directed by Lynne Parker

Set & Costume Design by Barbara Bradshaw

Lighting Design by Paul Keogan

Production Manager Padraig O'Neill

Stage Managers Annette Murphy and Paula Tierney

Produced by Siobhán Bourke

Photo: Sophie Flannery as Cactus and Eileen Walsh as Dolores © Amelia Stein.

Dramatis Personae:

Dan (Danti-Dan), aged 14 with a functioning age of 8

Ber, aged 16

Cactus, aged 13

Dolores, aged 14, Ber's younger sister

Noel, aged 18, Ber's boyfriend

The action takes place in summer 1970, ten miles from Cork City.

Note re. music: All of these fab songs were used in the original production and worked wonderfully. Those specified without brackets are integral; however, those within brackets are only suggestions.

Act One

Scene One

Afternoon. Early summer 1970. Ten miles from Cork City. Bridge, low parapet, with a five-bar gate alongside leading to the riverside and cornfields. Nearby is a phone box and a monument to those who died locally in the civil war.
Music: 'In the Summertime' by Mungo Jerry.
Lights Up.
  Dan *enters. He is fourteen, and has a functioning age of eight. He has a downy moustache. He's wearing shorts and a tee shirt, a gun and holster, a length of rope over one shoulder and slung across his chest, and a battered cowboy hat. He's riding an imaginary horse.*

Dan: Danti-dan, ti dan dan dan, danti-dan, ti dan dan dan, danti-dan, ti dan dan dan, danti-dan, ti dan dan, daaan, daaaaanti-dan dan dan.

  He rides the length of the bridge, slapping his backside as he goes, the other hand holding the reins in front of him. He anxiously looks behind him. He whips off the rope from around his shoulder, makes a slip knot in it and skirls it above his head. He gallops towards the monument and lassos it, lifts himself off the horse and swings around behind the monument. He shoos the horse away, coils the rope and peeps out. Gun at the ready.
  Ber, *aged sixteen, wearing a nylon shop coat, zipped up the front, sits at the far end of the bridge. She takes a ten-pack of 'Major' cigarettes from her pocket, takes one and puts it in her mouth. She takes a Ronson lighter out of her bra, lights the fag, kisses the lighter and puts it back in her bra. She inhales down to her toes.*

Dan: Stick em' up.

Ber: I come in peace, didn't you see the smoke signals. Stop it now boy, I'm in fierce form, so don't be bugging me.

> **Dan** *puts his gun away and goes towards* **Ber**, *arsing his way along the bridge.*

Dan: Sorry Ber.

Ber: S'alright. Jesus, a power cut. Whoever heard of a power cut in the summer? And I would have to be on, oh yeah, of course.

Dan: Give us a drag, will you?

Ber: Here, have a full one, you'll only be horsing it.

Dan: I'd never go a whole one.

> **Ber** *passes him her cigarette.*

Ber: More fool me. They'll ruin your chest. (*Laughs*)

Dan: Is it out all morning?

Ber: (*Nods*) The register and everything. And you know me, I'm useless at sums. My head's shagging hopping. The shop is boiling. (*She unzips her shop coat to cleavage level.*) And nylon is useless in this weather. Mum, me arse, I'm saturated. And I wouldn't mind like, but I've nothing on under it even. Stop gawking you. You're miles too young for me. I better get back. What time is it?

Dan: Fifty-six minutes apast one.

Ber: What's that? Oh yeah. Listen, if you see Dolores tell her to call up. Tell her get money off Mammy, we'll have to get rid of the meats by this evening. That ham'll be humming if it's there any longer.

Dan: She went swimming with Cactus.

Ber: I thought that snobby little bitch wasn't talking to her. I wish she'd make up her mind. She had Dolores bawling last night.

Dan: Over what?

Ber: God knows boy. God knows. (*She goes to leave*)

Dan: Will you be around after?

Ber: I might, then again I mightn't.

Dan *is embarrassed.*

Ber: See you so. Oh and Dan, the moustache is coming on lovely.

He twirls his gun on his index finger.

(Music: 'In the Summertime' by Mungo Jerry.)

Scene Two

Dan *is sitting on top of the gate. Sound effects of cars passing. Good gap between each car.* **Dan** *notes the registration numbers in a notebook. He has a bundle of similar books on his lap. His head goes from right, looking at the oncoming car, to left, clocking its number, to centre, writing it down. Occasionally he waves at a passing motorist. His concentration is supreme.*

Scene Three

Cactus, *aged thirteen, tomboyishly dressed, sticky-out hair, climbs through the gate from the riverside and very carefully arranges slices of ham in a line along the parapet of the bridge.* **Dan** *is still taking down numbers. The angelus bells ring six o'clock .* **Dan** *checks his watch and* *tidies away his notebooks. He goes to* **Cactus**. *She stares at him, then gives him a mad smile. He retreats to the monument.* **Dolores** (**Ber**'s *sister*) *aged fourteen, an innocent, slightly gawky, climbs through the gate.*

Dolores: Flip's sake, Cactus, what are you doing?

Cactus: What?

Dolores: The ham. The good cooked ham. I'm going to be murdered all over you. Oh flip. What did you do that for?

Cactus I thought it looked nice, that's all.

Dolores: Ah God. You're lousy, you are. That's just pure stupid. (*She tries to peel the slices off the bridge and pile them neatly*)

Cactus: Eh Dolores …

Dolores: What?

Cactus: Don't say what, say pardon.

Dolores: Shut up you. Pardon, what?

Cactus: Your frock is caught up in your knickers.

Dolores: Oh God. Am I puce? Thanks. Did any cars pass? Was he looking?

Cactus: Don't mind that langer. He hasn't a clue, him.

Dolores: I know, yeah. Ah God love him.

Cactus: You sound like your Granny, 'sure gawney love him'.

Dolores: Don't forget your togs.

Cactus: Who said I'm going anywhere?

Dolores: Well … your tea.

Cactus: I'm not hungry.

Dolores: You need it. We're not finished growing you know.

Cactus: Jesus, I hope not. I must, I must, increase my bust.

Dolores: Ber's a 34C already.

Cactus: I know.

Dolores: You man's ears are out on stalks. How do you know?

Cactus: (*Shouts at* **Dan**) Danti-dan, ti dan dan dan.

   Dan *slopes off.*

I know because I can read dummy. I saw the label when you were taking in her bra for yourself.

Dolores: Remember, I had more under my arms than I had on my chest. Where's Ber? Mammy'll lacerate us for being late. She's like a bear.

Cactus: Over what?

Dolores: She heard Ber calling her a cunt behind her back. Ber swore on the bible that she said 'can't'. Daddy gave her an awful clatter. I wouldn't mind like, but I'm sure Mammy doesn't even know what it means.

Cactus: Not half, I'd say. She's not that thick is she?

Dolores: I never said she was thick, Cactus, I just said she didn't know what cunt means, that's all.

Cactus: Ooooooh touchy.

Dolores: I only said …

Cactus: Here's her nibs. Look at the walk of her. Septic. She thinks she's it.

Dolores: She's breaking in her new shoes.

Ber *sits by them.*

Cactus: Hiya.

Ber: Hello.

Dolores: We'd better be going.

Ber: I'm sitting down for a fag for a minute. I'm crippled. 'Twasn't a power cut at all in the end. Yer man made a balls of the wiring trying to do it himself. Langer. Serves him right. We could've all been blown up though.

Cactus: And you with your good shoes on. That would've been desperate.

Ber: I don't know what you hang around with her for.

Dolores: I don't. She hangs around with me!

Ber: When she has no one better.

Cactus: Ah no seriously though, are they leather?

Ber: Look.

Cactus: What?

Ber: Look.

Cactus: Look?

Ber: Leather look, you fecking thick. Leather look, okay.

Cactus: They look it.

Ber: Watch it you.

Dolores: Come on.

Cactus: Give me a pull before you go.

  Ber *yanks* **Cactus**'*s tee shirt.*

You're hilarious. Ah go on.

Ber: No Cactus, you're the one who's hilarious. You're the one who's loaded the whole time. I'm up there sweating bricks in the mini-market all day to make enough money for my keep, not yours.

Cactus: Ah Ber, go on. It's just I have none on me. Go on, go on, go on. I'll get you back, ten for one. Ah go on.

Ber: You have my heart scalded. I pity that poor man putting up with you. Now this is the last time. Honest to God, I'm worse. Here.

Cactus: Match.

Ber: Your face and my ass. (*She takes the lighter from her bra and flicks it expertly*)

Cactus: You can be so common sometimes.

Ber: Shift. Look at the time it is.

Dolores: I'm waiting for you. God's sake.

  Ber *links* **Dolores** *and marches her off.* **Cactus** *gives her the two fingers,* **Dolores** *catches it out of the corner of her eye.*

Cactus: And hey, you shouldn't call your mother a cunt.

  (*Music: 'All Kinds of Everything' by Dana.*)

Scene Four

Night. **Cactus** *is in the phone box, on the phone but not speaking. She hangs up and taps another number. Again she doesn't speak. Sound effects of a bus stopping and pulling off again. It fades into the distance.*

Ber *and her boyfriend* **Noel** (*Eighteen, wiry, sharp dresser*) *come into view.* **Cactus** *ducks down in the phone box.*

Noel: (*Off stage*) G'luck John Jo, and thanks.

Ber: So?

Noel: So what?

Ber: I mean like ... are we saving or what? Jesus.

Noel: Yeah, we're saving ... then I can flah you cross-eyed whenever I like.

Ber: You will in your hole. Ah get off me, you animal. Listen will you Noel, Noelie.

Noel: Fuck's sake. Ease up will you girl. We'll get engaged, alright. We'll get fucking well engaged. We'll get fucking well engaged for your birth-fucking-day, alright? Loosen your top.

Ber: Noel.

Noel: Just for a minute. Go on, will you. (*Cupping her breasts*) Oh dear ol'Flo, I love you so, 'specially in your nightie, when the moonlight flits across your tits, oh Jesus Christ almighty.

Ber: Langer. Who taught you that?

Noel: The Brothers.

Ber: You're hand'll stick up out of the grave for lying.

Noel: (*Opening her bra*) You're on the last hook.

Ber: June is bursting out all over.

Noel: Come on down to the cornfield, will you.

Ber: They're after cutting it I'm sure. It'd be all stubbly.

Noel: That's not all'd be stubbly.

Ber: Naw. I'm sure I saw Mammy at the curtain. She'd have heard the bus Noelie. I better go in.

Noel: Don't be lousy Ber. Come on, two fucking minutes, that's all. I have an awful horn on me.

Ber: I don't know what you think you'll be doing for two whole minutes. It usually only takes you thirty seconds.

He sticks his tongue in her ear.

Stop it will you boy, you have me weak.

Noel: Come on, you're gasping for it, admit it.

Ber: I told you Noel, I'm due my Auntie Jane. My friend, do you get me?

Noel: Again?

They separate. **Ber** *ties her bra. They light fags.*

Ber: I was thinking, a solitaire, with a white gold band. Or just the shank white and the rest ordinary yellow gold. I can't make up my mind. What do you think?

Noel *shrugs, and blows rings of smoke.*

I don't want it too high though. It snags your tights when it's too high, apparently. And not too wide either. Then the wedding ring'd look like a washer next to it. Am I going to have to get you one?

Noel: Put your hand in me pocket there a minute.

She puts her arm around his waist and her hand in his arse pocket.

The front one, you fucking eejit.

Ber: I should've known. Would you say the Topaz suite at the airport would charge a bomb for the reception?

Noel: Arm and a leg. Oh, that's the fucking business.

Ber: It'd be dead handy though, to be in the airport already. Like if we were going somewhere.

>   **Ber** *steps on a bundle lying at her foot. It's difficult to make out what it is.*

Oh sweet Jesus Christ almighty.

Noel: What? In the name of fuck…

Ber: Oh, Jesus no. It's a baby. I just know it's a baby. Is it dead? Oh Jesus, that's desperate. Oh God love us.

>   **Noel** *pokes at the bundle.*

Noel: It's alright. Fuck's sake. It's nothing Ber. Only someone's togs and towel.

Ber: It's after putting the heart crossways on me. (*She unrolls the towel and examines the togs*) Cactus's. I should've guessed. Christ. I'm not the better of that. I don't know why I thought it was a baby. Feel my heart, it's pumping.

>   *He does readily.*

Ah Noel. Cop yourself on, will you. I'm in no humour now. What's she doing leaving her togs here, stupid bitch. I wouldn't be surprised if she did it on purpose to scare the lard out of me.

Noel: You're the one who should cop on.

Ber: She's a queer hawk that one. Jesus.

Noel: There's your old lady at the window. I never knew she had teeth like stars.

Ber: Whah?

Noel: They come out at night. Get it?

Ber: Jesus, you're pathetic. Call up tomorrow?

Noel: (*Nods*) Hobble a few fags for us.

> **Ber** *nods.* **Noel** *wiggles his tongue at her, she wiggles hers back at him and runs off.* **Cactus** *emerges from the phone box.*

Cactus: (*Throws a ten-pack of Major*) Hey, give them to Ber from me, will you?

Noel: No bother, thanks very much. What has you out at this hour?

Cactus: Not a lot. I have as much right to be out as you have.

Noel: Is that a fact?

Cactus: Yeah, that's a fact.

Noel: Little fucking smartie pants, huh.

Cactus: You're entitled to your opinion, even if it is wrong.

Noel: I don't need you to tell me what I'm entitled to.

Cactus: I'll try and remember that.

Noel: Think you're great huh? All fucking grown up. And look at you, two fucking blackberries up your jumper.

Cactus: Couldn't be. It's too early for them yet.

Noel: Sure what matter, any more than a handful is a waste. Am I right or am I fucking right?

Cactus: Again it's a matter of opinion. Hey, would you say the weather would hold up?

Noel: I wish someone would hold something else up.

Cactus: Whatever that's supposed to mean. Would you say it would be a good summer or not?

Noel: What the fuck are you talking about? Every summer is good, that's what summers are for.

Cactus: Oh! I remember my mother saying that every summer when she was small was raining. Day in, day out. Lashing the whole time. Imagine.

Noel: You should go on away in home girl and take them togs with you.

Cactus: Those togs. Not them togs, those togs.

Noel: Watch your fucking lip you, I'm warning you.

Cactus: You and whose army.

Noel: Just watch it.

He backs away from her, pointing at her. She stares at him smirking.

(Music: 'Down the Dustpipe' by Status Quo.)

Scene Five

Cactus *is sitting on the gate next to* **Dan**. *He's taking down car numbers. She tries to distract him.* **Dolores** *appears, walking briskly.* **Cactus** *jumps off the gate and danti-dans her way to* **Dolores**.

Cactus: Get it?

Dolores: Got it.

Cactus: Good. Show.

Dolores: Hang on, yer man's gawking down here the whole time.

Cactus: Hey (*Whistles*) Danti-Dan. Dan. Hey, your mother is looking for you. She said to send you home if we saw you.

Dan *obediently puts his books away and heads home.*

Come on, give us a sconce.

Dolores: The page where they're shifting, kissing like, is bent down.

Cactus: Is it the first time?

Dolores: Ehm. Yeah. I think so. I only read as far as the page after that. I think anyway. She's Janet and he's Richard.

Cactus: Thanks. I can read. Right, so who do you want to be?

Dolores: I don't mind.

Cactus: We better get away from the monument, your ma can see us.

Dolores: Down there for dancing.

They walk to the far end of the bridge.

Cactus: Okay, which one?

Dolores: You know me, I'm easy.

Cactus: But Dolores, you've read it already. You know what happens.

Dolores: Yeah, but ... well, you pick and then we can swop. Then the two of us are the two of them.

Cactus: Do it twice?

Dolores: It's only fair really, I suppose. D'you know what I mean like?

Cactus: Yeah. I suppose. From here ...' Janet's chest was rising and falling, she had no control over it ...'

Dolores: Flip's sake, here's Ber. Shove it up your jumper.

Cactus: Sugar.

They look very suspicious as **Ber** *comes level with them.*

Ber: What are ye up to?

Cactus: Us?

Dolores: Us?

Ber: Well, there's no one else shagging well here, is there? Take that brazen puss off you, you. What have you up your jumper?

Cactus: Two blackberries. Ask Noel, he knows all about it. Sorry, it's two fucking blackberries?

Ber: Sounds like him alright. Are you sure it's not two fucking black-fucking-berries?

Cactus: Maybe that's it.

Ber: What are you wearing a jumper for anyway? It's boiling.

Cactus: I hate my arms.

Ber: Jesus.

Dolores: Were you on time this morning?

Ber: Just.

Dolores: Mammy said you're not going out during the week anymore. You're too hard to get up.

Ber: Fuck her.

Dolores: Ber.

Ber: I won't have to put up with her much longer.

Dolores: How do you mean like?

Ber *kisses her ring finger.*

Serious?

Cactus: To Noel?

Ber: We're going into Kings on Saturday.

Dolores: Kings? I thought there was a better selection in O'Reillys.

Ber: Mmmm, there's the back room in Kings though where you can pick your ring in private.

Cactus: Sounds sore.

Ber: A solitaire.

Dolores: Not too high though.

Ber: No.

Dolores: Snags your tights.

Ber: Apparently.

Dolores: When did he ask you?

Ber: What? Oh, ehm … last night.

Dolores: At the pictures?

Cactus: What did you see?

Ber: Haven't a clue what was on.

Cactus: How come, didn't you go?

Ber: Listen love, you don't go to the flicks with a fella if you want to watch the film.

Dolores: Did ye get the twin seats?

Ber: Yeah. I got me ration of passion alright. I was hardly finished my golly bar and he was at me. Look at the state of my stomach after him.

She unzips her shop coat to her waist. She's covered in love bites.

Cactus: Oh God. It looks like shingles. Does it hurt?

Ber: It sort of hurts for a bit, but then you get all, I don't know, jiggly or something. Hot anyway. You couldn't give a fuck about anything.

Dolores: Ber.

Cactus: He doesn't use his teeth though, sure he doesn't.

Ber: No. Just a good suck.

Dolores: Yeuch.

Ber: No, you'd get used to it. It's not disgusting, I swear. I mean like, I've a weak enough stomach. No, it's nice ... ish.

Cactus: How hard does he have to suck?

Ber: Do it there on your arm and you'll find out.

Cactus: Ah, I was only wondering.

Dolores: Curiosity killed the cat.

Cactus: Who asked you?

Dolores: God. I only said ...

Cactus: I only said.

Ber: Jesus H Christ, give us a break would you. My lunch time is short enough without having to listen to ye.

Cactus: You're right, shut up Dolores will you.

Dolores: Flip's sake.

Cactus: Joke. Jesus. Fag Ber?

Ber: No, you can feck off. Anyway you owe me.

Cactus: I do not.

Ber: You do so. You said ten for one the other day, when was it? I'm not as green as I'm cabbage looking, you know.

Cactus: Oh, I gave them to Noel for you.

Ber: When did you meet him? This morning?

Dolores: He never saw morning.

Ber: Shut up you.

Cactus: Last night actually.

Ber: When? Where were you?

Cactus: Hanging round just.

Dolores: Liar. That late?

Cactus: I was. Proof? Okay … you gave him a hand shandy. You looked bored rigid.

Dolores: Is that true? Bored? Naw, Ber's mad for it, aren't you?

Ber: Where were you, you spying little bitch?

Cactus: I'm like God, I see anything. Watch out.

Ber: You give me the willies sometimes, you do.

Cactus: I thought it was Noel was giving you the willies.

Dolores: That's a good one. Never thought of it like that.

Ber: It's none of your business what I do with my fiancé. So watch your face or I'll burst you.

Cactus: I'm quaking. Hold me up.

Dan *arrives.*

Dan: My mother didn't want me.

Cactus: So what? Mine didn't want me either.

Ber: That's an awful thing to say. God rest her. Don't mind her love. You walk me back to work, will you?

Dan: She's not even there. She's gone to town.

Cactus: We must've been hearing things. Or seeing things, is it Dolores?

Ber: What's he on about?

Dolores: Yeah, sorry about that. A mistake.

Ber *lights a fag, lighter from her bra, as usual. She links* **Dan**.

Ber: Dolores, say nothing to Mammy about you know what. I might just keep the, ahem, ahem, on a chain around my neck for a bit. She's like a dog these days, isn't she? Can't wait to move out, to give up work.

Cactus: For ever?

Ber: I might try for a secretarial course in the School of Comm. There's loads of sums though, I don't know if I'd be able for it. Sure, Noel might get something. You'd never know, maybe one of the dogs will get lucky.

Dan: It's nearly one fifty eight, Ber.

Ber: What? See. Sums again.

Dan: I … have to get back to my post.

Ber *gives him a peck on the cheek. He rides off.*

Ber: Be good. And if you can't be good be careful.

Dolores: And if you can't be careful buy a pram.

Ber: Where did you hear that?

Dolores: Off of you. Where else.

Ber: Are ye going swimming?

Dolores: Naw.

Cactus: She has her friend.

Ber: I'm usually around the same time as you, aren't I? I thought I was getting it yesterday but naw. My chest is killing me. Shag it anyway. I'll probably get it Friday and I wanted to wear my white pants going out.

Dolores: Why can't you?

Ber: You can see the shape of the S.T.

Dolores: Use tampoons.

Cactus: Tampons, isn't it?

Ber: Mmm. Mammy'd kill me if she caught me with Tampax.

Cactus: Why?

Dolores: 'Cause you're not a virgin anymore after them or something like that.

Cactus: Sure you're not anyway, are you? Have you gone all the way?

Ber: Listen girl, this is the kind of place that if you lost your virginity somebody would find it and bring it home to your mother. C'mon, walk up along. I'm dead late already. I'll be slaughtered.

Cactus: Have you gone all the way or not?

Ber: Jesus, keep your hair on. Well, I sort of have. Not lying down like only standing.

Dolores: What'd you do if you get preggers?

Ber: Shut up would you. I'm far too young for that. Anyway, it was only standing.

Cactus: Go on anyway.

Ber: About what?

Cactus: What it's like. What does he do?

Ber: Jesus, I don't know. I wasn't looking.

Cactus: Had you your eyes closed?

Ber: Yeah. When you're weak for someone you sort of go … (*She closes her eyes, head to one side, breathing heavily*)

Cactus: Do you have to close your eyes though?

Ber: No, you don't have to, but … this is like a what do you call it, a court case. Fuck's sake.

Cactus: Does he have his eyes closed?

Dolores: Couldn't have. Or else how would he know where you were? Flip's sake, you could get your nose broken that way.

   Cactus *tries out what* **Ber** *was doing.*

Ber: You look more like Saint Bernadette.

Cactus: Fuck off you.

Ber: Jesus, the time. I'm gone (*She goes off in a hurry*)

Dolores: Me too. See you.

Cactus: Where are you going?

Dolores: In home. I promised Mammy I'd do the ironing for her. I don't mind it too much really, do you? I love the smell of it.

Cactus: Mrs Breen does ours. I think it's even her iron. I don't know.

Dolores: See you after.

Cactus: Hey, the book.

Dolores: Hang on to it. Or plank it somewhere till after.

Cactus: Yeah. See you after so. Definitely.

> **Dolores** *goes and* **Cactus** *starts to give herself a love bite on the arm.*
>
> *(Music: 'Sugar' by the Archies.)*

Scene Six

Dan *is car watching.* **Noel** *is hanging around kicking at stones. A car passes.*

Noel: Renault. CZT 520. Wouldn't take one of them fucking yokes if you gave it to me on a plate.

Dan: That's her third time passing today.

Noel: Who?

Dan: Miss McInerney.

Noel: Miss fucking Mc-a-fucking-nerney. A tiger in her tank, that's what she needs, and I know who'd give it to her too.

Dan: Esso.

Noel: Oh yesso. Esso blue.

Noel *ferrets around for five white stones of a similar weight and shape. He starts playing gobs (jacks).*

Yeah, I fancy the notion of America too. Maybe the two of us should fuck off out west together Dan, what do you think, huh? Riding the fucking range, boy, huh? Saloons bursting with young ones called Lulu, their tits falling out of their frocks. Bottles of whiskey all over the gaff. Shoot the shit out of anyone who looked at you crossways. You could flah the ol'doll without even leaving the place. In the back room like, not in front of the whole town. Yeah. Now that's what I call a pub. And poker with a massive pot.

Dan: I can't play cards.

Noel: Oh man. You have to be able to play fucking cards if you want to be a cowboy. You have to be able to play fucking cards. They won't let you in otherwise like.

Dan: That true?

Noel: Gospel boy. The honest to God truth. Cross my heart and hope to die. Rawhide Dan, raw fucking hide. What are you up to boy? Coming down to watch the young ones swimming? Wouldn't mind being an eel in that water, huh? Would not.

Dan: Naw. I'll stick here till six o' clock.

A car passes.

Noel: Wolsey. Don't see many of them now. Great fucking car. Say what you like about the shagging Brits, and I'd agree with you, but they can put a decent car together. I'll give them that. Do you take down every number or what?

Dan: Just the ones coming from town, that's all.

Noel: Why like?

Dan: 'Cause the gate is on this side and I can tie Trigger up at the monument. I could stand on the other side alright, I suppose. Naw, I like the gate side the best. If there's no cars I can do bucking bronco for a bit. The gang sits this side. As well, there's more people coming out from town than going in. The going in is in the morning and I'm mostly here in the afternoon time.

Noel: I mean like, what are you taking them down for, at all?

Dan: For my books. I have to keep my books up to date. If I miss one the whole thing is ruined on me. I have a place at home, in a hide, and I put them in there at night-time. During the daytime I have them with me, mostly. You'd have to shoot the shit out of me to get them.

Noel: You're fucking mad, young fella. Fucking mental you are.

Cactus *comes along, sits to one side of* **Dan.**

Dan: Hello.

Noel: Well, look what the cat dragged up.

Cactus *just stares at him.*

What are you gawking at?

Cactus: Not a lot, obviously.

Noel: Right fucking smart arse here, Dan.

Cactus: I wasn't being smart at all, actually. I wouldn't give you the soot of being smart. You probably wouldn't understand it anyway. You can't even think of a name for your dog, I heard. If that's not thick, I don't know what is. Why don't you call him Blackie? That's nice and easy.

Noel: Because, fuck face, it's a bitch and it's a brindle.

Cactus: Oooh, excuse me.

Noel: And, fuck face, she has a name, she's called Naked Lady. Yes and she's running in the Bitch Classic next Friday night and that lady is going to fucking well win. Then we'll see who's shagging well thick, alright.

Cactus: Phew. Who ate your cake?

Noel: No one ate my cake, you little prick teaser. No one ate my cake. I just don't like being fucking called thick. Alright? Don't call me thick, alright.

Cactus: Yes Noel, no Noel.

Noel: I'm warning you.

Cactus: Is that a threat? Dan, you heard him.

Noel: You're bugging me, I tell you. Really getting on my wick.

Cactus: You could always go away. It's a free country you know. Right Danti-Dan?

Dan: Dan.

Cactus: See. No one's making you stay. You're a big boy now. Go if you want.

Noel: (*Winks at* **Dan**) Bigger than you're able for.

Cactus: Ah just fuck off, will you. A langer, that's all you are. A langer.

He exits, making lewd and threatening gestures at **Cactus.**

Thinks I'm weak for him. The langer.

Dan: And are you?

Cactus: No way. God.

Dan: Can you play poker?

Cactus: Eh no, can you?

Dan: No. Just beg of my neighbour and snap. Oh and memory. I have to learn poker though.

Cactus: God, would you look at them. Doing that out on the road. Common. And I wouldn't mind but they're nearly engaged, there's no call for that.

Dan: Who?

Cactus: Ber and that langer. Don't know what she sees in him.

Dan: Ber? Getting engaged?

He gathers up his stuff and goes and sits alone by the monument . He's on the verge of tears. **Cactus** *watches* **Ber** *and* **Noel** *as they approach.*

Cactus: Oh God. He has her bra open. That's ... oh God ... look ... Dan, Dan?

She continues to watch them. It's clear that **Noel** *is doing this for* **Cactus**'s *benefit. They come close,* **Ber** *is laughing, aroused.*

Ber: Tell her Noel. Ah go on, it's a good one.

Noel: Cactus doesn't know how to laugh, sure you don't Cactus? Come on, smile and give your face a fucking holiday.

Ber: Just tell the bloody joke, would you.

Noel: Okay. O-fucking-kay. Right, Why don't big trains have little trains?

Cactus: I don't know Noel. Why?

Noel: Because they pull out in time.

Ber: Good isn't it? D'ya get it?

Cactus: Of course I get it.

Noel: Why aren't you laughing so?

Cactus: Didn't find it funny, that's all.

Noel: You couldn't have fucking got it so.

Ber: You tarry bastard, take your hand out of there.

Noel: I thought you said you had the curse.

Ber: Thought made a fool of you. Got my dates mixed up.

Noel: Oh good. This is my lucky day. Yabba dabba fucking do Freddy.

Ber: Noelie. Stop will you, she's only a young one.

Noel: That one was here before.

Ber: Where's Dan?

Cactus: Up by the monument. Don't know what's eating him, went off in a huff. Anyone any fags?

Ber: Noel.

Noel: They're in my pocket there. Take one if you want one.

Ber: You're desperate. Ah give her a cigarette. (*Shouts to* **Dan**) How's my boy?

Noel: She knows where they are. Come and get it. Don't try and tell me you're shy.

Cactus: Stuff them. I'll get my own thanks.

Noel: Please yourself. Don't say I didn't offer.

Ber: Dan. Come down here love. Dan. He's deaf, is he?

Cactus *leaves.* **Ber** *and* **Noel** *kiss.*

Scene Seven

There's a transistor radio balanced on the bridge, the top twenty programme is on and 'I'm Going To Make You Love Me' by The Temptations & Supremes is playing. **Dan** *is teaching* **Dolores** *to twirl a gun and shoot. They have competitions to draw the fastest.* **Dan** *wins by a long shot,* **Dolores** *is only humouring him. She takes* **Dan**'s *hand and checks the time. They hear somebody coming and duck behind the gate guns at the ready.* **Cactus** *appears and sits on the gate. They shoot at her from either side. She falls to the ground.* **Dan** *clears the wall and checks the body. The game goes on too long and* **Dolores** *begins to try to revive* **Cactus.** **Dan** *is getting worried. He checks the guns. They check her breathing. Suddenly* **Cactus** *leaps up on* **Dan** *when he's not looking. She twists his arm behind his back and whispers into his ear.*

Cactus: Don't ever shoot anyone in the back again. Do you hear me? I'm warning you.

She pushes his arm until he's almost on his knees. She's getting a sexual charge from this, without really knowing what it's about. Giddy and confused, she lets him go. All three are aware that something has happened. They sit on the bridge. The record on the radio changes to 'My Cherie Amour' by Stevie Wonder.

Dolores: Anyone any fags?

Cactus: I thought you gave them up.

Dolores: I know yeah. I think I'll take them up again for the summer. There's nothing else to do like.

Cactus: I know yeah. Dan, run up to the shop for us, like a good boy.

Dan: Ah no. They won't sell them to me.

Cactus: Danti-dan. Danti-dan. You wouldn't be a minute. We'd let you hang around with us all evening. Wouldn't we Dol? Here, I'll give you money to get something for yourself even.

Dolores: Where did you get a fiver?

Cactus: Found it. Here Dan. Say they're for your Da. Get whatever he smokes.

Dolores: You're always finding money. It's not fair.

Dan: Aftons.

Cactus: Flow gently sweet Afton.

Dolores: Players please. Thank you so much.

Cactus: What are you talking about? Here Dan. You can buy whatever you want. Whatever you want. Imagine.

Dan *puts his guns in the holsters, saddles up and takes off.* **Dolores** *and* **Cactus** *look at each other and shrug.*

Did you have your tea already?

Dolores: Mammy is in bed sick. Cramps or something. There was blood all over the toilet. She was in there with the holy water bottle, firing it down the jacks as if it was Harpic. Then Ber started going on about someone taking her rollers and not putting them back and how was she supposed to get ready to go out if Mammy wouldn't get out of the bathroom. Then Daddy said she wasn't going out. Ber started roaring. Daddy gave her a clatter. Then Mammy started bawling crying and went into the bedroom and shoved the wardrobe against the door. Flip's sake, it's like Our Lady's loony bin over there.

Cactus: I planked the book. Will I get in before Danti-dan comes back?

Dolores: Ehm. I don't know like.

Cactus: Fuck you. Make up your mind.

Dolores: Alright. I'm easy.

   Cactus *retrieves the book from behind the bridge wall. The radio plays 'Make it With You' by Bread.*

Cactus: I'll read, okay. Sit next to me. Nearer. Right. 'Janet's chest ... blah, blah, blah'.

Dolores: Who's who?

Cactus: You be her ... right ... eh ... 'no control over it'. Right. 'Richard was silhouetted against the window, his Adam's apple bobbed in a sea of emotion' ...

Dolores: Langer.

Cactus: Yeah, ah no ... 'His brow furrowed, trying to read her thoughts, her mind.'

   Cactus *furrows her brow and looks into* **Dolores***'s eyes.*

'Like magnets they drew closer. Janet raised her hand to touch the outline of his square jaw. He caught her and pulled her to him.'

They do likewise.

'It felt good'.

Dolores: It!!!!

Cactus: Shut up ... 'She surrendered to him, (**Dolores** *puts her hands up,* **Cactus** *withers her with a look*) sinking into his chest. He brushed her chestnut curls back to reveal her neck, like alabaster, bare but for the velvet choker at her throat. They were breathing as one. Their eyes locked, their lips parted, their bodies trembled.'

* **Cactus** *is really getting aroused,* **Dolores** *is trying but has trouble not laughing.*   ,

'Janet had often wondered whether Richard's moustache would prove an irritant, if and when they ever kissed. The only irritant right now was James. "Take me, oh God, Richard," moaned Janet'...

Dolores: Take me, oh God, Richard.

They are so close to kissing that it's difficult for **Cactus** *to read the book.*

Cactus: ...'moaned Janet, "take me to the hospital." The hospital was a sprawling grey affair, built in 1879 ...' Jesus, is that it? What's wrong with him?

Dolores: Who?

Cactus: James.

Dolores: He's after falling off his horse.

Cactus: That's all? They don't even shift. That's no shagging use. You said they shifted in it.

Dolores: More or less though.

Cactus: Where exactly? Show.

Dolores: Well, ehm …

Cactus *fires the book into the river.*

Cactus.

Cactus: Kiss.

They stare at each other, move closer, close their eyes and kiss very quickly.

Dolores: God.

Cactus: The mirror is better than that. It's useless if you keep your mouth closed so much. There should be that pwawppy sound.

She practices on her hand. **Dolores** *is feeling awkward.*

Come here.

She pulls **Dolores** *to her a bit too quickly. They bash teeth. Both hold their mouths.*

Dolores: Ouch. God. I don't think that's right anyway.

Cactus: You've seen Ber and Noel millions of times, how come you don't know how?

Dolores: That's different. He nearly chokes her with his tongue. He's like a camel.

Cactus: Try, just a small bit.

Cactus kisses **Dolores**, *softer and longer.* **Dolores** *wipes her mouth and makes a face. Radio plays 'Something' by Shirley Bassey.*

Dolores: Crisps.

Cactus: Cheese and onion. That was better wasn't it?

Dolores Ehm, yeah. I don't know. Suppose so. Sort of.

Cactus *kisses her again. They separate, both hot around the collar. They listen to the radio..* **Dolores** *avoids* **Cactus***'s eye.*

Cactus: Love that song. Clinger.

Dolores: I know, yeah. It's ancient though.

Cactus: Oh God.

Dolores: Phew. Roasting are you? Boiling.

Cactus *is tracing her lips with her fingers.*

Cactus: Was that how, do you think?

Dolores *shrugs, embarrassed.*

What did it feel like to you?

Dolores: Tickly, inside my lips. Quakey kinda. Funny. You?

Cactus: Did it make you want to go to the jacks?

Dolores: Eh ... no. For a pee like? No.

Cactus: And what about your chest? Did you feel anything there?

Dolores: In my chest? A while ago, you mean ... Eh ... no.

Cactus: Wasn't your heart thumping?

Dolores: My heart? Yeah, I think I could feel my heart alright.

Cactus: And that's just with you. God.

Dolores: Here's Dan. He took his time. Hiya.

Dan rides up, dismounts and ties his horse up.

Dan: I'm going to be caught. I think he knows they're not for my Dad. You'll have to say you made me, Cactus. I'd be murdered. I got a Tiffin for myself, okay. Here's the change.

Cactus takes the cigarettes and change. She kisses Dan full on the mouth. He pulls away and wipes his mouth.

Cactus: Take me. Oh God Richard, take me to the hospital.

Dan is gobsmacked. Dolores is nearly crying with mortification. Cactus lights a cigarette. The two are transfixed by her. She walks off moving with the music. Dan looks at Dolores.

Dolores: What are you gawking at? Langer.

She switches off the music and runs off, opposite direction to Cactus, with the transistor in her arm.

Scene Eight

Dan is sitting on the monument, fastidiously covering a new notebook with wallpaper. He has a geometry set, pencil case, rubber and ruler. When he's finished covering the book, he starts to rule columns, slowly and methodically. A car is heard in the distance, Dan's hand slips as he grabs the relevant notebook, leaving a squiggle across the new book. The car approaches and he checks his watch, it's too early for him to be taking numbers. He hits himself quite hard with his knuckles on the temples, stops and waits for his breathing to return to normal. He gingerly picks up his new book and the rubber and starts to erase the unwanted mark.

Blackout.

Scene Nine

Cactus *and* **Dolores** *are walking along the parapet of the bridge.* **Dolores** *is smartly dressed in her Sunday best.* **Cactus** *is in her usual duds, and wearing sunglasses.*

(Music: 'Je t'Aime' by Serge Gainsbourg and Jane Birkin.)

Cactus: There's a pike, look.

Dolores: Where?

Cactus: There. Look would you

Dolores: Naw, can't see it. Give me a go.

   Cactus *gives her the glasses.*

Groovy baby.

Cactus: Gravy booby.

   A car approaches, **Cactus** *snatches back her glasses. They peer at the car and wave frantically.*

Dolores: Hiya handsome.

Cactus: Hiya handsome.

   The car passes.

Dolores: The look on his face.

Cactus: Yeah. I thought he was going to stop there for a minute.

Dolores: God. What would you say?

Cactus: Nothing. What would you have to say anything for? Langer. Who does he think he is?

Dolores: Who?

Cactus: Your man.

Dolores: Oh yeah.

Cactus: Shhh. Listen. Car coming.

The car approaches, they stand, one hand on hip, waving with the other.

Dolores: Hiya sexy.

Cactus: Hiya s ... oh sugar, it's a woman. Go on Dol, you lezzer.

Dolores: Come off it girl, you thought it was a fella too.

Cactus: Lesbe friends and go homo.

Dolores: Ha ha very funny. You think you're it don't you.

They sit on the bridge, **Cactus** *firing stones into the river.*

Cactus: Pike. Filthy ugly looking things. What's the use of them?

Dolores: They eat shite. (*They sit a while, bored*) Here's Ber. (*Shouts*) Hiya.

Cactus: Brilliant. I don't think.

Ber *joins them.*

Ber: How are ye lads?

Dolores: Where's Noel?

Cactus: Give us a look at the famous ring.

Ber *takes it off the chain around her neck and gives it to her.*

Ber: Twiddle it three times and make three wishes. He's at home. He can stay there for all I care. Christ almighty he's like a dog himself over Naked Lady.

Cactus: She lose? (*Hands back the ring*) Bit gaudy, isn't it.

Ber: It's only for now, till he gets the money, then I'll get a good one. Yeah, Naked Lady, she got her leg caught in the trap.

Dolores: (*Mimicking* **Noel**) Stupid fucking bitch.

Ber *thumps her on the back.*

Ber: Shut up you, you pup you.

Dolores: He said it, not me. God.

Cactus: You pup you!

The girls snigger. **Dolores** *rubs her back. Fags all around.* **Ber** *gives one to* **Dolores** *reluctantly, sorry to have hit her.*

Ber: I'm up the fecking walls girls. I swear I'll give every bob I have to Concern if I get my friend.

Cactus: You're mental.

Ber: I'm crooked from praying for it. I even had Dol digging me in the stomach last night, didn't I Dol? No word of a lie.

Dolores: She did. I didn't want to like but she made me. Didn't you Ber?

Ber: God forgive me. I couldn't be, sure I couldn't?

Cactus *shrugs and goes to sit on the gate post, the capping stone of which is loose.*

Dolores: I wouldn't say so, no. Not really. Naw, you're just late. God, you'd be killed.

Cactus: Well, how far did you … you know, was he on top of you or what? Like had ye clothes on?

Ber: I told you before we were standing up. Jesus. Watch yourself up there you. That stone thing is awful wobbly.

Cactus: Only once you did it.

Ber: Would you ever shag off. Loads of times, but I always got my auntie Jane before, didn't I?

Cactus: Well, it couldn't have been the whole way so. I thought you said you did it.

Dolores: She did. Didn't you Ber?

Cactus: Did you have to touch his thing? His knob!

Dolores: Ol' King Cole (**Cactus** *joins in*) stuck a penny up his hole but he never got his ha'penny change, he pulled his knob and got five bob but he never got his ha'penny change.

Ber: Jesus, ye can't remember 'Hickory Dickory Dock' and ye have that off by heart.

Cactus: Well, did you touch it or not?

Dolores: Ah stop, the thought of it.

Ber: One of the charms on my bracelet sort of got caught in his zip. I felt it then alright.

   Dolores *puts her hands over her ears.*

Dolores: La la la la la …

Cactus: And …

Ber: He was real randy and pushing up against me like that and sticking his tongue in my ear and you know me, that always makes me weak. I don't know where my skirt was, around my oxters I suppose. Ah lads, I'm not, sure I'm not. My savings even I'll give them, the Biafrans is it?

Cactus: Ah no, what did 'it' feel like?

Dolores: Flips' sake Cactus.

Ber: Wait till I think ... ehm ... sorta like white pudding. Yeah.

Dolores: God Ber, that's disgusting. I'm going to puke.

Cactus: What? I like white pudding. And black pudding.

Ber: Cooked, yeah. This was raw.

> *Laughter.* **Danti-dan** *comes along, stops short of them. He's wearing trousers.*

Cactus: Look at him in the long pants, he's like an old man cut down.

Dolores: Ah God love him.

Ber: Here's my boy. Come over here and give us a kiss.

Dan: Howdy. (*He doesn't budge*)

Ber: Who ate your cake?

Dan: No one. No one ate my cake. Alright. No one.

Ber: Moods now you see. That's more of it. Jesus, you couldn't be up to them. They're all the shagging same if you ask me. Come on, come on in home with me Dol, will you? I don't want to be in there on my own with Mammy.

Dolores: Oh yeah, right. See you later, bye.

Cactus *and* **Dan** *are left alone.* **Ber** *links* **Dolores** *as they walk off.*

Cactus: (*Shouts*) Hey Dolores ....

Dolores: What?

Cactus: Come here, quick.

Ber *stops,* **Dolores** *returns.*

Dolores: What?

Cactus: Bye.

Dolores: Flip's sake. Cop yourself on would you.

Pissed off with being caught out, she runs back to **Ber** *and they leave.*

Cactus: How's Danti-dan, the little man?

Dan: Dan. The horses go Danti-dan. Danti-dan, danti-dan, danti dan dan dan.

Cactus: Ah shut up would you, cranky pants. Hey, come here. Guess what?

Dan: What?

Cactus: Come here. I have something to tell you.

Warily he goes to her.

I found out how to play poker. Want me to show you?

Dan: Yeah. Sure.

Cactus: Don't believe me? (*She takes a deck of cards from her pocket*) See. Doubting Thomas. I know, come on down under the bridge and I'll teach you.

Dan: I'm not allowed down there, Mammy says it's too skeety, I might fall in.

Cactus: Sure who'd tell her? (*She flicks the cards*) Come on Dan. Come on. Dan. Come on.

She walks ahead of him. **Dan** *ties up his horse, pats its nose etc.*

Dan: Rawhide Trigger. Raw fucking hide boy.

The song 'Rawhide' by Frankie Lane begins gently as he follows **Cactus**. *She looks around to check that nobody is watching, then they both climb over the gate and disappear towards the riverside.*

Blackout.

End of Act One

Act Two

Scene One

Music: 'Gimme Dat Ding' by the Pipkins.
   Dan *climbs over the gate from the riverside. He looks around to see if anyone is watching, the coast is clear, he whistles and* **Cactus** *comes into view. She sits on the gatepost. She's wearing different clothes, a little sexier, nothing too obvious. She's holding* **Dan**'s *books.* **Dan** *is subdued, while* **Cactus**, *full of adrenaline, rocks on the loose capping stone.*

Dan: Give me them. You said you'd give them back now. Give them to me.

   She holds the books out and snatches them back before **Dan** *can grab them. This happens a couple of times. She stands on the post and holds them out again. It's far too high for* **Dan** *to reach. He's getting frantic.*

Give them back or I'm telling on you. You swore.

Cactus: Oh, tell tale tattler, buy a penny rattler. Don't be such a bloody baba. Here they are. Look, I'm giving them to you. Come on, Danti-dan, jump. Woops nearly got them there. Jump. Ah not high enough Dan. Here, jump. You little squirt, you can't reach.

   Dan *starts to cry.*

Dan: I'm straight telling on you.

   Cactus *holds the books out over the river.*

Cactus: Oh no you're not. You're not telling anyone anything, sure you're not Danti-dan?

 Dan *is fixed to the spot, his eyes glued to his books.*

Dan: (*Whispers*) No.

Cactus: Can't hear you.

Dan: No.

Cactus: What? Still can't hear you.

Dan: (*Shouts*) No.

Cactus: No, what?

Dan: No, I'm not going to tell anyone anything.

 Cactus *hands him his books. He hugs them to himself.*

Cactus: That's more like it. Good boy Dan.

 He heads for home.

Where do you think you're going?

Dan: I have to get Trigger and go home. I have to go in for my tea.

Cactus: You don't have to do anything Danti-dan, except die.

Dan: I'll be killed if I'm late. Mammy'll get worried.

Cactus: Mammy Mammy Mammy. Jesus.

 She jumps down and grabs him by the arm.

Come under the bridge after.

 He doesn't answer and won't look at her.

Tell you what, I'll ring the man in the County Council now, alright. Hang on, alright. And I'll ask him.

She runs to the phone box. She doesn't put in any money and talks very animatedly. She gives **Dan** *a thumbs up sign during the call. He walks to the box, half crying but full of expectation.* **Cactus** *comes out.*

Well …

Dan: What? What did he say? Tell me.

Cactus: He said … eh … he said, yeah he said he'd buy them. A pound for each book. Imagine. A whole pound. They need all sorts of statistics he said, that's figures, numbers like, for how many cars are passing. As well they want to know other stuff like, ehm, like how many white cars, say, there are, and red and grey ones too. What else? And ehm, like how many drivers are wearing glasses or are baldy and loads of other stuff. I'll remember it, don't worry. I better mind them for you. (*She takes the notebooks from him*)

Dan: A pound. Phew. For one book. I could do a one of hubcaps and one of … loads of things. I'll get enough to go the Wild West soon so, will I?

Cactus: Oh yeah. Real soon, I'd say. And you know how to play poker and all now. See Danti-dan. Don't be stupid now and go telling anyone anything or else I'll have to ring the man. Then he'll change his mind and get somebody else. Swear?

Dan: Swear.

Cactus: Cross your heart?

Dan: Cross my heart and hope to die.

Cactus: See you after tea so.

Dan: Okay.

She kisses him full on the mouth and puts one of his hands on her breast. He pulls away.

Does it have to be in pencil or biro?

Cactus: Biro. Yeah, he said biro definitely.

Dan *goes off full of excitement;* **Cactus** *laughs at him.*

Stupid langer.

She throws stones in the river.

(Music: 'You Can Get It If You Really Want' by Desmond Dekker.)

Scene Two

Noel *is in the phone box.* **Ber** *and* **Dolores** *are sitting on the monument.* **Ber** *is putting nail varnish on* **Dolores**'s *toenails.*

Ber: And Sinead's salon is gone unisex, if you don't mind.

Dolores: Go away. Who said?

Ber: Miss McInerney. She was in this morning. She's as mean as get out that one. One slice of corned beef. Jesus, gumming up a slicer for that. Still, it took my mind off ... you know. She was giving out about the word sex being plastered up all over the gaff, and the last thing she wanted to be faced with under the drier was sex.

Dolores: That's the closest she'll get to it.

Ber: Did you ever notice how thick her glasses are?

Dolores: You're desperate. There's not an ounce of truth in that, sure there isn't?

Ber: If there was, Noel would be led around by a bloody dog by now. Jesus, what's keeping him?

Cactus *passes the phone box en route to the monument.* **Noel** *leans out.*

Noel: Where did you get legs all of a sudden?

Cactus: Lucky bag ...

She wiggles her backside, **Noel** *returns to his call, watching* **Cactus** *all the while.*

Dolores: Long time no see. Were you in town or what?

Cactus *shrugs.*

Ber: Well?

Cactus: Just around.

Ber: Don't mind her.

Cactus *starts messing with the laurel wreaths on the monument, undoing the tricolour ribbon and twirling the wreaths on her fingers till they fly off.*

So which do you think?

Dolores: What?

Ber: Shoes. Jesus.

Dolores: I don't know really like. I'd prefer egg-cup heels to Cubans, I think.

Ber: The ones I liked were fairly pointy. Slingbacks.

Dolores: You could always get them for your going away outfit. In patent. And get Sinead to cover the others in the same stuff as your frock.

Ber: Yeah. Jesus knows where I'll be going away to. Bessborough. Yeah, scrubbing shagging floors for the nuns till I'm out to here.

Dolores: Ah Ber, stop. They'd never do that to you. Don't worry. He'll get something and you'll be grand.

Ber: We'll see. Here's his lordship. Say nothing. Well dreamboat, how did you get on?

Noel: Not bad, not bad at all. He said to call some day during the week and he'd try to fix me up. No bother.

Ber: That's fabulous now. Thanks be to God.

Cactus: Do you have to see a man about a dog?

   Noel *tickles her.*

Noel: She's very fucking funny this one, isn't she?

Dolores: He's going for a job in a chewing gum factory, actually, if you must know.

Cactus: For the summer just?

Ber: Full time, what do you think? Do you hear her?

Cactus: 'I'm forever blowing bubbles.' Jesus, I'd be bored rigid.

Ber: Who's asking you? Put them things down, you'll break them.

Cactus: Those things.

Dolores: Mammy'll have a stroke if you do. She doesn't even like us sitting on the monument, sure she doesn't Ber?

Ber: Put them down, I'm warning you.

Cactus: I'm quaking. (*She puts them on the ground but continues to fiddle with them*) So I heard Naked Lady was useless.

Noel: Stupid fucking cunt, got her leg caught in the trap.

Ber/Dolores: We know.

Noel: Jesus, I'm only telling the girl. I tell you, that dog is only fit for the Chinese place, what do you call it?

Dolores: The Yangtze.

Noel: Yeah. Sweet and sour naked lady and chips.

Dolores: No, flied lice.

Noel: Rice, Christ no. That's where I draw the line. Couldn't look at the stuff.

Ber: Don't mind him, he had it only last week.

Noel: Who did? Me?

Dolores: No, the cat's aunt.

Noel: Ah yeah Ber, that was after a feed of pints. That's different. I'd eat shite if I know I'm not going to remember it.

Cactus: You're obviously not marrying him for his mind, Ber.

Noel: We're only talking about the poxy dog, who said anything about getting married?

Cactus: Oooops. Did I say something wrong? Am I not supposed to know, Ber? Sorry, sorrreee.

Noel: Supposed to know what?

Ber: Don't mind her, she's talking through her arse.

Dolores: It's lovely again today isn't it? We're haunted.

Noel: Hang on a minute, just hang on a fucking minute.

Cactus: Oh God. Sorry sorry sorry. It's all my fault. I just thought since you were engaged, that you had the ring and everything …

Dolores *pinches* **Cactus**'s *leg.*

Ouch. What did you do that for? That hurt you know.

Noel: What load of shite have you been telling them? Answer me.

Ber: Nothing Noelie boy. I swear. She's only making it up. Mind your own business you or I'll give you a proper dig.

Cactus: You and whose army?

Noel *catches* **Ber** *by the arm, almost lifting her.*

Noel: Ring? What fucking ring is she talking about? What fucking ring? I bought you no ring.

Dolores: Let her go you. Let my sister go.

Ber *fumbles for the ring around her neck.*

Ber: Here look. It's only a stupid ol'thing I got myself. It's only mock.

Noel: You dopey fuck, what did you do that for?

He reefs the chain from her neck.

Ber: Ouch. The girls at work … sorry Noelie. I told them we were getting engaged.

He throws the ring into the field behind him.

A bastard. That's all you are. Fuck you anyway.

He pushes her and she falls down the steps of the monument.

Dolores: (*Whispers*) The baby.

There is silence. **Noel** *shakes his head, the others are stock still.*

Noel: Tell me I'm hearing things here. The what?

Nobody answers. **Noel** *lights a fag and walks around in a circle.* **Ber** *edges her way back onto the steps.* **Dolores** *comforts her.*

I said, the what?

Cactus: The baby! Are you deaf or something? The baby. Alright. Did you hear that?

Noel *stares at* **Ber**. *She nods.* **Cactus** *is peeling the leaves off the wreaths.*

Ber: I think I'm up the pole.

Noel: You are in your hole.

Ber: I'm not sure yet like, I think I am though.

Dolores: She's three weeks late, is it? And her chest is killing her.

Noel: That's all I fucking well need. Jesus H Christ. Oh no, no no no, hang on a minute here. I get it now; you're only saying that so as to get married. (*Laughs*) What kind of an eejit do you take me for? You can go and fuck yourself.

Ber: Jesus Noel. I swear. I wouldn't do that Noelie. I am, really.

Noel: You lying little pox bottle. I wouldn't believe daylight out of you. Sweet lamb of divine fuck. Even if you are, don't think I'm marrying any ol'flah bag who's after getting herself in trouble. Christ like t'would kill the fucking mother.

Cactus: That's lovely, that is.

Noel: And you, you shut your face if you know what's good for you.

Ber gets up and heads back to work, crying. Noel goes off in the opposite direction, shouting after her.

And you needn't think I'm going to waste my fucking time making bubble gum either. Fuck bubble gum. Do you hear me? I'm not having some bastarding Yank telling me what to do. They can stuff their jobs up their holes.

Ber runs after him, he pushes her away. She turns and goes on her way to work. Dolores follows her.

Ber: Leave me alone. Oh Jesus God help me. Leave me alone, will you. Just leave me alone.

Dolores comes back to the monument, near tears herself.

Cactus: What a gutty boy. You know, the phone isn't even working. Dirty liar. Still, that was good hack wasn't it?

The wreaths are shredded.

(Music: 'Wonderful World, Beautiful People' by Jimmy Cliff.)

Scene Three

Dan has Cactus on his back and is running up and down behind the gate. Cactus has his rope and is slapping him on the bottom with it.

Cactus: Giddyup Danti-dan, giddyup. Danti-dan, danti-dan, danti-dan dan dan.

He runs towards the gate. When they reach it she leaps off his back and onto the gate.

Naw, no use. You have to go faster coming up to it. Again.

She climbs back over the wall to him. He stoops for her to get on his back.

(*Whispers*) Richard, take me to the hospital.

Dan *straightens up slowly. She walks towards him trance-like. He's rooted to the spot.*

It's James, Richard. He's fallen from his horse.

Dan *doesn't react.*

What's wrong with you, are you deaf or something? Is that it? (*She shakes him*) You are aren't you? Can't even give someone a decent higgy back. Fat lot of use you'll be in the Wild West. That's if you ever get there of course. Only I know that. (*She flicks at his nose with her fingers*) Love to know wouldn't you, nosey baa.

Dan *does his best not to react, though she's obviously hurting him. She makes a lasso out of the rope and starts skirling it.*

Dan: Alright.

He makes to go under the bridge. She stops him.

Cactus: No. Here. What are you afraid of? I told you, everyone does what I tell them to do. Did you forget? Hmmm? Did you? Come on, I haven't got all summer you know. Do it Danti-dan.

*He kisses her, his arms stiffly by his sides. She thumps him to make him more active. He clumsily fumbles inside her shirt. She gropes in his pockets and down his trousers. **Dan** starts coughing and breaks away.*

Dan: I'm suffocating.

Cactus: I told you to breathe through your nose. How many times do you have to be told everything?

Dan: I can't, it's blocked.

Cactus: Ah shut up will you, you little moaning minnie.

She grabs him, he pushes her away. She loses her temper.

Right. That's it. I'm going to ring the man this time. Definitely. I'm going to ring him and tell him. Then you'll be sorry. (*She heads towards the telephone box*) I should've known you couldn't keep your word. The man's going to be real disappointed. No books — no money. No money — no Wild West.

Dan *pinches his nostrils and tries to breathe through them.*

Dan: Hang on Cactus, hang on. I think they're after clearing.

Cactus: They better be Dan. They better be. I'm warning you. (*She stands on the wall looking down at him, snapping the rope at him*) You're sure Danti-dan?

He nods, she jumps down next to him and dances around him.

Dan: When's the man going to give me the money?

Cactus: Oh ... ehm ... let me think. When I ask him for it I suppose. So ... you better watch it Danti. You better watch out, you better not cry, you better not pout, I'm telling you why ...

She holds up a notebook and waves it in front of **Dan***. She kisses him ferociously. Gasping for breath, he separates.*

Dan: Here's Ber, coming over the bridge.

Cactus: Do you know what? Kissing you is like kissing a holy water font. (*She kisses the notebook and shoves it in her waistband*) You better watch out, you better not cry ... see you later Danti and remember ... (*She puts her finger to her lips*).

She walks off towards the cornfields. **Dan** *picks up his rope and is doing bucking bronco on the gate as* **Ber** *comes level.*

Ber: There's my boy. I'd've been better off with you than that other langer. I'll tell you this much, boy, I'm brassed off with fellas, full stop. Don't ever grow up, do you hear me. It's cat, cat melojun.

Dan: (*Chanting*) Rolling, rolling, rolling, keep them dogies rolling, rolling, rawhide. Rolling, rolling rolling rolling, keep them dogies rolling, rawhide. Du du du du du du ...

Ber: Will you quit that, you're giving me a pain in the brain. Fuck's sake ... thanks. Sorry I nearly ate you. I'm in awful crabby form. Over Noel like, it's all off, but I suppose you heard that.

Dan shrugs. Some cars pass.

What's bugging you? Christ almighty, this place is gone mental altogether. Everyone has a puss on them over something.

Dan looks like he might cry.

Why aren't you talking to me? Where's your books, you should be doing them, shouldn't you? Look there's cars coming and all. What's up with you love? There's a van, hurry up or you'll miss it. Dan.

Dan: I ... I don't have to take them all ... the man ... see ... no ehm ... Cactus is minding them. Is Noel coming back? Is he gone away for good?

Ber: He'd be delighted to know someone's missing him. He's gone nowhere boy, he's hanging around with that shower by the grotto, drinking himself stupid. Stupider than he is already. Bad company, that crowd. Mammy is right for once.

Ber takes out ten fags. She offers one to Dan.

Go on, I'll tell no one. They'll hardly stunt your growth at this stage.

He sits with her on the bridge and takes a cigarette. She notices what looks like a love bite on his neck.

Come here a minute, show us your neck. Jesus. What's that? What happened to your neck?

Dan *shrugs and rubs his neck, then puts the rope over his shoulder.*

Ah the rope, must be a burn off the rope. I thought for a minute there … naw.

She takes her lighter from her bra and they light up.

Dan: Can you play poker?

Ber: Naw, ludo is my limit. (*Reading inscription on her lighter*) 'Light of my life' , I ask you. A dirty louser, that's all he is.

Dan: You must, I could teach you then …

Ber: He gave Eileen … what's her name, from in the back road.

Dan: Hurley.

Ber: Hurley, yeah, Eileen Hurley. Mrs Hurley's precious sliotar. He walked her home last night. All the ways from town.

Dan: I have Cact … cards here and all, look.

Ber: It won't last like. She's too grand for him, she even got honours in her Inter, and she's useless at jiving. You'd want to see her like, it's a panic.

Dan: But Ber, listen. If you knew how to play he'd bring you with us. To the Wild West. Me and Noel are going, I'm saving up.

Ber: Yeah, and I'm getting married. (*Laughs*) And I didn't believe it when the teachers told me I was thick. He's a lying bastard, Dan. (*Throws the lighter away, near tears*) Don't believe daylight out of his mouth. Jesus, look at me, up the pole without a paddle.

She breaks down in tears. **Dan** *gets panicky and upset.*

Dan: Ah Ber, Ber. Stop Ber. Will you stop. Stop. He'll come back for us. He swore. He said riding the range we'd be. Round 'em up and brand 'em. Rawhide, Ber.

Ber: Don't you start. Thick as pig-shit plaited the pair of us. (*She hugs him*) Sorry love, I'm grand again. Right so, are you any use at snap?

She takes the cards and starts to deal them. **Dan** *grabs them back.*

Dan: Not snap, poker, I said. You have to know poker.

Ber: Alright, alright. Jesus. Just don't ask me to remember what a trick is, or what do you call thems, suits. Alright.

Dan: Our ranch is going to be called Fort Knox, you know. Come on, we have to go under the bridge.

Ber: Ah Jesus, play if you're going to play.

Dan: Here?

Ber: No, I'd love to play in Tim-bloody-bucktu, only I've no car. Hand out the shagging cards or we'll never get anywhere. I'm worse, I'll be knitting next.

Dan *deals, putting the cards into two ultra neat piles.*

Dan: One two, one two. One two, one two ....

Ber: Shut up counting if you're not going to go any higher than two, will you?

He finishes dealing, mouthing 'one two'.

Jesus, one two, one two. I thought I was bad at sums. Now what?

Dan *plays a number card, as does* **Ber**. *This happens a couple of times, then* **Dan** *plays a king.*

Dan: Now, you have to … you must kiss me. 'Cause it's a King, see. I'm the King and the girl must …

Ber: That's a good one, Jesus. If I knew poker was this much hack, I'd've been at it long ago. (*She gives him a cursory peck on the cheek*) Come here, Dan, 'tisn't a ranch we'll be going to at all boy, but Las Vegas. Do I play again now, or what?

Dan: Properly.

Ber: What? How do you mean? Oh, it's your go, is it?

Dan: (*Getting upset*) No. You're supposed to kiss, I said, properly. On the mouth. Play properly.

Ber: Poker or no poker, you're a bit young for that. Sure look at the trouble it got me into. A kiss is just a kiss, me eyeball. Come on.

They continue to play, like snap. **Dan** *throws his cards down each time, in exasperation. There is a run of number cards.*

Dan: We won't get in if we don't play by the rules. It'll be your fault then.

Ber *has lost whatever interest she had in the game, and is picking nail varnish off her nails.* **Dan** *is getting a bit frantic.*

Play will you. Play for God's sake.

Ber: Jesus wept bitter tears of mercy, ye haven't the patience of a worm between ye. All the bloody same. Here.

Dan *plays a jack and* **Ber** *puts an ace on it.*

Dan: You're supposed to wait, you're ruining it.

Ber: Ah for feck's sake. Come on, two colouredy ones, what's that supposed to mean now?

Dan *grabs* **Ber**'s *hand and puts it on his crotch, he puts his hand up her skirt.* **Ber** *begins to laugh initially, then* **Dan** *starts to bang against her, trying to kiss her. She tries to get past him but he persists. She slaps him hard across the face.*

You little bollix you. Don't you ever, ever, do that again. Do you hear me? Ever. Or I'll fucking well tear you to shreds. Jesus, Mary and Joseph. I'd tell you mother on you only I wouldn't know what to say to the poor woman. Who showed you that?

Dan *shrugs. He's stunned by* **Ber**'s *reaction.*

I have a bloody good idea, you needn't bother protecting her.

Dan: No one showed me. I made it up myself.

Ber: You couldn't make a bed, boy, let alone make that up.

She walks off, dropping her cards as she goes. **Dan** *slaps himself with the rope.*

(Music: 'Band of Gold' by Freda Payne.)

Scene Four

Dolores *and* **Cactus** *are washing the monument. They have two buckets and are scrubbing with deck brushes.* **Cactus** *isn't exerting herself too much.*

Cactus: If she's blaming me over the wreaths, what did she make you wash it for?

Dolores: She said I was to blame as well because I should have stopped you.

Cactus: Fantastic. She should have been a scientist or something.

Dolores: What's that supposed to mean?

Cactus: Eh, that your mother is very intelligent, Dolores. Pity she's such an old bitch as well.

Dolores: Excuse me, Cactus.

Cactus: You're excused, Mrs bloody wash the monument. They were withered away. They're there since Easter.

Dolores: That's not the point actually, they're a mark of respect to the dead. You wouldn't do it in a graveyard, would you?

Cactus: Depends.

Dolores: Flip's sake Cactus, you liar. You would not.

Cactus: I said it would depend, alright. Do we have to do the sides as well.

Dolores: And the back. When she says the monument, she means the whole monument.

Cactus: Shut up will you, you're as bad.

Cactus *sits and lights a cigarette.* **Dolores** *scrubs the inscription with an old toothbrush.*

I hate to break it to you Dolores, but they're dead, there's no good in brushing their teeth.

Dolores: Very funny, I don't think. Are you going swimming after?

Cactus: No.

Dolores: How come? The water's meant to be lovely today.

Cactus: Just.

Dolores: A quick one even. You never come down these days hardly.

Cactus: So.

Dolores: Well, what are you doing so?

Cactus: That's for me to know and you to find out. Naw, I'm going to teach Danti-dan how to fart the National Anthem. Okay?

Dolores: Get lost. Since when are you great with him, I thought you said he was a langer.

Cactus: I never said he wasn't. He's an alright kisser though. Better than you, that is.

Dolores: Pull the other one, it has bells.

Cactus: Swear.

Dolores: I don't believe you. Oh God.

Cactus: Yeah, I taught him to play poker, with my rules though. He hasn't a clue. He'll do anything I tell him. Langer, is right.

Dolores: Like what?

Cactus *whispers into* **Dolores***'s ear. She is incredulous.*

Oh mammy. And is it like … you know, white pudding?

Cactus: Naw. More like a cocktail sausage.

Dolores: Ah no. That's disgusting. Ah God, no. I don't believe you.

Cactus: Come down after so, and we can all have a game of cards.

Dolores: Sure he wouldn't let me. I'd be morto like.

Cactus: It's grand. Only a bit of laugh. He'd let you alright, if I told him to. Don't worry.

Dolores: I might so, for a look like.

Cactus: It's good practice. Better hack than swimming anyway. I'm sick of this. (*She flings her bucket of water at the monument*) There now, we're finished.

Dolores: She'll inspect it.

Cactus: Fuck her.

Dolores: Yeah. Fuck her.

Cactus: About half past so?

Dolores: Yeah. Okay.

   Cactus *goes off,* **Dolores** *tidies up.*

   (*Music: 'Let's Work Together' by Canned Heart.*)

Scene Five

A phone is heard ringing, faintly. **Ber** *is looking up and down the road.*

Ber: (*Shouts*) Dolores. Dolores. It's working. It's ringing. Dolores.

Noel *comes from the bridge end and stands watching her. She turns.*

I thought I got the smell of Harp. Well?

Noel: Water.

Ber: You never lost it.

Noel: What?

Ber: Nothing.

Noel: What's news?

Ber: We're after getting the phone in at long last.

Noel: And I thought that that was your drawers ringing. Well, it'll save me walking up to the mini-market if I want to talk to you. What's the number? Just in case.

Ber: Eh, eight, seven … something. I don't know it off yet. We only got it in today like.

Noel: That a new frock?

Ber: It's a skirt, actually.

Noel: You're after filling out a bit, are you?

Ber: Must be all the Weetabix I'm eating.

Noel: No, on top like.

Ber: Bigger than Eileen Hurley anyhow, of course you'd know all about that.

Noel: I'd say she never saw her own fucking chest, not to mind anyone else seeing it. She wouldn't give you the steam, that one.

Ber: My heart pumps piss for you. I don't know what you're telling me for, I couldn't give a sugar about her.

Noel: That makes two of us. Dozy cow nearly clattered me. I told her the joke about the two pencils. You know the one. It's eejity.

Ber: No, go on.

Noel: Ah you do. Why don't big pencils have little pencils?

Ber: No, I don't know.

Noel: Because they have rubbers on the end.

   Ber *laughs. They stare at each other.*

Did you hear the news?

Ber: Don't tell me. I'm pregnant.

Noel: Ah Jesus no, I know that. No, I got a job above in the chewing gum factory.

Ber: That's brilliant Noelie. I'm delighted for you.

Noel: Brilliant? That's fan-fucking-tastic girl. You'll be mad after me now I'm loaded.

Ber: That's what you think. I better go in and do the delph or she'll be out on her broomstick after me.

Noel: Will you be around tonight?

Ber: I might, then again I mightn't.

Noel: I might see you so.

Ber: You might.

Noel: Right.

Ber: See you so. Oh listen, if you see Dolores tell her I was looking for her. She's dying to have a go of the phone.

Noel: She was up at the bridge, while ago with Dan. That poor fella's not the full shilling. He was going on about the Wild West, America. I hadn't a bog what he was talking about. I just said 'yeah yeah'.

Ber: He's not as green as he's cabbage looking, I can tell you.

Noel: That Cactus one is turning into a right little sex pot, isn't she? The go of her, trying to get me to go playing cards with them. Wiggling her arse and all. Fuck's sake.

Ber: The brazen little bitch, she has Dolores at it now. I'll reef her out of it. Walk up along and I'll catch up with you, I have to put on my shoes.

She runs home. **Noel** *dawdles.*

(Music: 'Sex Machine' by James Brown.)

Scene Six

In front of the gate, **Ber** *has* **Cactus** *by the arm,* **Cactus** *is holding a bundle of* **Dan**'s *books.* **Noel** *is standing to one side.*

Cactus: Would you mind letting me go please. I don't know where they are. She's your sister, not mine.

Noel: They were with you earlier.

Cactus: So.

Ber: So where are they? You better tell me or I'll break your fucking arm, I'm warning you.

Cactus: I'm scared shitless.

Ber: Jesus, but you're a bad piece of work. (*Shouts*) Dolores. Dolores. Dan.

Cactus: I told you, they're not here.

Dolores appears on the other side of the wall, followed by Dan. They both look dishevelled and guilty. Cactus is raging that they've surrendered but smirkingly brazens it out.

Ber: Get out here, the two of you. (*To* **Cactus**) You lying little bitch you.

Cactus shrugs. They get over the wall. Noel starts laughing.

Noel: She's the image of the mother when she's roused.

Ber: Shut up you. What were ye doing? Come on. Tell me. What were ye doing under the bridge?

Cactus is rattled but silences them with a look.

Cactus: God. Alright. We were playing cards, okay? Since when is that a sin?

Ber: I know what kind of cards you were playing alright.

Cactus: What would you know? You can't even add two and two without using the cash register.

Noel: There's no call for that now.

Ber: Come over here and look me in the eye Dolores, and tell me, were you playing cards?

Dolores comes closer, but doesn't look her in the eye.

Dolores: Yeah.

Ber: You filthy little scut you. Dan, is it the same rules as you showed me?

Cactus: Don't mind her Dan, she has no right to be bossing you.

Ber: Shut up you. Is it?

Cactus runs to the bridge and holds Dan's books over the river. Ber grips Dan. Cactus starts to wave the books.

Cactus: Dan. Yohoo. Danti-dan.

Ber: Is it Dan? Did she make you do that.

Cactus opens one of the books and reads mockingly.

Cactus: Renault. Blue. CZT 520. 2.39. Lovely joined up writing and all, Danti-dan. Zetor. Red and Black. No number plate. 2.44.

Ber: Stop tormenting him you.

Dan: Leave my books alone. They're mine.

Dolores: It was only french kissing, I swear Ber.

Ber: You better tell me, Dan, do you hear me? Or I'll call your mother down. You don't want that, do you? Then she'll send you away somewhere.

Noel: Ease up girl.

Dan: She said …

There is a splash as Cactus let slip one of the books, exercising the only control she has left over him.

Cactus: Ooops.

Dan: No.

He starts to hyperventilate, on the verge of a panic attack. He tries to go to stop Cactus, Ber grips him and shakes him roughly.

Ber: Go on Dan.

Dan: Noel said you have to know poker. They're my statistics. She made me take ... Lulu with her tits falling out. That's for a queen.

> **Cactus** *can't believe that* **Dan** *is spilling the beans. She desperately tries to deflect.*

Cactus: See. It's all your fault Noel.

Noel: Christ like, I never said nothing.

Cactus: Anything.

Ber: Listen, I'm warning you, you better tell me what she made you do.

> **Dan** *is gulping for air.* **Cactus** *is frantic. She climbs onto the wall.*

Dan: She made me ... made me take out my winkie. The man's going to give me money for my books. For Fort Knox. She was pinching it.

Cactus: Liar, liar pants on fire.

Ber: Shut up, you filthy little bitch you.

Noel: Christ al-fucking-mighty.

Ber: Go on, Dan.

Dan: She was minding them. Now they're in the river. They're all in biro even. She said if I didn't ... kiss ... she'd ...

> **Cactus** *lets go of two more books, there's a splash. She retains one.* **Dan** *screams.*

Cactus: Oh sorry, they just slipped.

Dolores: Flip sake Cactus.

Dan *succeeds in breaking away from* **Ber,** *he lunges at* **Cactus** *trying to grab the remaining book. In doing so he pulls her to the ground. They roll around fighting like cats and dogs.* **Dan** *is extremely traumatised and viciously pulling* **Cactus***'s hair and clothing.* **Cactus** *lashes back, well able for him.*

Ber: Jesus, Mary and holy Saint Joseph. You're just … an animal, that's what you are.

Cactus: Takes one to know one.

Dolores: Will I go down and try to get them out?

Noel: I would, only I can't swim like.

Ber: I'm telling your father on you. The poor child.

Dolores: Will I Ber?

Ber *goes to where the two are fighting and pulls* **Cactus** *off* **Dan***.*

Ber: Come on love, you'll be alright. We'll get you more books.

Cactus: Dan.

Cactus *runs to the bridge, gets up on the gate and throws the remaining book into the river.* **Dan** *lets out a blood-curling roar, pushes* **Dolores** *out of the way and gets up on the wall. He leans across the capping stone and screams at* **Cactus***.*

Dan: I'm telling on you, I'm telling on you, I'm telling on you.

Cactus: Just shut up, shut up, shut up.

She tries to push him off the wall, he hangs onto the capping stone. With unmerciful strength she pushes the capping stone off the pillar. **Dan** *and the stone disappear behind the wall.*

Langer, you're not telling anyone anything.

There is a thud, then silence. **Dolores** *looks from where* **Dan** *has fallen to* **Ber**.

Dolores: Oh God.

Ber *and* **Noel** *join her, and look over the wall.*
(Music: 'Wanderin' Star' by Lee Marvin.)

Scene Seven

Epilogue. One month later.
Dolores *is returning from swimming, through the corn field.* **Cactus** *is sitting on the gate.*

Cactus: Long time no see. Oh, you're still not talking to me either.

Dolores: I'm not let.

Cactus: God. Do you always do everything you're told?

Cactus *offers her a cigarette.* **Dolores** *declines.*

Dolores: I gave them up, for swimming like. I'm training for the medals.

Cactus: In the river?

Dolores: No, the baths. I'm in a club now. How come you weren't at the ... you know, the funeral?

Cactus: *(Laughs)* They wouldn't let me. Sure everyone's saying I did it on purpose. I suppose you are too.

Dolores: No. I'm saying nothing to no one about it.

Cactus: It's the County Council's fault. That thing was broken for ages. Something was bound to happen.

Dolores: Yeah, I suppose. No, I don't think they own the wall though.

Cactus: Did you end up touching his ... you know what, at all?

Dolores: That's desperate Cactus. How can you say ... that's awful.

Cactus: Only asking, Jesus. Listen, I heard Ber's getting married.

Dolores: Next Saturday, yeah.

Cactus: They're made for each other. Two beauts. And Dan's ma is making her dress.

Dolores: She offered like. Couldn't say no.

Cactus: She'll need yards of stuff, I'd say. Ber must be out to here by now.

Dolores: And ye're moving.

Cactus: Yeah. Limerick. My father got a transfer. At least we'll be in a town though, not like this boring old kip.

There is an awkward silence. **Cactus** *smokes.*

I'll send on my address when I know it.

Dolores: You better not. It's Mammy, she'd have a fit like. I have to go. My tea. It'll be ready.

Cactus: If you gotta go, you gotta go.

Dolores: See you so.

Cactus: See you.

Dolores *walks away.* **Cactus** *shouts after her.*

Cactus: Hey, Dol, Dolores, come here a minute.

Dolores *returns.*

Dolores: What?

Cactus: See you.

They stare at each other.

Music: 'Everything is Beautiful' by Ray Stevens.

The End

Author's Note

One of the most self-defining things you learn as a child is to memorise and write your own address. This is me and I am of this place. This is my place in the world. And while *Danti-Dan* is set at a cross-roads in the middle of nowhere, that nowhere is in Cork.

Corkonians have an innate sense of their County's superiority and the cockiness of a community who decided to build their city on a marsh. A place where the accent reflects the ups and downs of the landscape, the intonation vacillating between panic and coma, where if you dared to have notions of upperosity you'd quickly be brought down to size, where even the river forks when it hits town. But it's far too sophisticated to be dismissed as being merely provincial. The wit can be viciously pass-remarkable and the slang is peppered with come-downs. A friend of our family was asked on her return from holidays what she thought of Canada. 'Not great really like, everyone's going around in shorts.' And so the second largest country in the world was written off purely in sartorial terms. That's the kind of hard to impress place Cork is, one false move and you'll be dismissed as a langer. You daren't show your ignorance about anything, you find out on the sly.

Enough of the travelogue. I just wanted to give some idea of the background that informs the people of this play. While their language and attitudes are necessarily local, their inexperience is universal.

It is deeply flattering to be asked to write a play, particularly if you haven't written one before. I'm forever indebted to Lynne Parker and Siobhán Bourke for their foolhardiness in asking me in the first place and for their continuing support and encouragement. The Rough Magic production was given life by a wonderful, hugely talented cast. I thank them from the bottom of my heart. My regrets to the thirty-odd ladies from

Bandon who walked out of the show in Cork. My guess is that they couldn't hack looking at themselves. Then again a hand shandy isn't everyone's cup of tea.

Gina Moxley
Dublin
August 1998

MRS SWEENEY

Paula Meehan

Rough Magic produced *Mrs Sweeney* at project @ the mint in May 1997 with the following cast and production team:

Thug Emmet Dowling

Thug Barry White

Lil Sweeney Ger Ryan

Mariah Neilí Conroy

Father Tom Tim Ruddy

Sweeney Mick Nolan

Frano Gina Moxley

Oweny Anto Nolan

Jimmy O'Reilly Anto Nolan

Directed by Kathy McArdle

Set & Costume Design by Barbara Bradshaw

Lighting Design by Paul Keogan

Sound Design by Bell Helicopter

Production Manager Stephen McManus

Stage Manager Jennifer Crawford

Produced by Siobhán Bourke

Photo: Mick Nolan as Sweeney © Amelia Stein.

Dramatis Personae:

Lil Sweeney, 42

Sweeney, 44, her husband

Frano, 41, her friend and neighbour since childhood

Mariah, 20, her late daughter's friend

Oweny, 38, Sweeney's friend

Father Tom, 32, Catholic priest

Place: 22 E Maria Goretti mansions

Time: The recent past.
Act 1: End of September
Act 2: Halloween

Act One

The flat. Living room / kitchen which looks as if it has recently been ransacked – drawers, cupboards emptied. Prominent on and over mantelpiece, like a shrine, are photos of **Lil** *and* **Sweeney**'s *daughter Chrissie through all her ages, including large one of her swaddled in bedclothes lying in the armchair, taken shortly before she died. Said armchair, very large, upended, and table. One window broken and curtains gone. Sounds from bedroom of room being thrashed.*

Enter **First young thug** *from bedroom .*

First young thug: C'mon willya. C'mon.

Goes to mantelpiece and sweeps everything off it. Pulls pictures of Chrissie from wall to floor. Picks up trophy and stashes it in his jacket.

Enter **Second young thug** *lugging loot wrapped in curtain.*

Give us a hand with this.

First young thug is now fiddling with old-fashioned radio, finds station. Song is playing low.

Second young thug: Leave it. It's a piece of crap.

First young thug *highers it up. It's Bob Dylan:*

Princes on the steeple and all the pretty people / They're drinkin', thinkin' that they got it made / Exchanging all kinds of precious gifts and things / But you'd better lift your diamond ring, you'd better pawn it babe / You used to be so amused / At Napoleon in rags and the language that he used / Go to him now, he calls you, you can't refuse / When you got nothing, you got

*nothing to lose/ You're invisible now, you got no secrets
to conceal …*

*The music continues at full blast. They gather swag in curtain
between them and leg it. As they pass window outside they crash
into approaching* **Lil** *and knock her to the ground.*
   A few seconds later **Lil**'s *head appears over sill and then her
face at broken window. Scans room. Enters shortly after carrying
plastic bag of messages. Goes to radio and turns it off. Looks into
bedroom. Rights big armchair and sits on edge of it head in
hands.*
   *Noise from outside: pneumatic drill, sirens, evening Angelus
bells, child bawling her heart out, kids at play, a father from a
balcony calling his kids for their tea.*

Sha-ron, Jim-my, Na-tal-ie. Get up here this instant. Now.

Absolute silence for three seconds, then **Lil** *screams.*

Lil: Jesus.

*More silence then ice cream van chimes. She comes to. She
notices rag rug with turd at the centre of it.*

Lil: The idea of it. The idea. Savages.

*She puts small plastic bags on her hands and folds rug up
gingerly and puts it in large plastic bag.*

Lil: A desecration, Chrissie.

*She begins to straighten up room, righting chairs and picking up.
Goes to mantelpiece and retrieves photos of Chrissie. During next
speech she is reassembling shrine, dusting off photos and placing
them in spots they occupied before. She is manically exact about
this.*

Lil: You're better off dead, Chrissie. Ah now don't be
looking at me with your big sad eyes. I don't mean that. I
don't mean that at all. I didn't even get a chance to clock
who they were. They were on top of me before I knew it.

What am I going to do Chrissie? Look at it. Just look at it.
Could be worse. I could've been here.

She finds this hilarious.

Do you hear me Chrissie? I'd've slit them belly to neck and
gutted them. The little shites. And where was your Da?
That's what I'd like to know. Where was he, Chrissie?
Oweny Burke was saying the other night … What was he
saying? That the dead are all around us, looking out for us.
Keeping an eye. You're falling down badly on the job
Chrissie. Or maybe you're doing a grand job. We could've
been murdered alive in our beds.

She goes to window.

Four times. Four times this month Chrissie. Well I'm not
putting glass in it again. They'd rob the eyes from your
head if you didn't blink now and then.

*She fetches a couple of sheets of plywood and hammer, picks sheet
nearest in size to smashed pane of glass, balances plastic milk
crate on chair, climbs up precariously and begins to hammer
wood to window frame.*

And did you see what they took Chrissie? Eh? One radio
alarm clock (*Hammer*) one Magimix blender (*Hammer*) the
remote control to go with the telly they robbed the last time
(*Hammer*) me new coat (*Hammer*) me snaky earrings
(*Hammer*) Sweeney's drill (*Hammer*) Sweeney's leather
jacket (*Hammer*) Sweeney's Trophy, his shaggin trophy with
the golden pigeon on it, Leinster Champion 1989. King of
the Fanciers. Ugly fucking yoke. King of the Avoiders
would be more like. Head in the Sand Award. Eyes closed
and up to the neck in shite award. Creek with no paddle
award. (*Sings:*) 'O where are you now when we need you,
Da da da da da da da dee, Da da da da da da da da da, And
only our livers are free.' (*Hammer*) Not much for their
trouble, hardly worth the effort, Chrissie. Now if they'd any
sense they would have waited until we'd built up a few
more bits and pieces. Left us a couple of months, at least

until we replaced the telly and the vid, maybe a CD player, make it worth their while. Rule number one – don't hit the same flat too often. Flat Breaking for Beginners: wait until the inmates have got over the shock of the last break-in. Just when they're breathing normally again and their hearts have stopped hammering at the slightest noise in the night, and they are lulled completely into a false sense of security – then – strike! Robber's Etiquette: do not shit in the bed, do not smear excrement on the kitchen walls, do not piss in the wardrobe. (*She begins to weep*) Jesus Chrissie. (*Hammers last nail in and closes window. Sudden silence. She climbs down and surveys her work*) They took the curtains. Curious that. What would they get for a set of old curtains and a few nets? Are their minds gone with the drugs? If it *was* the junkies. Was it Chrissie? Old pals of yours up to their junky tricks, eh? What they got here wouldn't fix them up for a day. You'd think they'd go out to Howth or Rathgar or ... Sure they wouldn't even have the energy to get the bus out. This was the work of kids. For the hell of it. On their own people, but! Preying on their own people like animals. No. Animals is too good for them. Vampires. Ha! Blood from stones. Blood from fucking stones.

Lil goes towards and into bedroom as **Mariah**, *dressed as usual to the nines, appears at window, peering in. She raps on pane.*

Mariah: Lil! Lil! Lil Sweeney are you in there?

Lil: (*From bedroom*) Hang on. I'm coming. (*Crosses stage, her arms full of bed linen. Drops it. Opens window*) Mariah. You're not going to believe it. We've been robbed again.

Mariah: Will you listen for a minute, something terrible's after happening.

Lil: Huh, tell me about it.

Mariah: Lookit, I was sent on up ahead. They're on their way up now. It's the pigeons. Well, it's Sweeney, I mean. And the pigeons. The pigeons are done for. Sweeney's okay. Not okay exactly, but not done for. What I mean is ...

Lil: You better come around.

Enter **Mariah**.

Lil: Sit. Take a breath. Now.

Mariah: Me nerves. We found Sweeney ... no, I tell a lie, Father Tom found Sweeney, what with all the blood and feathers ... What happened here?

Lil: Let's get this much straight. Sweeney's alive?

Mariah: Sweeney's game ball. Well. Not game ball exactly. O God Lil he's very shook. Very shook. Father Tom knocked in to me. He found Sweeney at the pramsheds with his pigeons. Well, without his pigeons. What I mean is the pigeons were there, only they weren't if you see what I mean. The loft is totally wrecked. A write-off.

Lil: He'll be sorry he's not dead when I get my hands on him. If he'd of stayed here like he said he would none of this would've happened. We've been robbed. Whoever did it shit on the rug. Their calling card.

Mariah: They're all slaughtered, Lil. All his pigeons. The sight of it. It'd turn your stomach. The blood. The feathers. The guts. A massacre. Here, don't shoot the messenger.

> **Father Tom** *and* **Sweeney**, *bearing a heap of dead pigeons on a board, troop past the window. They enter with the air of solemn procession.*

> *Dusk begins to fall and full night, stars, and lights of other flat blocks should fill the windows by the end of this passage.*

> **Sweeney** *and* **Father Tom** *place the board on the ground and they stand in silence regarding it.*

Lil: (*Eventually*)We've been robbed again Sweeney. How're you Father.

Mariah: Who'd do such a thing?

More silence. **Lil** *is tidying shambles throughout.* **Mariah** *joins in.*

Lil: Who'd beat up old Nedser Casey for his few bob pension? Who'd hang the Doyles' cat from a lamppost until it was dead? And stick darning needles in its eyes? Who'd rape Mary Murtagh's granny?

Mariah: Mary Murtagh's granny? I never heard about that.

Father Tom: A shocking occurrence. Deeply distressing to her family.

Mariah: Will someone cover that up? Me dinner's going to come up.

Father Tom: I'm sorry Lil. I just didn't know what to do with them. Sweeney wouldn't leave the pramsheds without them.

Lil: (*With edge of hysteria*) I'll make a cup of tea. (*She doesn't move*)

Mariah: I'll make it.

Lil: You said you were staying in. If you hadn't of gone out ... What's the use. Sit down for God's sake. (*She guides him to Chrissie's chair where he perches tensely on edge of it*) Will you have a seat Father. And thanks for ...

Father Tom: Do you want me to get the guards, Sweeney? (*No response*) Eh, Lil?

Lil: Don't make me laugh.

Father Tom: I know you've no faith in them Lil, but at the very least it would be on the record. Eh? Sweeney, it might be as well now to eh dispose of the eh remains. Sweeney?

Lil: We can't just shag them down the rubbish chute. And there's no bins until Thursday.

Father Tom: Have you a black plastic bag? Perhaps I could ...?

Lil: Could what Father?

Father Tom: Eh, well, take them off in the van.

Mariah: Bury them. Burn them. Cremate them. Before
they start to smell.

Lil: Will you keep it down. Look at the state he's in. Give
us a hand with these.

Mariah: I'm not touching them. They're filthy anyway.
The smell passing those pramsheds. It's just as well, a
grown man fiddling around with birdseed, morning noon
and night. I don't know how you stick it, Lil.

Lil: To be fair to Sweeney, he kept them birds immaculate.
It was the Taj Mahal of pigeon lofts.

Figure passes by windows.

Lil: Trouble loves company. Here's (*Knock on door*) Frano.

Enter **Frano**. *She takes in scene.* **Sweeney** *is staring off into the
distance, very out of it.*

Lil: You missed all the excitement Frano. We've been
robbed again.

Frano: I know. Of course I heard all belonging to you were
dead Lil Sweeney. There was nothing of *him* left. The lads
up in Becketts have him in the Meath, or stretched out in
the morgue by now. How're you doing, Sweeney? Taking it
bad is he? Here, Sweeney, the lads sent this up. (*Produces
bottle of Jameson from bag*) They're drinking themselves into a
stupor of condolences. My Jimmy's half locked already.
What they're not …

Mariah: Bad news travels fast.

Frano: … going to do when they get their hands on the
perpetrators. They're rounding up the posse. And Oweny
Burke'll be up to you Lil. He said Sweeney and him have a
nixer on for tonight, the old one over the shop wants a
carpet put in. She wants a good puck in the mouth if you

ask me, the wagon. Do you know what she said to me this
morning, 'Your account Mrs. O'Reilly has reached the
maximum credit I allow to customers in this area'. As if
there were any other shaggin' customers, excuse my French
Father. It's like Fort Knox in there. There's more wire than
in the H Blocks. (*Sings:*) 'The fags behind the wire, the
sweets behind the wire.' Little Jason nearly got the hand
taken off himself. (*She's filling cups & mugs with whiskey
throughout and passing them round*) Well here's to ... may
their souls ...

Father Tom: Just a taste for me, Frano, please. I've a, eh,
meeting to attend shortly. Of course I'll see to the eh,
(*Gestures to pigeons*)

Lil: There's a conundrum for you Father Tom. I always
worried about that in school. Like, the Holy Ghost. Do you
remember the picture, Frano, in Miss Shannon's class. Over
the back table. Mary kneeling there and the big dove on the
windowsill with the light coming out of him. I was terrified
of birds for ages after that. You'd look at them twice. I
thought the rays of light were like a kind of special grace,
only they'd make you pregnant. Funny. Haven't thought of
that place in years.

Frano: It was an awful kip.

Father Tom: (*Feeble attempt at a joke*) You're not suggesting
that's a pile of Holy Ghosts on the floor, Lil. Listen, why
don't we just get them wrapped up and I'll come for them
later with the van and eh see to the disposal. I'd seriously
consider the guards for this.

Lil: Sweeney, lookit. What do you want to do with the
pigeons. Jesus Sweeney, are you hearing us at all? (*She goes
to* **Sweeney** *and tries to gently shake him out of it*)

Mariah: Earth calling Sweeney. Come in Sween–

Lil: Will you ever leave him?

Father Tom: ... best leave him Mariah. The shock has
him. It'll pass after a good night's sleep.

Frano: The burglary and then the massacre. It's a shocking thing alright.

Lil: We've been robbed Sweeney.

Father Tom: I don't think he's taking anything in.

Lil: He lived for them birds Father Tom. As Chrissie was fading away there in that very chair in front of our eyes with the full blown Aids, he nearly moved in with them. It got so as you wouldn't see him from one end of the day to the other. He could never stand suffering, anything like that.

Frano: God rest her soul.

Lil: I'll have to find something to wrap them in. A sheet. I've an old sheet somewhere in here. (*Rummaging in cupboard*) It's not here. They wouldn't of taken an old sheet?

Frano: (*Topping up cups and mugs*) It's the least you could do for them.

Father Tom: Was there much taken, Lil?

Mariah: (*On the verge of exploding with laughter*) You'd have to see the funny side. The funeral cortege is now leaving Maria Goretti Mansions, winding its way slowly past the telegraph wires they loved so well. A hush has fallen over the Mansions as neighbours and friends pay their last respects. Pigeon fanciers from all parts of Ireland have flocked to say a fond farewell, the guard of honour holding aloft their trophies. I'm sorry Lil. I can't resist it.

Lil: (*Giving up search for sheet*) Stuff you'd sell quick. A solid gold pair of earrings, Sweeney's leather jacket – Sweeney, your good jacket's gone – Electric gear. They didn't take me pictures thank God.

Frano: Stick them in a sack.

Lil: (*Poking at heap of pigeons with tongs*) They're Red Chequers, and look, the Grizzle. That one, he's Theobald Wolfe Tone, there's James Connolly (**Mariah** *sniggers*) well

he always called them after the great patriots. Brian Boru
there, he was new. A Blue Barred. He'd great hopes for
him. And James Clarence Mangan …

Mariah: He wasn't a patriot, he was a poet. And a junky.
We did him in school. '*Tick-tick, tick-tick – not a sound save
Time's, / And the wind-gust as it drives the rain – / Tortured
torturer of reluctant rhymes, / Go to bed, and rest thine aching
brain! / Sleep no more … sleep the dupe …*' No. That's not it.
Phit! Gone! I used know the whole thing off by heart.

Lil: Well then, Michael Davitt, or one of them. What does
it matter? They must of stabbed them. Look. Do you see
the slits? Will you listen to me – Hercule Poirrot. Here
Frano. You're not squeamish. Give us a hand. Me last
black bag.

They pack pigeons into plastic bag.

Mariah: Into thy hands O Lord I commend …

Father Tom: I'll have to be off … I'll be back for the …
eh..

Lil: They're not going anywhere anyway. Their flying days
are done. Father, could you drop this down the chute for
me. (*Giving him rubbish bag with rug in it*) On your way past.
I'd be grateful.

Father Tom: Maybe it would be an idea to call a special
meeting of the Development Group. Or the Drugs Group.
See what could be done and …

Frano: Another meeting! This wasn't the junkies. This was
the kids from the new flats. They're on a rampage.

Mariah: Lookit. There's some fellahs around here'd like
nothing better than to tool up and strut around these flats
persecuting people. Look at the last time. We ended up
with the pushers *and* the shagging vigilantes who went
around beating up the poor junkies. The fellah I was with
got the shite beaten out of him for smoking a joint at the
end of the soccer pitch. You couldn't get into the flats some

nights without having to explain yourself to any Tom Dick or Harry who called himself Mr Neighbourhood Watch. The pushers just kept a low profile until the hards went back to the bars, or to beating their own wives at night.

Mariah *stares at* **Frano** *who won't meet her look.*

Father Tom: It's a community issue and we should try to tackle it together as a community –

Frano: Mariah means no disrespect Father. She grew up with the nuns …

MARIAH: (*Angry*) Mariah means …

Lil: Okay Mariah, keep it down. You're agitating Sweeney.

Father Tom: I eh better be off, ladies. Listen, I'd get him to bed if I was you, Lil. I don't like the look of him. And don't worry about the … the … remains. God Bless now.

Exit **Father Tom.** *The women stiffen slightly to attention, wave as* **Father Tom** *passes by windows.*

Mariah: Does she take sugar!? Mariah means no disrespect Father. Nhyeh, nhyeh, hijnnhyeh, nhyeh. Lickarse.

Frano: What a waste!

Mariah: You're welcome to him. Creep.

Lil *goes to* **Sweeney.**

Lil: Sweeney, he's gone. Father Tom is gone now. Do you want a drop of whiskey? No? Here sit in there and take it easy. (*Settling him further into chair*)

Frano: You shouldn't have got so het up with him Mariah. Didn't you put in for that job to run the women's project? I bet you anything he'll be on the interviewing committee. You'll blow it if you don't watch your tongue.

Mariah: Sure amn't I a model for it? And I did me interview last week. And did very well too, I'd say.

Lil: I wouldn't put it past them to bring in an outsider. All that funny money coming into the flats and the only local getting paid is Rose Doyle for cleaning the community centre two mornings a week.

Mariah: Where do you want these Lil? (*Armload of cloths*)

Lil: The basket in the bedroom. Thanks Mariah. I'll have to wash everything. I can smell them off everything. (*She picks up ornament, smells it, puts it in place. Smells her hands*)

Mariah: Didn't Father Tom encourage me to apply. And asked me all the right questions. He told me after that I 'shined'. That was the word he used – 'shined'. Though you wouldn't know. Ten to one, it'll go to a plainsclothes nun. He told fat arse Moran she did very well too. She couldn't organise a piss-up in a brewery. If, if, if brains were chocolate she wouldn't have the makings of two Smarties.

Lil: It looks good on paper, interviewing locals. That's how they do it. Just don't go getting your hopes up. Frano would you ever gather those papers up? I'm going to dump them. Sweeney do you want to keep any of these? Sweeney? (*No response. To* **Frano**) You can leave any British Fanciers you come across on the side. Dump the rest.

Mariah: Givvus a fillyup there. (*Sings:*) '*In Glendalough there lived an oul saint / Renowned for his learning and piety / His manners exceedingly quaint / He fucked boy and girl with propriety.*

Lil: Do you think you'd get the shift out of him? Father Tom?

Frano: Do you fancy your own chances?

Mariah: He gives me the willies. He's always eyeing me tits when he thinks I'm not noticing.

Lil: They're all at it. Holy families everywhere. What can you expect? You send these boy priests off and they come back up to their eyes in Christ the Liberator and the next you know they're crawling all over the flats finding us every bit as exotic as the Ballubas. (*Drinks*) That tastes like more. I should put Sweeney to the *leaba*. Go on in Sweeney. The room's in bits but at least this time they didn't shite in the bed.

Enter **Father Tom.**

Father Tom: The van it seems was borrowed. I'll try and get up later. I'll have a word anyway with the Garda Community Liaison chap. Rogers. He's not a bad old skin.

He exits.

Lil: (*After him*) It's a waste of time. For all the good …

Mariah: Big deal in Dodge City. Givus another drop of that. You too Lil. Look at the face on Sweeney.

Lil: Sweeney. Sweeney. Would you not go in, love? I'm going to have to fumigate this place. Scrub it from top to bottom. I can feel them off everything.

Mariah: There's not a drop left. Jesus, I'm into the scabby leg phase now. Come on and we'll all go out.

Lil: Yous go on. I'll have to sort out a few things. I don't feel very sociable, but I can't believe we're after drinking a bottle of whiskey. Look at the state of him. Do you think he's with us at all?

Frano: Was he ever?

Mariah: Sure you'd not notice the difference. You could hardly get a peep out of him at the best of times. Words in edgewise, edgeways? (*Hiccup*) was never a problem with Sweeney.

Frano: He lived for them pigeons.

Lil: You could carve that in stone. It's very handy for him all the same. Sweeney, go on in to bed and get your head down.

Mariah: Come on and we'll get a drink.

Lil: Yous go on. I haven't the heart.

Cronies leave. Shortly after, they pass by window. **Mariah** *mimes they'll be back.*

Lil: You and me babe. (*Circles* **Sweeney**, *scrutinising him*) Creature. Creature. You poor demented creature. What'll we do with you? Should I get the Doctor? Sweeney are you hearing me? (*Begins to put up sheets over windows, again balanced on rickety box on chair. Wobbles*) Whoops. Nearly went that time, Sweeney. I shouldn't of drank that whiskey. Listen. You can start over, Sweeney. Go down to Puck O Malley first thing in the morning. You were saying he had some real beauts. Some Mealys. And maybe the Irish Homing Union would help, love. We'll get on to them. Is the bird market on this Sunday? Maybe there's someone selling up? Look on the bright side. Sorry Sweeney. I'm not going to have enough in these. Let's see. The bedspread'd be too big. The green tablecloth? No, it'd be a foot short at least. I wonder now … (*Climbs down, goes to cupboard, Takes out Starry Plough*) The very thing! (*Up and fixes it in place. Down and admires work*) Isn't that just gorgeous. I knew it'd come in useful sometime. I love that flag. Sweeney. Sweeney. Do you read me Sweeney? (*Shouts*) Ah, for Jaysus sake Sweeney will you answer me. (*Silence. She walks around the room tidying away cups and mugs*) You're as bad as a holy picture. You're like a sacred bleeding heart with your blue eye on me. Are you putting this on, Sweeney? Look love, I'm sorry about the birds. If I could bring them back I would, but fuck it, it's not my fault, do ya hear me, Sweeney? (**Sweeney** *begins to make jerky movements and tremble*) Will I get you the Doctor love? What about a bath? Hmm. That'd be good. (*Trying to humour him*) The water's on. I'll run you a nice bath. With bubbles. You'll be a new man. You won't know yourself. (*Silence*) Listen fuckface you're not the only one is suffering. And it'll be me has to put Humpty Dumpty together again. Come on. I'll have to get that muck off you. Okay. Okay. (*She goes to sink and fills bucket.* **Sweeney** *is shaking violently*) There, there, you poor creature. Hush, hush, hush. Shush. Now. There. (*Begins to sponge him down gently. Croons what emerges as song*)

> *I'll have stockings of silk,*
> *Shoes of fine green leather,*
> *Combs to buckle my hair*
> *And a ring for every finger.*
>
> *Feather beds are soft,*
> *Painted rooms are bonny;*
> *But I'd leave them all*
> *To go with my love Johnny.*

Fades back to croon, rocking him and loosening his clothes. She has his trust and she takes his shirt off. Examines it.

Lil: For the bin, I'd say.

Rap on window. Silence. Rap on window.

That's Oweny Burke's knock. (*Deciding*) He knows we're in. (*Loud*) Is that you Oweny? Be with you in a tick. (*Soft*) It's Mister Mouth Almighty. You better deal with him. I'm in no humour. (*She lets* **Oweny** *in*)

Oweny Burke *is constantly in motion, curious. He moves about picking things up, fiddling with things and reading things, packages, the underside of ornaments, bills, anything lying around. You get the feeling he'd happily root in the drawers if he was on his own.*

Lil: You probably heard the ins and outs. Do you have any word on who did it?

Oweny: Kids from the new flats. No bout adoubt it. Where is he? Sweeney! You bollix! Tarzan himself what. Are you fit? The old one is up to ninety. Terrible business about the birds. Terrible. She's threatening to sue us. That's a good one. Anyway if we don't put the carpet in tonight me life is not worth living. I drank the money she gave us last week and I couldn't get the solution. Some little fucker nicked the half a tin I'd left up in me Ma's house. Sweeney's bad is he? Anyway me old pal I've appropriated the ammunition from the quartermaster so to speak and we're game ball now.

Together.

Lil: He's not going anywhere. No. Oweny. N. O.

Oweny: Just what he needs to take his mind off his troubles. We'll be in and out like a light. She has the room bare. We don't have to lift a thing. C'mon partner.

Lil: He's helping me put this place back together and that's a fact. Partners me arse.

Lil *empties bucket and continues sorting things while* **Oweny** *prowls about fiddling.*

Oweny: We'll get the news. (*Looking around for TV*) Where's it gone. Sorry. I forgot. Sure yous're better off. I was reading in this article where they're beaming in sublimnial messages from outer space through the TV stations. Wave particles. And they can't be detected! That's the worst part. See you can trace sublimnial messages say from advertisers – EAT BURGERS, BUY MORE – but these boys have it beat. They beam waves directly into the reptilian part of the brain where our most ancient and primitive instincts are stored. Rape. Yes. Rape, and child abuse and murder and, you name it. Notice how tense things are in the world, right now? Notice how on edge everyone is? Huh? Now do you remember before TV came. Go on. When you were a boy. A callow youth Sweeney. And even after. Because it was a while before these boys cottoned on to the potential. That's right! So Mrs Lavin is sitting there knitting, night after night zzhat into her reptilian and then one day she picks up the hatchet and skulls Bartie. Just like that. There's this American Professor has proof only the C.I.A. are onto him and have him under

house arrest. Of course they could lock him up in the
nuthouse. Who'd believe him? Or liquidise him to stop him
encouraging other nuts getting on the bandwagon. But.
And it's a big but ...

Lil: (*Getting a word in edgewise*) Oweny, you're doing me
head in. Do you want tea? Did you hear of anyone selling
stuff around the flats today?

Oweny: Nah. And also no. To the former inquiry. I'm all
tea-ed out. Of course the tea is not what it used to be. Do
you know what I'm going to tell you?

Lil: No Oweny, I don't know what you're going to tell me.

Oweny: Your average cup of tea nowadays is a chemical
timebomb. Amn't I right, Sweeney? It's the systemic
pesticides they use. They don't spray them on. They water
them in, put them straight into the ground and the tea bush
soaks the whole caboodle up. Any bugs or flies or bacterias
come along and suck at the bush, that's the end of them.
Now. Think of the implications for us. How many cups a
day do you drink? Let's see. Three at breakfast, four or five
by lunchtime, another four at least over lunch or your
dinner, whatever you call it, now *I've* always called it
dinner, that's nine at least and it's only two in the
afternoon. You add them up. What you're drinking, what
we're all drinking day in day out, is nothing more nor
nothing less than cancer soup. Highly toxic. Especially to
the pancreas and the kidneys. It also makes your tits droop.
It's a fact. Always did, even before the systemics. (**Lil**
groans) I was reading the other day where no woman is
satisfied with the size of her bust. Them with the big ones
get bits cut off; them with flat chests get the implants. O it's
very big business in the States. Half the women over there,
that's 50%, who are over forty years of age are only 75%
their original selves. Bits of bone out here (*Nose and cheeks*) a
silicone job here (*Breasts*) hip job, a few slash and tucks
(*Neck and belly*). It all adds up. The men are as bad. Look at
that pop star, the black fellow who turned himself into a
white man. I'd say he's only about 10% himself. Sure even

you are not the person you were seven years ago. Every
seven years the human organism has renewed itself so
completely that very few of the original molecules remain.
Curiously enough in astrology they say that every seven
years with Saturn back in the area it was in when you were
born you can expect huge change. Them astrologers knew a
thing or two, Sweeney. I can tell you that for nothing. I got
this great book at the Hill last week. *Ancient Wisdoms and
Interpersonal Growth*. By a fellow called Bannor. No.
Bingham. No. No. Flagstaff. That was it. He has this theory
you see ...

Lil: I bet he has, Oweny. For the love and honour of
Jaysus will you put an a zip on it for a minute. Me head is
wrecked. (*Deep breath*) Sweeney has not uttered one single
solitary word since he discovered his murdered pigeons.
Not only that but he's acting very peculiar. If I was not his
devoted and loyal wife I would say he has flipped his lid.
But I'll not say it. I'll say he's in a state of shock and
everything in the garden will be rosy in the morning after a
good night's sleep.

Oweny: Well, excuse me for breathing. I was just about to
tell you something that may be very useful for you Sweeney
in your present state. He's on another planet Lil. In the
chapter called Bereavement or Life in the Bardos, this
fellow Bannor, no, Flagstaff, claims that to get over a
sudden and especially a violent death, you must actively
help the dead find their way out of this world. Right.
Instead of lying back and bawling your eyes out you get
involved. Because the poor dead fuckers don't realise
they're dead. It all happened so fast like. That's why you
have ghosts. Whereas if you prepare for your death every
minute you're alive – his motto is Learn To Die A Little
Every Day – when the big number is up, it's a walkover. No
problem. Now ... where was I. What am I telling you this
for? O yea. Sweeney. Now admittedly this guy doesn't say
anything about pigeons, or any other birds or animals for
that matter, but he gives this old Tibetan chant. A sutra as

they're known. You chant it every day for as long as it takes
to release the dead from you.

Lil: Oh brilliant. That's what I love about you Oweny
Burke. You're a great listener. An ear for the troubled,
friend of the afflicted. Why, you can come down Oweny
with your sutures and your witchdoctor kit and chant the
bejaysus sense back into him.

Oweny: He hasn't been the same since Chrissie died. It
was watching her die like that. Sure she was like a little
pigeon herself towards the end. He couldn't handle it at all.
Amn't I right Sweeney?

Lil: (*Going to photo of Chrissie*) Except he didn't. Watch her
die I mean. He was up and out to those shaggin' pigeons
first thing every morning. It was like she wasn't there,
Oweny. Like she was invisible. He wouldn't even talk
about it. Would you Sweeney? You'd come in and throw
your jacket up on that hook and scuttle into the bedroom.
Sure he had his dinner and all in there. She must have been
very hurt. She never said. (*Silence*) She never said a word
against you. She'd just follow you with her big eyes. She'd
be looking at that door for hours like she was willing it to
open.

Oweny: Isn't that what I'm saying.

Lil: What?

Oweny: You know. Eh. Eh? What *was* I saying Lil?

Lil: Six months it took her. From the moment she walked
in this room. I was watching Eastenders with me feet up.
I'd just scrubbed down the balcony and the hall, I'd the
front door open to air the place, a lovely warm spring day. I
remember it because it was the first good day we'd had in
months. Valentine's Day. The fourteenth of February. She
was there in front of me like an apparition. 'Ma', she said,
'I'm dyin'. As simple as that. I thought it was a dream. Six
months it took her to die. God, Oweny, it's hard to believe
she's more than a year dead. Where did it go?

Oweny: Was it six calendar months or six periods of 28 days? Twenty-four weeks in other words? Of course the lunar would be more natural. We should be keeping time by the moon. Our bodies are even unbeknownst to us in tune with the moon. Lookit women. Menstruation! Ha! I was just reading about this tribe of Indians, oh Hopis, I think, or was it the Navahos? Anyway the women all went off on their own to little huts and just sat down on the moss till it was all over. Every month off they went. On their moon. That's what they call it. I am on my moon, you'd say. Begging your pardon Lil. She is on her moon. See? Well do you see? No stress. No PMTs. Women are timebombs. Explosive. They can get away with murder. Murder. Sorry sir I had the curse. It wasn't me who stuck the knife in his heart officer. It was me hormones. No officer I can't explain what I'm doing with me fellah's mickey in me hand and it dripping blood all over the gaff, I've me monthlies. Yis get away with murder. Yis do, Lil.

Lil: We'd maybe get a grant to convert the pramsheds Oweny. Pack them up with moss. That'd be marvellous. We'll stick all the bleeding women in the flats in them. Throw the keys away. You should bring that one up at the next meeting. Through the chair. You're some tulip. Would you ever cop on to yourself.

Oweny: Ah now Lil, no offence meant.

Lil: (*Going back to photograph of Chrissie*) Six months. We buried her on the 16th of August. And where was he? Where were you Sweeney? Your own daughter's funeral and you were in the fucking pramsheds with your fucking pigeons. All that summer and Chrissie dying there in that chair before me eyes. The only one to darken the door was Mariah. She sat with Chrissie day after day. I have to hand it to her. It was a beautiful summer. The best we had in years. Do you know Oweny hardly a week goes by but we're burying some young one or young fellah from the flats.

Lil: Shush. What's that? Listen?

Scuffles outside windows. Large shadows thrown on sheets.
Mutters. Loud crash of breaking glass. Shouts:

Leg it!

Noise of three sets of running feet down stairs. Shouts,
indistinguishable. Simultaneously:

Lil: Jesus Christ. Me heart!

Oweny: What the ...

Lil: O me heart. I'll get those little ... (*Runs out*)

Oweny: Come back here. Come back. They'll be well
gone.

Lil: (*From the balcony*) Yis whore's melts. I'm on to yis. I'll
have the Shinners after yis. A few bullets in your poxy
kneecaps, we'll see who's the brave men then. Yis're the
hards alright.

Meanwhile, **Oweny** *has gone to window, pulls back sheet*
revealing **Lil**. **Sweeney** *agitated at commotion. Takes up*
boxer's stance and makes swings at the air. He manages to pull
sheets and Starry Plough completely off window. Goes for
Oweny *and tries to land a punch on him.*

Oweny: Ah here Sweeney. Get a hold of yourself. Do you
not know me man. It's me. Oweny Burke. Now Sweeney.
Hang on a tick.

Lil *returns. Pandemonium reigns.* **Oweny** *finally gets*
Sweeney *in flying tackle to the floor and wrestles him into*
submission.

Oweny: He's worn himself out Lil. Let's get him to bed.
Sleep knits up the unravelled jumper of care as the bard
said.

Lil *&* **Oweny** *carry* **Sweeney** *off to bedroom.* **Lil** *emerges*
seconds later. Over her shoulder ...

Lil: I wouldn't even attempt to put those pyjamas on him.
Just get him under the covers. I'm going to have to get the
Doctor.

*She gets pieces of hardboard and cardboard from hall, hammer
and nails and goes to window. Measures until she finds a piece of
hardboard that fits.*

Lil: Fucking lovely behaviour. The whole place is gone to
the dogs. And everyone in it is cracked, or half-cracked or
doing a very good impersonation of a nut. It's no life,
Oweny. I should just get the whole she-bang cemented
over.

Oweny *comes out of bedroom, closing door behind him.*

Oweny: He's asleep. At least I think he's asleep. His eyes
are closed in any case. That was some performance, what?
He's not himself and that's for sure. I've never come across
the like. Although there was a programme on demonic
possession on Channel Four the other night, in the
Carríbbean, or the Carribbéan, I'm never sure which it is.
How do you say it?

Lil: How do I say what?

Oweny: Do you say Carríbbean or Carribbéan? Anyway
this fellow starts acting strange, eating dirt and curling up in
a ball on the floor of the hut, gibbering out of him in a
foreign language. It turns out not to be so strange after all.
He's only talking in classical Greek. Would you believe
that? Fellow's never been to school, he's a kind of slave on
the sugar plantation and there he is speaking fluent classical
Greek.

Lil: And what about me, Oweny. I'm a bit shocked myself.

Oweny: There's this nurse at the hospital is Greek and
recognises it. Now there are two theories as to what's going
on.

Lil: Two? Only two?

Oweny: One, he's a reincarnation of Aristotle, you see he was reciting whole chunks of a book this ancient Greek guy wrote or he wa –

Lil: Oweny. Do us a favour. Would you? Go out and see if you can get the Doctor to come down. He'll probably not come till the morning, but would you ring him? His number's up beside the phone in Becketts. It says Doctor Joyce in black marker round eye level.

Oweny: Your eye level is of course a different kettle of fish to my eye level. That's a curious thing …

Lil: Just explain the situation. No. On second thoughts just say Sweeney is taken very bad. He'll not come though, I bet. They won't come into the flats after dark. You could be bleeding to death here. Do that for us, would you?

Oweny: Leave it to me. I'll be eh discrete. I'll have to go over now and face this old one. I'll get one of the lads down in Becketts to come along. I better go to the pub first so. I know. I'll ring her from there when I'm ringing old Joyce. Right. No sooner said than done. (*Exits. Passes window. Salutes*)

Lil: (*Goes to bedroom door, opens it softly, listens*) He's deep. (*Closes it*) I'll risk the hammer. I'm not leaving that gaping all night. (*Begins to hammer board in place as before. After about five hammer strokes there's a banging on the ceiling above*) Bless you too. (*She resumes hammering. Louder banging on ceiling*)

Mrs Earwig Mack: Shut the fuck racket up!

Lil: (*Shouts*) Sorry. Won't be a minute now. (*Softly*) You miserable wagon. You've probably had your ear glued to the floor all night, Mrs Earwig Mack. (*Hammer strokes*)

Mrs Earwig Mack: (*Banging on floor again*) I'm warning you Lil Sweeney. Shut the fuck racket up. Have a bit of consideration.

Lil: Yeah. Yeah. Yeah. Yeah. You old termagant. Nobody's putting your windows in, Mrs High and Bleeding

Mighty with your glass shagging swans in the window and your twitching shagging nets. (*Rising*) Mrs Butter Wouldn't Melt with your fitted shagging kitchen, which Mrs Crucifix Up Your Arsehole, you had put in when my Chrissie was dying. No consideration then with the noise going through Chrissie's brain. O yes. Drills, and hammers. Hammers? Lump hammers! Kango hammers! Pneumatic drills. 'My Joey is having a kitchen put in for me. My Joey is having the bedroom carpeted. My Joey is sending me off to Costa Del Poxo for a week.' My Joey (*Shouts*) and *you* know bloody well where he gets his money. (*Hammers last few nails in*)

Mrs Earwig Mack *bangs on ceiling again.* Silence. **Lil** *surveys her work, anger spent.*

Lil: (*Goes to photos on mantelpiece*) You're as well out of it, Chrissie. No. I don't mean that. I'm glad you came back. Even to die. I'd've lost my reason if you'd died in some London hospital on your own. Or at the side of the street in a cardboard box like you see on the telly. How could I live with that? O me heart. I think there's a bruise inside from it jumping. At the end you were just a handful. Funny word. Your Granny used say that. 'Your Chrissie is a right handful.' Thank God she didn't live to see it. I thought I could lift you in the palm of me hand. I'd be trying to get a smile out of you. You'd a beautiful smile. You got that from Sweeney alright. He was a terrible serious youngfellah with his pigeons and his bicycle and his union meetings. He was going to change the world; always on about the Russians. I used call him Ivan the Terrible. I was mad about him. I must of needed me head examined. From the minute I met him. Your Granda sent me down to him with a thing he'd cut out of the paper 'Carrier Pigeons To Win Cold War'. I remember it as clear as day. He was ringing the young pigeons. He was all excited. Some new Belgian wonderbird he'd got to breed. And these were the first brood, all strong and healthy. He was so gentle with them. That's what did it. Watching his hands stroking the birds. I wonder now ... And then the big smile he gave me. 'I'll have him,' I said to myself, 'a man like him will never do you any harm.' There's harm and there's harm, Christ knows.

> **Frano** *at window tapping with fingernails, trying to attract her attention but not wanting to make any noise, looking down balcony in highly nervous state.* **Lil** *sees her. Motions her to door.*

Frano: Quick Lil. He'll be up after me. (*Drags* **Lil** *over beneath window*) O Jesus keep down. We should have turned off the light. Don't move Lil. (**Lil** *makes a dash for it and knocks off light. Crawls back to spot below window*) I swear he'll murder me if he gets his hands on me. Shush, listen. Do you hear it. (*Faint, in distance, noise of house been broken up. A man screaming indistinctly*) He's roaring drunk, Lil. He's like a mad bull.

Lil: This is ridiculous. (*Goes to move, gets sheets and flag*) I'll stick these back up.

Frano: Please Lil. I beg you. Don't give us away. There he is now. Do you hear him.

Lil: OK, OK. Relax. (*She tucks flag around* **Frano**'*s body*) Listen to me: you'll be alright. He's not going to lay another finger on you.

Frano: (*Panicky*) O Mother of Jaysus, there he is. (**Lil** *covers* **Frano**'*s mouth. Shadow looms into room. Mr O: visible, stupid drunk, swaying and trying to get a good view into the room*)

Mr O: A man's got some rights around here. Are you there Lil Sweeney? Where's my wife? Where's Fran O'Reilly? Fucking Frankenstein. I want her. Yis are all the same. Cunts. Lil Sweeney! Lil Sweeney! I told her. I warned her. There's only so much a man can take. No respect. The poxy cunt has no respect.

Mrs Earwig Mack: Shut the fuck racket up.

Mr O: (*Pugilist stance towards above*) Say that to me face. Come on down. Come on down. I'm ready for you.

Coward. You're yellow. Say it to me face. Nobody says a word to Jimmy O'Reilly. (*Back to window. Peers in. Crafty*) Ah, Lil, me old flower. I just want a word. Everything's cool. Everything's A 1 with Jimmy O'Reilly. A 1. No problem. I just want a word. She wouldn't listen. I swear. I swear on the kids' life. She wouldn't listen to me. I told her. I says have a bit of respect. (*Roars*) Yis are all cunts. (*Loses momentum. Shambles off*) Cunts! (*Fading*) Cunts! (*Fading*) Cunts!

Silence. **Lil** *crawls to mantelpiece and back with cigarettes. Lights two. Gives one to* **Frano**. *Silence. They smoke.*

Lil: You're safe now I'd say. He'll not be back.

Frano: He has me demented. I'll have to go down. The kids are in bits.

Lil: The kids know well to stay out of his way. He'll crash out soon. You'll only set him off again if he sees you.

Frano: He gets a bee in his bonnet and there's no reasoning with him. Respect is the latest. It was Manners last week. Before that it was Cop On. No Cop On! You – Have – No – Cop – On. He went straight into Becketts from the dole. When I showed up with Mariah he was all sweetness and light. Drinks all round. Mr Bleeding Big. He turned, just like that. 'What kind of wife would turn up to the pub in a pair of old jeans,' he asked Mariah. Showed a lack of respect. No Respect. Of course Mariah is done up to the nines. It was dig, dig, needle, needle.

Lil: You should have walked away from it.

Frano: You're beginning to sound like the Personal Development course. I got me seed breed and generation thrun in me face. 'You've let your self go.' Do you know that, Lil? Ha. I've let meself go! Mariah put her foot in it then. Asked him how he liked his new job with the Chippendales, he must have terrible trouble beating off the women, she could see how they'd be mad for him, why she could hardly resist such charm herself, such sensitivity. I had to laugh. That went down a bomb I can tell you. Un-fucking-believable.

They laugh.

Frano: It's not funny.

They laugh again.

Lil: He's not going to change, you know.

Frano: I should have got out years ago. Something always came up. I'd say I'll wait till after Jason's communion, or till Sandra's finished the primary. Then it was me Da sick, and then I didn't want to leave me Ma on her own. I'm sorry I didn't do it. I saved up nearly two hundred pounds once in the Credit Union. Me Fuck-You-Money I called it. For the great escape. I was going to write 'No Frances. No Fucking Frances' on the mirror in lipstick. Like in the films. Do you remember the time he put in the butcher's window? The cops found him with his pockets stuffed with meat and a big sack of frozen chickens. A string of sausages round his neck like a scarf. He took out a black pudding and said to the cop 'Reach for them clouds pardner. Prepare to meet your maker.' The cops had a great laugh. The Fuck-You-Money got him out of it.

Lil: You never told me that one.

Frano: What can you do? You'd have to laugh.

Lil: Will we risk the sheets?

They put sheets back up between them. Knock on door. **Frano** *panics.*

Lil: It's alright. That's Mariah's knock.

Frano: She was milling into young Flynn when I left. Wrapped around him she was.

Lil: You let her in, I'll check on Sweeney.

Frano *lets* **Mariah** *in.* **Lil** *goes into bedroom.* **Mariah** *is well on and carries a six-pack.*

Mariah: I'd of worn black if I'd known you were in mourning. Get a life, baby! Tempus Fugent! Where's the opener? Where does she keep the opener? You missed the crack in Becketts. It was nine hundred and ninety nine point nine percent brilliant. Oh yay. There was killing outside. Franco Nugent's bit on the side versus Franco Nugent's regular mot. Anyway the regular mot was in the wrong place at the wrong time, or maybe the bit on the side was in the wrong place at the wrong time, though mind you it's only ever the bit on the side he drinks with most nights in Becketts. The regular mot usually flutters around him up in The Elephants, Friday nights and Saturday nights. Only on Friday and Saturday nights, get this, cos they're saving up to get married. Well the regular mot's Da dropped dead this morning. He's just about to get on the number thirty nine and bang. The heart just blew. She comes up looking for Franco babee. His little brother Benito tells her where he is. Franco manages beautifully for a few hours – both the women skulling pints at different ends of the bar. Until time now gentlemen please, and the piece on the side wants the ride at the back of the chipper and the regular mot wants to mourn her dearly departed father in the arms of her true love. A right pair of scaldy arses when they got going. There you are Lil. Here. Get that in to you. (**Lil** *slumps in chair*) You're wrecked. (*Silence.* **Mariah** *begins to roll joint*)

Sounds of various groups coming home from pub. Odd scream. Inexplicable crash. Crying woman. Someone staggers past window giving a passionate if murderous rendition of 'Dublin in the Rare Old Times'. They listen.

I courted Peggy Duignam
As Dublin as can be
A rogue and Child of Mary
From the rebel Liberties
I lost her to a student chap
With skin as black as coal

When he took her off to Birmingham
He took away my soul

Ring a ring a rosy
As the light declines

Fading off ...

Frano: Peadser had a beautiful voice in his day it has to be said.

Lil: I'll have to take your word for it.

Mariah: Was there a pissup here earlier? (**Frano** *and* **Lil** *look at her*) Was I at it? Did I enjoy myself?

The three women crack up laughing. Long and sustained howl is heard from outside.

Lil: It's nearly a full moon. It explains a lot.

Mariah: I used to be a werewolf but I'm alright noo-o-o-o-w!

Long and sustained howl again.

Frano: That'd give me the creeps. It makes me skin crawl.

Mariah: It's only some lunatic practising for the song contest. Wry – O – Muni Tri Pwah. Kagorny-Karabakh Sex Pwah. Maria Goretti Mansions Deh Pwah. Come in Outer Mongolia, may we have the results of the Mongolian jury. Dah Dee Dum Gurn Da Dum Dum. Baby, baby baby, baby.

Frano: What's that?

Mariah: The Irish entry this year. Change Me Nappy Like Me Mammy Used To Do.

Frano: No. Hang on. I can hear something.

Scrabble. Scrabble. Then noise of **Sweeney** *knocking into things.*

Lil: It's Sweeney. Take it easy now. Not a word. God knows what form he's in. Right? Yous are not to make a laugh out of him. (**Mariah** *mimes zipping her lips*)

> **Lil** *goes to bedroom door. Opens it.* **Sweeney** *comes in. He's extremely agitated and moves about the room as if he's in another dimension. Women freeze and watch intently as he moves about the place, twitching occasionally. They tense noticeably when he comes near them.* **Frano** *goes to speak.* **Lil** *silences her with a finger to her lips.* **Lil** *begins to gently shush him in the direction of the bedroom and he eventually goes in. They are silent but intermittent scrabbling from bedroom is heard for next few minutes.*

Mariah: (*Eventually*) Nice weather for this time of year.

Frano: Did I see what I just saw or am I after hallucinating?

Lil: (*Desperately*) Typical. It's just fucking typical. Just when you need a bit of support. Sweet Divine Jesus.

Mariah: Holy Cow Batman. You have your hands full. I'm going off.

Frano: Would he be putting it on, Lil?

Lil: What am I going to do with him?

Frano: He could turn on you. He might be dangerous.

> **Lil** *gives her withering look. Silence.*

Lil: It's suspiciously quiet in there. It might have been a bad dream though he's been acting strange since the massacre. Am I acting strange?

Frano: A good night's sleep.

Lil: I was hoping Doctor Joyce would … Oweny Burke was going to … Jesus what'll I do?

Mariah: I'd keep me clothes on going to bed if I was you. (*Snigger*)

Frano: I better get back.

Mariah: Have another bottle for God's sake. Fuck Jimmy. If he was mine I'd have him put down. Put him out of his misery. Humane killing I think they call it.

Frano: I'll just have the one, then.

Lil: The three most told lies in Dublin: I'll just have the one; me mammy's not in; I'll only put it in a little bit.

Mariah: There's this fellah going round the flats. He calls in to see Frano there. 'I'm doing a survey to ascertain decision-making patterns in Irish households,' says he. 'Well. My husband Jimmy makes all the important decisions, and I make all the rest.' 'O' says your man, 'how's that?' 'I decide how we spend the dole. So much for food, so much for rent, so much for the E.S.B. Whether we have fried mince for dinner, mince stew, hamburgers, boiled mince, roast mince, grilled mince. Where the kids go to school. What colour wallpaper we'll have in the living room. What time the kids go to bed. Whether the doctor should be got if one of the kids are sick.' 'And tell me madam, what decisions does your husband make?' says your man. 'O, you know. The big ones. Who should run for president, what should be done about the North, whether the UN should get heavy with the Serbs ...' Did I tell that right? It was very funny when I heard it.

> **Mariah** *is cracking up laughing all the way through but nobody else laughs.*

Lil: That was a fast one Bolger pulled at the Development meeting the other night.

Frano: What's the story there?

Lil: The only man in G Block with a job.

Mariah: You could sing that if you had a tune.

Lil: The only man in G Block with a job. (*To the tune of 'The Only Living Boy in New York'*)

Mariah: Oweny Burke reckons it's a plot.

Frano: It probably is.

Lil: Though not the plot *he* thinks it is, I betcha.

Mariah: You watch. A picture will turn up in *An Poblacht* soon enough. The pramshed with Bolger and this newfellah gawking into it. Blah blah blah what they're doing for the People. Whoever the fuck they are. They're probably writing up Sweeney's martyred pigeons even as we speak. Them being called after the great patriots and all.

Frano: Are you the People?

Mariah: I am in me bollix. If I had any.

Frano: Are you the People, Lil?

Lil: Naw. I resigned. Handed in me uniform. The People, don't make me laugh.

Mariah: (*Sings:*)

> Put on yer docs
> Trouble on the blocks.

Knock on door.

Lil: That's Oweny Burke's knock.

Frano: Don't answer it.

Lil: It's Oweny I'm telling you. It'll be about the Doctor.

Frano: You can let me out anyway. I better get back.

Mariah: Jimmy should be assumed into heaven by now.

Lil: Would you not stay here tonight?

Frano: You've a lot to answer for Mariah.

Mariah: To who? And to what army?

Oweny Burke's knock again, louder.

Frano: You wound him up. You're always winding him up. I'm the one has to deal with it.

Mariah: Get a life Mrs.

Lil: (*Getting door*) Leave it out Mariah.

Frano *exits in huff.*

Oweny: What's up with yer one? (*Leers*) How're ya Mariah?

Lil: Did you get Joyce? Is he going to come over?

Oweny: Not exactly but …

Mariah: You either did or you didn't.

Oweny: O saucy.

Mariah: I'm on to you Oweny Burke. All talk. No action. If it was as big as your mouth now …

Lil: So what's the story? For Jesus sake Oweny!

Oweny: I got a bit side-tracked. Forget Joyce. I ran into a very interesting bloke …

Lil: Fuck you and your interesting bloke. I can't ask anyone to do anything. I have to do every single thing myself.

Oweny: Hang on there a minute. (*Produces box of tablets. Rattles them*) Never fear. These'll do the trick. Guaranteed. These are very good Mariah. This bloke, Folan, I got into company with, very intelligent fellow. Knows all there is to know about pharmaceuticals. They'd cost you fifty quid in the chemists. Two, three times a day and he'll be right as rain. Or was it three, two times a day. In any case it was six a day. Six a day altogether, definitely. Space them out.

Lil: Space them out! Givus a look. Hypno-Ver. Jesus Oweny, you're something else. I'm not putting this shite into Sweeney.

Mariah *takes box, opens it, sniffs, takes out a few, examines them.*

Mariah: I've never come across them. They must be new.

Oweny: O the very latest …

Lil: Hypno-Ver. What are they supposed to be for?

Mariah *pockets a few tablets, recaps box and leaves it on table.*

Oweny: Well you know. For Sweeney. Exactly. Stress. Nerves. Insomnia. That class of stuff. Yer man Folan gave a load of them to May Clancy. Her youngone's very bad. The eldest girl. You can tell when they go full blown. It's the eyes. All in the eyes. The eyes, Mariah, as the poet said, are the portals to the soul.

Lil: The eldest? That's Ger. Little Ger.

Mariah *lifts up mirror and is retouching make-up. And examining her eyes.*

Mariah: Ger was in the class under me. They're sending her home to die.

Oweny: May said it was only a matter of days. Days at the most. An experiment gone wrong – that's my theory. And there's evidence. Only they're not letting on. A military experiment in the States. Out in Nevada where they used do the atomic bomb blasts. They had the very same stuff in England over in that army place … Hunton Downs. I was only just reading about it. It's a way of purifying society. Eugenics – like if all the homos and junkies, or even anyone having a bit of extra-marital shenanigans – do you get the drift? Clear out the runts from the litter, so to speak. Just like Sweeney and his pigeons. Sure it was them started it. The pigeons! Charles Darwin, the evolution man, he based all his theories on pigeons. O he did. Darwin made an exhausting study of the pigeon. I bet you didn't know that? Now where was I? Pigeons – o yea, the virus. The military complex. They covered their tracks very well of course. Blaming the Haitians …

Lil: No. I'm not listening to another one of your Aids theories. It was monkeys. The Simian Conspiracy.

Mariah: It's the funerals would get to you. Lenno Roach last Monday.

Lil: He'd a horrible end.

Mariah: The story is his sister helped him out. Got him the big fix. The last fix. Not that he'd long to go.

Lil: I nearly took a pillow to Chrissie. It'd get so you couldn't stand it. You couldn't watch the pain. Some of those kids have no one to mind them.

Mariah: I hope someone'd do that for me if it came to it.

Lil: Come on, I'm throwing yous out. I'm going to bed. Here Oweny would you ever take them pigeons and dump them down the rubbish chute on your way. I think Father Tom is after forgetting about us.

Oweny: There's all kinds of avian diseases you can get off of them. The species barrier is a very thin wall indeed, I'll have you know.

Mariah: Let me penetrate *your* species barrier Oweny. Oooogh skin.

Lil: Okay. Okay. Okay. They're well wrapped up. (**Lil** *gives him bag of pigeons and ushers him out*)

Exit **Oweny.**

Lil: It doesn't seem right somehow, just shaggin them down the chute.

> **Mariah** *scrutinises herself again in mirror.* **Lil** *goes to window. Pulls sheet aside and cranes up to get a view of the sky.*

Lil: It's a beautiful night. Listen. Do you hear it, Mariah?

Mariah: Do I hear what?

Lil: The silence. That's rare. (*Pause*) I was born in a ballroom. The whole eight of us were born there. Would you credit that? One room. My Ma was delighted to move here. See, these flats really were mansions then. Long before your time. The ceiling in that ballroom. Dripping with fruit and angels and these long trumpets and scrolls of paper with musical notes writ on them. One of the angels fell down into the baby's pram once in the middle of the night. Me Ma thought it was a sign Git was going to be a bishop at least. The pram was one of those big black ones – like a shaggin tank it was. Me Ma used be wrecked from lugging it up and down the stairs. Funny I remember that ceiling clear as day. I used dress up in me Ma's old dance dress and spin round and round. Then I'd stop and the ceiling would go on spinning. It was a blue yoke with sequins. She'd turn in her grave if she could see us now. Me Ma. I'm only glad she didn't live to see Chrissie suffer. She'd never put all that together.

Mariah: You're getting a bit maudlin there Lil.

Lil: It comes back so clear. I wish sometimes I'd no memory. I'm always comparing things to the way they used to be. If I could remember ahead to the future. Do you know what I mean? If I could only ... see this clearly ... into the times to come.

Mariah: You've lost me. You should talk to Oweny about that one. I'd say he's an expert on remembering the future.

Lil: Do you see that new barbed-wire stuff they've put on the wall between us and the houses. The flats look like one of those concentration camp films in the moonlight. They'd gas us if they could, Mariah. Seal up the flats and pump in the gas. You should get out Mariah. Go away. While you're still young and you have the energy.

Mariah: I'll wait and see do I get the job. Twelve thousand a year. Imagine. (*Pause*) I haven't a snowballs, sure I haven't Lil? Honestly now?

Lil: I can smell a stitch up.

Mariah: (*Sings:*)

> '*The working class can kiss me arse*
> *I've got the foreman's job at last.*'

Jesus. I'm going to turn in. Me head is splitting apart. No.
No, stay where you are.

Lil: Goodnight love.

Exit **Mariah.** **Lil** *checks bottles. Finds one half-full. Settles on a*
chair with her feet up.

Lil: Here's to you Ma, wherever you are. I hope it's the
heaven you prayed for. The grace of a happy death. All
those years on your knees – I hope there's some pay-off and
you're reaping the reward. And here's to you Chrissie,
wherever you are. Only the good die young. Whisper a few
words in God's ear for us, would you Chrissie? Like for a
few bob, or a win on the Lotto. And I'll take Sweeney out
of the shagging place. Where he can have thousands of
pigeons and race them to his heart's content. Do you hear
me Chrissie? Where we can keep the key in the door. Have
a word for us. How does the prayer go? Hail our life our
holiness and our grace? No. No. Hail Holy Queen – is that
the same one? (*Gets it*)

> *Hail our life our sweetness and our hope*
> *To thee do we cry poor banished children of Eve*
> *To thee do we send up our sighs*
> *Mourning and weeping in the valley of tears*
> *And after this our exile*
> *Show unto us the blessed fruit of thy womb Jesus.*

Is that right? Are you hearing me, Chrissie?

End of Act One

Act Two

The flat. Dim and tidy. Sense of entombment, which will grow throughout this act. Windows almost completely boarded up with just occasional pane left intact showing strong daylight outside. Shafts of light stream in through these intact panes. Some light from open bedroom door. A fire burning in the grate. Two boxes, one on table, one on floor, both with coloured silky stuffs and glittery stuffs spilling out of them, this colour and texture startling against the drabness. Noise: occasional banger and fireworks, rhythmic thump of two balls against boarded window, hammering from bedroom – obviously windows at rear of flat are also under attack. At first drowned out by hammering , then coming to fore as hammering tails off – the thump of two balls being played against outside of boarded up windows.

Girl: (*With chant as* **Lil** *enters living room*) One two three and over, four five six and over, seven eight nine and over, ten and over, I love you. One two three and uppy, four five six and uppy, seven eight nine and uppy, ten and uppy, I love you. One two three and downy, four five six and downy, seven eight nine and down ... oops. Quick! Get it!

Second Girl: Me. Me now. It's my turn. Me. One two three and over, four five six and over (*Continues on with chant as* **Lil** *enters living room with hammer and scrap plywood.* **Girl** *turns on light and picks up two oranges from bowl and begins juggling, synchronising her movement and speech to game outside. It reaches*) seven eight nine and twirly, ten and twirly, I love you.

Sound of banger loud.

Third Girl: Yous are wanted for your tea.

First Girl: Fuck off.

Third Girl: You wait. You just wait.

Second Girl: Go and fuck yourself.

Third Girl: You wait. You won't be allowed go to the Festival. I'm telling on yous. I'm telling.

Lil: (*Crosses to window. Bangs loudly and ghoulish voiced*) Amanda Dempsey, Lorraine Dempsey, go home for your tea. This is the ghost of Maria Goretti Mansions. Go – home – for – your – tea. And wash your mouths out with soap you filthy tongued little rips.

Girls: Run. Jaysus. Get me out of here …

> **Lil** *starts sweeping up. Shifts armchair to discover pile of shredded newsprint behind it. Hard going to sweep it up. Lifts long tablecloth and discovers even bigger pile of shredded newsprint. Gives up. Sweeps what she has under.*

Lil: He must be nesting. That's the only explanation. Maybe he'll start laying eggs. That'd be a good one. Free range. Ach, I'll leave it. It's the least I could do. It's not doing any harm and nobody'd notice it under the table. (*She resumes sweeping.* **Sweeney** *enters from bedroom and follows her around room executing a formal mating dance behind her*) Here Sweeney, I know what you're after, you old divil. (*Holding him off with brush*) A rub of the relic. Or to be exact, you want me to give the relic a rub. I can't get used to it. What's in your head at all Sweeney? Huh? What do you see? Am I all feathery to you? Is that how I look? Do you see a beak? Do I look like another pigeon to you? (*Entering spirit she begins to respond and join in the mating ritual, laughing at first, then growing solemn and enrapt. Ritual continues until* **Sweeney** *enfolds her in his 'wings' from behind. Murmuring, billing and cooing interrupted by knock on door*) Let them knock. (*More knocks.* **Lil** *shakes herself out of it. Comes to.* **Sweeney** *manoeuvres himself under the table, scrabbles in the shredded newsprint and settles himself comfortably*)

> **Lil** *gets door. Enter* **Frano** *and* **Mariah** *with wrapped parcel.*

Lil: I gave up answering the door. I thought yous were more kids. It's been 'help the halloween party' all day. Any apples or nuts cigarettes or butts. Still it's better then them pulling a knife and demanding it. As long as they're still asking.

Frano: We're just dropping this off now. It's for tonight. Solly Burns is dead. Where's his nibs. (**Lil** *gestures under table*) And he was only full blown less than a month.

Lil: Solly! That was fast alright.

Frano: I met his sister down at the corner. She doesn't look too hot herself. She's in bits.

Lil: We'll have to send a wreath from the Development Group.

Frano: Maybe we should cancel tonight. It doesn't seem right with the Burns in mourning.

Mariah: We can't cancel. You'd end up cancelling everything. Let's cancel the rest of our existence now and save us all the bother. Pass the razor blades. (*Changing subject fast*) Yo man. Give us a claw. You're looking very perky today Sweeney. (*To* **Lil**) No developments?

Lil: What am I going to do with him?

Mariah: I'd lock the bedroom door at night for a start. You have to watch yourself with cocks.

Frano: I saw chickens at it once.

Mariah: You were never further than Finglas in your natural.

Frano: No, no, no. Me Uncle Harry kept them up in a pal's back garden in East Wall. Eight of them there was and a huge cock. He'd a big red comb and these jowly bits dangling down. Harry'd send us kids up with the corn. Mad yokes they were. It took about two seconds.

Mariah: Is that with or without foreplay?

Frano: Wat dat? The cock gets all strutty. Hops up on the bin. Starts puffing out his chest. Yodelling out of him to beat the band. Then he goes to it.

Mariah: And?

Frano: And nothing. He comes behind a hen, any hen, pushes up against her. She just goes on pecking. She wouldn't even seem to notice.

Mariah: That sounds familiar.

Frano: Lil should be counting her blessings its not a rottweiler he thinks he is. Or a pit bull terrier. He coulda turned into a vulture.

Mariah: A buzzard.

Frano: A bleeding dodo.

Mariah: A turkey. Gobble, gobble, get stuffed.

Frano: Eaglema-a-a-an! That'd be something. Swooping down on you from the wardrobe, pecking out your eyes.

Lil: O yous are very funny.

Mariah: You'll be scraping the shite off the mantelpiece morning, noon and night. Wait'll he starts moulting. Up to your oxters in feathers. Do the males moult?

Frano: What you need is a birdcage.

Knock on door.

Everyone: That's Oweny Burke's knock.

Mariah *gets door.*

Lil: I've something to show yis all. You'll appreciate this, Oweny. My sister brought this up to me last night. You know Ellie, you met her at Chrissie's funeral. She wears those weatherglaze aluminium glasses. She's as blind as a bat. Now close your eyes. Turn out the light there, Mariah. Keep them closed now till I say. (*She removes cardboard cover*

*from statue of the virgin lamp already plugged in. She switches it
on and the halo around the virgin's head flashes and a greeny glow
comes from her body. Her sacred bleeding heart is also lit up)*
Now! She's after being over on a pilgrimage to Lourdes.
She brought this back for Sweeney. That he'd go back to
normal. Did you ever see anything like it? Even Oweny
Burke is flabbergasted. Not a word out of him. Have you no
theory for us Oweny?

Mariah: Your sister needs her head examined.

Lil: She got religion in a big way after she had her womb
removed. I can't see the connection myself.

Frano: (*About* **Oweny**) Jesus Lil don't give him any
excuses. You'll set him off.

Oweny: I was just going to take Sweeney down for a pint.
And you're wrong Lil. There is a connection.

Lil: No. No. Help.

Oweny: Your sister's made a fundamental connection. I
was listening to this programme the other day. On the
World Service. Sex is at the very heart of all our religious
impulses. There're these guys off in India, the Tantras, they
have it all sussed. The Catholics got it arseways. Now what
you have to do to see the face of god, and he might be
female, probably is female, though I missed that bit cos me
Ma came in the bathroom door at that point with a cup of
tea. I was doing up the bathroom for her. Anyway, where
was I? The bathroom … me Ma … oh yeah, the face of
God. See, your sister's womb – it'd be like the repository for
belief. That's where one of the most important chakras is.
The Hindu name means jewelled city. Just there at the
navel. You've another one at your heart and there's a head
chakra as well. You yank out the womb and she'd be
looking all over for something to replace it.

Mariah: Stop Oweny.

Oweny: I only came up to bring Sweeney out for a pint.

Lil: What time is it? Look come back in a while, an hour or so and he can go with you. We've something to do first.

Mariah: You can take us Oweny. We'd love a drink. Wouldn't we Frano? C'mon we'll leave you in peace Lil.

Father Tom *passes window.*

Lil: Yous better all be off. I have a visitor.

They leave and **Lil** *re-enters with* **Father Tom**. *She furtively shakes down tablecloth in line with his vision but* **Sweeney** *remains on view to audience. Embarrassed silence. He takes in Virgin lamp.* **Lil** *gestures him into large armchair close to table. He lays a folder on the table and takes out notebook.* **Lil** *clocks this, nervous of his power.*

Father Tom: Right Lil, I've, been doing a bit of research.

Very loud banger outside. He jumps.

Lil: This is not official or anything? Sure it's not?

Father Tom: Oh this ... (*Indicating notebook*) just a habit, I suppose. Do you mind?

More bangers and noise of fireworks.

Father Tom: Just a few details about tonight, eh, Lil, before we, eh, eh start. We agreed on seven for the bunting. I think it's a brilliant idea to put it on the washing lines.

Lil: That was Mariah. Though she'd some job getting everyone to agree. It'll look only great. And we'll have a gang of youngfellows out minding the stuff once it goes up. Though it cost us.

Father Tom: If they're busy on patrol ...

Lil: Exactly. Though I'm a bit worried about the bonfire. The McAuley youngfellows drove a bus into the side of the Community Centre and legged it. The other kids had all the seats out and on the heap before anyone could do a thing.

It's the fumes you'd be worried about. Any word yet on who got the job in the women's project, Father?

Father Tom: (*Not meeting her eye*) Well it *is* about to be announced. But eh, you know. Confidential. Just until all the letters have gone out. Today, I think they're going out, but you understand, I can't really say anymore. Yes. Today in fact.

Lil: (*Realising* **Mariah** *hasn't got job, looks at* **Father Tom** *with contempt*) You could have waited until tomorrow. She did so much work for tonight. It's her way of staying clean. To have something to get up in the morning for. Have you any idea what it's like?

Embarrassed silence.

Father Tom: Well now, to Sweeney. I've been doing a bit of research, as I said. Making phone calls mostly. And I met with an old friend of mine, I was in college with him, Pete Lawler. A psychologist and psychotherapist. A very sound bloke, good head on his shoulders.

Lil: Had he ever come across anything like this before?

Father Tom: He'd really need to assess Sweeney. That is have a look at him in person. He'd be too cautious to hazard an opinion without a full examination. Which he's willing to undertake.

Lil: What did he think we should do?

Father Tom: Every case is different and the regime varies. Treatment depends on many factors.

Lil: I don't want him locked up.

Father Tom: This is all preliminary, Lil. No decisions will be made without full consultation with all parties concerned. Pete would see you initially for a chat, with Sweeney. An informal setting.

Lil: I tried the few prayers, Father. I'm developing a particular devotion to the Holy Paraclete.

Father Tom: O very good Lil. Ha. Ha. Now, I made it clear to him that you were not prepared to go through regular channels of the psychiatric service …

Lil: I don't want Sweeney locked up.

Father Tom: … at least at this point in time. I appreciate that.

Lil: It's nearly a whole month he's been out of it. Gone into himself. Gone somewhere. I don't know where he is.

Father Tom: Traumatic shock can bring on the strangest behaviour.

Lil: Who are you telling? I'm almost seeing feathers myself at this stage of the ball game. He's no trouble mind. He's terrified of dogs and the youngfellows two doors down are mad on pit bulls at the minute. When they come sniffing at the door he gets into a desperate state altogether. But then who wouldn't? I get into a desperate state meself. Pure savages they are. They'd ate you alive.

Father Tom: Lil …

Lil: I know, I know. Stick to the point. I just don't want him locked up. I've seen those places. I've met ordinary everyday people who've been perfectly all right, maybe a bit bad with the nerves or hearing things or something. They go inside. And that's the end of them. Whatever was wrong with them to start with, when they get out they're well and truly round the twist. Packy Farrell, Father. Sure there was nothing bad there. A touch of the poet maybe, always rawmayshing, talking to himself, muttering and spluttering about the flats. Everything was a sign to him. If a seagull flew over the canal in a certain way he knew that it would be raining by four o'clock. Amazing when you think about it. He's like a zombie since he got out. Or Annie. Remember Annie, Father, from B Block? Her nerves went after Kylie was born. She came out zonked up to the eyeballs. (*Pause*) And they were the ones that got out!

Father Tom: I think you'll find the whole approach to psychiatric treatment in this country has changed …

Lil: I'm talking *recent* here. Very recent! Annie's only out about six weeks!

Father Tom: To get back to your troubles Lil …

Lil: I don't know how much he's taking in. Although he understands some of what is going on. Of that I'm certain.

Father Tom: How's do you mean?

Lil: There's been a few things. Do you remember last week you came back with us after the meeting with the corporation?

Father Tom: O yes. The lighting wasn't it?

Lil: They're still banjaxed. Well that night you were talking about some rare bird you saw on the missions. The male carries the egg tucked up under its wing and mooches around the river edge feeding. Thing is he stands on only one leg. Wasn't that it, Father? For days after Sweeney'd be standing around for ages at a time on the one leg, and he was without a doubt favouring something under his wing. So. I believe he's definitely taking some things in.

Father Tom: Has he been seen again by your family doctor?

Lil: Old Joyce? Don't make me laugh. Oh he has, he has. But when Joyce came up Sweeney was very quiet. No. Joyce was a bad idea. He did write *me* a perscription though. For Ativan. And sleeping pills. 'A little hypnotic, Mrs Sweeney, to help you go over at night.' Hypnotic. I was mesmeric. He said I'd have to expect a bit of discomfort now that I was going through the Change. He's more of a danger to society than Sweeney. I can tell you that for nothing.

Father Tom: I better have a look at the man himself. Inside is he?

Lil: No. He's under the table.

Father Tom: (*Lifts cloth and comes face to face with* **Sweeney**. *Gets a terrible fright*) Agh!

Lil: Just keep nice and cool. That's right, isn't it Sweeney. (*Stroking him gently*) It's only Father Tom. Friend, Sweeney. It's okay. There, there.

Sweeney scrabbles tensely in the newsprint. It goes all over the place. He fixes **Father Tom** *with a beady eye, and begins to make cock aggression motions towards him. He backs him up into a corner.* **Father Tom** *turns back to him and* **Sweeney** *takes a bite at his upper thigh.*

Father Tom: Christ Almighty. He bit me. He bit me. He bit me.

Noise of sustained bursts of bangers and fireworks. Each burst panicking **Sweeney** *more.*

Lil: Shoo. Shoo. Away. Sweeney. Back, back. It's those shagging bangers. He's just a bit jumpy. Father, will you close off his escape there. Father! Father! Quick! That's it.

Lil *nods towards bedroom and she and* **Father Tom** *manoeuvre* **Sweeney** *back into bedroom.* **Lil** *goes in with him to settle him and closes door.* **Father Tom** *listens to flapping and commotion from inside for some seconds, then –*

Father Tom: (*Trying to get trousers rolled up to examine bite and failing. Finally takes trousers down*) The man is a nut.

Re-enter **Lil**.

Lil: What *would* normally happen in a case like this?

Father Tom: That man should be getting treatment. I'm serious now Lil. Normally? You must be joking! A committal order. I hope he didn't break the skin. Did he? Tell me he didn't. Will you look at that bruise. Look at the teeth marks. Thank God he didn't break the skin.

Lil: Don't worry. You won't get Aids or anything.

Father Tom: I'm sorry Lil. I didn't mean …

Lil: Maybe psittacosis. It's a disease you get from handling birds. It's a joke, Father. Here's a drop of Dettol.

Father Tom: There's no two ways about it. He should be committed. Even to give you a break.

Lil: Absolutely not. As long as I'm alive …

Father Tom: We could get you linked to a bereavement group. I'm sure that's at the root of all this.

Lil: Whatever happens I'm not letting them take Sweeney away. He's all I've got left in the world.

   Father Tom *pulls back up trousers and pulls his professional dignity back into place. Sits back on edge of chair.*

Father Tom: I'm sorry about all that Lil. I got a fright I can tell you. I'm over-reacting. I must be tired. I've had a lot on my plate recently. I'm afraid I'm burning myself out. I'll end up with a Messiah complex.

Lil: It's alright Father.

Father Tom: Meetings, meetings, meetings. I thought I could organise the people, empower them, you know, Lil, the basic Christian community stuff. Live amongst the people, share their shelter and their lives, release their spirit, direct the anger, fight injustice. I feel more like a politician than a shepherd these days. I may have to channel my energy back into pastoral care.

Lil: Sounds like you need a holiday.

Father Tom: The first mass I said in these flats was over in C Block. Just after I moved in. I brought a bottle of wine. We drank it around the table. I used a batch loaf for the communion. I was so full of it. Spiritual pride, really. It dawned on me that people were – as they say – pissing themselves at the offertory. I suggested they offer up their struggle. Made a speech ... never mind. I'd be embarrassed to repeat it. But the amazing thing was, they stuck it out, they put up with me. Not out of respect for the cloth, though there may have been some residual respect left. No. Out of kindness.

Lil: You've done good work in these flats. Don't be giving yourself such a hard time.

Father Tom: I'm full of shit, I'm afraid. I've learned more about love here than I learned in my entire formation.

> **Father Tom** *goes to statue and begins examining it, turning it on and off.*

Lil: Strange times eh?

Silence.

Father Tom: You'll have to seriously consider ...

Lil: No. He just got a fright. I don't know what it was. He just took a turn against you. The bangers have him confused.

Father Tom: Maybe Lil, you'd like to, em, mull it over and ... I think that'd be for the best. You can get back to me. We'll look at all possible avenues of help.

Lil: I don't want Sweeney locked up. That's the bottom line.

Father Tom: Believe me, Lil, there are some very progressive facilities in the State. There's not the same stigma attached to having a member of the family under psychiatric care these days.

Lil: Well thank you for your time anyway. What do you think of my new lamp?

Silence.

Father Tom: (*Finally*) It's very unusual. Very ... very ... Mexican. Exuberant!

Lil: It's been specially blessed and all. You get a plenary indulgence every time you turn it on.

Lil on impulse disconnects statue of Virgin.

Lil: Here Father. I'd like you to have this. For your flat.

Father Tom: I couldn't possibly Lil. I'm very moved by your gesture but I couldn't take it off you.

Lil: It would be an honour.

Father Tom: What can I say? Thank you Lil. Thank you so very much.

Lil lets them out. She returns and lights ball shaped candle before shrine of Chrissie.

Lil: Thank you so very much. Did you see his face? He nearly fucking died when I gave him that yoke. I'll have to visit him and see has he got it out on show. I'm a terrible hypocrite, God forgive me. Poor Mariah. What's she going to do, Chrissie? He thinks I'm worried about the stigma! Stigma! It's competence I'm worried about. Competence. I wouldn't trust some of those guys to scramble eggs. Sweeney'd crack up if he was put away. Of course we might have to face the fact that he's gone savage on us. You know what your Da used do to pigeons who got lost? I didn't know for years. If they went astray and didn't come home straight? Your Da would wring their necks. He said he couldn't have the straying blood getting into his stocks. He'd be cold as ice then. Your Da. One day he'd be like Florence Nightingale, mending a broken leg with a couple of lollipop sticks and the next ... (*She mimes wringing neck*)

She goes to bedroom door and looks in.

Lil: Come on out. He's gone. That's right. Come on. You sure blew that one, Sweeney. Come on Sweeney. There's nothing to be frightened of now ... (*She coaxes him out. He gradually relaxes and begins mooching around the room. She watches him. And take the brush yet again to sweep up the mess*

he's made. He's now in a playful mood and gets in her way) Ah
Sweeney. I'm trying to get this finished. (*He ruffles up her
neat pile of newsprint. Her temper's getting up*) Enough is
enough. Did you not hear him? The drift of it? You'll be
taken from me. Locked up. Do you understand? Will you
get that through your skull. Gone. Straightjacket. St
Brendan's. Tablets. Do you get it? Stop that now, Sweeney.
Stop messing. You're fucking up me head. I'll sign *myself* in.
Do you not understand, Sweeney? Is there anything human
at all left in your head? Is there anything left? Can you
answer me that, me fine feathered friend? (**Sweeney** *makes
more of a mess*) Right that's it. I give up. You've won. I give
up. Do what you want. Do exactly what you want. I resign.
Here's me resignation.

*She's in a rage. She smashes brush across her knee and flings
pieces at **Sweeney**. He takes fright at this and scuttles out of her
way, whimpering. She picks up a chair and thrashes it. When
her anger subsides she comes out of it, sweating and panting. She
gives way to sobs, ends up crouched in a foetal position. No
sound but her loud wracking weeping. **Sweeney** begins to circle
her tentatively, then gaining confidence, picking at her clothes,
nudging at her until she is in his arms. Finally comes to rest with
her enfolded in his wings, cooing, soothing her. Her sobs subside.
Then she is breathing peacefully.*

   Oweny Burke *presently appears at window, carrying a
fermentation jar full of blackberry wine and a black plastic bag.
He can only see **Sweeney** from his angle. He taps in.*

Oweny: Sweeney, my old son. Is your missus in?

*Louder raps till **Lil** composes herself and gets door.*

Oweny: I saw Father Tom leaving? Up about the
arrangements for tonight was he? How's the boy, hah? Jeez
you're looking better Sweeney, if I do say so myself. Here
Lil, I was wondering if you'd put a few stitches in me outfit
for tonight. (*Hauls out of bin liner a pink ball dress*) The back
burst when I put it on. It's a well known fact that people

unless they suffer from anorexia imagine they are smaller than they really are. The anorexic, on the other hand ...

Lil: What are you going as?

Oweny: A woman. What did Father Tom want? Was ...?

Lil: A woman? You can't just go as a woman. That's too ... vague. You'll have to be a particular woman and going by this dress I'd say you'd be on the bimbo end of the scale.

Oweny goes to window and fiddles with the coverings.

Oweny: It's like the tomb of Tutenkhamum in here. Did you know that the ration of daylight you absorb every day determines your whole outlook on life? It's a fact. But you're as well hanging on now till they put the aluminium windows in. They're only at D Block but. You could have a long wait. I was reading there about this new transparent plastic they've developed. The hardest substance known to man. It can withstand kilotrons of pressure, a small nuclear blast. Though there's small and there's small if you get my drift. If you're talking nuclear you're talking ...

Lil: We could do with some of that stuff round here. Where (*Gesturing to wine*) did you get that?

Oweny: An offering, a sacrificial offering.

Lil: Looks like Ribena. It smells like shite.

Oweny: That's the bouquet, you ignoramus. You know Feeley. Frankie. Mr F in F. In F Block – it's his. Blackberry. Chateau Maria Goretti. The left-hand-side of the canal bank.

Lil: He made it himself?

Oweny: So he says. His gaff is like a brewery. He has a new formula he invented himself. He can have it brewed up and clear as a jewel in one month flat. They're only this year's blackberries. Very scientific you know, the process. The trick is in the clearing or the finings. That's the technical term for it. That's the secret. The smell I grant you

isn't the best. But this is only the proto-batch: when he's
perfected the method all those little kinks will be ironed out.
It's fantastic stuff. It'd blow your head off.

Lil: Will you try a drop?

Oweny: You must be mad! Well, I mean, I'll pass for the
minute. It's a pint I'm after. I thought I'd bring Sweeney
down for an airing. Are you on Sweeney me, old mate.

Lil: Will you be able to handle him? I think he might be
turning, Oweny.

Oweny: Turning?

Lil: (*More to herself*) Savage. I think he might be turning on
us.

Oweny: Sure look at him. He knows he's going out. He's
dying for it. Aren't you Sweeney? Sniffing the air. Cock a
rookie.

Lil: You're worse to encourage him. Don't lose him again.

Oweny: Look. Sweeney'll be grand. There's no fear of
losing Sweeney. Now the homing instinct of birds is one of
the great mysteries of nature. If we could figure out …
millions have been spent on it, millions. If we could figure
out the migratory instinct of the swallow for instance. The
common swallow, we'd … we'd … what am I on about. O
yeah. Sweeney'll be game ball. Just a couple of quiet pints.

Lil: Take him the long way round. To be honest I could do
with a break. It's crazy out there.

Oweny: There was an article in the paper the other night:
Did you know that it is safer to walk down the Main Street
of Sarajevo than it is to walk down O'Connell Street? Now
I walk down O'Connell Street every day of my life and have
I ever seen anything? Even remotely violent? I have not.
That's the Law of Randomicity. It's a new concept you see
that proves that there is absolutely no truth in statistics.
Some other person could walk down O'Connell Street
every day of his, or for that matter, her, life and see

mugging shooting stabbing rape every time. The universe is random you see. But we all from time to time go through periods of Synchronicity – or as it's known technically – Periodic Synchronicity. Where the random seems to have a pattern. So we all act as if you could plan out your life. As if there were a future. Ha! And that's the major fuck up of Western civilisation.

Lil: I'll have to take your word for it Oweny.

Sudden blast of sound. Sound check of band outside. Drowns out conversation. **Sweeney** *is very startled and panicked by the noise but relaxes as sound moderates and lowers into rhythmic pattern.* **Oweny** *gets a grip on* **Sweeney** *and they make for the door.*

Lil: They're called The Effin Eejits. At least that's what Mariah calls them. And, Oweny, don't you let any of them reprobates down in Becketts make a laugh of Sweeney. Do you hear?

Mariah *is seen to pass window. Laughter at hall door.* **Mariah** *bursts into living room. She's carrying an assortment of plastic bags –Dunnes, Guineys, bin liners, one large heavy duty black number. But something anxious, furious, underneath her gaiety.*

Mariah: (*To rhythm of sound check number*)

> *I'm dustin down my angel wings*
> *flying tonight, flying tonight,*
> *above the city and its broken dreams*
> *flying tonight, flying tonight,*
>
> *shake down my dusty wings*
> *shake down, shake down*
> *all you behold you will own*
> *so high, so high into the light*
>
> *black angel dream child*
> *ain't never coming home*
> *bound for the other side of space*
> *ain't never coming home*

Aren't they great? If we can keep them straight enough to
play tonight. They're warned. If they fuck up I'll kill them. I
sicced Harry Brady on them. He'll have them riveted with
all his stories of the great rock stars he's met in his day.
There's some little fucker out there with a stash of E's,
dishing them out like smarties. (**Lil** *is pouring out blackberry
wine into two tankards while* **Mariah** *unpacks from plastic bags
motley, tat and gimcracks*) That's Frank Feeley's moonshine.
Try a drop of this. It'll put a kick in it. (*Producing naggin of
vodka. Sings:*)

> *Put some fuel in my tank*
> *we'll ride the dark night down*
> *Put some fuel in my tank*
> *we're gonna take on this whole town.*

Yihaw! Let's get this show on the road.

Lil: We better go easy. Pace ourselves.

Mariah: This place'd drive you to drink. I swear. Oweny
Burke'd have your brain mangled.

Lil: He's very good to Sweeney but. Did he say something
to you?

Mariah: I'd say it was hanging out with Oweny Burke
drove him mad in the first place, Lil. I'm serious! You
know Oweny's problem? He got stuck in a trip. When he
was growing up there were only two kinds of acid. One-
way and return. He took the one-way tab.

Lil: Any word?

Mariah: It was delivered. (*Taking out letter*) By hand. Huh.
Someone snuck it in the letterbox more like. Afraid to tell
me to me face. Bastards. Listen. – Dear Mizz Donohue,
Blah blah to thank you blah blah blah extremely hard
decision blah blah blah huge number of applicants blah blah
blah. Here it is ... and regret to inform you that we have
decided to offer the position to another candidate ... blah
bleeding blah. Regret. I'll regret them. That's me out, Lil.

After tonight. That's it. They can stuff their community work up their holes.

Lil: Who signed it?

Mariah: On behalf of the Maria Goretti Mansions Development Group Subcommittee for the Women's Community Leadership Project, Eamonn Lynch.

Lil: He's lick-arsing his way onto everything around here. The sleeveen.

Mariah: Sure I never even clapped eyes on him before in me life until I walked in the door to the interview. The Three Muskateers. There they were: Father Tom, Eamonn Lynch and the Fás fellow. Martin – sorry, I beg your pardon. Martín. He was called Martín. Martín O Fuckface. He was Irish.

Lil: I'm sorry Mariah. I'm really sorry.

Mariah: You knew all along the way the wind was blowing. Well fuck them all.

Then from largest, sturdiest black plastic bag she produces the decorations for the washing lines. These are an extraordinary assortment of colourful buntings recalling juggernaut adornments, ships pennants, flags of undreamt republics, textless banners for libertarians.

Lil: Wow!

Mariah: Amazing what? Yours is the last. C'mom.

They drape bunting around set. A space on rope is left free for **Lil**'s *piece. She goes to a drawer and ceremonially unpacks a magnificent banner. The space for it needs to be arranged so that it occupies a dominant position on stage when it's hung with the others. Where possible a pulley system so that when all is arranged a rope can be pulled and the whole thing can be hoisted like a ship getting ready to sail. It should be like the ceiling of the flat opens up to the sky.*
Silence of adoration.

Mariah: Ah look. Ah look. (*At* **Lil***'s piece*) That blue stuff's from Chrissie's kimona. (*Closer examination*) She loved that velvet dress. Do you remember she wore it, there! there! she wore it with that goldy waistcoat! Our docs 'n frocks days. (*Dawning on her*) These are all Chrissie's things. She wore that the day we were thrun out of school. You should of seen the nun's face when we walked in with the leather gear. Our skirts up around our fannies and the chains! I'd a big skull and crossbones on the back of me jacket. She freaked. Her moustache started twitching. A sure sign. I'd say she was sorry she couldn't whip out her cane and tan our arses. Dirty-minded old bitch. (*They both surrender to a fit of laughter that gradually turns into tears; then laugh and cry at the same time*)

Lil: Do you remember yous were hiding out in the pramsheds around at K block for a week?

Mariah: Did you know about that?

Lil: Where do you think all the fish and chips came from? (*Pause*) Chrissie could be a terrible wagon. She hocked her granny's wedding ring on me. At least she didn't sell it like the trophy. The trouble that trophy cost me. She flogged it to Ernie Byrne. I'd to lash out forty quid to get it back. I don't know if Sweeney ever even noticed. He was very good at not noticing things. I was in bits. Sure what could I have done, I keep asking meself. If I'd gone around and reefed her back out of it she'd only've bided her time and legged it the first chance she got.

Mariah: I wonder what happened to my leather jacket. I sold it for a hit I think.

Lil: Get out of here Mariah. I'll help you get the money. I'm serious.

Mariah: It's the same everywhere. (*Sings:*)

> no where to run
> no where to hide
> from the monkey man.

Or something like that. I keep thinking I should go for the test. It wasn't only the needles. We shared everything. I was mad about her, Lil. Look at her up there listening to us.

Lil: I blame meself for not getting out years ago. When Chrissie was a youngone. Me brother Git would've put us up. He could've got Sweeney a job on the buses. They've a lovely house in Manchester. If only ...

Mariah: If only. If only. If me aunt had a micky she'd be me uncle.

> *They don't notice* **Frano** *passing window. Knock at halldoor.* **Lil** *gets it. Enter* **Frano**, *hair down around her face and made up to try and hide black eye and other bruises. Silence.*

Lil: When did this happen?

Mariah: That's a lovely fucking start to the night I must say.

Frano: Nobody asked you.

> *Silence.*

Lil: Come on. Do you think we're blind love?

Frano: He couldn't find a match for a red sock.

Mariah: The fucker.

Frano: I have No Organisation, d'ye see. No Organisation.

Mariah: The fucker.

Lil: Mariah ...

Frano: He was in the horrors from last night. He fell over Jason's bike in the hall on his way out and ripped the arse out of his trousers. Sandra laughed. Then he lost his balance taking the trousers off. He smashed into the coffee table and split his skull. And then he grabbed a cloth off of the airer to stop the blood, only it was his new T-shirt, the one with Ian Paisley fucking the Pope on the front.

Mariah: Your heart'd break for him.

Lil: (*Giving her drink*) Where are the kids?

Mariah: You're the eejit to stay with him. It wouldn't be me. No siree.

Lil: Leave it rest, Mariah. Where are the kids?

Frano: Sandra's up in me Ma's and the boys are with the Murphys. Though I'd say they're around at the bonfire by now. Did you see the size of it? The last news I had on him he was stupified down in Becketts. And he left me without the price of a cigarette. I stuck my head in a few minutes ago to check but, and there was no sign of him.

Lil: (*Giving her cigarette*) You're taking your life in your hands going within a hundred miles of him when he's like that.

Frano: I was hoping to catch him when he was comatose and relieve him of a few shillings. You can get him sometimes between waves. The thing is he could snap wide awake like that (*Snapping fingers*) And turn on you. Jesus. What am I going to do?

Mariah: I know what I'd do, I'd …

Lil: I said OK Mariah. It's alright for you to talk.

Mariah: Well. Excuse me. Imagine having to dip the father of your children for the price of a packet of fags. I was only …

Frano: Who do you think you are? Just who the fuck do you think you are? Lady Bleedin Muck.

Lil: Lookit. Will you two give over. I can't take much more aggro. From any quarter. (*Striking table*) Whatever happens we're going to have a ball tonight. Yes you are coming. And that's that. He won't recognise any of us anyway, and you can crash here. Tomorrow is time enough to worry about what any of us is going to do. Agreed? But tonight, we're going to let rip. We haven't had a decent night out in how long? Jesus it feels like years.

Mariah: (*Refilling glasses*) Grab a hit of the community spirit. (*Sings:*)

> *Put some fuel in my tank*
> *we'll ride the dark night down*
> *Put some fuel in my tank*
> *we'll take on this whole town*
> *Love has got some business*
> *on the dark side of the tracks*
> *Some sweet and shady business*
> *a mean man and his sax.*

Frano: There's some crack though in Becketts. It's like the zoological gardens in there at the minute.

Lil: (*Suspicious*) How so?

Frano: They're getting a good laugh out of your Sweeney. I don't know how it started but they're all mad into it. Tommy Smith was up on the bar crawling the length of it barking his head off; Séan the Box was oink-oink-oinking; there was cock-a-doodling to beat the band; even old Shamy who hasn't been known to speak a word since his missus ran off with the moneylender was in on it like he'd resurrected from the dead. Do you know what he was singing? Skippy Skippy/ Skippy the Bush Kangaroo. A menagerie. When I left they were screeching Old Macdonald Had a Farm out of them to raise the roof.

Lil: I'll kill Oweny Burke. I warned him.

Mariah: That just sounds like an ordinary teatime session. Yessir. Happy Hour in Becketts.

Frano: Maybe what Sweeney has is infectious.

Mariah: Like the chicken pox? The Pigeon Tox!

Angelus bells from outside. As if on cue the women begin poking in the bags and amongst the bundles. **Lil** *pulls out long mirror*

and smaller ones are produced from bags. **Mariah** *is singing,
humming, or beating time on some surface as she gathers what
she needs,* **Frano** *gives herself two red and black circular designs
around her eyes, disguising her bruise. The three of them
independent of each other stake a space on stage with their bits
and pieces and begin transforming themselves into exotic birds.*

Frano: (*Sings:*)

>*Sold my soul to the devil in red
>Sold my body to the man in black
>Gave my heart to a boy of sixteen
>But he ain't never coming back
>Dig my grave, dig it wide and deep*

All join

>*Put a marble stone at my head and feet
>And in my fist put a jug of rum
>And Paul McGrath's prick shoved up me bum*
>
>*Dum dum dum dum
>Da dee dee dee*

Yis are no use. You've got to lively up yerselves and don't
be no drag.

Others: Oooh ah! Oooh ah ah! Oooh ah! Oooh ah ah!

Frano: Do you remember (*To the tune of 'The Sash My
Father Wore'*)

>*They were old but they were beautiful
>And they made me want to score
>I would trade Ruid Gullet's garters
>For the shorts Packie Bonner wore.*

*Repeat verse, all lost in it, harmonising. At end they've
mesmerised themselves by their own voices.*

Lil: We had the *craic* then alright. (*Knock at door*) That'll be
them now.

Enter **Sweeney** *and* **Oweny.** **Sweeney** *is excited by the colour
of the banners and sets about exploring them.*

Lil: Oweny, this (*Pink dress*) won't be fixed. It's burst.

Mariah: We'll do a sash over it. A cummerbund. It can double as a corset to hold in your beer belly. Take your clothes off Oweny Burke.

Oweny: That's an offer I couldn't refuse. And this (*Patting belly*) is what we call the balcony over the toyshop.

Mariah: Be careful Oweny or I might short circuit your Scalectrix.

Frano: Isn't that disgraceful.

Lil: (*To* **Mariah**) You told me this morning you were going as the Virgin Mary.

Frano: Where's the statue gone? The lamp?

Lil: I gave it to Father Tom.

Mariah: A pity I didn't know that. I could've booby trapped it with a pound of semtex.

Oweny: You'd make a lovely virgin.

Mariah: Yeah that was the plan alright. But I couldn't get the bleeding heart or the halo. Sure I didn't have time. I nearly had to give your man a blow job for the sound system. I didn't tell you about that. A real filtho. I'm a bit long in the tooth for an immaculate conception.

Oweny: Now there's a curious and little known fact. The immaculate conception, or I should say, *an* immaculate conception is a perfectly ordinary everyday occurrence. The motility of sperm is such that they can cross all kinds of barriers to get to the target so to speak. In fact ...

All: Oweny!

Oweny: Wha ... right.

They get his clothes off. They get him into the pink number and plonk a blonde wig on his head and force his feet into some red shoes. As they're dressing him up–

Lil: So. Did Sweeney behave himself down in Becketts?

Oweny: Not a bother. Sure it was very quiet down there.

Lil: Quiet?

Oweny: Dead quiet. Well quiet enough. Very civil.

Lil: Civil?

Oweny: The best of order.

Mariah: Pink really suits you Oweny. You look like a right queen of the fairies. We'll have to keep a strong grip on you tonight. You'll be driving the men wild.

Oweny: Get away out of that Mariah. Though there's a curious thing. Did you know that you can change your whole mood by the colours you wear? Chromatics. I met this fellow in the hardware on Monday explained it all to me. Like aromatics – you know with the smells. Moodchange. All that stuff. You're into that a bit, aren't you Mariah? Well this is the same. No. Similar, to be precise. Only with colour. Every colour under the sun registers on a tinctorial scale that directly affects the emotional response. These walls now. Wrong. All wrong. They should be a pale shade of green.

Lil: That's what they were when we moved here. Puke green in the living room and vomit pink in the bedrooms. The Corpo only had two colours in them days.

Oweny: You see. I bet you were happier then. You didn't realise it. Your trouble is that little purple fleck in the wallpaper pattern. O bad that. Purple. Very dangerous. And it's probably got too much red in it. Anger you see. The ruddy, or rubicund end of the spectrum's a real bummer.

Frano: (*Putting lipstick on* **Oweny**) You talk an awful lot of shite Oweny Burke. Did anyone ever tell you that?

Oweny: (*Looking in mirror*) Jays. I look like Gypsy Rose Lee.

Frano: In her decline. You've a face only a mother could love.

Mariah: Tell us our fortune Lil. Go on. Lil can remember the future. Amn't I right?

Lil: Will you get away with yourself.

Frano: Yeah. Go on, Lil. For the *craic*.

Lil: Ah I'd need a crystal ball.

   Mariah *brings ball-shaped candle to table.*

Mariah: Here, use the candle. Madame Sweenio.

Oweny: Yous may laugh in your ignorance which is, as the sage said, a form of bliss. But time is a loop, and a mere nudge sideways could be enough to catapult you into a different dimension of chronology. Things are not always as they seem. What are we all but a collection of molecules buzzing around held together by the transcripted laws of the universe? A little wobble and pidang, I'm into the seventeenth century, Mariah could be caroomed whop into post-millennial Siberia. You Frano, could at this very moment be in Africa dreaming you live in the Mansions. We don't even know if we're here, for Christ's sake. We don't know where we are, let alone when we are.

Mariah: Will someone please pull the plug?

Lil: It's coming through. I can see it.

Frano: Shush!

Lil: I can see it. Wait. It's Father Tom.

Mariah: He's pregnant right. He's having Oweny Burke's baby.

   They move close in a huddle around candle, all staring into the flame.

Lil: Father Tom will be in South America by Easter. A postcard from Peru. Saving the savages for Coca Cola.

Mariah: Well good riddance ...

Frano: Will you listen.

Lil: Oweny Burke will have grown a beard before the year is out. There'll be a theory about that too.

> **Oweny** *moves away towards mirror. Scrutinises himself in it.*

Lil: Frano will get one of the new houses up the canal in six months' time, the ones they're building now. She'll be pregnant on her last child. There's a beating in store that'll make sure she never has another and that she'll limp for the rest of her life.

> **Frano** *moves over to window.*

Lil: Mariah will be back on gear within months and strung out to fuck, living here, living there. Ducking into the flats with her hollow cheeks and her big eyes and ducking out with whatever she scrounges. Pretending not to see me.

> **Mariah** *moves away to side opposite window. Just* **Lil** *and* **Sweeney** *left in strong light. Others in shadow.* **Sweeney** *is watching* **Lil** *intently while she speaks.*

Lil: Sweeney will be dead within a year. Not peacefully in his bed. O no. The green room, St Brendan's. His lovely wings all crumpled up in a straitjacket. Myocardial infarction it will say on his death cert. A broken heart I'd call it.

> **Sweeney** *nudges* **Lil** *insistently.*

Lil: I'll be ... I can't see it. My own future's a blank to me, a darkness.

> *The sound system gives a few screeches and comes to life. Blurred announcements are made and the band strike up. It disperses mood of solemnity that has grown through the fortune telling.*

Lil: Come on now folks. Give us a hand with Sweeney.

She produces from a black plastic sack a peacock costume made of feathers. This is for **Sweeney** *who looks absolutely magnificent when they finally manage to coax him into it. They have a final drink.* **Frano** *pours some wine into a saucer and puts it on the table for* **Sweeney** *who jumps up and sucks it from the saucer.*

Mariah: Let's get out into it.

Oweny: Cock a rookie doo. Sweeney's mad for it. Aren't you, you little bollix.

Lil *tidies up the shrine and toasts Chrissie.*

Frano: (*Seeing* **Lil**'*s gesture*) A bit of hush. Order. Order. A toast.

They all face shrine and raise drinks.

Lil: To you Chrissie. My beautiful daughter. The souls of the faithful departed are supposed to come out tonight. If you're there and looking down on us it must be like a dream to you. It's like a dream to me. Look at the flats, Chrissie. The banners and the colourdy lights and the people dancing in their fancy dress. Do you see the bonfire? The kids whirling around the flames. And there's May Clancy with Ger in her arms. Little Ger. See? She's brought her out to look at the fire. For the last time. As I once carried you in my own arms out that you'd see it all. Do you remember? The last morning I carried you outside? I tucked you up in a duvet in the big armchair. You were watching the pigeons for hours up over the flats. The way the pigeons would be wheeling in big sweeps. How they seemed to disappear when they turned, whatever way the light caught them. Now you see them. Now you don't. And then they'd be back. Magic. That's what you said Chrissie. Magic. The last thing you ever said. Magic.

They all knock back their drinks. **Lil** *blows out candle. They exit to loud music.*

The End

Author's Note

Mrs Sweeney

I cast my song on the water.
The sky stirs,
clouds are driven under the trailing willow.

I cast my song on the water.
The sky in your hungry eye, you drop
to meet the cloud's image.

Your eye most nights is sparrowhawk.
So strike. Flip me over. Pin
my wings with your talons.
Pluck, then, my breast feathers
to the creamy skin over my heart.
Flash of beak as you stoop to pierce.

(from *Pillow Talk*, Gallery Press)

*

This is the poem that was the genesis of the play. I've
always been fascinated by the ancient legend of Sweeney
and his exile amongst the birds. It spoke across the
centuries to me and, though I identified strongly with the
cursed king himself, I wondered what it must have been like
to be his woman. I also wanted to capture something I saw
at close quarters in Leitrim – a sparrowhawk taking down
and killing a magpie. It was the picture of ravishing I
reached for when I needed such an image for a poem.

Immediately I'd finished the poem the thought flashed –
*get a grip, woman, it wouldn't be songs cast on water at all, at all.
Scraping the shite off the mantelpiece you'd be.* The whole shape
and smell of the play came immediately into mind. A room
came into focus. And Lil Sweeney entered.

The next day when I saw a call for scripts from Rough Magic I sat down and began to write.

The play allowed me draw on my experience of living in Fatima Mansions during the 1980s. There's a gesture in the old tale – the cook Muirghil would make a hollow with her heel in a cow pat and fill it with milk for the bird man to sip from. I witnessed that tender gesture again and again in contemporary guise many times when I lived there.

I dedicate *Mrs Sweeney* to the memory of the lost children of that community who, like Chrissie in the play, are ghosts long before their time. I also dedicate it with love and thanks to director Kathy McArdle and producer Siobhán Bourke who made it all happen.

Paula Meehan
Dublin
August 1998